# A CLASS DIVIDED

# A Class Divided

Appeasement and the Road to Munich, 1938

Robert Shepherd

MACMILLAN
LONDON

First published 1988 by
MACMILLAN LONDON LIMITED
4 Little Essex Street London WC2R 3LF
and Basingstoke

Associated companies in Auckland, Delhi, Dublin, Gaborone,
Hamburg, Harare, Hong Kong, Johannesburg, Kuala Lumpur,
Lagos, Manzini, Melbourne, Mexico City, Nairobi, New York,
Singapore and Tokyo

**British Library Cataloguing in Publication Data**

Shepherd, Rob
A class divided: appeasement and the road to Munich, 1938.
1. Great Britain. Political events.
1933–1945
I. Title
941.084

ISBN 0–333–46080–4

Typeset by Columns, Reading
Printed in Great Britain by Richard Clay Ltd,
Bungay, Suffolk

# CONTENTS

*List of Illustrations*                                    vii
*Acknowledgements*                                          ix

 1   Chamberlain's Hour                                      1
 2   Pacifists and Appeasers                                13
 3   Hitler's Challenge                                     27
 4   A Shock to the System                                  44
 5   'Their Own Back-Garden'                                58
 6   Rebels and Rearmers                                    69
 7   'And I Remember Spain'                                 85
 8   Appeasers in Command                                  105
 9   A Sudden Departure                                    124
10   'The Micawber Strain'                                 144
11   'The Bleak Choice'                                    167
12   'Fly, Fly, Fly Again'                                 189
13   Munich Week                                           204
14   'Shame and Relief'                                    223
15   'A Vote for Hitler!'                                  251
16   End of Illusion                                       272

*Select Bibliography*                                      298
*Index*                                                    303
*Picture Acknowledgements*                                 323

# LIST OF ILLUSTRATIONS

Neville Chamberlain briefs the press during his shuttle-diplomacy with Hitler, September 1938.

Trenches dug as air-raid shelters in London's Hyde Park.

Winston Churchill with Brendan Bracken.

Anthony Eden and Sir Samuel Hoare on their way to an emergency Cabinet meeting during the Abyssinian crisis, 1935.

Union leaders Ernest Bevin and Walter Citrine.

George Lansbury.

Malcolm MacDonald and Buck de la Warr of the National Labour Party with Hugh Dalton and Clem Attlee.

The Duchess of Atholl – 'Red Kitty'.

Sir John Simon.

Leo Amery.

Sir Austen Chamberlain.

Sympathisers of Hitler's regime Lord and Lady Redesdale and their daughter Unity Mitford, with Dr Fitz-Randolph.

The Cable Street riots, October 1936.

Foreign Secretary Lord Halifax does the goose step with Ribbentrop and the Marquis of Londonderry.

The images of Chamberlain: Low's 'Appeasement Umbrella', and the expert angler.

Lord Halifax and Sir Robert Vansittart leave Downing Street as the Czech crisis flares, August 1939.

Sir Nevile Henderson and Sir Alec Cadogan arrive at Number 10 as war looms.

A. D. Lindsay campaigns during the Oxford City by-election, October 1938.

*Times* editor Geoffrey Dawson with his deputy Robert Barrington Ward.

# ACKNOWLEDGEMENTS

I should like to thank Gillian Shepherd for her invaluable help with the research for this book. I am also grateful to Philippa Harrison, Tom Weldon and Juliet Brightmore at Macmillan, and Michael Shaw at Curtis Brown, for their advice, encouragement and enthusiasm.

I wish to express my gratitude for the friendship and support of my colleagues at Brook Publications, both on Channel Four's drama-documentary about the 1938 Oxford City by-election and on *A Week in Politics*. In particular, I should like to thank Anne Lapping, Paul Bryers, Jean Kerr and John Ashworth.

I am grateful to all those who have discussed with me the events and personalities of the 1930s. For their generosity with their time and their recollections, I particularly wish to thank Lord Home of the Hirsel, Lord Blake, Lord Jay, Lord Sherfield, Lord Thorneycroft, Lord Zuckerman, Sir Isaiah Berlin, Sir Frank Roberts, and the late Sir Con O'Neill.

I am indebted to the many historians who have undertaken detailed research on the period covered in this book. I have endeavoured to ensure that their work is acknowledged in the select bibliography.

To the staff of the London Library I owe an appreciation of their courteous and efficient assistance.

Extracts from Hansard, the Official Report of the House of Lords and House of Commons Debates, and from Cabinet and other official papers are Crown copyright and are quoted by permission of Her Majesty's Stationery Office.

I am grateful to the following for permission to quote copyright material: the BBC, for *The Chamberlain Trilogy* (Radio 4, 1988); Brook Productions (1986) Ltd and Channel Four Television, for access to the interviews for the drama-documentary about the Oxford by-election; Lady Avon, for the late Lord Avon's diary; Lady Butler, for the late Lord Butler's diary; Jonathan Cape Ltd, for Anthony Howard's *RAB: The Life of R. A. Butler*, Frank Pakenham's *Born to Believe* and Philip Williams's *Hugh Gaitskell*; Cassell Ltd, for Winston S. Churchill's *The Gathering Storm*; Century Hutchinson Ltd, for Hugh Dalton's *Memoirs 1931–1945: The Fateful Years* and Christopher Mayhew's *Time to Explain*; Collins Ltd, for *The Diplomatic Diaries of Oliver Harvey, 1937–40* edited by John Harvey, *Harold Nicolson: Diaries and Letters, 1930–39* edited by Nigel Nicolson, Barbara Cartland's *Ronald Cartland*, John Colville's *Footprints in Time*, and Jack Jones's *Union Man*; Faber & Faber Ltd, for T. S. Eliot's 'East Coker' and Louis MacNiece's 'Autumn Journal'; Victor Gollancz Ltd, for Jessica Mitford's *Hons and Rebels*; Robin Gordon Walker and Churchill College, Cambridge, for the papers of Patrick Gordon Walker; Grafton Books, for Duff Cooper's *Old Men Forget*; Elaine Greene Ltd, for Ted Willis's *Whatever Happened to Tom Mix?*; Hamish Hamilton Ltd, for Edward Whitley's *The Graduates*; Sir Rupert Hart-Davis, for Duff Cooper's diary; Heinemann Ltd, for Alan Bullock's *The Life and Times of Ernest Bevin*, Martin Gilbert's *Winston S. Churchill*, Vols V and VI, and Francis Williams's *A Prime Minister Remembers*; David Higham Associates Ltd, for *The Diaries of Sir Alexander Cadogan, 1938–1945* edited by David Dilks, A. J. P. Taylor's *Beaverbrook* and *A Personal History*, Douglas Jay's *Change and Fortune* and L. S. Amery's *My Political Life*; The Hogarth Press Ltd, for *The Diary of Virginia Woolf* edited by Anne Oliver Bell and *The Letters of Virginia Woolf* edited by Nigel Nicolson and Joanne Trautmann; Longman Ltd, for George Hutchinson's *Edward Heath: A Personal and Political Biography*; Macmillan Inc., New York, for Anthony Eden's *Facing the Dictators* and *The Reckoning*, and Roy Lewis's *Enoch Powell: Principle in Politics*; Macmillan Publishers Ltd, for Keith Feiling's *The Life of Neville Chamberlain*, Roy Harrod's *The Prof*, Harold Macmillan's *Winds of Change* and *The Blast of War*, and Philip Snow's *Stranger and Brother: A Portrait of C. P. Snow*; John Murray, for *The Letters of Conrad Russell* edited by Georgiana Blakiston, and Kenneth Clark's *Another Part of the Wood*; Viscount Norwich, for Lady Diana Cooper's *The Light of the Common Day*; Oxford University Press Ltd, for Thomas Jones's *A Diary with Letters*; A. D. Peters & Co. Ltd, for Storm Jameson's *Journey from the North* and Evelyn Waugh's *Vile Bodies*; Robert Rhodes James, for *Victor Cazalet: A Portrait*; Ruskin College, Oxford, for the records of the Oxford City Labour Party; Solo Syndication, for *Low's Autobiography*; Mrs M. E. Tree, for Ronald Tree's *'When the Moon Was High'*; Lord Tweedsmuir, for John Buchan's letters; Vallentine, Mitchell & Co. Ltd, for *Baffy: The Diaries of Blanche Dugdale, 1936–1947* edited by N. A. Rose; Weidenfeld & Nicolson Ltd, for *Chips: The Diaries of Sir Henry Channon* edited by Robert Rhodes James, C. M. Bowra's *Memories, 1898–1939* and Robert Rhodes James's *Anthony Eden*; and the trustees of the John Wheeler Bennett settlement, for his *King George VI*.

Every effort has been made to trace the holders of copyright. I apologise if any copyright material has been inadvertently quoted without permission.

*Robert Shepherd*
*London, 1988*

# CHAPTER ONE

# CHAMBERLAIN'S HOUR

**Neville Chamberlain**

As Priam to Achilles for his son,
So you, into the night, divinely led,
To ask that young men's bodies, not yet dead,
Be given from the battle not begun.

(Tribute to Neville Chamberlain by the Poet Laureate, John Masefield, published as the leader in *The Times*, 16 September 1938)

Crowds had gathered from mid-afternoon on Friday 30 September 1938, although the flight was not due to arrive for a couple of hours. Thousands thronged the airport entrance, eager to greet the homecoming hero.

Heston was one of London's principal airports, but this was a time when only a tiny minority travelled by air. As more and more cars converged, the narrow approach roads became virtually impassable. Inside the gateway, in an appropriately privileged position, 120 boys from Eton College lined up on each side of the road leading from the airport buildings to cheer the man of the hour.

On the aerodrome, an impressive array of VIPs – Cabinet ministers, high commissioners, ambassadors – had assembled long before the flight was due. One of the first to arrive was the Lord Mayor of London, Sir Harry Twyford, who had good reason to feel a deep sense of relief as he scanned the sky. Only three days earlier, when war seemed unavoidable, the sky had held the main menace for his city. Londoners had seen the Luftwaffe's destruction of Spanish towns and villages on the newsreels. London had seemed doomed to become Britain's own Guernica, writ large.

Shortly before 5.40 p.m., after a heavy downpour of rain, the silver airliner was spotted against the grey clouds. The twin-engined Lockheed was smaller than today's airliners, more the size of an executive jet, though far less comfortable and considerably slower. A couple of minutes later the plane landed and taxied to a standstill. The cabin door opened to reveal the man everyone was waiting for. To loud cheers, he smiled and waved the familiar black homburg.

As soon as the Prime Minister stepped to the ground, he was handed a message from the King, asking him to 'come straight to Buckingham Palace, so that I can express to you personally my most heartfelt congratulations on the success of your visit to Munich'. The invitation to the Palace was the ultimate accolade, confirming Chamberlain's place among the nation's heroes.

Viscount Halifax, the Foreign Secretary, was the first to congratulate his Prime Minister, rushing forward to shake him by the hand. Prominent among the other dignitaries greeting Chamberlain were the London representatives of the other signatories to the Four-Power Agreement which had finally been reached at Munich, in the early hours of the morning – the Italian Ambassador Count Grandi, the German Chargé d'Affaires Dr Kordt, and the French Ambassador M. Corbin, whose Prime Minister, Daladier, had dreaded his own return to Paris earlier that same day. When Daladier first saw the crowds gathered at le Bourget aerodrome, he assumed that they had come to express their disgust, and was astonished to be greeted as a hero.

Amid continuous cheering Chamberlain stepped forward to face the world's press and photographers. Elated, though weary, he thanked people for the 'immense number of letters during all these anxious days . . . letters of support and approval and gratitude' which he and his wife had received. He then delivered his historic message: 'the settlement of the Czechoslovak problem which has now been achieved is, in my view, only a prelude to a larger settlement in which all Europe may find peace.'

It was as he spoke the next sentence that he performed the act for which he will always be remembered, producing a sheet of paper and briefly waving it in his hand. He then told the crowds, 'This morning I had another talk with the German Chancellor, Herr Hitler, and here is a paper which bears his name upon it as well as mine.'

Chamberlain was an astute manager of the media, despite his dated appearance and manner – his Victorian garb, winged collar, umbrella and lugubrious delivery in the House of Commons earned him the nicknames 'The Coroner' and 'The Undertaker'. His dramatic gesture was captured by the world's press and newsreel cameras, and even by an early BBC television crew. When the scenes of his return were shown in cinemas up and down the land, people applauded and cheered.

The Prime Minister read out his 123-word joint declaration with Hitler, pledging to 'continue our efforts to remove possible sources of difference'. There was a further burst of cheering as the police cleared a way for him to his car.

Chamberlain set off on his drive to Buckingham Palace, and the crowds sang 'For he's a jolly good fellow'. His car passed the cheering Etonians, and at the airport gateway was mobbed as the police could not hold back the cheering crowds, including many small children waving tiny Union Jacks. Many tried to open the car doors to shake him by the hand. Eventually mounted police had to clear a way through the mass of people. All along the route from the airport to central London crowds filled the streets and people were cheering from their windows.

Outside the Palace, as dusk approached, a crowd of several thousand had been waiting for over two hours. *The Times* captured their mood: 'Indifferent to the heavy rain, they stood, densely packed, a happy throng, their hearts full of relief and a deep sense of thankfulness towards the man who had lifted a great weight from their minds.' Rational judgement was easily suspended. Shortly before Chamberlain's arrival, there was an extraordinary moment when a rainbow appeared over the rooftops and was hailed as a good omen.

At 6.50 p.m., Chamberlain's car came into sight. Motorists sounded their horns and the crowd swept across the road, leaving only a narrow passage to the Palace gates. After the Prime Minister entered the Palace, the crowd began chanting 'We want Chamberlain!' and 'We want Neville!'

Ten minutes later, King George VI and his Prime Minister emerged, accompanied by Queen Elizabeth and Mrs Chamberlain, into the glare of the floodlights trained on to the balcony high above the Palace forecourt. It was a rare privilege for a monarch to accord a peacetime Prime Minister the honour of sharing the balcony.

They stood together for some minutes smiling and waving as the crowd cheered and sang 'For they are jolly good fellows'. The King motioned Chamberlain forward, and for two minutes the Prime Minister stood alone at the front of the balcony acknowledging his remarkable reception.

After the group returned indoors the crowd spontaneously sang the National Anthem. When the Chamberlains left the Palace the crowd again surged around their car, with men and women tapping on the windows and Chamberlain waving to them.

The most extraordinary scenes took place as the Chamberlains returned to Number 10 Downing Street. 'It was a scene charged with emotion,' commented *The Times*, 'and those who saw it and took part will not readily forget it.' Crowds had packed Downing Street and Whitehall from early afternoon. The police were unable to keep open even a small section of road, and mounted police had to cajole people to create the narrowest of avenues for the Prime Minister's car to squeeze through the Foreign Office arch to Number 10 opposite.

The Chamberlains had difficulty struggling from their car and on to the doorstep of Number 10. There was a great crush of people in the entrance hall and around the foot of the stairs. Among them were the Cabinet, who would soon meet to hear the details of the Prime Minister's historic mission. Outside, the chanting grew louder, 'We want Chamberlain!'

Lord Home (the former Sir Alec Douglas-Home, and in those days known by his courtesy title, Lord Dunglass) has recalled what happened next. As the Prime Minister's Parliamentary Private Secretary, Home had accompanied Chamberlain to Munich and was now with him inside Number 10. Chamberlain was on his way up the stairs to wave to the crowds from a first-floor window. Home was separated from him by a few steps in the crush, but he distinctly heard someone call out, 'Tell them it's "Peace with Honour"!' Home could not identify who had said it, but Chamberlain stopped, turned round sharply and replied, 'No, I do not do that kind of thing.'

Moments later Chamberlain and his wife appeared at the first-floor window. To cries from below of 'Speech! Speech!', the Prime Minister held up his hand and waited for a couple of minutes for the crowd to quieten. As he spoke he repeated his gesture from the aerodrome, waving the paper which he and Hitler had signed that morning: 'My good friends, this is the second time in our history that there has come back from Germany to Downing Street "Peace with Honour".' As the cheering eventually subsided, Chamberlain continued, 'I believe it is peace for our time. We thank you from the bottom of our hearts.'

He had, after all, been unable to resist repeating the words which had been uttered by Disraeli, an earlier Conservative Prime Minister, in July 1878, on his triumphant return after signing the Treaty of Berlin which had brought the Russo-Turkish war to an end. As Chamberlain later wrote to his sister, 'The scenes culminated in Downing St., when I spoke to the multitudes below from the same window, I believe, as that from which Dizzy announced peace with honour 60 years ago.'

Before leaving the window, Chamberlain paused, then said 'And now I recommend you to go home and sleep quietly in your beds.'

Chamberlain regretted saying 'Peace with Honour' almost as soon as he had said it. 'I should never have said that,' he told his wife shortly afterwards. Home believes that in the few moments between Chamberlain rejecting the idea on the stairs and his reaching the window, someone must have persuaded him to go against his better judgement.

As the Cabinet gathered to hear the Prime Minister's account of the talks at Munich, the crowds outside sang 'For he's a jolly good fellow' and the National Anthem, before slowly beginning to disperse. But the celebrations carried on throughout the West End till the early hours.

The release of tension after Munich was almost tangible. Pathé produced a documentary film, *Chamberlain, the Man of the Hour*, which was shown from the following Monday at cinemas throughout the country. *The Times* announced that it was issuing the photograph of the King and Queen with the Chamberlains at Buckingham Palace as a photogravure plate, 17½ inches by 16¾, 'suitable for framing', price 1s. There were Chamberlain dolls, even sugar brollies.

Munich was good for business. 'News of the signing of the Four-Power Agreement over Czechoslovakia brought members of the Stock Exchange to town early . . .', *The Times* reported. 'From Wednesday's last-minute reprieve and Thursday's renewal of hope the City passed yesterday in continued crescendo on to the capitalisation first of peace here and now, and then, after the joint declaration of Mr Chamberlain and Herr Hitler, to that of no more war in the future.'

It is difficult, many years later, to appreciate how real the threat of war seemed in September 1938.

It was a war which people believed would be even more terrible than the appalling carnage of 1914–18. The new terrors of the age were poison gas and bombing from the air. The victims of the gas attacks in the trenches twenty years earlier were still around to remind people of the horror. Next time, it was feared, gas attacks would be targeted on the civilian population.

In 1935, Mussolini had used poison gas against the Abyssinians. In 1937, Hitler's planes had attacked the Basque town of Guernica, causing death and destruction. Most people had seen the slaughter of the Spanish Civil War on the cinema newsreels. By 1938, many were convinced that it was Britain's turn next. Some people even contemplated killing their families if war broke out. 'I'd sooner see kids dead than see them bombed like they are in some places,' was the comment of one woman in a 'Mass Observation' survey.

There had been a false alarm in May. Reports of German troop manoeuvres on the Czech border had prompted the following 'cyclostyled appeal' to villagers in Sussex:

Dear Sir,
In case of invasion, the Cuckfield Rural District Council will need the use of extra road-vehicles as emergency ambulances. . . . *not* asked for are 1-ton Ford lorries . . . or any milk-delivery lorries or vans. Horse-draught carriages are asked for to be a reserve in case of petrol shortage. . . . Drivers are expected to enrol as A.R.P. volunteers . . . and be trained in first aid to the wounded and gas-infected.

One of its recipients, Harold Macmillan, later recalled that the instructions were received 'with a characteristic mixture of scepticism and alarm' by his Sussex neighbours.

That summer, the English had their traditional distractions. The Derby was won by Bois Roussel at 20–1. There was Ascot and Henley. At Wimbledon, the American, Budge, defeated Britain's Austin to win the men's singles for the second year running. Mrs Helen Wills-Moody returned after three years to win her eighth title. At the Oval, in August, Len Hutton scored 364 runs, the highest innings by an Englishman in Tests against Australia.

But as the summer drew to a close the crisis came to the boil. On 12 September, Hitler addressed the Nazis' Nuremberg Rally and demanded self-determination for Germans living in the Sudetenland area of Czechoslovakia. If others would not help them, Germany would.

By the last week in September, war seemed imminent. The threat affected everyone's lives. Air Raid Precautions, or 'ARP', were launched on a massive scale. The Government issued 38 million gas masks.

Virginia Woolf wrote to her sister, Vanessa Bell, who was in Sussex, telling her about the war preparations in the capital: 'In London it was hectic and gloomy and at the same time despairing and yet cynical and calm. The streets were crowded. People were everywhere talking loudly about war. There were heaps of sandbags in the streets, also men digging trenches, lorries delivering planks, loud-speakers slowly driving and solemnly exhorting the citizens of Westminster "Go and fit your gas masks".'

Everyone expected that the bombing attacks would have an enormous impact. The Government's private estimates predicted that in the first intensive air-raid up to 600,000 people would be killed, and twice that number injured. Lady Diana Cooper, wife of the then First Lord of the Admiralty, Duff Cooper, recalled that the scientist Victor Rothschild (later Lord Rothschild) 'took pleasure in watching me writhe at his calculations of blast and his reasoned prophecies of annihilation by gas and germ-warfare'.

As *The Times* reported, 'All over London yesterday [Sunday, 25 September] citizens were being fitted for their gas masks, and many of the depots were open for 12 hours. From motor vans equipped with loud-speakers which cruised slowly around London this sort of announcement was broadcast: "Will every citizen of Westminster get his gas mask fitted as soon as possible? Please do not delay. Your nearest station is —." '

In Westminster alone there were eight ARP stations open from 9 a.m. till 10 p.m. Another five were open from 5 until 9 p.m. At each one, there was a continuous stream of people. Lady Diana Cooper and Venetia

Montagu 'sat in the Tothill Street [Westminster] workrooms clamping snouts and schnozzles on to rubber masks, parcelling them and distributing them to queues of men and women. Mothers would ask me for small ones for children. There were none as yet.' As Lady Diana later wrote, she 'felt sick all the time, like many others, no doubt. It was a grisly job for a neurotic but better than inaction.'

The novelist Storm Jameson went to her sister's house to take in the gas masks being distributed:

> The woman handed over three, a small one for Nicholas. I signed for them.
>
> 'There's also a four-months-old baby', I said. 'What have you for her?'
>
> 'I'm afraid – nothing. You must wrap a blanket round her and run with her to the nearest gas-shelter.'
>
> 'Oh. Where is it?'
>
> That it did not exist was part of the lunacy, no more insane than the rest.

ARP impinged on every aspect of life. As *The Times* reported:

> Announcements on the screens at cinemas, from the stage at theatres, from the pulpit in churches, and at sports and social gatherings, and posters and postcards were among the methods adopted over the week-end to inform people that they should have their gas masks fitted.
>
> One station is Caxton Hall, and on Saturday a newly married couple went straight from the office of the registrar of marriages there to another part of the building to be fitted for gas masks.

In another instance, 'At the Football League match between Brentford and Sunderland on Saturday, 28,000 spectators heard a loud-speaker announcement saying that all residents of Brentford and Chiswick should report from yesterday morning to be fitted for gas masks.'

Press reports referred to ARP proceeding 'vigorously, though calmly'. But there was real anxiety, and in some cases sheer panic. False alarms were inevitable. Lord Blake, the historian, interviewed for Channel Four, recalls an incident in the Norfolk village where his parents lived. Blake was waiting to return for the start of the new academic year at Oxford. The peace was suddenly shattered by a friend of his mother's, who came rushing into the Blakes' home, clutching her gas mask, convinced that the Germans had launched an attack. On investigation, what she had supposed to be poison gas turned out to be a neighbour's autumnal bonfire.

Virginia Woolf had a fright while she was reading a back-copy of *The*

*Times* in the basement of the London Library, in St James's Square, London. As she wrote to her sister, an old man told her, ' "They're telling us to put on our gas masks, Madam." I thought the raid had begun. . . .' It turned out to be the 'loudspeaker once more addressing the citizens of Westminster'.

Afterwards, Virginia Woolf walked to the National Gallery in Trafalgar Square, 'and a voice again urged me to fit my gas mask at once. The Nat. Gallery was fuller than usual; a nice old man was lecturing to an attentive crowd on Watteau. I suppose they were all having a last look.'

Towns and cities were soon transformed by the ARP preparations. There were practice black-outs and rescue operations to cope with casualties following any air-raids. Protective trenches were dug in parks and open spaces, often by the unemployed and volunteers. The composer Constant Lambert helped dig the trenches in Hyde Park. Jessica Mitford later recalled that nannies complained that their little charges were always falling in.

By an unhappy coincidence a film based on H.G. Wells's *War in the Air* had been showing at cinemas, and as Francis Williams, then editor of the *Daily Herald*, has recalled, this 'added a macabre horror to the sight of slit trenches being dug in the parks by the light of acetylene flares as darkness fell'.

In London, *The Times* reported that 'Trenches were dug in Hyde Park, St James's Park and Green Park, and yesterday workmen were busy in all three taking measurements and marking with stakes the sites for more of these shelters against blast and splinters. The operations attracted much public interest. . . .'

The Home Office had prepared designs for a trench, which could be constructed in people's gardens, though they cannot have been very comforting to the majority of city dwellers who lacked them. 'The depth suggested is 4ft. 6in. and the width 4ft. 6in. at the top, narrowing to 3ft. 6in. at the bottom. For six persons the trench should be 10ft. long. It should be covered with corrugated iron or old planks resting on sandbags or sacks or old boxes filled with the earth which has been excavated. . . . The trench should be dug some distance from any building to avoid the risk of wreckage falling on it. . . . the occupants should have their gas masks with them, as the trench would not be gas-proof.'

Parents' meetings were hurriedly arranged to discuss details of evacuation for their children: 'The proposal is for the children, more than 500,000 of them, to be moved to camps from 50 to 100 miles away, but evacuation would not be compulsory, and one of the objects of the meetings was to obtain parents' views.'

Hitler's speech in the Berlin Sports Palace was billed as his 'last word'.

Britain's press reported the Nazis' proclamation of the speech, which was extensively displayed throughout Germany:

HISTORIC SPEECH
CALL TO THE POPULATION: MAN THE STREETS.
The Reich Propaganda Director of the National-Socialist Ministry, Reich Minister Dr Goebbels, announces as follows:
On Monday, September 26th, at 8 p.m., in the Sports Palace in Berlin, a great speech to the people will be delivered.
The Führer speaks.
This speech will be broadcast from all German stations. It will be heard in all towns and villages of the Reich, and for those who themselves do not possess a wireless set, through loud-speakers.
The local party directors will immediately begin preparations for this communal wireless reception.
There must be no one in the whole Reich who fails to listen over the wireless to the historic speech.

It seemed improbable that Hitler's intentions would be entirely pacific.

The Berlin correspondent of *The Times* concluded his dispatch for Monday's editions with the news that all Hitler's ministers had assembled in Berlin; he added, almost as an afterthought, 'The only other development of interest during the week-end was the ostentatious mounting of guns on roofs and buildings and in playing-fields and parks in all parts of Berlin.'

That most English of institutions, *The Times* personal column, then securely located on the paper's front page, served as a barometer of the rising sense of anxiety. The cryptic messages (for lovers or spies?) continued:

EROS noon today. Old erotics and newcomers welcomed from Adelaide. G.W.

But ARP impinged heavily even on these columns:

A.R.P. – 60 miles S.W. of LONDON, to be LET UNFURNISHED on confines of private park, a gentleman's RESIDENCE. . . .
A.R.P. AND DOGS. – The League is compiling a list of people who will take dogs as boarders during an emergency . . . remote places preferred . . . National Canine Defence League.
SAFETY FOR BOYS. – Sussex Preparatory School far from danger zone has immediate vacancies. . . .
REFUGE FROM AIR ATTACK. – Enjoy complete safety in unspoiled surroundings. The WEBLEY HOTEL, St Dogmaels, near Cardigan,

West Wales, is comfortable, fully licensed, and miles away from any
military objective. Shooting and fishing. . . .

Readers of *The Times* clearly expected their bolt-holes to keep them in the
manner to which they were accustomed. For many, however, there was no
escape from the cities and, as yet, precious little protection.

Chamberlain felt compelled to dissuade the King from accompanying
the Queen to attend the launch of the new Cunard liner, the *Queen
Elizabeth*, in Glasgow. Photographs of the launch in the press were
juxtaposed with scenes of workmen digging more trenches, gas masks
being fitted and anti-aircraft units being installed.

Large numbers were turning up at recruiting stations, causing a level of
activity not seen 'since the days of the Great War . . .'. The anti-aircraft
and coastal defence units of the Territorial Army were called up. 'By
nightfall London and its environs were dotted with guns and searchlight
detachments, already prepared for possible action should an emergency
arise. . . .' The Air Ministry was instructed to call up the personnel of the
Fighter and Balloon Barrage squadrons, which comprised the defensive
units of the Auxiliary Air Force, but not the bomber units.

The exodus from London gathered pace – for those with somewhere
else to go. As *The Times* reported:

At all the main railway termini the scene was much the same –
crowded trains, thronged departure platforms, husbands bidding
farewell to wives and children, piles of trunks and perambulators,
mothers and nurses carrying babies, buffets full to overflowing,
hurrying porters and harassed officials, soldiers, sailors and airmen
equipped with full packs. Many people took their pets with them.
Dogs on leads, cats in baskets, and even canaries and parrots were
seen. As each train steamed out, those left standing on the platform
were predominantly men. . . . The boat trains told an interesting
story. Practically every person travelling to the Continent was a
foreigner returning home. Inward trains were filled, almost without
exception, with British subjects. . . .'

The extra trains running to the West Country, Ireland and Scotland
were all packed. 'A surprisingly large number of people took tickets for
small villages in East Anglia' – presumably they were less than reassured
by the effectiveness of the capital's ARP.

In her diary that week, Virginia Woolf described the evacuation from
London,

the marvels of organisation recited on the BBC last night. All who wish to leave London to go to certain tube stations, with a thick coat & enough food for the day: children to bring no glass bottles: parents not to come. Public will then be taken free of charge to towns and villages 50 miles out of London. Each will be given a stamped card on wh. to write to friends. No choice of destination, etc. . . .

'But what a shave', Virginia Woolf wrote in her diary on Friday, 30 September 1938. The sense of relief, even euphoria, at the news of the Munich Agreement was understandable. Britain had been on the brink of war. No one was in any doubt that it had been a desperately close-run thing. Yet relief soon gave way to recrimination.

The bitterness of the disagreement over Munich shocked even a seasoned political campaigner like Winston Churchill. He had already experienced at first hand many fierce clashes since he was first elected to the Commons in 1900 – the disagreements over the Boer War, the clash over the power of the House of Lords in 1910, the threat of armed insurrection in Ulster in 1912, and the General Strike in 1926 – but he felt that none of them had caused as much ill-feeling as Munich. Yet as Churchill wrote in his account of the years leading up to the Second World War,

It is not easy in these latter days, when we have all passed through years of intense moral and physical stress and exertion, to portray for another generation the passion which raged in Britain about the Munich Agreement. Among the Conservatives families and friends in intimate contact were divided to a degree the like of which I have never seen. Men and women, long bound together by party ties, social amenities, and family connections, glared upon one another in scorn and anger.

Harold Macmillan later echoed Churchill's experience. As he recalled in his memoirs, 'There have been many conflicts in my political life which at the time were fought with energy and even anger, but they were quickly forgotten. It is only in this case that the memory dies hard.'

Duff Cooper said that, at that time, 'I could count among my acquaintances twelve happily married couples who were divided upon the issue of Munich.' And he added, 'in every case it was the husband who supported and the wife who opposed Chamberlain.' But Harold Nicolson, then a National Labour MP, found the exact opposite in his Leicester constituency. He was told that he had 'put the women's vote against me by abusing Munich'.

At one level it is understandable why Munich provoked angry dispute. Britain had been on the brink of European war and had only been saved at the eleventh hour. But some found the manner of the salvation unacceptable. Inevitably, the clash between those who welcomed Munich and those who criticised it was bitter.

But this is only a part of the explanation. The bitterness of the conflict, the depth of emotions and the lasting impact of the disagreements reflect the fact that the debate over Munich was itself the culmination of a much longer period of conflict and disagreement.

Within a period of less than six years there had been a convulsion in British attitudes and thinking. The question of how Britain should respond to the dictators had fragmented the bedrock of British society and politics, which was already under stress from the combination of economic slump and the burden of defending a far-flung empire. What many had thought sensible and morally right as recently as 1933, they found irresponsible and morally corrupt by the autumn of 1938.

Every shade of political opinion, and everyone who took an active interest in political debate, was affected. Every section of the British political class was riven by the bitterest conflict in generations – Conservative, Labour, Liberal, right, left and centre, civil servant and diplomat, trade unionist and boss, journalist, editor and proprietor, student and don. None of them escaped division or dissent.

# CHAPTER TWO

# PACIFISTS AND APPEASERS

Wars don't start nowadays because people want them. We long for peace, and fill our newspapers with conferences about disarmament and arbitration, but there is a radical instability in our whole ·world-order, and soon we shall be walking into the jaws of destruction again, protesting our pacific intentions.

(Evelyn Waugh, extract from *Vile Bodies*, 1930)

In Berlin, on the morning of Monday, 30 January 1933, President Hindenburg received Adolf Hitler, leader of the National Socialist German Workers' Party (Nazis), and appointed him Chancellor of the Reich. That night a torchlight procession of 100,000 Nazi supporters marched through the German capital in triumph. Hitler saluted them from the Chancellery balcony, while the eighty-five-year-old Hindenburg watched, bewildered, from the presidential palace.

Yet Hitler was one of only three Nazis in the Cabinet. The new Government was dominated by old-style nationalists, who thought they were reining Hitler in. As von Papen, the Vice-Chancellor, boasted to a friend, 'in two months we'll have pushed Hitler into a corner so hard that he'll be squeaking.'

This optimism was shared in Britain. The following day, *The Times*, then regarded around the world as unofficial mouthpiece of the British Government, observed that giving Hitler 'the chance of showing that he is something more than an orator and an agitator was always desirable'. *The Times* acknowledged that there would be misgivings about Germany's attitude on armaments. 'But in fairness to the Nazis it must be admitted that they have in fact said little more on the subject of German disabilities under the Treaty of Versailles than the most constitutional parties, although they have said it much louder.' The soothing message was that the Nazis might make more noise, but diplomacy and negotiation should do the trick. Concessions could be made, bargains struck, and the peace of Europe preserved.

This sanguine view of how to deal with Hitler was to prevail throughout much of British society and across all shades of opinion for much of the decade. At Oxford, although the don Maurice Bowra feared the worst about Hitler, he found that 'This view was not well received in England. Even the Murrays [Gilbert Murray, the classicist, and his wife] were inclined to think that things could not be as bad as I said and that Hitler might be restrained by Conservative colleagues such as Hugenberg and von Neurath. . . .'

In Britain in January 1933, the temptation to indulge in wishful thinking was virtually irresistible. Less than eighteen months earlier, a Labour Government had collapsed in financial chaos, and in the Far East the Japanese had invaded Manchuria. Britain had been simultaneously plunged into domestic crisis and confronted by an alarming threat to her far-flung empire. She was in no state to contemplate a threat from the Continent of Europe.

It was also a question of state of mind. The Great War had ended only fifteen years earlier, and people believed that it must remain the 'war to end all wars'. Britain alone had lost more than 750,000 men. Twice that number had been wounded. Their sacrifice was not to be in vain.

The appalling losses affected everyone. Neville Chamberlain had been devastated by the death of his young cousin, Norman, to whom he had been devoted. Lord Home, whose schooldays at Ludgrove and Eton coincided with the Great War, recalls 'scarcely a day going by without seeing one of the other boys in floods of tears', because an elder brother or father had been killed.

'Never again!' This was the emotional well-spring from which 'pacifists' and 'appeasers' were able to attract such enormous support.

Just ten days after Hitler was sworn in as Chancellor, the Oxford Union debated the motion 'That this House will in no circumstances fight for its King and Country'.

The meeting on the evening of Thursday, 9 February 1933, was one of the Union's regular weekly meetings. Although no one attending could have realised at the time, it was to become one of the most talked-about events of the decade.

Proposing the motion, Cyril Joad (the philosopher who became famous for his radio broadcasts) delivered an unremittingly pacifist speech. Among those speaking for the motion were Max Beloff (later a founder of the independent University of Buckingham and a Conservative peer), Tony Greenwood (a Labour Cabinet minister in the 1960s) and David Hunt (who fought in the Second World War and became Private Secretary to Attlee and Churchill).

The main speaker against, a former President of the Union, Quintin Hogg (later Lord Hailsham, the Conservative Lord Chancellor), argued in the assertive style which was to become his hallmark that pacifists were not the 'true friends of peace'. A strong Britain was 'a necessary factor for peace'. Among those who also opposed the motion was Angus Maude (later a Conservative MP and Cabinet minister in the Thatcher Government).

Hogg challenged the pacifists on what they would do if their wives were being raped. Joad's response was to quote Lytton Strachey, 'I should interpose my body!' Non-violent resistance was the cornerstone of Joad's case. This argument had considerable appeal in intellectual circles at the time. Gandhi had visited Britain during the autumn of 1931 for the Round Table conference on India, and his visit had aroused interest in the apparent effectiveness of a pacifist strategy, even against the might of the British Raj.

Joad gave brilliant expression to the deepening revulsion felt towards war in the early 1930s. In part this reflected the widespread anxiety that the horrors of any future war would be even worse than the carnage of 1914–18, and would be visited on the entire population. This fear had been encouraged in late 1932 by the Conservative leader in the coalition Government, Stanley Baldwin. Speaking in the House of Commons, he had warned of the 'terror of the air', and thought it as well 'for the man in the street to realize that there is no power on earth that can protect him from being bombed. Whatever people may tell him, the bomber will always get through . . .' (Hansard, 10 November 1932, col. 632).

Joad claimed that bombers would be over Britain 'within twenty minutes of the declaration of war with a western European power'. Aircraft defences were futile when 'a single bomb can poison every living thing in an area of three-quarters of a square mile'.

Joad's attack on the futility of war swayed the debate. The motion was passed by 275 votes to 153. Yet it was the reaction afterwards which transformed the occasion into a *cause célèbre*. The debate had been designed for intellectual amusement rather than as a serious test of opinion, but it soon featured in news stories around the world.

Two days after the debate, the *Daily Telegraph* published a letter expressing the shock felt by older generations of Oxford men at the display of 'Red tendencies' in the debate and urged that they should expunge the shameful motion from the minutes of the Union. The letter, written under the pseudonym 'Sixty-Four', was in fact written by J.B. Firth, one of the paper's leader writers.

At the Union's next weekly meeting, on 16 February, an unidentified group of about twenty people invaded the hall and tore the offending pages from the minute book. The *Oxford Times* suggested that they were supporters of Oswald Mosley's British Union of Fascists, formed the previous year.

Addressing the Anti-Socialist and Anti-Communist Union the following day, Winston Churchill lambasted *The Times* for allegedly not treating the 'King and Country' debate seriously. He described the debate as 'a very disquieting and disgusting symptom', and spoke of Germany 'with its splendid clear-eyed youth marching forward . . . demanding to be conscripted into an army', of Italy 'with her ardent Fascisti, her renowned Chief, and stern sense of national duty', and of France 'anxious, peace-loving, pacifist to the core, but armed to the teeth and determined to survive as a great nation in the world'. And he declared, 'One can almost feel the curl of contempt upon the lips of the manhood of all these peoples when they read this message sent out by Oxford Univeristy in the name of Young England.'

Churchill's son Randolph took up Firth's idea. He circulated a letter to all life-members of the Oxford Union, seeking support for the proposal that the 'King and Country' debate be expunged from the minutes. But on 2 March, his motion was defeated by a staggering 750 votes to 138. The class of '33 were not going to let their predecessors run the Union.

In his subsequent account of the period Winston Churchill attributed the most far-reaching ramifications to the 'King and Country' debate. In *The Gathering Storm*, he was as melodramatic about the event as he and his son had been at the time: 'It was easy to laugh off such an episode in England, but in Germany, in Russia, in Italy, in Japan, the idea of a decadent, degenerate Britain took deep root and swayed many calculations.'

The antagonisms stirred by the 'King and Country' debate were mirrored in another incident. Beverley Nichols, the popular writer and pacifist, was filmed making an impassioned speech at an Albert Hall peace rally. Nichols went to see his performance in the newsreels and met Noël Coward in the queue outside a cinema in Piccadilly. Nichols asked Coward why he had come. 'To look at your performance'. When Nichols replied that he hoped he would enjoy it, Coward proclaimed, 'I shan't like it at all', adding, with what Nichols described as 'a beady look', 'I have come to hiss.' Coward proceeded to sit in the front row and hiss. Nichols claimed, however, that Coward's hissing was drowned by the applause.

The 'King and Country' debate should not have come as any shock. In March 1927, the Cambridge Union had voted for a pacifist motion by 213 votes to 138. On Armistice Day 1932, the Debating Society of University College, London, resolved 'That in the event of a declaration of war, this House would not support the Government'.

The senior Conservative politician Leo Amery later recalled his experience in October 1932 when he had debated a motion, also at the Cambridge Union, 'That we should disarm down to the German level': 'What was significant was, not only that I was outvoted by four to one (377 to 89) in a crowded house, but that a passionately excited body of undergraduates found it difficult even to give me a hearing.'

What had particularly outraged conservative and patriotic sentiment about the Oxford Union debate was the inclusion in the motion of the words 'King and Country'. The *Daily Express* was provoked to blame the vote on 'practical jokers, woozy-minded Communists and sexual indeterminates'.

To students in the early 1930s, however, 'King and Country' conjured up the jingoistic excesses of 1914. It ran counter to the belief in internationalism, the new spirit of the age, which would banish the old nationalistic wars. It was this clash between diametrically opposed views which provoked the furore.

Defending the Oxford vote a fortnight later in the *News Chronicle*, A.A. Milne (now remembered as the author of the Winnie the Pooh stories), reminded his readers that 'There is no infamy for which the words "King and Country" do not provide adequate cover! "My Country, right or wrong!" How tragically easy war becomes waged in these mists of sentimentality.'

In the late 1920s and early 1930s, the pacifist mood was being fuelled by the flow of memoirs and novels exploring the horrors of the Great War – Richard Aldington's *Death of a Hero* and Siegfried Sassoon's *Memoirs of a Fox-hunting Man* were published in 1928, and Robert Graves' *Goodbye to All That*, Ernest Hemingway's *Farewell to Arms* and Erich Maria Remarque's *All Quiet on the Western Front* appeared in 1929. Lewis Milestone's film of Remarque's book had a powerful impact.

Economic slump and the rise of aggressive dictators revived the fear of war. In 1931, this was highlighted in *New Signatures*, an anthology by contemporary poets including W.H. Auden, Cecil Day Lewis and Stephen Spender. As one of the reviews commented, several of the contributors felt themselves living 'Under the shadow of future, nationalist war'. They were 'indignant that anything so idiotic and wasteful as war should menace the creative promise of their generation'.

In early 1933, Hitler's appointment as German Chancellor and a fresh Japanese offensive in China increased the anxieties about war. When Vera Brittain delivered the manuscript of *Testament of Youth*, itself a memoir of the lost generation of 1914–18, to her publisher, Victor Gollancz, in March 1933, she was greeted with the comment, 'I hope there won't be a war before your book comes out.' The year 1933 also saw the publication of Storm Jameson's pacifist memoir, *No Time Like the Present*, and Beverley Nichols' *Cry Havoc!*, which predicted another war within a year.

The wave of pacifist sentiment and the sudden menace of war in early 1933 lies behind the outcome of the Oxford Union debate. As the historian of British pacifism Martin Ceadel has argued, the vote mingled anger at the folly of 1914 with an impulsive reaction against the sudden threat of war – a classic case of 'Never again!'

Within a short time of the Oxford Union debate, even some of the most influential pacifist writers were already having their doubts. It was all very well to protest against war, but how could war be prevented in the first place? Storm Jameson later confessed her own confusion. In *Cry Havoc!*, Beverley Nichols emerged as a supporter of an international peace-keeping force, while later in the decade he was to take an increasing interest in the British Union of Fascists and the Anglo-German Fellowship, which attracted many pro-Nazis.

Britain's political leaders, whether of the right or the left, were as uncertain as anyone else about what to do at the sudden threat to world peace.

The ministers and civil servants who were having to grapple with Britain's new predicament were, with remarkably few exceptions, members of that same ruling class who had governed the empire for decades before 1914. Although Ramsay MacDonald, the former Labour leader, was Prime Minister, he was a captive of the Conservative Party, which dominated the coalition National Government.

The governing class of the 1930s were the products of that suddenly distant late-Victorian and Edwardian era. At the close of the nineteenth century and the start of the twentieth they were being sent to the same public schools as their fathers and grandfathers – Eton, Harrow, Rugby and the like. When they went up to Oxford and Cambridge, they read the same subjects as their forebears, and no doubt heard some of the same lectures.

They spoke in the same idiom as their predecessors, thought the same way, tried to govern with the same paternalist approach, and shared the view that the British had a special civilising mission in the world. They had the same perspective on the world scene. Britain was a great power, which should maintain her position without risking another major war. But in the last resort Britain should 'buy off' other countries thrusting for world power by making limited concessions, rather than face a show-down.

Sir Samuel Hoare and Viscount Halifax, Foreign Secretaries in the 1930s, would have been perfectly at ease had they been able to swap places with the Marquis of Lansdowne or Sir Edward Grey, who held the office in the 1900s. Whether any of this equipped them to cope with the complexities of economic policy, or to deal with Adolf Hitler, Benito Mussolini and the militaristic Japanese, was another matter.

The opposition were in disarray. The Liberals were split three ways, between the Lloyd George faction with four MPs, the free-traders led by Sir Herbert Samuel, and the National Liberals led by Sir John Simon, who remained supporters of the Government. Both the Samuelites and the Simonites each had only thirty or so MPs.

On the left, the growing threat from the dictators was beginning to reveal divisions between pacifists, internationalists and rearmers, which had been submerged during the more peaceable 1920s. After their rout at the 1931 election, when only fifty-two Labour MPs were returned, the Labour Party was led in the Commons by George Lansbury, the seventy-two-year-old Christian pacifist. Lansbury's fiercest critic, the union leader Ernest Bevin, is reputed to have commented, 'The trouble with George is that 'e lets 'is bleedin' 'eart rule 'is bloody 'ead.'

Besides Lansbury, the only other Labour MP with any ministerial experience was Sir Stafford Cripps, who had served as Solicitor-General before 1931. Cripps was a left-winger who regarded the League of Nations as a tool of capitalist Britain and France, and maintained that in a capitalist society socialists had no alternative but to oppose rearmament.

On 15 February 1933, the Cabinet reviewed Britain's defences at home and throughout the empire. It was a disquieting occasion. All three ministers for the armed services – the First Lord of the Admiralty, Sir Bolton Eyres-Monsell, and the Secretaries of State for War and Air, Viscount Hailsham and the Marquis of Londonderry – warned their colleagues that Britain's defences were seriously deficient.

The ministers seated round the Cabinet table were faced with a problem whose origins went back over a decade. In the aftermath of the Great War, British strategy had been dictated by the need to spend less on arms. The enormous debts incurred during the war had to be paid. Industry was switched from war production to earning hard cash.

At the same time, there was immense pressure to spend more on social welfare, notably health and housing. These demands were exploding as more people won the vote – in 1906 the electorate totalled only 7¼ million, but by 1918 there were over 21¼ million voters, and by 1929 nearly 29 million.

The British had also emerged from the Great War with far and away the most extensive empire, stretching through the Near and Middle East, Africa, Asia and the Far East. Defending these interests would inevitably entail huge costs, despite the overriding need to cut back. Every effort would have to be made to avoid any 'entanglement' on the Continent of Europe.

From 1918, constraints on defence spending were so tight that military chiefs had to plan on the basis of an extraordinary assumption that there would be no large-scale war for at least ten years, the so-called Ten-Year Rule. In keeping with this policy, Winston Churchill, Chancellor of the Exchequer from 1924 to 1929, was niggardly about defence spending – as his opponents pointed out when he later campaigned for rearmament. The Ten-Year Rule was carried forward each year, so that by the early 1930s Britain's defences were based on the assumption that there would be no war until the early 1940s.

By the time Hitler came to power, disarmament and the desire to distance herself from Europe were the twin pillars of Britain's diplomacy. She desperately wanted the peace preserved, but at least cost to herself. She was prepared to use her diplomacy in Europe, but not to back it up.

Britain was schizophrenic about the League of Nations, the new international organisation established by the Treaty of Versailles. On the one hand, an effective League with a workable system of collective security would restrain potential aggressors and help Britain reduce her defence commitments. On the other hand, an open commitment to the League ran the risk that she would become embroiled in other people's disputes, and end up having to spend unspecified sums.

Principally on Britain's initiative, the World Disarmament Conference had been launched at Geneva in February 1932. At home, it enjoyed wide support across the political spectrum. It was largely the brainchild of the Conservative politician Lord Robert Cecil (later Viscount Cecil of Chelwood), and its President was the former Labour leader and ex-Foreign Secretary Arthur Henderson.

Within a month of its opening, the growing threat from Japan led Britain to rescind the Ten-Year Rule. But there was no question of any increase in defence spending. When the British Prime Minister Ramsay MacDonald addressed the Disarmament Conference later that month, he called for general disarmament, and chose to single out the need for the well-armed French to cut their arsenal.

Earlier in April, Hitler had won over 13 million votes in the German presidential election. The Foreign Secretary Sir John Simon was soon expressing sympathy for a disarmed Germany looking across her border at France. In June, Britain agreed to end economic reparations against Germany. At the Reichstag elections the following month, the Nazis emerged as the largest single party.

By the autumn of 1932, Britain's confusion seemed complete. The new Government in Berlin called for an end to German disarmament. At first, this was rejected by Sir John Simon, who reiterated Britain's commitment to the Versailles Treaty. In protest, Germany withdrew from the

Disarmament Conference. But two months later Simon reversed his position. He was prepared, after all, to consider Germany's case. Suddenly, the Treaty of Versailles was negotiable. This helped woo the Germans back into the Conference.

Britain had, however, acted decisively to distance herself from Europe. In the Ottawa Trade Agreement of August 1932, she gave preferential access to foodstuffs from the Dominions – Australia, Canada, New Zealand, South Africa – in return for the Dominions giving preference to British manufactured goods. Neville Chamberlain, the Chancellor of the Exchequer, was cock-a-hoop that he had given practical expression to 'Imperial Preference', the great dream of his father Joseph Chamberlain.

The upshot was that Britain had turned her back on the Continent and tightened the bonds of Commonwealth and empire. As a result, her influence was reduced in Central and Eastern Europe. In turn, this increased the risk that the smaller countries in the region – Czechoslovakia, Hungary, Poland, Rumania, Yugoslavia – would fall into the orbit of a resurgent Germany.

Inevitably, it also meant that Britain would have to give even higher priority to protecting her imperial interests at a time when they were coming under ever-increasing threat. The troubles in Palestine, the rise of the nationalist movement in India, the menace of Mussolini's Italy in the Mediterranean, and a militaristic Japan determined to establish an empire of her own – all added to the burdens on Britain when she was already severely overstretched.

But there was one consideration which British ministers believed was overriding. The nightmare of the financial crisis of 1931 was still fresh in their minds. Under no circumstances would the Cabinet put at risk Britain's financial stability. At their defence review in February 1933, the Chancellor of the Exchequer Neville Chamberlain countered the warnings from the three ministers for the armed services by arguing that financial considerations were paramount. In the Treasury's view, 'other risks [would] have to be run until the country has had time to recuperate.' MacDonald, haunted by the way the markets had toppled his Labour Government, backed his Conservative Chancellor. The Cabinet concurred. There could be no extra defence spending. Within existing budgets, priority was given to defending bases, and to the Far East.

British diplomacy was having to depend more and more heavily on bluff. But ministers had decided that there was nothing they could yet do about it, apart from hoping that the Disarmament Conference would let them off the hook.

★

No sooner had the Cabinet ruled out any extra spending on defence than events in Germany took a dramatic turn. On 27 February 1933, the German Reichstag burnt down. At the elections on 6 March, amid great fear and unprecedented intimidation, Hitler won an overall majority.

Far from being reined in, Hitler now held the reins. In Britain, although few found Hitler attractive, some positively welcomed the prospect of a German revival – not least, in the wake of the Russian Revolution, as a bulwark against the spread of Soviet Communism. It would be good for business as far as some in the City and industry were concerned, though others remained protectionist.

One of the most influential supporters of a stronger Germany was the editor of *The Times*, Geoffrey Dawson. So it was hardly surprising that *The Times* should identify a 'new spirit' in Germany in its leader on 22 March, the day after the newly elected Reichstag met in the highly symbolic setting of the Garrison Church in Potsdam, where Frederick the Great lies buried.

*The Times* was actually better informed than most about the true nature of the Nazis. This superior knowledge was a tribute to the daily telegrams sent by their correspondents in Berlin, Norman Ebbutt and Douglas Reed. But the paper's knowledge remained superior because it was not always fully shared with its readers – though anyone reading the paper in the 1930s would still have been able to establish a comprehensive picture of events in Europe.

From 1931, Douglas Jay (later a Labour Cabinet minister) worked at the paper's old offices in Printing House Square, as a sub-editor of foreign news. He recalls being filled with 'mounting pessimism' at the dispatches from Ebbutt and Reed, 'all the more so because it did not seem to me that the full import of what they were saying was being allowed to percolate through to the readers . . .'. As Dawson himself was to write later in the 1930s, 'I did my utmost, night after night, to keep out of the paper anything that might hurt their [i.e. German] susceptibilities.'

Jay left the paper in early 1933, but by then he was convinced that 'Hitler and Goering were not so much political extremists as desperate maniacs who would shrink from no sort of violence or duplicity to achieve their criminal aims.' This was 'implicit' in the telegrams which Ebbutt and Reed sent for publication, and was even clearer from the background notes they sent for the guidance of the London office.

Nonetheless, in its leader on the Reichstag opening, *The Times* sedulously developed the case for making concessions to Germany, a case which Dawson was to plead through its columns for the following five years. A speech of Hitler's in which he had proclaimed 'I am for force, because in force I see strength . . .' was discounted on the grounds that it had been intended for domestic consumption. The paper preferred to trust Hitler's comments at Potsdam, where he had spoken of the desire of the German people to be 'true friends, of a peace which would at last heal the wounds from which all suffer'.

With the reassuring conclusion that there was no evidence that 'the new Chancellor intends to be immoderate in his foreign policy' *The Times* declared,

> It is his [Hitler's] set purpose – and in that he has much sympathy outside his own country – to re-establish Germany on a footing of equality with other nations; and the internal excesses of his regime should not debar foreign statesmanship from examining with an open mind the external claims of the German, as they would of any other, Government.

There was undoubtedly a feeling in some quarters that Germany had suffered injustices at the Treaty of Versailles, and that these should be put right. There was also a general belief that disputes should be resolved through negotiation and conciliation, whatever the nature of the regimes involved – the traditional diplomacy of secret deals and power blocs was held responsible for the 1914–18 war.

Nancy Astor, who had become the first woman MP in 1919, preached negotiation with both Hitler and Stalin. As a Conservative, the latter course took far more political courage, setting her apart from others on the right who agreed on the need to treat with Germany under the Nazis, but who could not accept the thought of any dealings with Soviet Russia. Her fierce commitment to appeasement reflected her hatred of war.

Feminist concern also led Nancy Astor to emerge as an early critic of the Hitler regime's repressive measures. At a meeting of the National Union of Societies for Equal Citizenship, chaired by the Independent MP Eleanor Rathbone, at the end of May 1933, Nancy Astor won unanimous support for a resolution expressing 'dismay' at the Nazis' dismissals of women from government service. The resolution declared that 'any injury done to the women of one nation must be deeply felt by the women of all nations', and was duly sent to the German Ambassador.

Nancy Astor and Geoffrey Dawson were leading lights in two groups, centred at Cliveden and All Souls College, Oxford, whose number included some of the strongest advocates of concessions to Germany. Both groups subsequently attracted notoriety (and achieved immortality) through the writings of Claud Cockburn, editor of the 1930s scandal sheet *The Week*, who coined the phrase the 'Cliveden Set'; the cartoonist David Low, who caricatured Nancy Astor and her friends as the 'Shiver Sisters';

and the historian A.L. Rowse, who published his memoir *All Souls and Appeasement* in the 1960s.

The 1920s and 1930s were still the era of country weekends and dinner parties. Both the Astors' country home at Cliveden in Berkshire, and All Souls, where Dawson was a senior fellow, were close enough to London to enable busy men to escape from the capital without having to travel for more than a couple of hours. Rowse, then a young fellow at All Souls, has this recollection of Dawson: 'I can see him now on a summer day coming into the smoking-room in full Ascot kit, grey topper and tails, chaffing me whether I wouldn't come too.'

Any notion of conspiracy is far-fetched, not least because some of the regulars at both places were noted 'anti-appeasers'. The independent-minded Conservative MP for Stockton, Harold Macmillan, was a frequent visitor at Cliveden. Another friend of the Astors was Lord Cranborne, heir to the Marquis of Salisbury, who like the rest of the Cecils was vehemently opposed to appeasement.

Robert Boothby, a passionate anti-appeaser and close associate of Winston Churchill, wrote of 'that fatal dinner table' at All Souls, implying that appeasement was dreamt up over the evening meal in an Oxford college. Yet some senior fellows, and almost all the younger fellows, including Isaiah Berlin, Douglas Jay, Rowse and John Sparrow, opposed appeasement. This led to some heated arguments, as Maurice Bowra, himself a committed anti-appeaser, later recalled:

When Simon [Sir John Simon, Foreign Secretary 1931–5] visited Wadham, I avoided politics as far as possible, but at All Souls I found myself in company of the younger Fellows arguing against Geoffrey Dawson and his friends. What particularly embittered me was the cold-blooded indifference which the appeasers showed towards the barbarities of the Nazis.

All Souls and Cliveden regularly brought together the leading appeasers, and they were extremely well connected. Although they were not responsible for the British Government's subsequent pursuit of appeasement, which was largely determined by powerful economic and strategic considerations, they nonetheless helped reinforce the policy and create a favourable climate.

Among the senior fellows at All Souls, along with Dawson, were two Foreign Secretaries, Simon and Viscount Halifax, who were among Neville Chamberlain's most trusted colleagues. Dawson and Halifax were particularly close – both had country homes in Yorkshire and were eminent members of the strongly independent, provincial 'society' – quite distinct from London society – which still flourished in the 1930s. Dawson and Halifax would sometimes travel together on the train between London and Leeds.

At Cliveden, Viscount (Waldorf) Astor and his wife Nancy held court. Waldorf Astor owned the *Observer*, his brother John *The Times*. The editors of the Astor papers, J.L. Garvin and Dawson, were members of the group. Other regulars included Tom Jones, former Deputy Cabinet Secretary and confidant to Lloyd George and Stanley Baldwin, and Philip Kerr, the diplomat. From 1930, when Kerr came into his inheritance as the Marquis of Lothian, his country seat – Blickling Hall in Norfolk – became another centre for the group.

The most striking feature about the appeasers at All Souls and Cliveden is the predominance of men who had been acolytes of Lord Milner, the right-wing Conservative politician. Milner had been British High Commissioner in the British Cape during and after the Boer War, a leading member of Lloyd George's War Cabinet, and Colonial Secretary in the early 1920s. He had died in 1924, but his influence lived on through 'Milner's Kindergarten', the corps of young civil servants who had served him in South Africa.

On their return to Britain, members of 'Milner's Kindergarten' founded a quarterly magazine, the *Round Table*, to spread their belief in the ideals of the British empire, the English-speaking world and social reform. Milner's commitment to the supremacy of the British empire was remarkably similar to that of Joseph Chamberlain, Colonial Secretary during the Boer War.

Four of Milner's disciples and founder members of the Round Table group were senior fellows at All Souls, where they dubbed themselves the 'Establishment' – Geoffrey Dawson, Dougal Malcolm, chairman of the Chartered Company, Lionel Curtis, an Oxford academic, and Bob Brand, a managing director of Lazards, the merchant bank – though Brand was not an appeaser. The 'Establishment' were also friends of Waldorf Astor from their student days together at Oxford, and became the nucleus of the regulars at Cliveden, along with Lionel Hichens (an anti-appeaser) and another old friend from Oxford, Philip Kerr (Lothian), whom Nancy had converted from Catholicism to Christian Science.

Others associated with the Round Table and Cliveden were Garvin (besides editing the *Observer* he was biographer of Joseph Chamberlain), John Buchan (the novelist and author of *The Thirty-Nine Steps* and later, as Lord Tweedsmuir, British Governor-General in Canada) and Edward Grigg (a Conservative MP). Among these, Grigg was an anti-appeaser, and Garvin, though believing in appeasement, also backed rearmament on the ground that Britain should bargain from strength.

The strong influence of Milner's thinking on his 'disciples' often impressed Douglas Jay during his weekend visits to All Souls. Milner had made himself into an apostle of the British empire, yet he was German by birth and had been educated in Germany.

Before 1914, Germany had been the great rival, but in October 1918, before the Armistice, Milner had proposed a peace settlement. He became a strong critic of the Treaty of Versailles, and felt that the Germans had been unjustly treated, a view which others came to share, most notably the economist John Maynard Keynes. The terms were not as harsh on the Germans as many claimed, but during the 1920s and 1930s the perception that the Treaty was unjust undoubtedly gained force. Among the Round Table group, Philip Kerr (Lothian) had special reason to feel remorse – as chief aide to Lloyd George he was one of the Treaty's authors.

Milner's thinking was dominated by the impact of the Russian Revolution in 1917. His biographer, John Marlowe, has written that after 1917, Milner 'held that the real enemy was Communism and the Allied war aim should be to get themselves in a position of sufficient strength to negotiate with Germany "a draw in our favour" which would leave both West and Central Europe sufficiently strong to combat the menace of Communism.' Jay has observed that it would be hard to find a better description of British appeasement as it developed during the 1930s.

# CHAPTER THREE

# HITLER'S CHALLENGE

At present the mood here is most pacific, especially among the youth of the country. . . . And one of the perplexities of those statesmen who think that we shall have to re-arm is how to bring the country to that point.

(Tom Jones (former Deputy Secretary to the Cabinet), writing to Dr Abraham Flexner of Princeton University, 1 March 1934)

During 1933, Britain was still the prisoner of her commitment to disarmament. As the Government would discover, most people were willing inmates.

In mid-March, a few days before the ceremonial opening of the new Reichstag at Potsdam, the British Government announced further cuts in spending on the Royal Air Force. As a result, not even 'the modest programme approved as long ago as 1923' would be met.

This was presented by the Under-Secretary of State for Air Sir Philip Sassoon as 'practical proof' of the Government's commitment to the Geneva Disarmament Conference. They were 'prepared to accept the continuance of the serious existing disparity between the strength of the Royal Air Force and that of the air services of the other great nations' for as long as the talks continued at Geneva (Hansard, 14 March 1933, col. 1796).

Winston Churchill, one of the Government's most senior back-benchers, strongly criticised Sassoon's arguments. The previous autumn, Churchill had urged that, while attempts should be made to meet Germany's grievances, disarmament should be abandoned. He had deplored Baldwin's readiness to spread anxiety about the new threat from bombers while doing nothing about it. He now argued that Britain must have the capacity to retaliate against any air attack.

But Churchill was already embroiled in another major row with the Government, over their plans to grant dominion status to India. Less than a month earlier, he had led a rebellion in which more than forty Conservative die-hards voted against the Government. His attack on the state of Britain's air defences was derided in Cabinet as being 'prompted to some extent by political motives'.

The Government persevered with their pleas for disarmament. In Geneva, on 16 March, Ramsay MacDonald proposed limits on the length of military service, the size of guns and tanks, and the number of aircraft. Bombing was to be forbidden. The French Army would be reduced and the Germans allowed to re-establish theirs, so that each country would have 200,000 troops. The same limits were set on the Polish and Italian armies.

A week after MacDonald's speech, and just two days after the ceremony at Potsdam, Hitler seized absolute power. Challenging the new Reichstag to declare for 'war or peace' with the Government, he forced through an Enabling Act which gave him the right to make laws (even if they were unconstitutional), enact the Budget, take up loans and conclude treaties with other countries.

Repression proceeded apace. On 10 May 1933, the Nazis burnt thousands of books, including the work of Professor Albert Einstein, then Germany's foremost scientist, along with works by André Gide, Proust, Zola and Thomas Mann. In July, trade unions were banned. Thousands of the Nazis' opponents were imprisoned, and many were sent to concentration camps.

Details of the Nazis' brutality and persecution of minorities or political opponents were published by Victor Gollancz in an anonymous book *The Brown Book of the Hitler Terror*, sponsored by a committee of which Einstein was president. In early September, Douglas Jay reviewed the book for the *Economist*, drawing attention to the reliable evidence that '60,000 have been subjected to violence since 27th February, and that over 35,000 were in concentration camps in July'. The committee had evidence of 500 murders perpetrated by the Nazis since 3 March, and at least forty-three Jews had been murdered for no other reason than their religion. Jay concluded that the report would 'raise the question whether the right to equality of status among the nations can be claimed by a Government which disregards the ordinary canons of justice and humanity in revenging itself on its own fellow-countrymen'.

The German Finance Minister, von Krosigk, immediately demanded an apology from the editor of the *Economist*, Walter Layton. When Layton retorted that he would ensure fair coverage of the impending trial of those charged with starting the Reichstag fire, von Krosigk replied that no journalist from the *Economist* would be allowed into Germany.

Reports that Germany was covertly rearming, against the terms of the Treaty of Versailles, prompted an emergency meeting of the Cabinet in September. But ministers decided that even if the news of Germany's rearmament was to be confirmed and made public, they would take no action in response.

On 14 October 1933, Hitler announced Germany's withdrawal from the League of Nations and the Disarmament Conference. The walk-out at Geneva was deliberately planned to follow the speech by the British Foreign Secretary Sir John Simon, in which he proposed a fresh initiative for world disarmament. The proposals, which the British had agreed with France, Italy and the United States, involved progressive disarmament down to the level imposed on Germany at Versailles. It was therefore less favourable to Germany than the plan put forward by MacDonald the previous March.

Germany's walk-out was a brilliant propaganda exercise. It created the impression that Simon was to blame for going back on an earlier British commitment. This was the line taken that evening in a BBC Radio broadcast by the popular commentator on foreign affairs, Vernon Bartlett. His criticism of the Foreign Secretary cost him his staff job at the BBC, although his message was a plea for appeasing Germany and against any British rearmament – views which Bartlett was later to reject.

The British Government had suffered a major setback. Unwilling to invest any spending in rearmament, they had invested their political capital in disarmament. Now it seemed that they had wrecked their whole strategy on defence and foreign policy.

The crisis coincided with the start of the by-election campaign in East Fulham, which seemed a safe Conservative seat with a majority of more than 14,000. The Conservatives had held the seat since 1922, including their bad year in 1929. It was the sort of seat the Conservatives counted as one they should hold, barring disaster.

But the Liberals, who had come third at the previous two general elections, were not fielding a candidate. In 1931 the Liberals won only 1788 votes. But in 1929 when the Conservative majority had been cut to only 1705 the Liberals had won over 5500. The Labour candidate John Wilmot assiduously set about wooing the Liberals, and shortly before polling day the local Liberal Association recommended that their supporters vote for him.

Wilmot was far superior as a campaigner to his Conservative rival, Alderman W.J. Waldron, a past mayor of Fulham. Waldron was a Tory die-hard, hampered by a weak and divided local party, identified with the council's wage cuts and, as a landlord, with the housing problems in the borough. Wilmot skilfully exploited concern about poor housing and the fear that the National Government had put at risk peace in Europe by provoking the German withdrawal.

When the result was declared, the large Conservative majority was wiped out and Labour won with a majority of almost 5000. It was the worst of the by-election results for the Government during the winter of 1933–4. 'It was a nightmare,' Baldwin later told his biographer, G.M. Young, who related that in his experience this was the only time that Baldwin spoke 'of the past with passion'.

Neville Chamberlain wrote to his sister Ida soon after the result that 'Fulham made the PM [MacDonald] very miserable but I confess I did not lose a minute's sleep over it. The press put it all down to Housing and lies about War. . . .' Chamberlain added his own suspicion that 'the real attack was on the means test.'

Two days after polling, the *West London and Fulham Gazette* wrote that 'the masses were scared at the prospect of another European war, or the possibility – however remote – of Hitlerism gaining ground in this country.' People at the time shared John Wilmot's description of his victory in his Commons maiden speech 'as a symptom of what is a general feeling, a passionate desire for peace, not merely a nebulous desire for peace, but a demand that that desire should be translated into some practical disarmament accomplishment' (Hansard, 13 November 1933, col. 613). The lesson was not lost on Baldwin.

'Thank God for the Blackshirts!' This headline appeared in the *Daily Mail* on 8 January 1934, over an article written by the paper's owner, Lord Rothermere. Fascism appealed to those on the right who were disillusioned with democracy, as Richard Griffiths has shown in his study *Fellow Travellers of the Right*. Rothermere was both an admirer of Mussolini and strongly pro-German, as was the first Director-General of the BBC, John Reith. In 1935, Reith told Marconi, 'I had always admired Mussolini immensely and I had constantly hailed him as the outstanding example of accomplishing high democratic purpose by means which, though not democratic, were the only possible ones.'

Oswald Mosley's British Union of Fascists, the 'Blackshirts', were enjoying their 'respectable' phase, for the two years following their formation in 1932. They were posing as a form of Conservatism, and at this stage, Mosley reflected Mussolini's approach rather than Hitler's.

But in June 1934, at the Kensington Olympia, the Blackshirts' rally degenerated into a riot as BUF stewards resorted to violence in the face of organised disruption. A few extreme right-wing Conservative MPs defended the BUF, but other sympathisers were shocked. Mosley was finished as a serious political figure – as Baldwin commented to Tom Jones, a few days after the Olympia riot, 'Mosley won't come to any good, and we need not bother about him.' During the summer, Rothermere and the eccentric right-winger, Lady Houston, editor of the *Saturday Review*, decided that they would have nothing more to do with Mosley.

As the influence of right-wing Conservatives faded, the Blackshirts came under the sway of pro-Nazi fanatics like William Joyce (later nicknamed 'Lord Haw-Haw' when he was broadcasting from Germany, and subsequently executed for treason), though the BUF were not entirely Hitlerite – in the autumn of 1935, MI5 reported that Mussolini had agreed to pay the BUF £3000 a month. But as the Blackshirts' anti-semitism became more pronounced, they turned to the streets for support, and frightened others away. Some who might have supported Mosley were scared off by the mounting evidence of Nazi repression in Germany.

More significant than Britain's own fascists were the strongly pro-German sympathies felt by many people. They partly developed from the feelings of guilt about the Treaty of Versailles which grew during the 1920s. Before Hitler came to power, those wanting closer links with Germany included strong pacifist and internationalist elements – the likes of Lord Allen of Hurtwood, who had been imprisoned as a conscientious objector during the Great War; a Liberal, the Marquis of Lothian; the Labour politician Philip Noel-Baker; the Liberal chairman of the *News Chronicle* and editor of the *Economist* Sir Walter Layton; the broadcaster Vernon Bartlett; and the Conservative MP Vyvyan Adams. With the exception of Lord Allen and Lord Lothian, all of the above quickly realised that hopes of better relations between London and Berlin were made impossible by the nature of Hitler's regime.

Others were less perturbed by Hitler's accession to power. In March 1933, John Reith was warned about the horrors of the Nazis by his friend Dr Wanner, head of broadcasting in South Germany, who wanted to leave Germany. But Reith was 'pretty certain, however, that the Nazis will clean things up and put Germany on the way to being a real power in Europe again. They are being ruthless and most determined. It is mostly the fault of France that there should be such manifestations of national spirit.'

A minority became positively enthusiastic about Hitler. From 1933, Ribbentrop, one of Hitler's closest advisers, sought to woo influential British opinion. He had some effect on those who were less than fastidious about events in the Third Reich and was able to cultivate a number of people who became Nazi apologists.

Ribbentrop, a former champagne salesman and wine exporter, had a penchant for aristocrats, the City and smart society, where he soon found a small band of Nazi admirers. He befriended the merchant banker Ernest Tennant, who regularly visited Germany on business and became an early defender of Hitler's regime. Similarly, Lord Brocket, a former Tory MP,

landowner and, like Tennant, a figure in the City, was a frequent recipient
of Nazi hospitality.

Brocket's Hampshire estate at Bramshill was close to Basingstoke, the
home of Neville Chamberlain's sisters. By the end of the 1930s, Brocket
had become a friend and confidant of Chamberlain, the latter being
a guest on several occasions at Bramshill and Brocket Hall in Hertford-
shire. Brocket later told James Lees-Milne about his friendship with
Chamberlain, which led Lees-Milne to write in his diary during the war:
'Chamberlain ought not to have been so intimate with a man of his
[Brocket's] calibre. One infers that the fleshpots of Brocket and Bramshill
were a bait. At any rate Chamberlain made a confidant of Brocket who
found himself in an exalted position undeservedly.'

Lord Redesdale and his daughter Unity Mitford were impressed by
Hitler's strong leadership and approved of the way he dealt with
Communists and socialists. This divided the Mitford family, quite
literally. Unity ('Boud' as she was nicknamed) backed the Fascists,
and would not talk to her anti-Fascist sister, Nancy. Unity did, however,
share a sitting room with another sister, Jessica, who was a Communist.
But as Jessica later wrote:

> We divided it down the middle, and Boud decorated her side with
> Fascist insignia of all kinds – the Italian 'fasces', a bundle of sticks;
> photographs of Mussolini framed in passe-partout; photographs of
> Mosley trying to look like Mussolini; the new German swastika, a
> record collection of Nazi youth songs. My side was fixed up with my
> Communist library, a small bust of Lenin purchased for a shilling in
> a second-hand shop, a file of 'Daily Workers'.

When Lord and Lady Redesdale visited Germany they 'were given a royal
time'. As Jessica wrote, 'They were lent a chauffeur-driven Mercedes-
Benz and shown all the gaudy trappings of the new regime, and they
returned full of praise for what they had seen.' In 1936, another of their
daughters, Diana, was married in Germany to the leader of the British
Fascists, Oswald Mosley.

In London society, the hosts and hostesses of some of London society's
most exclusive parties were pro-Nazi. Churchill's cousin the Marquis of
Londonderry, his wife and daughter were converts to the Hitler 'fan club'.
So too was Churchill's friend 'Bendor', the Duke of Westminster, who
developed strongly pro-German and anti-semitic views.

The society hostesses Emerald, Lady Cunard, and Mrs Ronnie Greville
were adulatory about the Nazis. Ribbentrop cut a dash at their lavish
parties, a 'suave man', as Lady Diana Cooper has described him, with 'a
certain elegance'. According to Kenneth Clark (the art historian, later

Lord Clark), Mrs Greville was 'the only hostess who had any political power, not simply on account of her wealth, but because she was a shrewd and forceful personality'. As he later wrote,

The conversation at these parties was not even about money: mere generalities. But afterwards Mrs Greville would draw aside Sir John Simon, Sir Sam Hoare or some of her other regulars, and talk to them seriously. She sat back in a large chair, like a Phoenician goddess, while the cabinet minister or ambassador leant forward attentively. I have no doubt that she had considerable influence.

Other socialites, however, remained positively hostile to Ribbentrop and his entreaties. Sybil, Lady Colefax, another society hostess, whose soirées were held at her home, Argyll House, in the King's Road, was vehemently anti-Nazi.

Lady Diana Cooper recalled a luncheon from which Ribbentrop took his leave, 'kissing the shrinking hands of the ladies, and as the door shut on his departure Winston and Duff [her husband] and some other patriots dancing and shouting with glee at having been sent so despicable a German Ambassador'. But when Lady Diana and her mother, the Duchess of Rutland, were leaving one of Ribbentrop's parties at the 'atrociously decorated' German Embassy in Carlton House Terrace, the Duchess pointed at a bust of Hitler and whispered to the Ambassador, 'You know I can't help rather admiring him. *Please* don't tell Diana.'

In 1934 pro-German feelings were so strong in some quarters that justification was sought for almost anything Hitler did. On Sunday, 1 July, news broke of the 'Night of the Long Knives', Hitler's bloody night-time purge of the SA, or 'Brown Shirts'. The British press was full of the details – Hitler's allegations of homosexuality among the SA, the shooting of its Chief of Staff Röhm, the murder of the Nazi sympathiser General von Schleicher and his wife, along with dozens of arrests and summary executions.

The Director-General of the BBC was undeterred by the news. Reith noted in his diary, 'I really admire the way Hitler has cleaned up what looked like an incipient revolt against him by the Brown Shirt leaders. I really admire the drastic actions taken, which were obviously badly needed.'

Harold Macmillan has revealed that Reith's views were by no means untypical. As he later wrote,

I remember being at a house-party in the country when the news came through. Some of those who were present were ultimately to be the protagonists of the policy of appeasement. I recall that they were trying to find some comfort in the excuse that Röhm and his friends were guilty of immorality, as well as treason: Hitler might be a tyrant; but at heart he was a puritan.

Kenneth Clark was a guest at Trent, the country home of the junior Air Minister, Sir Philip Sassoon, along with several Cabinet ministers, 'when news of the Röhm murders appeared in the evening papers. It was a complete surprise to them. "What do you think of your playmates now?" said Mr Churchill. But this, and the subsequent horrors, seemed to make no impression at all on these rich, respectable men.'

But some who respected German culture, if not Hitler, were stunned. One was a twenty-two-year-old classics scholar at Cambridge University, Enoch Powell. He has since recalled that 'the decisive date for me' was 1 July 1934:

I still remember clearly how I sat for hours in a state of shock, shock which you experience when, around you, you see the debris of a beautiful building in which you have lived for a long time. . . . So it had all been illusion, all fantasy, all a self-created myth. Music, philosophy, poetry, science and the language itself – everything was demolished, broken to bits on the cliffs of a monstrous reality.

That same year, Powell recognised that 'it would soon come to war. . . . About the enemy and about what was at stake there was no doubt. The enemy was to be Germany, and at stake was the freedom of England.'

Virginia Woolf wrote of her shock to the composer Ethel Smyth, but noted that many were unperturbed:

For the first time almost in my life I am honestly, without exaggeration, appalled by the Germans. Can't get over it. How can you or anyone explain last weekend! Their faces! Hitler! Think of that hung before us as the ideal of human life! Sometimes I feel that we are all pent up in the stalls at a bull fight – I go out into the Strand and read the placards. Buses passing. Nobody caring.

Ribbentrop persevered. In December 1934, he persuaded Hitler to give a private dinner party in Germany for the pro-German banker Ernest Tennant and, from the British press, Lord Rothermere, Esmond Harmsworth and the foreign correspondent of the *Daily Mail*, George Ward Price.

Pro-German sympathies existed in far more exalted circles than Fleet Street. On 11 June 1935, the Prince of Wales caused a sensation in a speech to the British Legion, of which he was patron. On the eve of their visit to Germany, he told them, 'I feel that there could be no more suitable body or organisation of men to stretch forth the hand of friendship to the Germans than we ex-servicemen, who fought them and have now forgotten all about it and the Great War.' King George V was furious, sent for his son, and told him that he should not comment on controversial matters without first consulting ministers.

The speech was a boon for Hitler's propaganda machine. There were to be many further successes.

Britain's hopes for disarmament had looked forlorn even before Hitler's walk-out at Geneva in October 1933. That same month, the British Chiefs of Staff, in their annual review, had warned ministers that Germany had already started rearming, and within a few years would represent a serious military threat.

In response, the Cabinet set up the Defence Requirements Committee, to report on putting right Britain's most serious defence deficiencies. The Committee consisted of three Whitehall mandarins (the chairman, Maurice Hankey, and the Permanent Secretaries of the Foreign Office and the Treasury, Sir Robert Vansittart and Sir Warren Fisher) and the three Chiefs of Staff. As the military historian Brian Bond has revealed, the Chiefs of Staff acted as the moderating influence, while the civilians demanded stronger rearmament – Vansittart had extensive contacts in Germany, in effect his own intelligence network, and was aware of the scale of Hitler's unpublicised rearmament programme.

In February 1934, the Committee reported to Cabinet. They acknowledged the seriousness of the Japanese threat, recommending completion of the naval base at Singapore. They urged that Britain should seek better relations with the Japanese, even if this gave offence to the USA, an approach which was strongly favoured at the Treasury by the Chancellor Neville Chamberlain and Sir Warren Fisher.

But the main threat identified by the Committee was Germany. All Britain's long-term defence planning should now be directed against the risk of German aggression. This pointed to the overriding need to defend the Low Countries, and prompted the Committee to call for the creation of a small British Expeditionary Force as a deterrent on the Continent.

After three months, the Cabinet eventually referred the report of the Defence Requirements Committee to a ministerial committee. The Chancellor of the Exchequer Neville Chamberlain led the attack on the call for an Expeditionary Force.

Plainly, the military were shocked at their encounter. Following the first meeting with ministers, the military secretary of the Defence Requirements Committee Colonel Pownall noted in his diary that 'Chamberlain is going to be trouble.' The trouble was the Chancellor's 'deadly dangerous belief' that the country could go to war depending entirely on the navy and air force, and 'cutting out all land contribution' – the doctrine of 'limited liability'. Pownall concluded that Chamberlain's 'ideas on strategy would disgrace a board school'.

At a further ministers' meeting in June, Chamberlain argued that economic and political considerations made it impossible to implement the Defence Requirements Committee report in full. The Treasury feared that large-scale rearmament would increase imports and weaken the country's credit. As a result, Britain would be seriously weakened before any war had even begun. A more immediate constraint was the run-down state of British industry. An ambitious programme would be impractical, and strict priorities would have to be imposed on any rearmament.

Besides stressing the financial constraints on the Committee's recommendations, Chamberlain argued that the public would regard any increase in spending on the army as making preparations to take the country into war. But he accepted that Germany represented the greatest danger, and argued that home defence should therefore be given top priority. This pointed to the need for a strong, home-based air force.

Rearmament was still opposed by all shades of opinion. In early July, Churchill had again warned of the unique threat posed by Hitler and of the need for a doubled, then a redoubled air force. But the leader of the Liberals on the opposition benches, Sir Herbert Samuel, described Churchill's plea as 'rather the language of a Malay running amok than of a responsible statesman'.

In the end, the Cabinet agreed to allow the army an extra £20 million (only half the sum originally proposed) to put right its deficiencies over the five-year period up to 1939. Only £12 million was allocated to an Expeditionary Force. The principle of a Continental role for the army had been accepted, but its funding was puny. Whether ministers would ever agree to put it into effect was another matter.

Speaking in the House of Commons on 28 November 1934, Stanley Baldwin rejected Churchill's attacks on the inadequacy of Britain's air force. Baldwin asserted that the RAF would retain parity with the German air force at least up to the end of 1936. He dismissed any need for larger-scale rearmament, and rejected the notion that Britain and France should work much more closely together to deter the threat from Germany.

Not everyone in Whitehall was so sanguine. The Foreign Office had received further details of Hitler's programme of rearmament. On the basis of this information, Sir Robert Vansittart reckoned that if Britain were to begin rearming immediately, in the late autumn of 1934, she might be in a position to go to war with some chance of success four years later.

*

Prevarication over Britain's defences was matched by drift in her foreign policy. The assassination of the conservative Austrian Chancellor Dollfuss in July 1934 and the attempted Nazi coup demonstrated how real the menace in Central Europe had become. Just two days later, the Foreign Secretary Sir John Simon wrote to the Prime Minister, 'Our own policy is quite clear. We must keep out of trouble in Central Europe at all costs.'

By January 1935, Hitler had reason to feel confident with the way events were going. That month, one of Germany's territorial grievances was resolved when the people of the Saarland voted by an overwhelming majority to be reunited with Germany. The plebiscite had been held under the terms of the Treaty of Versailles, but Hitler would take what he could from the Treaty without feeling bound by it.

In early March, the Government's defence White Paper explicitly drew attention to German rearmament, which could put peace 'in peril'. This marked a major shift in policy, but the size of the increase in spending scarcely met the scale of the threat. An extra £10 million was earmarked for the armed services.

In retaliation at British rearmament, Hitler cancelled the proposed visit to Germany by the British Foreign Secretary Sir John Simon and his junior minister Anthony Eden. On 16 March, Hitler flouted the Treaty of Versailles by introducing compulsory military service. His announcement that there were already 500,000 in arms, well in excess of the limit imposed on Germany, demonstrated that he had been acting in breach of the Treaty for some considerable time. The Geneva Disarmament Conference had merely given cover to Hitler while he rearmed.

Hitler was soon claiming that his air force, the Luftwaffe, had already achieved parity with the RAF and would soon exceed it. Hitler's claims were false, but at the time they had the effect of undermining Baldwin's reassurances on parity. Later that spring, Baldwin admitted that although he had been correct about the relative strengths of the British and German air forces when he had spoken about parity in November 1934, he had been wrong about the future.

A flurry of diplomatic toings and froings followed in the wake of Hitler's dramatic announcements of German rearmament. The British protests at Hitler's action were accompanied by a request that the planned visit by Simon and Eden should be allowed to go ahead. But the talks produced absolutely no progress.

The meeting did, however, lead Eden to change his mind about Hitler. He had met him the previous year and had formed quite a favourable impression – he had thought that Hitler was someone with whom the Government could do business. But after the meeting in 1935 Eden realised his misjudgement.

The increasing danger from Germany prompted Britain, France and Italy to meet in April 1935 at Stresa, where they discussed the threat to Austrian independence. The prospect of appeasing Mussolini in an effort to restrain Hitler was to become a recurrent theme throughout the rest of the decade. Eden, who became increasingly opposed to the idea, could not attend Stresa because of exhaustion after his travels to Germany, Russia, Poland and Czechoslovakia earlier in the spring.

But by the time of the Stresa conference Mussolini's build-up of troops in East Africa was becoming obvious. In discussions outside the formal sessions one of the British representatives warned the Italians that it would be impossible to foresee the consequences of any attack on Abyssinia.

That spring, Czechoslovakia signed defensive treaties with France and the Soviet Union. The commitment by the French to defend Czecho-slovakia was to have a profound impact on British diplomacy later in the 1930s, as the British Government strove to follow Sir John Simon's dictum that Britain 'must keep out of trouble in Central Europe at all costs'. The British were desperate to prevent the French dragging them into another European war.

In June 1935, Ramsay MacDonald finally retired from Number 10. In Stanley Baldwin's new Administration, Sir John Simon was moved from the Foreign Office (much to Eden's relief) to become Home Secretary. Sir Samuel Hoare succeeded as Foreign Secretary, following his achievement at the India Office, where he had successfully managed India's accession to dominion status.

Eden stayed on at the Foreign Office. He did not object in principle to plans which would meet German demands and pave the way for a settlement, but he was sceptical about the prospects when Britain had to negotiate from a position of military weakness.

The only progress in Anglo-German relations during 1935 came in June, when the Anglo-German Naval Agreement was signed. Ministers felt that they had prevented a new arms race by pegging the strength of the German navy to 35 per cent of the Royal Navy. But this was above the limit imposed by the Treaty of Versailles. More significant than the precise terms of the new Agreement was the fact that the British had willingly joined with Hitler in renegotiating the Treaty.

Rearmament was a thorny issue on the left. As the historian A.J.P. Taylor has recalled,

> People like me who opposed re-armament under the so-called National Government are written off nowadays as impractical idealists, blind to the threat of Nazi Germany. It was not as simple as

that. We were aware of the Nazi peril long before the National Government and its supporters were. But what were we to do? We believed, not I think wrongly, that the British government were helping Nazi Germany to survive and even to re-arm. . . . in opposing the National Government we were opposing Hitler's potential allies, or so we thought.

During 1933, some socialists and trade unionists were coming to the conclusion that pacifism was no answer to the threat from the aggressive and authoritarian regimes flexing their muscles in Europe. Douglas Jay, despite all his internationalist and pacifist sympathies, concluded that it might be necessary to use force against the Nazis. His personal testament of conversion appeared as an anonymous leader in the *Economist* on 2 December 1933.

For others, the turning point came in February 1934. In Austria, the conservative Chancellor Dollfuss had extended the ban on the Communist and Nazi Parties to the Social Democrats, who put up armed resistance. Dollfuss ordered an attack on their strongholds, and democratic Europe was horrified by the bombardment of the municipal workers' flats in Vienna. This shocking incident alerted some British socialists and trade unionists to the dangers, including Hugh Gaitskell (Labour Party leader 1955–63), who witnessed the attack while working in Vienna, and Ernest Bevin, the powerful leader of the Transport and General Workers' Union, who became a strong advocate of rearmament.

The Labour Party were split. Some, like Bevin and Hugh Dalton, were rearmers. Others, including Lansbury and Ponsonby, the leaders of the Party in the Commons and the Lords respectively, remained pacifists. And others like Attlee backed collective security, while still calling for reductions in national armaments.

In mid-1934, publication of the document *War and Peace* heralded an important shift in policy. The Party had backed collective security in its earlier call for economic sanctions against Japan during the Manchuria crisis. But now it recognised that in certain circumstances collective security might involve the use of military force – a point which had always been recognised in the Covenant of the League of Nations.

Accepting that the use of force might be justified inevitably raised other questions. How much force might be required to restrain an aggressor? If the threat from the dictators grew, the League would need to be able to put a bigger force in the field. And this in turn opened up the issue of national rearmament, since there was no international peace-keeping force.

The main problem for the left was that supporting rearmament would inevitably mean placing enormous trust in the National Government – a trust which many on the left felt simply was not justified. It would mean trusting a right-wing government not to deploy the extra weapons at home, and trusting them abroad to support the League of Nations.

There was as much concern about the threat of Fascism from within as there was about the growing menace in Europe. This was not simply a matter of worrying that Mosley and his British Union of Fascists would attract increasing support. As Margaret Cole, the socialist thinker, commented,

> We were willing to accept the arming of our country, if it meant saving Europe and ourselves from Fascism; but we were not willing to give those armaments into the control of Baldwin or Chamberlain and their friends, lest when zero hour arrived the guns should be found pointing the wrong way.

Some feared that Churchill and the other Conservatives pressing for speedier rearmament would be even more inclined than the National Government to resort to military force to suppress the unions and crush any political opposition. Many rank-and-file trade unionists still remembered Churchill's role as Home Secretary in 1912 (which gave rise to the myth that he ordered troops to crush strikes in South Wales) and as Chancellor of the Exchequer, when he was the hammer of the trade unions during the 1926 General Strike. These recollections, coupled with the recent experiences of trade unionists and socialists at the hands of conservatives on the Continent, led many on the left to reach opposite conclusions from those drawn by Labour's rearmers, Ernest Bevin, Walter Citrine, General Secretary of the TUC, and Hugh Dalton, who won back his seat in the Commons in 1935 and became Shadow Foreign Secretary.

Others suspected that rearmament might have the very reverse effect to the one which its proponents intended. Far from strengthening the National Government's support for the League, Britain's expanded armoury might well embolden Baldwin and encourage him to feel that he could cut loose from collective security and 'go it alone'.

A serious worry on the left was that the Government of a rearmed Britain might be tempted to forget about the League and drive a bargain with the dictators. If that were to be the result of Britain's rearmament, Labour would be accomplices to the crime. A.J.P. Taylor summed up the problem: 'The National Government were in their acts more anti-Communist than anti-Nazi, as indeed they remained until the outbreak of war, and perhaps even after it. . . . I believed that if Great Britain were involved in war it would be on Hitler's side against Russia. How could we advocate armaments that were likely to be used against Soviet Russia?' Taylor, however, was supporting rearmament by 1936.

While Labour remained in opposition, there was no escape from their basic dilemma. They could control neither foreign policy nor the use to which any extra spending on defence might be put.

In May 1935, the Parliamentary Labour Party had to decide how to vote on the defence estimates. At a meeting chaired by Lansbury, the PLP, the TUC's General Council and the party's National Executive Committee discussed what line they should take. Citrine and Bevin, speaking for the unions, were joined by Dalton in arguing that it would be difficult for the PLP to vote against an increase in spending which was merely designed to restore the RAF's parity with Hitler's Luftwaffe.

But the meeting was adjourned until the following day because Hitler was due to deliver a speech in the Reichstag that evening. Labour leaders wanted to hear what Hitler had to say before reaching any decision. The German Chancellor duly promised that Germany would honour her obligations under the Locarno Pact, which guaranteed the Belgian, French and German borders, and stated that his sole objective was to restore Germany to 'equality of status' with other powers.

Hitler's speech was well timed. When Labour's leaders reconvened, most were agreed that the situation had been completely transformed. Their ready belief that one speech could change everything overnight revealed more than a trace of wishful thinking.

It was reckoned that the German Chancellor's comments had made a fresh start possible – negotiations between the powers could be resumed and a new effort made at disarmament. The Labour Party therefore urged that the Government should summon an international conference and, in the meantime, should suspend their planned expansion of the air force.

Accordingly, the PLP would vote against the defence estimates. During the subsequent Commons debate, Attlee told the House that 'Our policy is not of seeking security through rearmament but through disarmament.' Rearmament had proved too big a stumbling block.

Voting against the defence estimates appealed strongly to the Party's activists, and might have been justifiable in terms of parliamentary tactics. It has been argued that voting against the defence estimates no more implied opposition to all armaments than voting against educational supplies meant that Labour were opposed to education. All that Labour were doing in voting against the defence estimates was to oppose Government defence and foreign policy as a whole.

It was not easy, to say the least, to explain Labour's position in Parliament to ordinary Labour supporters and floating voters. Its chief effect was to undermine Labour's case against the National Government's

handling of foreign policy. It seemed contradictory for Labour to lambast
ministers for failing to stand firm against the Fascist threat while opposing
any increase in Britain's defences.

Labour supported collective security, but were not yet ready to swallow
all the consequences. They were supporting the ends without being
prepared to will the means.

Throughout 1934 and 1935, the growing threat from the dictators had
forced people not simply to espouse peace as an ideal but to face the
practical problem of how peace could be preserved. Some remained
thoroughgoing pacifists, opposing the use of force under any circumstances. Canon 'Dick' Sheppard was able to win sizeable support from
October 1934 for his campaign of pure pacifism. About 50,000 people
responded to his request for postcards stating their support for the 'peace
pledge' that 'We renounce war and never again, directly or indirectly, will
we support or sanction another.' In 1935, over 7000 attended a Peace
Pledge Union rally at the Albert Hall. The writer Aldous Huxley was
attracted to the movement – the hero of his novel *Eyeless in Gaza*,
published in 1936, was a pacifist.

But many more realised that they were not pacifists in the narrow sense.
They accepted that in some situations force should be used to stop an
aggressor.

On 27 June 1935, the results of the 'Peace Ballot' were declared. What
gave them such force was that 11.5 million people had taken part in this
referendum on foreign policy and defence. This was about half the
number voting at the previous general election – a staggering response to a
voluntary questionnaire.

The Ballot had been conducted over seven months from November
1934, and was backed by the League of Nations Union. During the latter
stages, Mussolini's war preparations in East Africa gave added force to its
questions. Above all, they prompted a great groundswell of popular
enthusiasm for the League and for 'collective security', on a scale
unparalleled by international organisations in more recent times. Such was
the strength of response that no party could afford to ignore the Ballot
when the Abyssinian crisis broke.

There was overwhelming support for British membership of the
League and for international agreements to limit the production and
possession of armaments. But the most striking feature was the strong
support for collective security. Over 10 million agreed that nations should
take 'economic and non-military measures' in order to stop one nation
attacking another. Only 635,000 were opposed. As many as 6.8 million

were even prepared to support military measures 'if necessary', with 2.4 million opposed.

As the moderate Conservative weekly, the *Spectator*, commented the day after the results were declared, 'Henceforth, there can be no reasonable doubt about the conviction of the mass of ordinary people of this country; no Government will dare to flout public opinion by flouting the League, or by refraining from efforts to secure agreed disarmament and collective sanctions against peace-breakers.'

This shift in attitudes coincided with the Government's search for a credible policy. The Disarmament Conference, on which they had pinned their hopes, had proved an embarrassing failure. They had been forced to eat their words and start rearming, however modestly. Mussolini was threatening Abyssinia.

A general election was due within eighteen months. Ministers desperately needed a good tune to whistle.

# CHAPTER FOUR

# A SHOCK TO THE SYSTEM

It is placing the Executive [of the Labour Party] and the Movement in an absolutely wrong position to be taking your conscience round from body to body to be told what you ought to do with it.

(Ernest Bevin, attacking the Labour Party leader George Lansbury, Labour Party annual conference, Brighton, October 1935)

There was a bitterness such as was afterwards only equalled in the weeks and months that followed Munich. Conservative Members whose views on politics were normally divergent came together in indignation.

(Harold Macmillan, *Winds of Change, 1914–39*)

From the first outbreak of fighting between Italian and Abyssinian troops in December 1934, opinion in Britain was confused and divided.

On the one hand, there was a feeling that aggression must not succeed, and that the League should be supported. After the failure to deter Japanese aggression in Manchuria, the League and collective security could ill afford a further setback.

On the other hand, it was felt that a backward country like Abyssinia should not have joined the League in the first place, while supporting punitive measures against Italy might backfire. Britain could not risk any naval engagement in the Mediterranean when the fleet was already under pressure as a result of Japanese action in the Far East. Mussolini might also prove a useful ally against Hitler, since the Italians were concerned about German ambitions in Central and South-eastern Europe.

There was admiration on the right for the efficiency and organisation of Mussolini and his troops, in contrast to the 'primitive' regime in Addis Ababa – a view which was to be reflected in the dispatches from the novelist Evelyn Waugh, when he became war correspondent in Abyssinia for the *Daily Mail*.

Others on the right were more cynical. In the summer of 1935, 'Chips' Channon, who was elected as a Tory MP that year, confessed in his diary to being 'bored by this Italian–Abyssinian dispute'. He wondered, 'Why should England fight Italy over Abyssinia, when most of our far flung Empire has been won by conquest?'

The socialist weekly, the *New Statesman and Nation* – not renowned as Mussolini's greatest fan – acknowledged that although Abyssinia was a member of the League, the regime in Addis Ababa was 'a barbarous affair. It is doubtless not governed in accordance with the best European ideas. It contains a number of unruly tribal chieftains. It has not purged itself of the abomination of slavery.'

In London, the Foreign Secretary Sir Samuel Hoare and the Minister for League of Nations Affairs Anthony Eden sought all-party advice from an impressive array of talents, consulting Lansbury and Attlee from the Labour Party, Sir Herbert Samuel and Lloyd George from the Liberals, and fellow Tories Lord Robert Cecil, Sir Austen Chamberlain and Winston Churchill. Churchill and Lloyd George were concerned that Italy would cease to be a bulwark against Germany if she became alienated from France and Britain. For the main part, the others argued that priority had to be given to deterring Italian aggression, and that collective security through the League offered the most effective deterrent.

Hoare and Eden plumped for the League. In August, the Cabinet approved their conclusions as a firm commitment. Addressing the League's General Assembly at Geneva on 11 September, the Foreign Secretary delivered a ringing endorsement of the League and collective security. Significantly, the text of Hoare's speech had been seen beforehand by Neville Chamberlain and vetted by Baldwin.

When Eden and his Under-Secretary Lord Cranborne – both thorough-going supporters of the League – first saw the text of Hoare's speech they were both so shocked that they persuaded the Foreign Secretary to moderate his language. But they remained baffled by the firmness of Hoare's statement.

Nonetheless, the final version was heady stuff. Hoare declared:

> The attitude of His Majesty's Government has been one of unswerving fidelity to the League and all that it stands for, and the case before us [the Abyssinian crisis] is no exception, but, on the contrary, the continuance of the rule. The recent response of public opinion shows how completely the nation supports the Government in the full acceptance of the obligations of the League membership,

which is the oft proclaimed keystone of its foreign policy. . . .

. . . In conformity with its precise and explicit obligations the League stands, and my country stands with it, for the collective maintenance of the Covenant in its entirety, and particularly for steady and collective resistance to all acts of unprovoked aggression. The attitude of the British nation in the last few weeks has clearly demonstrated the fact that this is no variable and unreliable sentiment, but a principle of international conduct to which they and their Government hold with firm, enduring and universal persistence.

Hoare's speech was well received in Britain. Victor Cazalet, the Conservative backbencher, was spending the weekend at Sissinghurst with Harold Nicolson and his wife Vita Sackville-West. All three were thrilled at the line Hoare had taken, Cazalet noting that 'Harold agrees one hundred per cent with Sam Hoare's speech at Geneva.'

But the Foreign Secretary's conversion to the League was less wholehearted than it had seemed from his speech. Lord Sherfield (then a Foreign Office official at the League when Hoare spoke) is convinced that Hoare had approached his speech in the way that a lawyer regards his brief – he set out to give the most convincing performance of a particular line on a particular occasion. If the circumstance changed, so would the speech.

The key to Hoare's speech to the League lay in his references to British public opinion. The National Government would have to face the electorate within the next year or so, and the results of the Peace Ballot had demonstrated overwhelming support for the League. Neither Hoare nor most other ministers had undergone any lasting conversion to the League. Their new-found support reflected political pressures at home. In June, a secret Government review had concluded that British interests in the area were insufficient to justify opposition to an Italian invasion of Abyssinia – the Italian intelligence service had soon passed a copy of the report to Mussolini.

Leo Amery was later told by Neville Chamberlain that 'we were bound to try out the League of Nations . . . for political reasons at home, and that there was no question of our going beyond the mildest of economic sanctions.' Amery himself saw Italy as a potential ally against Germany. As he told his constituents in Birmingham Sparkbrook, he was 'not prepared to send a single Birmingham lad to his death for the sake of Abyssinia'.

On 3 October 1935, Italy invaded Abyssinia. In the parliamentary debate on the crisis later that month, Churchill chose to concentrate on the growing German threat. He referred to the Abyssinian crisis as 'a very small matter compared with the dangers I have just described', and hoped that the Foreign Secretary might achieve some compromise solution in Abyssinia.

But by the autumn of 1935, the National Government had apparently embraced the League and in the process had stolen the opposition's clothes.

There was a bonus for the Government. The Labour Party was in turmoil. The Abyssinian crisis had delivered its first shock to the system.

When George Lansbury rose to speak at the 1935 annual Party conference, delegates stood and greeted him with prolonged applause and sang 'For he's a jolly good fellow'. Lansbury occupied a special place in the affections of Labour activists during their bleakest years.

From his days on Poplar Council in the East End of London, Lansbury personified municipal socialism, which was seen to have improved the conditions of ordinary working people – in 1921 he went to prison in defiance of restrictions on local authority spending. His pacifism, informed by Christian principles, epitomised the abhorrence of war after the appalling experience of 1914–18.

Lansbury did not disappoint his many supporters in the hall. His declaration of Christian pacifism was uncompromising: 'I would say in the name of the faith I hold, the belief I have that God intended us to live peaceably and quietly with one another – if some people do not allow us to do so, I am ready to stand as the early Christians did and say "This is our faith, this is where we stand and if necessary, this is where we will die." '

Lansbury was opposing the call from Labour's National Executive Committee to support economic sanctions against Italy as a response to Mussolini's attack on Abyssinia. Lansbury was a supporter of the League only as long as it stuck to peaceful mediation and world disarmament. He opposed any attempts to put more practical flesh on the bones of the Covenant. Economic sanctions were a first move towards the use of force. If they were to fail, the next step would involve military action, which Lansbury could never condone.

Lansbury and the pacifists were joined in their opposition to sanctions by the non-pacifist left. As Sir Stafford Cripps, chairman of the left-wing Socialist League, told the conference, the League of Nations was 'nothing but the tool of the imperialist powers'. He would not trust the National Government to pursue anything other than capitalist and imperialist objectives. Labour should not support ministers in their call for sanctions. The only course open to socialists was to continue the fight against capitalism, in all its manifestations.

Although Lansbury and Cripps were well supported in the hall, the tide was running against them. By the autumn of 1935, many ordinary trade unionists and Labour supporters were coming to feel that neither pacifist purity nor unbending socialism provided an answer to the growing threat from Fascism. The emergence of Mosley's Blackshirts at home and the rise of the dictators in Europe and the Far East demanded more practical measures.

Trade union leaders saw collective security as collective bargaining writ large on the world stage, and appreciated the need to bargain from strength. By 1934, union leaders were drawing an important moral from the brutal attacks on trade unionists in conservative Austria and Nazi Germany. Walter Citrine and Ernest Bevin were among the first on the left to argue that the use of force might be needed if the dictators were to be restrained. At their annual conference the TUC voted for sanctions by an overwhelming majority, 2,962,000 votes to 177,000.

But Labour's parliamentary leadership was unable to support sanctions. On 17 September, Lord Ponsonby, Lansbury's pacifist ally and Labour's leader in the Lords, informed Lansbury of his decision to resign. 'I cannot wait any longer!' wrote Ponsonby, arguing that it was no longer possible for a pacifist to continue as a Party leader.

At a stormy special meeting of Labour's National Executive two days later, some trade union members wanted Lansbury to resign immediately, but the majority disagreed. On 20 September, the *Daily Herald* announced Ponsonby's resignation and also reported that the left-winger Cripps had resigned from the National Executive.

Lansbury, however, continued as leader of the Parliamentary Labour Party. Yet he made no bones about his opposition to official Party policy. Hugh Dalton later wrote of Lansbury, 'He wouldn't resign on his own initiative, was asking us (the National Executive) to settle the question for him [and] was rushing about the country speaking against the Party's international policy.' It was an impossible predicament for Labour, and it would have to be resolved one way or the other.

Opening the debate at the annual Party conference, Dalton argued that the question boiled down to a basic one: 'Do we stand firm in this crisis for the policy to which we have so often pledged ourselves, or shall we turn tail and run away, repudiate our obligations under the Covenant of the League and signal "All Clear" to Mussolini?'

All the major unions were in favour of sanctions. If ever there was a moment to take on the pacifists and the left on their 'home ground', the annual conference, this was it. Ernest Bevin, then in his fifties and at the height of his powers, seized his opportunity with both hands. Ominously for the pacifists and the left, Bevin and his delegation had remained seated and 'glowering' when almost everyone else had risen to greet Lansbury.

By the 1930s, Bevin was a formidable figure in the Labour Party. At a time when the unions dominated the Party, Bevin was the most forceful personality among the union leaders. He wielded enormous power on the National Council of Labour, the joint Labour Party and TUC body which laid down the general lines of Party policy.

Within his own union, the Transport and General Workers, Bevin's supremacy was unquestioned. He had strengthened the T&G through amalgamations in the 1920s. The result was that by the early 1930s Bevin effectively controlled a block vote at Labour's annual Party conference approaching 250,000, almost 10 per cent of the total vote.

His influence was pervasive. It was Bevin's initiative that led, during the 1920s, to the building of Transport House in Smith Square, Westminster. From its opening in 1928, it not only served as the T&G's headquarters, but also housed the TUC and the Labour Party. The *Daily Herald* with a circulation of a million was nominally run by the TUC and the Labour Party, but it was effectively under Bevin's control.

After Lansbury's speech, Bevin made his way to the platform. As he did so, there was what the *New Statesman and Nation* described as 'a singularly apposite hailstorm which beat a tattoo on the Dome'. Bevin launched a furious attack on the Party leader, delivering the tirade quoted at the head of this chapter. Those are Bevin's words as reported in the official conference report, but according to people there at the time Bevin actually accused Lansbury of 'trailing' or 'hawking' his conscience around.

Although Bevin was booed and heckled by delegates, he pressed home his attack: 'There is one quotation from the Scriptures which George Lansbury has quoted today which I think he might apply to himself – "Do unto others". I have had to sit in conference with the leader and come to decisions, and I am a democrat and I feel we have been betrayed.'

Bevin then turned the full force of his fury on Cripps, a middle-class theoretical socialist. Trade unionists had good reason to object passionately to the overriding priority which Cripps placed on attacking capitalism rather than being concerned about the defence of ordinary people against authoritarian regimes. Bevin was to the point: 'People have been on this platform today talking about the destruction of capitalism. The thing that is being wiped out is the trade union movement. . . . It is we who are being wiped out and who will be wiped out if Fascism comes here. . . .'

The conference duly gave their conditional support for sanctions, by 2,168,000 votes to 102,000. A few days later, the conference heard the news that Italian troops had invaded Abyssinia. The National Council of

Labour immediately demanded that Parliament should be recalled to debate the emergency. The following week, Lansbury finally resigned. Clem Attlee became acting leader of the Parliamentary Labour Party.

When Bevin was later taken to task over the viciousness of his attack on Lansbury, he replied, 'Lansbury has been going about in saint's clothes for years waiting for martyrdom. I set fire to the faggots.'

The consequence was that pure pacifism would no longer be espoused by the Labour leadership. But the Party was still far from the commitment to rearmament, which Bevin and his supporters believed was essential.

Labour was in no state to fight the general election, which followed within weeks. During the campaign, Roy Harrod, the Oxford economics don, spoke on Labour platforms, although he was himself a Liberal. His experience indicates the degree of confusion among the Government's opponents:

> I dealt mainly with the question of Abyssinia, holding that we should take all steps to check Mussolini's aggression. . . . Then the candidate came in, and she made an impassioned speech in favour of disarmament. 'How could you', I expostulated, 'when I had devoted my speech to the need for taking a strong line with Mussolini and everyone seemed to favour that?'
>
> 'But we ought to disarm', she said, 'as an example to the others.'
>
> 'You think our example will cause Hitler and Mussolini to disarm?' I asked.
>
> 'Oh, Roy', she said, 'have you lost all your idealism?'
>
> I am afraid that, confronted by the spectacle of Hitler, I had.

Baldwin won a landslide victory on the slogan 'Safety First'. The National Government's candidates (the vast majority were Conservatives) received over 50 per cent of the popular vote (no party has done so since) and a massive majority of 249 in the House of Commons. Labour had staged something of a recovery. Although they won only 154 seats, they secured 38 per cent of the vote – a share of the vote on which they have twice won power.

On 18 November, just four days after polling, Britain imposed limited economic sanctions against Italy.

But within a month of their massive victory, the Government were rocked to their foundations. They faced a major backbench revolt and Stanley Baldwin was on the brink of resignation.

On 9 December news leaked out in Paris that the French Prime Minister Pierre Laval and the British Foreign Secretary Sir Samuel Hoare had discussed a compromise solution to end the war in Abyssinia. Hoare had been accompanied by his Permanent Secretary, Vansittart, who was keen to appease Italy. In the proposed Anglo-French peace settlement, Italy would keep a large part of Abyssinia.

The leak provoked a furore in Britain. 'There is a terrific crisis over foreign affairs – the most exciting and indeed critical that I've known in fourteen years', Cazalet wrote in his journal. The Government's opponents were outraged, and many of their own supporters were deeply shocked. As the quotation at the head of this chapter shows, Harold Macmillan later wrote about the 'bitterness' which the crisis caused.

In fact, the British Government had previously made a similar offer, and was not opposed to Mussolini taking some Abyssinian territory. The revelations from Paris showed that the Foreign Secretary was working towards a deal which would reward an attack on a member state of the League and completely undermine any attempt to enforce collective security.

Yet only a matter of weeks beforehand the Government had made a commitment to the League one of the central planks in their election campaign. Foreign policy was a key issue, and the National Government's unequivocal stand contributed to their huge victory. In their manifesto they had pledged that:

> The League of Nations will remain, as heretofore, the keystone of British foreign policy. . . . In the present unhappy dispute between Italy and Abyssinia there will be no wavering in the policy we have hitherto pursued. We shall take no action in isolation, but we shall be prepared to take our part in any collective action decided upon by the League and shared in by its members.

The manifesto did also refer to the Government's intention of continuing to seek 'a just and fair settlement', provided it was 'within the framework of the League and acceptable to the three parties in the dispute – Italy, Abyssinia, and the League itself'.

The Hoare–Laval Pact plainly did not fit the bill. Coming only weeks after the election, it appeared to expose Baldwin's apparent cynicism. It seemed that he had backed the League and attacked Mussolini purely for party advantage. Now that the election was safely won, the commitment to the League and opposition to Mussolini had been abandoned virtually overnight.

The Prime Minister's standing plummeted. After his election victory, the master political strategist had seemed in command of his party, but suddenly he was vulnerable. The National Government's backbenchers were sent reeling by the shock-waves. The more liberal-minded Conservatives were angered at the abandonment of the commitment to the League, the right wing by an apparent capitulation to Mussolini. Many felt that they simply could not 'get away with it' after what they had said at the election. As Victor Cazalet noted in his diary,

> Stories rage all this week, and everyone goes about with a sunken head at the shame of betrayal. What were we elected for three weeks ago? Violet Bonham-Carter is very violent and goes for me. Will I defend Baldwin? Can I? Where are my moral principles etc., etc.? It is all very difficult. An error of the first order has been committed. What is to happen?

As Macmillan has commented, many loyal Tory MPs felt that they had been 'swindled; and if they were to toe the line now, they would feel guilty of having swindled those who voted for them'.

Fifty-nine MPs on the Government's own backbenches signed a critical amendment to the main opposition motion. These critics among the Government's supporters declared that the Hoare–Laval terms were 'unacceptable' and urged the Government to 'resume the policy outlined in September by the Foreign Secretary at Geneva and overwhelmingly endorsed by this country at the recent general election'.

The National Government's majority was so large that they were unlikely to be defeated, but a sizeable backbench revolt could have forced Baldwin to resign. The Cabinet were due to discuss the crisis on 18 December, and that morning *The Times* published a letter from Macmillan. The progressive Tory could not resist drawing attention to the fact that it was only right-wingers, usually Baldwin's most bitter opponents, who were now supporting him:

> It must indeed be galling for the Prime Minister to reflect on the character of the limited support which his new foreign policy is receiving. In the House of Commons many members on the Government side are in open revolt; many more are anxious and distressed. The only whole-hearted supporters are to be found among the very men who for six years have been steadily engaged in fighting Mr Baldwin's main policies and undermining his leadership.

In Cabinet, Neville Chamberlain defended the Foreign Secretary, but most ministers felt that the Government could not afford to stand by the Hoare–Laval Pact. Lord Halifax argued that Hoare should resign, emphasising the damage that would be done if Baldwin was left exposed to bear the brunt of the attack: 'If the Prime Minister were to lose his personal position, one of our national anchors would have dragged.'

That evening, the Foreign Secretary resigned. Hoare had been sacrificed, enabling many Conservatives who might not otherwise have done so to support the Government.

Eden later told Victor Cazalet of an extraordinary incident at the Palace after Hoare's resignation: 'G.V. [George V] told A.E. [Eden] that Hoare had been to resign the day before. He said to him, "One policy one day, another the next, where are we?" and then told him everyone was saying "No more coals to Newcastle, no more Hoares to Paris", and he added to A.E. – "He [Sam Hoare] didn't see the joke!" '

Hoare had been made a scapegoat. Baldwin and his colleagues knew what the Foreign Secretary was trying to achieve, and had approved his efforts. A few days before the election, a meeting in Hoare's room at the Foreign Office had decided that a new effort should be made to find a settlement. Hoare and Eden were concerned that the Italians, who believed that the French would stand aside in any conflict, were about to attack the British fleet in the Mediterranean. And at Cabinet on 2 December, it was agreed in principle that, while Britain should join in the oil embargo against the Italians, an attempt should be made to begin peace talks over Abyssinia.

Although Hoare's resignation improved the Government's prospects, they were still at risk. But the rebels would need a leader. The most likely candidates were the Conservative Party's two most senior Privy Councillors in the Commons, Winston Churchill and Sir Austen Chamberlain. Only a month earlier Baldwin had felt able to exclude both of them from his Administration. Now, his fate would largely depend on what kind of lead they gave the backbenchers. Neither of them owed the Prime Minister any favours.

Churchill, however, was out of the country on holiday. He later wished that he had returned, as 'I might have brought an element of decision to the anti-Government gatherings which would have ended the Baldwin regime. Perhaps a Government under Sir Austen Chamberlain might have been established at this moment.' But at the time Churchill's friends advised him to stay away. Had he returned, he would have had some difficulty justifying his own recent call for a compromise solution in Abyssinia.

Sir Austen Chamberlain was undecided on what line he should take. As late as 15 December, just three days before the Commons debate, he wrote, 'Laval has behaved treacherously, but I fear Sam Hoare has blundered badly.' As to his own position 'Much will depend on the speeches of Hoare and S.B., but they will have an extraordinarily difficult task, for I have never known the political sky cloud over so suddenly nor have I ever seen blacker clouds on the horizon.' Baldwin saw Sir Austen, and gave the impression that he would be offered the Foreign Office.

On 19 December, the day of the Commons debate on the Hoare–Laval Pact, Earl Winterton tabled a motion which was almost certainly inspired by the Government Whips. It reflected what they felt the backbenchers would stomach and held that the terms of any settlement of the Italo-Abyssinian dispute 'should be such as the League can accept'.

Hoare was a sorry sight when he rose to make his resignation speech in the Commons immediately before the main debate. After his ill-fated talks with Laval in Paris, he had gone on to Switzerland for a holiday. Although he was a skilled skater, he had suffered a fainting fit, fallen on the ice and broken his nose. Heavily bandaged, Hoare sought to justify his actions. But his defence was inadequate.

Attlee spoke first in the debate itself and savaged the Government. It was not only the country's honour which was at stake, but also the Prime Minister's. Baldwin's reply was unimpressive. He apologised to his supporters for what had happened, arguing that neither he nor his colleagues had thought they were breaching their election commitment. He subsequently realised that he had been wrong only as a result of 'that deeper feeling which was manifested by many of my hon. Friends in many parts of the country on what I may call grounds of honour' (Hansard, 19 December 1935, cols 2028–9).

The House was on tenterhooks waiting to hear what Sir Austen Chamberlain would say. The Speaker recognised his importance in the debate by calling him directly after the Prime Minister, abandoning the convention that speeches should come in turn from Government and opposition benches.

Sir Austen himself wrote after the debate, 'Had I thought it compatible with the public interest I believe that after S.B.'s miserably inadequate speech and the initial blunder, I could have so reduced his majority as to force his resignation.' But instead of attacking his own front bench, Sir Austen delivered a stinging rebuke to Attlee for his attack on the Prime Minister's honour and rallied the backbenchers behind the Administration.

Many younger National Government MPs had been in an acute moral dilemma at the start of the debate. Harold Nicolson, who had entered Parliament a month earlier as a National Labour MP, explained to the House his own feelings when he first heard the terms of the Hoare–Laval Pact: 'I spent a sleepless night wondering in all honesty what I was to do, knowing that if this White Paper had been published on the 4th November, it would not be I who would be sitting in this House, but my socialist opponent, and I remember wondering and thinking, in stress of conscience, whether I ought not to resign my seat and return my mandate to those who had voted for me' (ibid., cols 2077–9).

Yet in the end, Nicolson and his backbench colleagues were able to resolve their crisis of conscience. The combination of Sir Austen Chamberlain's speech and the Government's acceptance of Winterton's amendment to the opposition motion had done the trick. The amendment was an ingenious manoeuvre, since it allowed Government backbenchers to express their constituents' opposition to the Hoare–Laval Pact while still voting for the Government.

But Sir Austen was not offered the Foreign Office. Instead, Baldwin chose Eden to replace Hoare. At thirty-eight, Eden was the first of the generation who had fought in the Great War to reach such high office. His support for the League and collective security reflected the seminal influence of his years at the front. As Eden himself later wrote, 'I had entered the holocaust still childish and I emerged tempered by my experience, but with my illusions intact, neither shattered nor cynical. . . .'

He had served with distinction, and had been awarded the Military Cross for his bravery. But he lost two brothers, one killed in 1914 and the other, aged only sixteen, at the Battle of Jutland. In the trenches, he fought alongside men from very different backgrounds to his own (County Durham gentry and Eton). They talked politics for hours, agreeing on the need to remove the old class distinctions after the war.

Eden entered the Commons in December 1923, and from 1926 was Parliamentary Private Secretary to the Foreign Secretary, Sir Austen Chamberlain. After the Conservative defeat in 1929, he had joined with other young, moderate, reforming Tories, including Neil Skelton, Oliver Stanley, William Ormsby-Gore, Walter Elliot and W.S. ('Shakes') Morrison. They developed their ideas for ridding Britain of its rigid class divisions, and originated the then near-revolutionary notion of a 'property-owning democracy'.

When Baldwin was in danger of losing the party leadership in 1931, Eden was among his strongest supporters. Later that year, when the Conservatives returned to power, Eden was appointed Under-Secretary at the Foreign Office, and from the end of 1933 was Lord Privy Seal. His years as Sir John Simon's deputy were a difficult period – Eden did much of the work, but had to watch Simon mishandle his brief. When Baldwin finally returned to Number 10, however, Eden was promoted to the Cabinet as Minister for League of Nations Affairs.

Eden's appointment as Foreign Secretary six months later, shortly before Christmas 1935, was welcomed across the political spectrum. On the left, the *New Statesman and Nation* regarded it as 'the best Christmas present the Prime Minister could have given us'. Reflecting the views of moderate Conservatives, the *Spectator* thought it 'demonstrates the will of the Government, and still more the will of the people, that the foreign policy of Great Britain shall remain based on the League of Nations, and that the policy shall be maintained not only in words, but in deeds.'

Yet the tide was already running strongly against the League. The Abyssinian crisis had demonstrated its ineffectiveness, a lesson which was not lost on Hitler. As Victor Cazalet later wrote, 'The rape of Abyssinia was perhaps the turning point in the triumphant era of the Dictators. Our promises to help, our failure to fulfil them, the complete cynicism and paralysis of forty nations confronted by the bombast of what we now know to have been a very feeble foe, constitute one of the saddest stories in European history.'

Instead of heralding a renewal of British support for the League, Eden's early months at the Foreign Office coincided with a distinct cooling towards it. The British Government had helped bring this about by their half-hearted application of sanctions, which were not effective enough to restrain Italy. When they failed to work, the response was to say that the League and collective security did not work. The fact was that the League could only be as powerful as its members would allow. Britain had judged that her vital interests were not at stake, and did not want to risk a wider conflict with Italy.

At the same time, imposing even these ineffective sanctions had antagonised Mussolini. The British Government had ruined any chance of developing closer contacts with Mussolini, which would have made sense in terms of the *realpolitik* of restraining Hitler, and the overriding need to avoid conflict on too many fronts at once. Yet the Italians were guilty of appalling atrocities in Abyssinia, as Eden soon knew.

Among the senior critics on the Government backbenches, Leo Amery had never supported the League. Sir Austen Chamberlain and Churchill were now both primarily concerned at the threat posed by Hitler. By the spring of 1936, as the League appeared to falter and its popularity waned, Sir Austen and Churchill became increasingly opposed to the continuation of sanctions against Italy, which could prove a useful ally against Hitler's Germany. Yet in their stance on sanctions they were helping to destabilise the League and its system of collective security, bulwarks which they themselves maintained would need strengthening if Hitler was to be checked.

The world which Eden surveyed as Britain's Foreign Secretary in early 1936 was one in which both the old- and the new-style diplomacy had failed. Traditional diplomacy, in which defensive alliances were formed against any country challenging the balance of power in Europe, had been discredited by the 1914–18 war. But, in turn, the new diplomacy, embodied in the League and based on collective security, had been undermined.

As a result, Britain's already strong desire to avoid being dragged into any involvement on the Continent of Europe was reinforced. British policy came to depend on a combination of modest rearmament and appeasement. The former would provide some kind of limited insurance, while the latter would obviate the need for a much more ambitious programme of rearmament, which would entail major changes in economic and social policy.

The likes of Sir Austen Chamberlain and Churchill were in a small minority. Many more Conservatives, and others, were inclined to believe that Hitler could best be dealt with through appeasement, satisfying his demands – which many felt were based on justifiable grievances – thereby pacifying him and preserving peace in Europe.

This was the backdrop against which the youthful Foreign Secretary sought to contend with the most serious challenge yet from Hitler.

# CHAPTER FIVE

# 'THEIR OWN
# BACK-GARDEN'

Public opinion here does, I think, draw a clear distinction
between the action of Signor Mussolini in resorting to
aggressive war and waging it beyond his frontiers and the
actions, up-to-date at any rate, of Herr Hitler which, much as
we may regard them as reprehensible, have taken place within
the frontiers of the German Reich. The public here draw that
distinction, and it is a proper distinction.

(Hugh Dalton, Labour Foreign Affairs spokesman, speaking in
the House of Commons, 26 March 1936 (Hansard, col. 1454))

During the first weekend of March 1936, the Marquis of Lothian was
relaxing with his guests at Blickling Hall, his country seat in Norfolk. But
before dinner on Saturday, their tranquillity was shattered when the early
evening news on BBC radio reported that Hitler's troops had entered the
Rhineland. Earlier that day, 10,000 German soldiers and 22,700 armed
police had marched across the border. Hitler had unilaterally torn up the
provision in the 1918 peace settlement establishing the Rhineland as a
demilitarised zone.

One of Lothian's guests was Tom Jones, friend and adviser of the then
Prime Minister Stanley Baldwin. As soon as Jones heard the news, he was
anxious to ensure that the Prime Minister should receive the 'right' advice
before the Cabinet could get at him.

Tom Jones strongly believed that the way to deal with Hitler was
through appeasement and he had little trouble in immediately organising a
like-minded 'Shadow Cabinet' at Blickling. Lothian, though a Liberal,
generally favoured appeasing Hitler, and his guest-list included several
other prominent sympathisers – Sir Thomas Inskip, the Attorney-
General, and his wife, the Astors and Arnold Toynbee, the historian, who
had just returned from Germany and a meeting with Hitler. Also there was
Sir Walter Layton, editor of the *Economist* and the *News Chronicle*, though

he was out of sympathy with his host and most of the other guests.

While German troops were marching into the Rhineland, Hitler had also announced a set of diplomatic proposals. Jones and his friends were impressed, though others regarded the diplomatic initiative as a smokescreen. The German Chancellor offered non-aggression pacts with Belgium and France, the introduction of limits on the strength of air forces, and the establishment of new demilitarised zones on *both* sides of the border between France and Germany (which would have required the French to demolish their new defensive fortifications, the so-called 'Maginot line').

On Sunday morning, Jones telephoned the Prime Minister to brief him on the line which he had thrashed out with Inskip and Nancy Astor. The gist of the advice from Blickling was that the British Government should welcome Hitler's diplomatic initiative 'wholeheartedly'. Germany's march into the Rhineland had to be condemned, but it should not stand in the way of 'the peace proposals which accompany it'. Britain's interest lay in giving these proposals a chance, and not being 'dragged at the tail of France'.

On Sunday, 8 March, the same day that Jones had contacted Baldwin from Blickling, the *Observer* came close to praising what Hitler had done. On Monday the 9th, *The Times*, in a leader entitled 'A Chance to Rebuild', endorsed Hitler's proposals as offering the best prospect for lasting peace in Europe.

The reactions from an aristocrat's weekend party seemed to reflect the mood in the country. 'After all, they are only going into their own backgarden,' a taxi-driver told Lord Lothian on his return to London, and another taxi-driver reportedly used almost identical words to Anthony Eden. As Victor Cazalet wrote in his journal, 'Personally I believe country would refuse to send a man to turn Germans out of their own territory.'

Ronald Tree, another young Tory MP, attended a dinner of exservicemen in Leicester a few days after the Rhineland was occupied. He was amazed to find that 'the ex-servicemen reacted totally on the side of the Germans, saying in effect, "Why shouldn't they have their own territory back; if they get it it's no concern of ours." '

The Rhineland crisis marked a turning point, yet it did not appear at the time as a black-and-white issue. 'England as a whole anxious to seize Hitler's new Peace offer,' wrote Cazalet. 'Opinion v. divided both in Cabinet and country.'

There was no great public outcry and nothing remotely comparable to the outraged reaction when Mussolini had invaded Abyssinia the previous year. As the Conservative MP Paul Emrys-Evans later commented, 'I received no notice of great Albert Hall meetings of protest, when agreements were broken, when the Covenant was defied, when Locarno was smashed' (Hansard, 23 June 1936, col. 1654). Harold Macmillan later recalled that 'In the House of Commons, nearly all my friends, whether on the Right or the Left of politics, seemed comparatively undisturbed.'

The differing assumptions about how to deal with Germany were to send people on divergent paths, but in the spring of 1936 the debate was far less clear-cut. Few people were confident about the right way to deal with Hitler. Even those who had identified him as a serious threat were not all agreed on what precisely should be done. Many were understandably confused.

It was widely felt at the time that Germany had legitimate grievances. Some who were less sanguine about Hitler's longer-term ambitions nonetheless accepted that the League was in no position for the time being to do much about it. Others acknowledged that in the short term Britain's lack of military preparedness, when she was already facing threats from Japan in the Far East and Italy in the Mediterranean, severely constrained the Government's options. The Cabinet had decided over a year earlier that the demilitarised zone was not vital to British interests, a conclusion they had felt able to reach without any advice from the Chiefs of Staff.

The Labour Party agreed to the postponement of any Commons debate on the crisis for almost three weeks. The pretext was that nothing should be said which might hinder efforts to reach a settlement with the other signatories to the Locarno Pact, or through the League of Nations. But many Labour supporters shared the view of the *New Statesman and Nation*, 'We all have bad consciences about Germany's treatment since the war.'

The Rhineland crisis had come at an awkward time for the Labour leadership. The defence estimates were due to be debated in the Commons. The previous week, the TUC's General Council, the Party's National Executive Committee and the PLP had spent three days agonising over their response to the Government's defence White Paper, which proposed extra spending on all three services.

Labour were reviewing their policy on rearmament in the wake of their election defeat three months earlier. In early 1936, the Party's National Executive set up its own Defence Committee, with Attlee, now confirmed as leader of the Parliamentary Labour Party, as chairman. The Committee was composed mainly of MPs and others who had served in the service ministries or who had military experience.

Their report reflected the widespread concern about the new threat from bombers in any future war. They concluded that the country required a powerful air force, and pointed out that Britain was spending less on defence, relative to national income, than other first- or second-rank European powers.

But in March Labour decided to oppose Baldwin's proposals for rearmament. The revelation of the Hoare–Laval Pact the previous December strengthened the feeling that the Government could not be trusted. Labour's worst fears had been confirmed by the Government's complete disregard for the League of Nations and their readiness to contemplate meeting even a part of Mussolini's demands. Morrison's later comment encapsulated the view of many in the Labour Party: '[the Government] are never short of money for the means of destruction. They are only short of money for the means of life.'

As a result, on the Monday and Tuesday after Hitler's remilitarisation of the Rhineland, the Parliamentary Labour Party forced votes on token reductions in the spending for all three of Britain's armed services. This setback for Labour's rearmers led Dalton, the Shadow Foreign Secretary, to lament 'We *are* unfit to govern. "He who darkeneth counsel by words without knowledge" abounds among us. . . . The Party won't face up to realities. There is still much more anti-armament sentiment and many are more agin' our own Government than agin' Hitler.'

In France and Belgium the reaction to Hitler's coup was far less sanguine than in Britain. In those countries, Germany's 'back-garden' was next door.

But the French were unwilling to take any action on their own initiative. Instead, they called for a concerted response, in which they clearly envisaged Britain playing a key role. Although the British Government were under no immediate pressure at home, this put them on the spot and opened up divisions in the Cabinet and among Conservatives.

At Cabinet on Wednesday, 11 March, Baldwin rallied his ministers against the French proposal, raising the spectres of war and Soviet Bolshevism. He argued that the French Government's proposal would lead to another war in Europe. Even if the French and their new-found allies, the Soviet Union, succeeded in defeating Germany, 'it would probably only result in Germany going Bolshevik.'

The Prime Minister's views, however, were at odds with those of his Foreign Secretary. Eden warned, 'if Germany were allowed to remain unmolested in military occupation of the Rhineland, war in two years' time was a certainty and would be fought under very unfavourable conditions.' Eden's concern was shared in the Cabinet by Duff Cooper, the Secretary of War, and in the Foreign Office most notably by the Permanent Secretary, Sir Robert Vansittart, and Ralph Wigram.

Baldwin had little trouble in winning the Cabinet's backing. The Prime Minister argued that Britain could no longer be bound by the commitment she had given in the Locarno Treaty to support France, because Germany was no longer 'totally disarmed'. Britain was left in a vulnerable position following the collapse of the Disarmament Conference, and it would take time to 'educate public opinion' on the need for stronger defences. France was thus being 'very unfriendly', and 'should welcome our coming rearmament rather than expose us to the present embarrassments'.

On Friday the 13th, at the League's Council meeting, Ribbentrop, the German Ambassador in London, claimed that his Government were ready to play their part in building a new peace in Europe. Baldwin told Flandin, the French Foreign Minister, beforehand that Britain could not support the French proposal for joint action, and Eden now welcomed Ribbentrop's statement on the Government's behalf. In that day's issue of London's *Evening Standard*, Churchill argued that only joint action through the League of Nations might stop 'the horrible, dull, remorseless drift to war in 1937 or 1938'. If there were no redress for France and Belgium, the 'whole doctrine of international law' would be undermined.

On Saturday the 14th, Baldwin announced his appointment of a Minister for the Co-ordination of Defence. This followed an extensive campaign for the appointment of a Defence Minister, and Baldwin's move might have suggested that rearmament would now be given higher priority. Yet the choice of Sir Thomas Inskip, the little-known and uninspiring Attorney-General, as the new Minister scarcely suggested that this was Baldwin's intention.

It was a massive snub to Churchill, who had still been hoping to return to the Government. His friend and adviser, Professor Lindemann, subsequently described the choice of Inskip as 'the most cynical thing that has been done since Caligula appointed his horse as consul'. The far-right *Saturday Review*, edited by the eccentric Lady Houston, which admired the efforts of the dictators but also wanted Britain to rearm, was provoked even beyond its normal immoderate tone: 'Mr. Baldwin likes to surround himself with spineless sycophants and nancyfied nobodies; like many other vain men he cannot tolerate the man who calls a spade a spade.'

Chamberlain, who was now clearly established as the heir-apparent to Baldwin, confided in his diary what he believed were the real reasons for the appointment of Inskip. A few days after Hitler's troops had marched, Chamberlain wrote that the Rhineland crisis 'afforded an excellent reason for discarding both Winston and Sam [Hoare] since both had European reputations which might make it dangerous to add them to the Cabinet at a critical moment. Inskip would create no jealousies. He would excite no enthusiasm but he would involve us in no fresh perplexities.'

In mid-March, the Cabinet endorsed a policy which would give no encouragement to the French and sought to 'utilise Herr Hitler's offers in order to obtain a permanent settlement'. Ministers were confirmed in their judgement by the report from the Chiefs of Staff the same week: 'We would at once emphasise . . . that any question of war with Germany while we are as at present heavily committed to the possibility of hostilities in the Mediterranean would be thoroughly dangerous.'

But others were less certain. 'A week of excitement and alarms, as the whole crisis heats,' wrote Cazalet. 'Opinion v. divided and constantly changing. Extreme Right both Pro and Anti Hitler. Labour and L. of N. U. [League of Nations Union] both in favour of accepting German offer and in favour of sanctions.'

Just three days after Inskip's appointment, Harold Nicolson attended a dinner at the Belgian Embassy, which was attended by the Tories Eden, Churchill and Sir Austen Chamberlain, the Labour leader Attlee and the Liberals Samuel, Sinclair and Snell. Nicolson wrote to his wife, relating that Eden had expounded his policy:

> We all agreed. Winston said, 'Now here we are, elder statesmen plus heads of Opposition. We could sign a manifesto this very minute pledging ourselves to an agreed policy. Yet the world outside imagines that the House of Commons and the Government are torn by dissension.' 'And so they are', said Anthony in a low, sad voice.

Later in March, the day before the Commons eventually debated the Rhineland crisis, Eden told his Cabinet colleagues that the Government should do more to combat the complacency about the Rhineland crisis. He would therefore take the opportunity:

> to enlighten public opinion which was assuming that Germany was the 'white sheep' and not the 'black sheep'. . . . Another idea which ought to be combated was the prevalent one that the occupation of the Rhineland was no threat to France. It was a threat because so long as the Rhineland was demilitarised the Germans, in order to invade France through Belgium, as in 1914, would have to use large forces to hold the Rhineland and their striking force would be reduced. After occupying the Rhineland they could fortify it, hold the frontier with a relatively small force, and greatly increase their striking force on the northern bank.

In his speech, Eden left MPs in no doubt about Germany's responsibility for the serious breach of the Locarno Treaty.

But Neville Chamberlain, winding up the debate for the Government, was more conciliatory, commenting, 'The German Chancellor has declared that he has no intentions other than peaceful intentions at the present time. Personally, I believe that . . .' (Hansard, 26 March 1936, col. 1544). Under challenge from Lloyd George, Neville Chamberlain reassured the House that the Government would not join France in any move to force German troops out of the Rhineland.

There was no pressure from the opposition for the Government to take a tougher line. Dalton, one of the Labour Party's most committed rearmers, conceded, 'It is only right to say bluntly and frankly that public opinion in this country would not support, and certainly the Labour Party would not support, the taking of military sanctions or even economic sanctions against Germany at this time, in order to put German troops out of the Rhineland' (Hansard, 26 March 1936, col. 1454). Whereas Eden and critics of the Government on their own backbenches were concerned at the public's complacency, both front benches, Government and opposition, appeared to regard the mood in the country as a crucial factor determining their response.

The formula which preserved Labour Party unity put all the emphasis on the League of Nations, and the continued desire for disarmament as opposed to rearmament. It was encapsulated by Attlee:

People are thinking all the time in terms of national defence. We say that you should seek your full security through the League. We do not think that we should say we are going to make ourselves strong for defence and then as collateral security have the League in the background. We want to see the League developed so that you will get a real reduction of armaments, so that no nation will feel it can stand by its own armaments, but all will have to depend on collective security. (Ibid., col. 1535)

By far the most striking feature of the Rhineland debate was that out of seven speeches from the Government's own backbenches, only one supported the Government – and that was a maiden speech from the Hon. W. Astor, the second son of Nancy Astor. The young Astor acknowledged 'the risk there is in making an agreement with the German Government at the moment', but argued strongly for a settlement with Germany. He combined the anxieties of most Conservatives that war would overturn British society, with the widespread fear of war felt by all classes and particularly by the young:

The people of this country feel, I believe, that if there is a war now, it is possible that England may lose her influence for good, through many years to come, by having her economic and social system crippled if not destroyed. . . . I have only dared to utter these sentiments because I am convinced that they are the sentiments of nine-tenths of the country and of most of my generation. (Ibid., col. 1493)

Ranged against the Government (and the young Astor) was a formidable array of experience and talent on their own benches. Sir Austen Chamberlain and Winston Churchill both urged a tougher stand against Hitler, and were joined by four other impressive parliamentary performers – the National Labour MP Harold Nicolson and the Conservatives Robert Boothby, Paul Emrys-Evans and Brigadier-General Sir Edward Spears.

In this debate, they mapped out the major themes which the Tory rebels were to reiterate over the next few years. Their approach shows the extent of the gulf which was opening between those like Chamberlain and the majority of the Cabinet, who were looking for some settlement with Germany, and the Tory rebels who believed in a stronger commitment to rearmament and closer co-operation with the French.

Sir Austen Chamberlain admitted that when he first heard the news of remilitarisation, he had been in some doubt about his own reaction. But he now echoed Eden's desire to alert the country to the real extent of the threat. Speaking with the authority of a former Foreign Secretary and co-author of the Locarno Treaty, Sir Austen declared that he hoped the debate would 'remove from the public mind the idea that what is at stake now is one of those internal squabbles between France and Germany which disturb the world' (ibid., col. 1484). The real issue was 'whether in future the law of force shall prevail or whether there shall be substituted for it the force of law' (ibid., col. 1485).

Sir Austen warned that Britain should not allow herself to be lulled into a false sense of security by Hitler's more reassuring comments: 'All the acts are forceful; only the words are reassuring.' He summed up the difference between the Government and their critics as being 'between those who take a short view of what lies in front of us and those who, looking further ahead, cannot feel it in their conscience to accept an easy settlement to-day if they know that it will bring disaster to their children a few years ahead' (ibid., col. 1487).

One of the principal problems for the critics was that the main alternative to a settlement with Germany – a policy of alliances and rearmament – was held by many to have caused the 1914–18 war. But Sir Austen feared that he was already witnessing a repetition of the events before 1914:

What happened then is ominously like what has been happening recently – an ultimatum here, an ultimatum there, another ultimatum, each time confronting this country or that with brutal force if it does not surrender each time, diplomacy by force with the mailed fist and the shining armour prevailing over reason, over argument, over treaty obligations in some cases; and then the same procedure tried once too often and a world in arms to resist the aggression. (Ibid.)

While Sir Austen urged on the Government a stronger commitment to uphold 'the force of law', Churchill's support for the League and collective security was clearly focused on the overriding need to contain Germany. With every triumph, Hitler was tightening his grip at home and strengthening his position in Europe: 'One year it is the Saar, another month the right of Germany to conscription, another month to gain from Britain the right to build submarines, another month the Rhineland. Where will it be next? Austria, Memel, other territories and disturbed areas are already in view' (ibid., col. 1525).

Faced with the 'enormous process of the rearmament of Germany', Churchill called for an alliance between Britain and France, and argued that collective security could be made effective through mutual assistance pacts. The allied powers would then be in a position to offer Germany 'an absolute guarantee of the inviolability of German soil', and negotiate with Germany from a position of strength on the question of her rearmament and any remaining grievances.

Robert Boothby, one of Churchill's few close associates in the Commons, argued that the Nazis were now deploying the same methods by which they had won power in their own country: 'They are following the method of the coup of the *fait accompli*. They give the greatest assurances, and smooth everybody down, and, when everybody is feeling happy and nobody is looking, they pounce' (ibid., col. 1496). In one of the earliest references to *Mein Kampf* in Parliament, Boothby quoted 'an interesting passage', which 'justifies in international affairs a policy of bluff, provided that the bluff is big enough. If a real big bluff can be brought off that is, according to Herr Hitler, the acme of statesmanship in international affairs' (ibid.).

Boothby attacked those in Britain who advocated concessions to Germany in the belief that in time Nazi Germany and Soviet Russia would fight each other and that 'somehow these two great menaces will "do in" each other.' He warned that Germany would instead take the 'most alluring road', beginning at Vienna and stretching to the south and east. At some point Britain would have to take a stand because 'This country can never in the long run tolerate a Nazi Germany astride the whole of Europe, omnipotent right across the Continent' (ibid., col. 1498). The

Government's reaction to the Rhineland was a crucial test. If they did not stand by France and the League, the smaller powers would conclude that their interests would be best served by making a deal with Hitler.

From the Government backbenches Spears and Emrys-Evans developed further the need for Britain to make crystal-clear where she stood. Brigadier-General Spears referred to the need to view with the utmost suspicion any assurances from Hitler. He had heard the argument advanced on the Continent that 'having invaded the Rhineland this year and offered a treaty of 25 years, next year they will take Austria and offer a treaty of 50 years; that after that it will be the turn of Memel and the Corridor, when they will offer a treaty of 75 years, and we can look forward to eternal peace once France and England have disappeared' (ibid., col. 1509).

The Rhineland was decisive because Hitler had successfully called the bluff of the British and French Governments. He had correctly judged that they were distracted by Mussolini's aggressive actions in the Mediterranean and were disinclined to take any retaliatory measures if he moved on the Rhineland.

As a result, Hitler had strengthened immeasurably his own position in Germany and made it all the more likely that he would launch similar coups in the future. The qualms felt by Germany's military leaders were made to seem groundless, his judgement had been proved right and his bravado had been seen to work.

Arguably, Hitler might have been deterred had he thought that the French would mobilise – in early 1936, their army was still far superior in strength to the German Army. But once the remilitarisation had occurred it was unlikely, to say the least, that Hitler and the German people would have accepted any withdrawal of their troops from their own territory without fighting.

The French, like the British, were simply not prepared to risk a war over the incident. There is little mystery in their own inaction and preference for talking with the British about concerted action. One factor was the heavy psychological toll taken by the bloodletting of the 1914–18 war. This was compounded by the severe political instability which marked the later years of the Third Republic. In such circumstances it was unrealistic to expect any resolute response from Paris.

At the same time, the British Government did nothing to encourage a firmer stand by the French. This is where Britain's failure to rearm adequately, her imperial commitments and the wish to avoid any European 'entanglement' were crucial factors.

The month following the Rhineland crisis, the Chiefs of Staff were arguing that even the limited co-operation of joint staff talks with the French were too risky:

> If they [the French] think that they are strong enough at the present time to undertake hostilities against Germany, we may find ourselves committed to participation against Germany with forces which are not only inadequate to render effective support, but incapable of assuring our own security, with grave consequences to the people of this country.

The Government's critics, however, were a little too quick to turn a blind eye to the failings of the French. The francophile Sir Austen Chamberlain, and Winston Churchill, who continually emphasised the need for a resolute Anglo-French stand, tended, rather conveniently, to overlook the more awkward facts about France.

The Government's opponents and critics were divided among themselves. Labour was deeply split between its pacifist wing and the rearmers, with the former still the dominant force within the Parliamentary Labour Party. Labour's outright opposition to rearmament militated against any closer co-operation with the Tory critics.

Indeed, during the debate on the Rhineland crisis, Attlee took issue with Churchill over the continuation of sanctions against Italy. Churchill had suggested that sanctions had strained relations between France and Italy, and argued that Europe now needed to pull together against the greater threat from Hitler. Attlee, however, stressed – as had Dalton – the importance of sanctions as 'the vindication of the League against Italy'. Turning on Churchill, Attlee declared, 'It is no good taking action against someone who offends against the League if when the next sinner comes along you give the first sinner absolution and enrol him in your police force if possible' (ibid., col. 1536).

After the turmoil of the previous six months, Attlee's rebuke signalled a tightening of the bonds of party loyalty during the spring and summer of 1936.

# CHAPTER SIX

# REBELS AND REARMERS

The general impression left was that the majority of the National [Government] Party are at heart anti-League and anti-Russian, and that what they would really like would be a firm agreement with Germany and possibly Italy by which we could purchase peace at the expense of the smaller states.

(Harold Nicolson, writing in his diary, following Churchill's speech to backbench MPs supporting the National Government, 16 July 1936)

'I give you my word there will be no great armaments.' This was the pledge given by the Prime Minister Stanley Baldwin when he addressed the Peace Society on 31 October 1935, during that autumn's general election campaign. Baldwin was seeking to counter Labour's accusations that the Government's rearmament programme was a threat to peace.

Neville Chamberlain had suggested that 'we should take the bold course of actually appealing to the country on a defence programme.' But Baldwin resisted, judging that public opinion was still not ready for the kind of campaign favoured by his Chancellor. Baldwin was walking a tightrope between the disarmers and the rearmer critics in his own party, who had been urging the Government to do more since the latter months of 1933.

The announcement of increases in defence spending before the 1935 election had gone some way to reassure the Tory rearmers. Although they still felt that more needed to be done, Baldwin's measures were at least a move in the right direction. Churchill won unanimous support at that October's Conservative Party annual conference for his call for a strengthened defence effort, but the significance of his speech lay in his apparent support for Baldwin.

The disagreement between the Government and the rearmers was not merely about the level of resources which should be spent on defence. It also went to the heart of the debate about how the economy should be run and the kind of society Britain should become.

In April 1936, during the Commons debate on Neville Chamberlain's fifth Budget, Churchill told MPs, 'You cannot do anything without a working agreement with the trade unions.' As he explained, 'I read in a paper to-day that no meeting had yet taken place between the Government and trade unions in regard to questions of apprenticeship and dilution and transference, without settling which you cannot possibly expand your munitions production' (Hansard, 23 April 1936, col. 336). As far as most Conservatives were concerned, however, Churchill's prescription should not be on the agenda for any Conservative-dominated Government. They had been returned to power with a resounding majority less than six months earlier. It was bad enough that the Chancellor had raised income tax by threepence in the pound to help finance the rearmament programme. Yet here was Churchill demanding a 'working agreement' with organised labour – what kind of *quid pro quo* would the unions demand?

And Churchill went further. He warned that the Government would need to curb profiteering by the arms manufacturers, and again his concern was to create the national unity required for the effective rearmament. 'You will not get the effective co-operation of the working people unless you can make sure that there are not a lot of greedy fingers having a rake-off' (ibid. col. 337).

Churchill's advocacy of these policies stemmed not from any desire to challenge the *status quo*, but from a conviction that national security had to override all else. He justified his demands by reference to the massive scale of Hitler's rearmament.

Much of Churchill's detailed information was coming from civil servants – 'moles' as they have come to be known – who were pointing to the apparently ever-widening gap in armaments between Germany and Britain, despite the increases in spending sanctioned by Baldwin's Government since 1935. Although there was some debate about the extent of the threat, the difference which sparked greatest controversy was what should be done about it.

Churchill also called for a Ministry of Supply to be set up in Britain, which would ensure that the necesssary armaments were provided. Implicit in this demand was the need for some element of state compulsion, which was the main reason that the idea had been rejected by the Government.

What chance did Churchill and other Tory rearmers have of bringing enough pressure to bear on ministers to change their minds? Baldwin had suffered a severe loss of personal authority over the Hoare–Laval Pact. The rumblings on the right had grown louder during the Rhineland crisis.

But the Tory critics faced a Herculean task in trying to effect any shift in policy.

The dissenter's path has never been an easy one in British politics, but in 1936 the route was particularly arduous. The National Government was in a virtually impregnable position, with a majority of almost 250 in the Commons and no need to face the electorate again until the autumn of 1940.

The majority of Conservatives were 'anti-' almost anything which would be involved in boosting the rearmament programme and adopting a different foreign policy. At home, they were anti-reform and anti-union, which ruled out the kind of economic and social changes essential in any large-scale rearmament. They did not trust either the French or the Americans, and were anti-Soviet, anti-sanctions and anti-League, a combination of 'antis' which effectively ruled out all the possible alternatives. In July 1936 Churchill addressed the Foreign Affairs Committee, open to MPs who took the National Government whip. Their unresponsive reception was described by Harold Nicolson (see the quotation at the head of this chapter).

The Government's message was essentially a comforting one. Most of their supporters wanted to believe it. After all, at the time of the Rhineland crisis, no one could be absolutely sure what Hitler's intentions were, and few wanted to believe the doom-laden predictions of the critics. It was much easier to accept that it was possible to preserve peace by treating each crisis as it arose, that Hitler could be appeased, and that only modest defence measures were needed.

Conservative critics of the Government were seen not only to be advocating radical change, but also to be allying themselves with some distinctly radical forces. After the Rhineland crisis, Churchill launched himself on a great campaign to unite people of all political persuasions – Tories, Labour, trade unionists, Liberals – in a single movement supporting collective resistance. But many Tories were wary of openly associating with the opposition parties.

The number of dissidents on the Government benches on defence and foreign policy usually numbered no more than twenty or thirty. By contrast, in the early 1930s, up to eighty Conservatives had voted against the Government on the India Bill. But on that issue the rebels were the 'conservatives', opposing any reform, while Baldwin and his colleagues were cast in the position of the reformers. Conservatives are naturally more at ease opposing change. The more the rearmers emphasised the need for radical policies as part and parcel of an expanded rearmament programme, the more difficult their task became.

Besides the natural pull of Party loyalty, Party discipline was enforced with regimental rigour by Captain David Margesson, the Government Chief Whip from 1931, and James Stuart, his deputy from 1935. There was little chance of the critics making much headway without clear leadership. Most of them were younger MPs, and some, like Harold Macmillan, were also critical of the Government's domestic policies, urging that more should be done to tackle unemployment and the problems of industrial decline and poverty.

Churchill was by far the most eloquent and outspoken of the senior critics. He was the obvious focus for the dissidents, the kind of figure around whom they might have built up their support. But Churchill's reputation denied him the backing of more than a handful of MPs.

As Barbara Cartland has recalled, her brother, the young Tory MP Ronald Cartland, received a warning about Churchill from an older Tory MP: 'Let me give you a word of advice, Ronnie, Winston's no good – keep away from him.' But according to his sister, 'Ronald replied in that voice that those who antagonised him knew so well – "Thank you. I must be allowed to choose my own friends." ' Cartland was one of the few who rejected such advice.

Lord Thorneycroft recalls that when he first entered the House at the Stafford by-election in 1938 he had no intention of becoming a rebel, but nonetheless received an unsolicited warning from the Whips. 'The floor of the House of Commons is strewn with the bones of young men who have associated too closely with Mr. Churchill,' was the chilling advice given to the young Thorneycroft and his like.

The Whips were reinforcing what many young backbenchers already felt about Churchill. In Lord Beaverbrook's phrase, he was seen as a 'busted flush'. By the mid-1930s, he seemed to belong to a different era. In fact, he was not all that old. He celebrated his sixtieth birthday in November 1934, and was five years younger than Neville Chamberlain.

But Churchill had been in the House since 1900 and had served in Governments since Asquith's day. Crucially, he had not held office since the Conservative defeat in 1929, which already seemed a bygone age to the new intake of young Conservative backbenchers. He did not help his cause by arriving in the Chamber of the Commons to deliver some great and lengthy peroration, and then promptly disappearing for the rest of the debate.

He was also condemned as lacking judgement. His reputation still suffered from the damage caused by his responsibility for the disastrous Dardanelles initiative in the 1914–18 war. It was recalled that as Chancellor of the Exchequer in 1925 he had put Britain back on the Gold Standard, which had not proved a great success, and that he had agreed to reduce defence spending. Worst of all for Churchill, his rebellion in the early 1930s over the National Government's India Bill branded him a reactionary and a trouble-maker. The Party managers did not easily forgive him the bitter struggles he fought with Baldwin.

Most Conservative MPs were wary of being seen to associate with Churchill, and all the more so because of his readiness to associate with the opposition parties. During the middle and late 1930s, his only close colleagues in the Commons were Brendan Bracken, an Irishman who had worked for him since 1923, Robert Boothby, his former Parliamentary Private Secretary at the Treasury in the late 1920s, and Duncan Sandys, his son-in-law.

As for the other most senior Conservative Privy Councillor on the backbenches, there was little prospect that Sir Austen Chamberlain would assume the mantle as the critics' leader. Sir Austen was not cut out for cabals or anything that might smack of intrigue. Churchill's aphorism about him, that 'He always played the game, and always lost,' was painfully true in the 1930s, notably when he failed to exploit Hoare's resignation for his own ends. He was a loner, an uninspiring figure, 'ossified, tedious, and hopelessly out of date' as Chips Channon cruelly described him.

There were others who did not agree with all that the Government were saying, yet disagreed with both Churchill and Sir Austen. Leo Amery, himself a senior figure on the backbenches, argued that Britain should pursue an imperial strategy, concerning herself with the maintenance of the British empire and Commonwealth. As an imperialist and isolationist, his views were similar to Beaverbrook's, though he did not embrace appeasement as wholeheartedly as the press baron.

Divided among themselves, the Government's critics and opponents found that the spring and summer of 1936 was a period of confusion and uncertainty. And in the wake of Hitler's successful coup in the Rhineland the German regime launched an effective propaganda offensive, designed to show that the new Germany had much to be said for it, and was not bent on war with Britain. The net result was that the Tory rearmers faced an uphill struggle.

The response of senior Tory critics like Churchill and Sir Austen Chamberlain to the Rhineland crisis was to urge collective action against the growing threat from Germany and, as part of this, to establish better relations with Mussolini. The trouble was that the best hope for collective action was the League of Nations, yet establishing better links with Italy would inevitably mean ending sanctions. And that, in turn, would represent a serious blow to the League's credibility.

There was also a political problem. Most Conservatives were now strongly anti-League, but the Tory critics could gain support on the need for collective action and the League from the opposition parties. Yet the notion of concerting with the Fascist regime in Italy, which both Churchill and Sir Austen Chamberlain advocated, was wholly unacceptable on the left, and also to some Conservatives.

Immediately after the invasion of the Rhineland, Churchill launched himself on a great campaign of speeches and articles in the press to alert public opinion to the extent of the German threat. He stressed the need for rearmament and sought to unite all parties on the need for collective action to resist Hitler.

The campaign was very much the brainchild of disillusioned senior officials in the Foreign Office. The Permanent Secretary, Sir Robert Vansittart, and the Head of the News Department, Rex Leeper, a bright Australian, were dismayed that ministers were not educating the public about the real nature of the German threat and the need for Britain to resist it. Vansittart and Leeper had realised that there was no prospect that their political masters in Whitehall would ever change their policy.

Vansittart personally put Leeper in touch with Churchill. Leeper duly visited Churchill and found him ready to play a leading role in the campaign. Together, the rebel politician and the dissident official planned a campaign to unite everyone in the country who opposed Hitler and believed that he had to be resisted. Churchill was soon in touch with the Anti-Nazi Council, where he met the leading rearmers in the labour movement, Sir Walter Citrine, General-Secretary of the Trades Union Congress, and Hugh Dalton, the Shadow Foreign Secretary.

Through Vansittart, Churchill also met the Soviet Ambassador in London, Ivan Maisky, for the first time in April 1936. Churchill and Maisky were to keep in regular contact from this time on. Moscow had recently signed a defensive pact with Paris, another factor which did little to convince the great bulk of Conservatives of the attractions of collective action. It merely served to confirm them in their view that the French were untrustworthy.

Despite these contacts across parties, and across ideologies, the bonds of party loyalty reimposed themselves in the conflict over Italy and sanctions. Most Conservatives were increasingly opposed to the League of Nations. Ironically, Churchill and Sir Austen Chamberlain were themselves helping to foster this antagonism through their opposition to sanctions against Italy.

The Foreign Secretary, Eden, was against attempting any *rapprochement* with Italy, and in Cabinet argued that sanctions were still having some effect. But Neville Chamberlain began pressing the case for lifting them, on the grounds that it would help bring Italy back within the

League, secure assurances about Mussolini's future conduct, and renew Rome's interest in restraining Germany.

Eden, however, eventually came round to the view that sanctions were ineffective and might as well be lifted, although he was still opposed to appeasing Mussolini. By June, Neville Chamberlain decided that the time had come to force a decision. In a calculated breach of collective ministerial responsibility, the Chancellor of the Exchequer launched an outspoken attack on the renewal of sanctions. He told a meeting of the '1900 Club' that it would be 'the very midsummer of madness' to continue sanctions. He later confided in his diary, 'I did it deliberately because I felt that the party and the country needed a lead, and an indication that the government was not wavering and drifting without a policy. . . . I did not consult Anthony Eden because he would have been bound to beg me not to say what I proposed.'

On 18 June 1936, the British Government announced their intention of terminating sanctions. In the opposition censure debate five days later, only two Conservative backbenchers, Vyvyan Adams and Harold Macmillan, voted against their Government. The latter resigned the Government whip to sit as an Independent Progressive in an attempt to unite progressive opinion in all parties, Labour, Liberal and Conservative, against the National Government.

Leo Amery later delivered his verdict on the ending of sanctions, and coined an epitaph for the League: 'So ended the years of delusion in this country. So also ended the League of Nations, killed by the wishful thinking of sincere but misguided enthusiasts and by the interplay of our party politics.'

With the demise of the League and collective security, the main alternative to the Government's policy had effectively collapsed.

That summer, rearmament caused renewed dissension. The Tory re-armers were embattled. Speaking in his constituency on 20 June 1936, Churchill described the pressures of rebellion:

It has not been a pleasant task. It has certainly been a thankless task. It has brought me into conflict with many former friends and colleagues. I have been mocked and censured as a scare-monger and even as warmonger, by those whose complacency and inertia have brought us nearer to the war and war nearer to us all.

There was in fact a heated debate raging within Whitehall over the scale and nature of the rearmament programme. Its outcome during the summer of 1936 largely determined the shape of British strategy for the rest of the 1930s.

A year earlier, the Defence Policy Requirements Committee (the reconstituted Defence Requirements Committee) had stated that Britain's defence deficiencies were so serious that only an immediate loan of £200 million could put them right. The Committee also emphasised the strategic importance to Britain of being able to hold the Low Countries in the event of any European conflict. The Chancellor, Chamberlain, objected to such a commitment, but the consensus at the time was that it was necessary for national security.

But little priority was given to implementing the report, and within months the Italian invasion of Abyssinia had shifted attention to the Mediterranean. With the British empire facing threats around the globe, the Chiefs of Staff advised ministers to buy time wherever possible, and to act in a conciliatory way in any international dispute.

When ministers discussed a further report from the Defence Policy Requirements Committee in February 1936, they felt able to endorse the role envisaged for the navy and air force, and to approve plans for expanding the Field Force and modernising the Territorial Army. Chamberlain, however, remained opposed to the idea of any significant Continental role for the army. Eden also expressed concern at the likely adverse reaction to spending more on the army. Increasingly the Treasury view came to hold sway, that resources were limited, and Britain needed to concentrate on key, limited priorities.

Britain's financial and economic strength came to be seen as the fourth arm of defence. The idea was that by maintaining a sound economy, Britain would be able to draw on those assets in the event of war to purchase arms abroad until industry was fully converted to the war effort. The upshot was that financial constraint became of paramount importance, and defence measures were limited to preventing Britain succumbing to a sudden knock-out blow, whether from an air attack or by the severing of her crucial sea-lanes – the concept of 'limited liability'.

Reinforcing this limited concept of defence was the reluctance, particularly on Chamberlain's part, to antagonise business interests by intervening in the economy. Since the spring of 1936, the row over state intervention had rumbled on within Whitehall. Less than a week after Churchill's speech in the 1936 Budget debate, calling for greater state intervention, Sir Thomas Inskip, the recently appointed Minister for the Co-ordination of Defence, was echoing Churchill's warnings in Cabinet.

The new Minister told his colleagues that rearmament, even on the limited scale envisaged, would require greater state intervention in the economy. Inskip warned that 'he might have to ask for the authority to adopt more drastic measures', by which he had in mind enabling 'manufacturers to give priority to Government orders in connection with the Defence Requirements Programme, and to postpone commercial orders whether for home or foreign account'. Intervention in the economy – or 'interference with trade' – on the scale proposed was anathema to Neville Chamberlain. The Government were pinning their hopes on co-operation with industry, not compulsion.

Ministers had met leaders of the main employers' organisation, the Federation of British Industry, in October 1935. The bosses made it clear that while they were happy to co-operate with the Government, they were opposed to any compulsion or direction. There was a veiled threat from business that, if the Government resorted to compulsion during peace-time, industry would withdraw its co-operation from the rearmament programme.

No similar approach was made from Government to the trade unions, although by 1936 skill shortages were a severe limitation on the rearmament programme, particularly aircraft production. These bottle-necks were the result of union restrictive practices in the engineering industry and of the lack of training in British industry.

The Government's response to skill shortages was to worry about the effects on the rest of the economy of the higher wages paid by employers to attract skilled labour. Ministers were not prepared to address the causes of the skill shortages, since the solutions would almost certainly entail further state intervention. Instead, higher wages became another argu-ment against further increases in the defence budget, on the grounds that it was fuelling inflation.

The unions, for their part, were unwilling to co-operate. They feared that the armaments boom would be short-lived and that their members would soon face unemployment again, as they had when the munitions firms laid off their workers after 1918.

The Government's contrasting attitude to business and the unions has been well summed up by Robert Paul Shay Jr in his study of rearmament: 'Industry was consulted, cajoled, and treated with every consideration, while labour was regarded as and treated like a natural resource that tended to be unfortunately expensive.' In 1936, the Air Minister Viscount Swinton launched a programme of 'Shadow' factories to produce aero-engines, built and equipped at the state's expense, but run by private industry at a profit.

Inskip's arguments in Cabinet in the spring of 1936 that more active inter-vention was needed had fallen on deaf ears. His colleagues accepted the suggestion from Chamberlain that the questions should be deferred. During the summer, however, the question of greater state intervention to speed the rearmament programme was again discussed in Cabinet. Inskip was supported by Swinton and by Vansittart, who had been invited to attend.

But the calls for greater state powers were opposed by Neville Chamberlain and Sir Samuel Hoare, the latter now restored to Government as First Lord of the Admiralty. Hoare claimed that the increased steps being suggested 'might come as a great shock to the country and result in an upheaval of industry'. The Chancellor felt that 'The disturbance of industry produced by acceleration might result in grave consequences, financial, economic etc., and any alteration could only be justified by over-powering conditions.' In his view, the public could only be persuaded to accept more drastic measures when there was a further deterioration in the situation in Europe.

When the Commons debated defence in July, Inskip claimed that there was a 'swelling tide of production', a claim which Churchill dismissed as being 'based on a larger measure of anticipation than of reality'. Churchill reiterated his call for greater state intervention – 'an intermediate stage between ordinary peacetime and actual war', which would involve reorganising industry and disturbing 'a good deal of the comfort and smoothness of our ordinary life'.

In his speech, Churchill burnt any remaining bridges with Baldwin and the Conservative Party establishment:

> We are going away on our holidays. Jaded Ministers, anxious but impotent Members of Parliament, a public whose opinion is more bewildered and more expressionless than anything I can recall in my life – all will seek the illusion of rest and peace.
>
> We are told, 'Trust the National Government. Have confidence in the Prime Minister, with the Lord President of the Council [Ramsay MacDonald] at his side. Do not worry. Do not get alarmed. A great deal is being done. No one could do more.' And the influence of the Conservative Party machine is being used through a thousand channels to spread this soporific upon Parliament and the nation. But, I am bound to ask, has not the confidence been shaken by various things that have happened, and are still happening? (Hansard, 20 July 1936, col. 109)

As the *Daily Telegraph* commented, with massive understatement, 'The breach between Mr Churchill and the Government was certainly not narrowed by his speech last night.' Churchill wrote to his friend Lord Rothermere, the press baron, who was a convinced rearmer, as well as being pro-German: 'As you will see I keep on trying my best. If as you say we are going to be vassals of Germany, I can only hope I shall not live to see it!'

At the end of July, Churchill, Sir Austen Chamberlain and the Marquis of Salisbury led a deputation of eighteen senior Conservatives to

Number 10 to express their worries about the lack of progress on rearmament. Baldwin told them that he was not going to get the country into a war with anyone: 'If there is any fighting in Europe to be done, I should like to see the Bolshies and the Nazis doing it.'

The debate over Britain's defence strategy coincided with a period after the Rhineland crisis when more people began to feel that Germany was not such a threat to Britain after all. This lull made it all the more likely that a policy of essentially limited defence measures would be adopted. It became more difficult for those advocating a much larger rearmament programme, designed to deter Hitler, to make a convincing case.

There had been a great deal of sympathy for Germany's position over the Rhineland. Although Hitler intervened in Spain from the early autumn of 1936, so too did the Italians and the Soviets. And in 1936 many on the right were a great deal more worried about the threat of Communism than they were about the menace of Fascism. Hitler's regime had also launched a determined propaganda campaign. Ribbentrop became Ambassador in London from the summer, and was wining and dining those whom he supposed had influence with Government. More visits to Germany were arranged.

By the summer, Hitler's public relations campaign was beginning to bear fruit. Churchill's cousin, the Marquis of Londonderry, a senior member of the National Government until Baldwin's reshuffle the previous November, had visited Berlin in the spring of 1936. In early May, he wrote to Churchill, regretting what he called 'the "defeatist" attitude of this country in assuming' that war between Britain and Germany was unavoidable.

Londonderry added, 'When I saw Hitler in the course of a two hours' interview he spoke chiefly of the Communistic menace and I found myself in agreement with a great deal of what he said.' Because there were so few Communists in Britain, people still felt that 'Germany is exaggerating the Communistic danger.' He ended with a personal plea to Churchill: 'I should like to get out of your mind what appears to be a strong anti-German obsession.'

An anecdote of Beaverbrook's suggests why Londonderry might have been more fearful than most of 'the Communistic menace'. The Londonderrys were renowned for their hospitality, which was lavish even by the standards of smart London society at the time. But the Londonderrys were none too pleased about any publicity:

At New Year 1932 Lord Londonderry complained of paragraphs in the *Daily Express* about the gay doings at Londonderry House. . . .

Londonderry then explained that he had cancelled the usual
festivities at his country seats and did not want his retainers to know
how he had been enjoying himself in London.

Churchill was to be disappointed in his hope that his cousin would 'not
become too prominently identified with the pro-German view'.

Londonderry was by no means the only visitor to Hitler's Germany that
year. The Olympic Games started in Berlin on 1 August. Ribbentrop was
expecting a 'friendly invasion' from London – Lord Monsell, Lord
Beaverbrook, Lord Rothermere and many more were invited. In
September, others went out to see the Nuremberg Rally.

But the mention of Germany and Hitler was still liable to spark
controversy. At the start of August, Chips Channon was staying with
Philip Sassoon:

> There was the usual German argument after dinner with Philip
> [Sassoon] and Duff [Cooper] attacking the Nazis with the violence
> born of personal prejudice. I said never a word. After dinner . . . a
> young R.A.F. pilot whispered to me 'Is Duff Cooper off his rocker,
> or what?' Indeed he seems obsessed at times.

A couple of days later, Chips was at a dinner party where it was thought
safe to talk about Germany only when Duff and Lady Diana Cooper had
left. Max Aitken had been at the opening of the Games and 'proceeded to
describe the scene. . . . Teenie [Victor Cazalet] tactlessly flew at him (he
hates the whole Beaverbrook crew) and a dreadful discussion ensued
during which everyone lost their temper.' On another occasion, at a
London dinner party, the Liberal MP Harcourt ('Crinks') Johnstone
proposed a toast: 'Here's death to Ribbentrop.' This prompted Duff
Cooper to add, 'I only hope he dies in pain.' As Channon noted, 'Then the
usual, long anti-German tirade began'.

The Channons saw Germany for themselves later that summer. In
September, the Nicolsons met the Channons while on holiday in Austria,
as Harold Nicolson noted:

> At luncheon we discuss the Nazis. The Channons have fallen much
> under the champagne-like influence of Ribbentrop. . . . They had
> been to the Olympic Games and had not been the least disconcerted
> by Goering or Goebbels. They think Ribbentrop a fine man, and that
> we should let gallant little Germany glut her fill of the reds in the
> East and keep decadent France quiet while she does so. Otherwise
> we shall not have only reds in the West but bombs in London,
> Kelvedon and Southend. [The Channons lived in London and at
> Kelvedon, and Chips was MP for Southend.]

Channon's concern to keep the Communist menace at bay was unlikely to be divorced entirely from self-interest. Extremes of wealth prevailed at the time, and he was at the very rich extreme. Channon was able to spend £6000 decorating one room in his house, at a time when some working-class men were supporting a family on less than £3 a week. Chips was an American by birth, and his ostentatious wealth and pro-German sympathies prompted the comment from Robert Byron: 'I suppose I should not be surprised to learn that you are prepared to sacrifice the interests of your adopted country in the supposed interests of your adopted class.'

But the most notable visitor to Germany that year was the former Liberal Prime Minister, Lloyd George. He had admired Hitler since he came to power and, if anything, that admiration had grown. He was completely fooled by Hitler. On his return to Britain, he wrote a glowing account of Hitler and his new Germany, and felt confident enough to declare, 'The Germans have definitely made up their minds never to quarrel with us again.'

Despite this advice from Britain's leader during the 1914–18 war, the debate about rearmament in Britain revived in the autumn.

The controversy over state intervention and rearmament was raised again in Cabinet, at the time of the opening of the new session of Parliament in early November 1936. Baldwin was unwell and resting in the country, and this crucial policy review was chaired by the Chancellor of the Exchequer Neville Chamberlain.

Following the demise of collective security, Inskip queried 'what our policy was'. He warned that the Government would need to take emergency powers, if they were to work 'for readiness for war in June 1937'. Eden and Duff Cooper echoed Inskip's concern. Against these arguments, Sir Samuel Hoare reiterated that emergency powers would disrupt the economy. It would be 'necessary to assume for a long time that we should be unprepared', and therefore Britain 'would have to proceed very quietly' in the world.

Chamberlain made it clear that anxieties about the state of the economy were more pressing than Inskip's worries about the state of the country's defences. As the Cabinet minute records, Chamberlain 'was concerned at the mounting cost of the programme', and warned, 'Before long he thought people would be talking about an unbalanced Budget, and we might find that our credit was not so good as it was a few years ago. He said this because while recognising that national safety came first our resources were not unlimited and we were putting burdens on future generations.' Resources were finite and Britain could not possibly contemplate simultaneously fighting Germany, Italy and Japan on her own. Again, however, these arguments were buttressed by an austere financial orthodoxy and resistance to any economic and social reform which might have eased the path towards a stronger rearmament programme, free from the constraints of production bottlenecks and skill shortages.

Five days after this crucial Cabinet discussion, the conflict between rearmers and appeasers sparked one of the most dramatic parliamentary occasions of the 1930s.

On 12 November 1936, the final day of the Commons debate on the King's Speech to the new session of Parliament, Churchill delivered what Harold Nicolson called a 'sledgehammer' attack on the Government's defence policy. Baldwin, stung by this onslaught and the references to his own culpability, responded with extraordinary – and historic – candour. Churchill had fastened on to a Biblical reference used by Inskip earlier in the debate. The unsuspecting Minister had spoken of 'the years that the locust hath eaten'. Churchill responded, 'Let us see which are these "years which the locust hath eaten", even if we do not pry too closely in search of the locusts who have eaten these precious years' (Hansard, 12 November 1936, col. 1101).

Churchill recalled that, following Hitler's rise to power three years earlier, at the Conservative annual conference in October 1933 Lord Lloyd had proposed a motion expressing 'grave anxiety in regard to the inadequacy of the provisions made for Imperial Defence'. As Churchill recollected, 'The resolution was passed unanimously, with only a rider informing the Chancellor of the Exchequer that all necessary burdens of taxation would be cheerfully borne. There were no locusts there, at any rate' (ibid., col. 1102).

The responsibility for the indecision and lack of action during those three years was laid at the Prime Minister's door. Referring to Hoare's comment earlier in the King's Speech debate that 'We are always reviewing the position' and that everything was fluid, Churchill retorted,

I am sure that that is true. Anyone can see what the position is. The Government simply cannot make up their mind, or they cannot get the Prime Minister to make up his mind. So they go on in strange paradox, decided only to be undecided, resolved to be irresolute, adamant for drift, solid for fluidity, all powerful to be impotent. (Ibid., col. 1107)

Churchill spelt out the consequences: 'So we go on preparing more months and years – precious, perhaps vital to the greatness of Britain – for the locusts to eat' (ibid.).

Churchill called for the immediate establishment of a Ministry of Supply and the introduction of special powers to enable the Government to redirect at least a part of industry towards defence needs. 'Some interference with the normal trade of the country would be inevitable, but I have never proposed to institute anything like war conditions in time of peace' (ibid., col. 1106). His concern to secure the support of working people was reflected in his further comment that in the event of war the laws granting the state extra powers should also embody the principle, 'Take the profit out of war.'

In a backhanded compliment to the effectiveness of the Government Whips, Churchill concluded that he had been 'staggered by the failure of the House of Commons to react effectively' as the country's plight worsened 'month by month, and year by year'. It was also a recognition of the isolation of the Tory rearmers.

Yet more remarkable even than Churchill's own speech was the reply it prompted later that evening from Baldwin. Rarely has a Prime Minister spoken so candidly about his political tactics. On rearmament, Baldwin explained, 'We started late, and I want to say a word about the years the locusts have eaten. I want to speak to the House with the utmost frankness' (ibid., col. 1143).

The Prime Minister recalled that Churchill's differences with the Government over defence dated from 1933. Baldwin and his colleagues had also been worried at what was happening in Europe at that time, but he reminded the House of his adage that 'a democracy is always two years behind a dictator'. Baldwin elaborated,

> You will remember at that time there was probably a stronger pacifist feeling running through this country than at any time since the War. I am speaking of 1933 and 1934. You will remember the election at Fulham in the autumn of 1933, when a seat which the National Government held was lost by about 7,000 votes on no issue but the pacifist. You will remember perhaps that the National Government candidate who made a most guarded reference to the question of defence was mobbed for it. (Ibid., col. 1144)

During that period, his 'position as the leader of a great party was not altogether a comfortable one'. He told MPs how he had asked himself, 'what chance was there within the next year or two of that feeling being so changed that the country would give a mandate for rearmament?' Baldwin argued, 'Supposing I had gone to the country and said that Germany was rearming and that we must rearm, does anybody think this pacific democracy would have rallied to that cry at that moment? I cannot think of anything that would have made the loss of the election from my point of view more certain'. He added, 'All I did was to take a moment perhaps less unfortunate than another might have been, and we won the election with a large majority' (ibid., col. 1145).

The Prime Minister's rationale was that the Government were thus re-elected with a mandate for essential defence measures: 'We got from the country – with a large majority – a mandate for doing a thing that no one, 12 months before, would have believed possible'. Had the Government followed Churchill's advice before 1935, and started large-scale rearm-ament during 1933 and 1934 – 'arming without a mandate' as Baldwin characterised it – 'it would have defeated entirely the end I had in view.' (ibid.)

In short, Baldwin justified his tactics on the grounds that they had enabled a steady build-up of rearmament, while carrying the country with the new policy. Given the state of public opinion before 1935, Churchill's approach would only have provoked rejection of the very policy Churchill advocated so passionately. And if Labour had won the election, there would have been no rearmament at all.

But since the 1935 election economic considerations had replaced public opinion as the key factor influencing the rate of rearmament. The emphasis placed on the need for strong finances elevated the economy to a position as the fourth arm of defence. Echoing his Chancellor's line at Cabinet, Baldwin dismissed Churchill's calls for state intervention: 'more is to be gained in this country by relying on willing co-operation than by adopting dictatorial methods.' Baldwin argued that 'the exercise of compulsory powers' by the state 'would so dislocate the ordinary free working of industry as to reduce our effective financial strength; and that financial strength, so carefully nursed and looked after through all these years, is one of the strongest weapons we have if war ever comes upon us' (ibid., col. 1149).

The Prime Minister and the Government had survived their parlia-mentary buffeting at Churchill's hands without any need to shift their stance. Later in November a deputation of senior Conservatives had a further meeting with the Prime Minister, who this time was accompanied by Neville Chamberlain, Lord Halifax and Inskip. During the discussion, the weakness of Britain's air force became even more apparent. The scale of rearmament was still believed to be inadequate to meet a German threat in 1937 or 1938.

# CHAPTER SEVEN

# 'AND I REMEMBER SPAIN'

And next day took the boat
  For home, forgetting Spain, not realising
That Spain would soon denote
  Our grief, our aspirations;
Not knowing that our blunt
  Ideals would find their whetstone, that our spirit
Would find its frontier on the Spanish front,
  Its body in a rag-tag army.

(Louis MacNeice, extract from *Autumn Journal*, 1939)

On 17 July 1936, a Spanish Army officer, General Franco, led a military rising in Spanish Morocco which spread to mainland Spain the following day. But Franco's coup met determined resistance from the Republican 'Popular Front' Government, which held large parts of Spain. The Spanish Civil War had begun.

On 20 July, Franco sought Mussolini's assistance in moving his rebel Nationalist forces across the sea from Morocco, while the Republican Government approached France to buy aircraft, arms and ammunition. Mussolini refused the Nationalists' request, but the French Prime Minister Léon Blum agreed in principle to a perfectly proper request from a neighbouring, democratic Government.

Franco tried Mussolini again, and also approached Hitler. This time he was successful, securing promises of support from both Italy and Germany – Hitler agreed to Franco's plea while attending the Wagner festival at Bayreuth. Foreign intervention in Spain had begun.

But the French Government were getting cold feet about being involved at all. Blum's Popular Front Administration was split and the country deeply divided. There were fears that if France played any part in Spain, unrest and even civil war might spread north across the Pyrenees.

On 1 August, the French Government called for an international agreement on non-intervention in Spain. A little over a week later the French announced that they were banning the supply of arms or even civilian aircraft to Spain. They were soon joined by the British

85

Government, who were anxious to avoid any involvement on the Continent of Europe and certainly did not want any part in a conflict in which the main combatants were Communists and Fascists. On 15 August, the Anglo-French Non-Intervention Agreement was signed.

At the outset, Harold Nicolson shared Churchill's anxiety, fearing that 'The pro-German and anti-Russian tendencies of the Tories will be fortified and increased.' But it was not only Conservatives who were taking a strongly pro-German line. In September, during their talks in Germany, Lloyd George and Hitler were agreed on the dangers of a Communist victory in Spain.

Conservative die-hards spoke up for Franco. 'I recognise General Franco to be a gallant Christian gentleman, and I believe his word,' declared Sir Henry Page Croft. 'I hope to God Franco wins in Spain and the sooner the better', proclaimed Sir Arnold Wilson.

Only two Conservative backbenchers advocated support for the Republican Government. It was not all that surprising that Vyvyan Adams should support the Republicans, since he was a persistent rebel and frequently agreed with the opposition parties on foreign policy. But the identity of the other rebel marked one of the most extraordinary political conversions of the decade.

Katharine, Duchess of Atholl, was among the die-hards who had rebelled with Churchill against the India Bill and had opposed the imposition of sanctions on Italy. But she embraced the Republican cause with the zeal of the convert. She appeared on many public platforms in the Aid for Spain campaign with left-wing socialists like Ellen Wilkinson and celebrities like the black singer Paul Robeson. For her pains, she earned herself the nickname 'Red Kitty'.

The Duchess attributed her conversion to *Mein Kampf*. As she told her fellow MPs, the circulation of Hitler's book was enormous, and it was 'impossible to ignore the possibility that this may still be the policy of Herr Hitler's Government'. In her view, if this policy were carried out, it would be 'one of such all-round aggression that Europe as a whole has a common interest in doing everything possible to prevent it being carried into effect' (Hansard, 29 October 1936, cols 337–42). She did not regard the British Government's policy of non-intervention as even-handed in its practical effect, and 'was perhaps bound to tell rather against the constitutional government' (Hansard, 1 December 1936, cols 1130–4).

What set the Duchess apart from the bulk of her fellow Conservatives was her assessment of the strategic consequences. She dismissed the notion that a Republican victory would represent a great strategic coup for the Soviet Union:

The fear that, if the existing Spanish Government won, we should be faced with a State which might be subject to the dictation of Soviet Russia seems to be a remote contingency. I probably would not like the form of government that might emerge, but I do not believe it would be a government that would be subservient to Russia. (Ibid.)

If, however, the Nationalists were to win, 'they have had the most valuable assistance from Fascist powers which could not well be repaid in money, and would therefore have to be repaid by some transfer of territory or the use of ports, air bases and so on' (ibid.).

Edward Heath, then making a name for himself in student politics at Oxford, was one of the few other Tories who backed the Republican cause. During a holiday in Germany in the summer of 1937, when he was just twenty-one, he took the opportunity to see what made the Nazis tick, spending three days watching the Nazis at their Nuremberg Rally. As he has since recalled, he 'saw it all – the military demonstrations and Hitler himself. This was when I realised what they were really like.'

The next summer, Heath was a member of a student delegation to Republican Spain. They went to the front and saw the forces, including the British battalion of the International Brigade. In Barcelona, their hotel was bombed, killing all those who had rushed down to the basement for shelter. During their travels, they were machine-gunned. Heath recalls:

Of course I had fairly clear ideas about it all – Franco was backed by Hitler and Mussolini, after all, and I think everyone realised that this was the first stage of the European war. They were all using it to experiment. It was obvious that the Social Democrats had Communist support, but I was just more than ever in favour of a Government that was trying to resist the Fascists.

But most Tory critics of the Government were in step with the vast majority of their loyalist colleagues over the Spanish Civil War. In the Cabinet, Eden favoured neutrality, as did the likes of Churchill and Harold Macmillan on the backbenches. Churchill was concerned that nothing should be allowed to divide Britain and France, and they were therefore better advised to keep out of Spain.

Conservatives generally shared Baldwin's fear that the 'two electric currents' of Communism and Fascism, 'beating across Europe', might 'set the whole of Western Europe on fire'. Many Tories were sympathetic to the Nationalists – Victor Cazalet visited Spain in early 1937 and talked at length with Franco, whom he thought was reasonable and not a Fascist.

But even those Tories who wanted Franco to win did not advocate that the British Government should intervene on the Nationalist side. Whether

Conservative backbenchers would have been as relaxed about non-intervention if the Soviets had seemed set to score a strategic victory is a moot point.

In the autumn of 1936, Churchill acknowledged that 'There never was any question so baffling as the attitude which liberal democracies should adopt towards Soviet Russia at the present time' (Hansard, 5 November 1936, col. 318). He attributed much of the blame for the Civil War to 'Russian propaganda and intrigues', and advised Eden not to include Russia in his considerations 'while everything is so obscure, so double-faced, so transitional in that enormous country' (ibid., cols 318–19).

By the summer of 1937, Churchill was urging recognition of the Nationalist regime, in the hope of placating Franco and removing the threat to Gibraltar. In November that year, Churchill argued that it was 'foolish in the last degree for neutral powers like Britain and France to deny that measure of recognition to the *de facto* Government of the greater part of Spain which is necessary to safeguard their commercial and political interests'.

The Government resisted this advice. A year later, Churchill had completely changed his tune. Although it was rather late in the day to be hoping for a Republican victory, he argued, 'It would seem today that the British Empire would run far less risk from the victory of the Spanish Government than from that of General Franco.' Churchill's *volte face* is explained by the priority he was again giving to the need for Soviet support to restrain Hitler.

But Churchill was once more out of step with most Conservatives. The main effect of the Spanish Civil War on the Government and their supporters on the right was to confirm their anti-Communist prejudices and harden their anti-Soviet attitudes during the last, crucial three years of the 1930s.

But it was on the left in Britain that the Spanish Civil War had the most dramatic and far-reaching impact.

The plight of the Popular Front Government immediately attracted the support of all shades of left-wing opinion. It was seen both as a war against Fascism and as a class war. As Macmillan later recalled, 'a degree of bitterness and class-consciousness developed to an extent of which I certainly had no previous experience.'

Spain prompted an enormous surge in support for left-wing causes and parties. Up and down the country, there were numerous Aid for Spain rallies, Medical Aid for Spain assemblies, and meetings attacking the French and British non-intervention policy. The generation who went to University in the latter half of the 1930s, cut their political teeth on Spain.

It was a black-and-white issue, right versus wrong, a battle against a great evil.

Spain was both the catalyst, and the focus, merging art and politics. Poets, artists, musicians, writers joined forces with trade unionists and political activists to campaign for the Republican cause. This gave the Labour Party and the Communists a hinterland which the other parties totally lacked.

Some young intellectuals and writers went to fight (John Cornford, George Orwell), others to help as medical workers (W.H. Auden). Young activists and trade unionists volunteered, including Bob Edwards, later a Labour MP, and Jack Jones, later General Secretary of the Transport and General Workers' Union. Jessica Mitford and her cousin Esmond Romilly fled to Spain together. Romilly was a nephew of Churchill's and had shocked his family and teachers by launching a pacifist, left-wing magazine at Wellington, his public school. He had already been out to Spain himself before returning with Jessica Mitford.

Over 2700 Britons fought with the International Brigades, and others like Orwell fought with the POUM, the radical socialist and anarchist group. About 80 per cent of Britons in the International Brigades were working-class. More than 500 British volunteers were killed, including John Cornford, and Julian Bell, son of Vanessa Bell and nephew of Virginia Woolf, who was driving ambulances. Orwell and Jack Jones were wounded. Only 450 of the British contingent survived without injury.

The Communist Party in Britain were determined not to miss a trick in exploiting the propaganda value of Spain. In February 1937, Virginia Woolf wrote in her diary that Stephen Spender 'said the C.P., which he had that day joined, wanted him to be killed, in order that there might be another Byron'.

The Communist newspaper, the *Daily Worker*, exploited the Spanish Civil War for all it was worth. It was able to sustain a regular flow of headlines – 'Film Stars [Chaplin, Gable, Dietrich, Bette Davis, Joan Crawford] all back the Spanish Republic'; 'Charles Laughton to Open Exhibition in Aid of Spain'; 'With Paul Robeson on the Spanish Front'; and a report that over 700 British artists, writers and musicians had petitioned the Prime Minister to restore to the Spanish Republic the right to buy defensive arms.

At universities, the left attracted support on an unprecedented scale. By the end of the 1930s, about one in five undergraduates at Oxford and Cambridge were members of the University Labour Federation. Douglas Jay has recalled that in 1929 the Oxford University Labour Club consisted of only 'three or four eccentric Wykehamists meeting in New College garden', but by the mid-1930s had swollen to between 500 and 600. By the

late 1930s, there were about 1500 members, according to Christopher
Mayhew, who was elected President of the Union in 1937.

The threat from Fascism was undoubtedly proving an effective
recruiting sergeant for the left. Frank Pakenham (later Lord Longford)
converted to socialism (he had worked in the Conservative Research
Department in the early 1930s) following a riot at a rally of Oswald
Mosley's in Oxford in the early summer of 1936. The audience was a
mixture of town people, dons and their wives, and Oxford busmen.

Mosley goaded the audience. The busmen shouted out 'Red Front!'
The audience applauded. Mosley retorted that anyone who repeated the
slogan would be thrown out. This was the cue for Basil Murray, son of the
classicist Gilbert, to rise from his seat and, in a very academic, mild-
mannered voice, utter the dreaded words.

All hell broke loose. Blackshirts, busmen and dons were suddenly
thrown into a pitched battle. Christopher Mayhew was reporting the
meeting for *Isis*, and later wrote to his parents:

> I saw my tutor of last term – the Hon. F. A. Pakenham, a pillar of
> the Conservative Association – attacked by three Blackshirts at once,
> who were hanging round his neck and hitting him while he swiped
> about with a chair. Another don from Christ Church, Patrick
> Gordon Walker, was fighting hard to defend him, and I saw too Dick
> Crossman, Vice-Warden of New College and a City Councillor in the
> middle of the fight.

Pakenham did not remain a pillar of the Conservative Association. As
his wife has recalled, as he lay recovering from the fight, his mind 'was
throbbing with plans to "break the fascists" power in Oxford forever.'

Communism was proving more attractive than at any other time. In the
early part of the decade, the curse of unemployment had led many to join
in the depressed regions. But by the mid-1930s, events in Europe were
attracting increasing numbers of young intellectuals, many encouraged by
the decision of the Communist International in Moscow in 1935 to support
Popular Fronts with other anti-Fascist parties. In fact, this provoked
infighting as much as co-operation on the left. Mayhew reckons that at
Oxford nearly 200 were members of the Communist Party, 'including
some of the ablest and most intelligent undergraduates'.

Many, like Denis Healey, who joined the Party at the end of his first
year at Oxford in the summer of 1937, felt that the Communist Party was
the only one prepared to combat Fascism. The novelist Iris Murdoch went
up to Somerville College, Oxford, in 1938, 'that strange year before the
war, full of anxiety and fear'. She joined the Communist Party in her

second term: 'there was a feeling that Europe was falling apart, and that the only thing that could save us was some kind of left-wing movement. There was a great deal of this sort of idealism in Oxford at that time, which led people into left-wing politics.'

But by far the most popular proponent of left-wing ideas was the Left Book Club, launched in May 1936, a couple of months before the Spanish Civil War began, by the publisher Victor Gollancz. The Club was such a success that its orange-covered paperbacks have come to symbolise the left in Britain in the 1930s. Its objective was 'to help in the terribly urgent struggle for world peace and *against* fascism'.

Gollancz was one of the most fervent advocates of an alliance between the Labour and Communist Parties. Until the end of 1938, the Club virtually served as the Communist Party's propaganda machine, supporting campaigns for Aid to Spain and for a Popular Front in Britain. So strongly did it favour the Communists that no criticism of Stalin's show trials, which began in Moscow in the summer of 1936, was permitted in its publications.

In return for an annual subscription of 2s 6d, members received a book each month, selected by a committee consisting of Victor Gollancz, Harold Laski, a lecturer at the London School of Economics, and John Strachey, the left-wing politician. Among its most famous authors and titles were Arthur Koestler's *Spanish Testament*, Ellen Wilkinson's *The Town That Was Murdered*, and George Orwell's *The Road to Wigan Pier*, although there was some controversy before Orwell's book was published, because it did not toe the 'party' line.

In February 1937, more than 7000 people attended a Left Book Club rally at the Albert Hall. By the end of 1937, the Club had spawned 730 local discussion groups. By March 1938 it could boast 58,000 members, largely from the middle and lower-middle classes. Many were young and new to active politics.

During the Club's first three years, its monthly choice put into circulation over 1.5 million anti-Fascist, anti-war, socialist and Communist books. Millions of leaflets were distributed, and tens of thousands of discussion meetings, lectures, demonstrations, rallies, plays and films were organised. Members were recruited for the Communist and Labour Parties. Money was raised for medical aid for Spain, and the Club organised hundreds of meetings throughout the country against non-intervention in Spain.

The Spanish Civil War put the Labour Party in an immediate quandary. The great emotional flood-tide of support for the Republican cause on the left led many activists to assume that Labour would urge support for the

Popular Front Government and oppose the Baldwin Administration's policy of non-intervention. But the leadership were divided. Non-intervention was, after all, the policy of a socialist Prime Minister and his Popular Front Government in France.

Herbert Morrison pressed the Spanish Government's case from the start of the rebellion. Ernest Bevin praised 'the heroic struggle being carried on by the workers of Spain to save their democratic regime', but was concerned that Britain could ill afford to supply arms when she needed to rearm herself.

On 28 August, the National Council of Labour decided, despite some misgivings, to back non-intervention. They did so with the proviso that the policy was immediately and strictly observed by other countries.

A Labour Party deputation, led by Dalton, went to Paris to see Blum. The French Premier argued that the Spanish Government would fare better under non-intervention, even if Hitler and Mussolini were to commit limited breaches of the policy, than in a free-for-all. And Blum reportedly asked the deputation 'to urge my British colleagues to support *my* policy of non-intervention'.

Dalton was open to Blum's persuasion: 'I value France above Spain, both as a civilised modern state, and as a friend and pledged ally of Britain. I was not an admirer of the Spanish approximation to demo-cracy. . . .' As Dalton added, Labour politicians had close contacts with French socialists, but not with the Spanish. 'And there were other elements in the Spanish Left, including Anarchists, who did not inspire much confidence.'

At the annual Trades Union Congress at Plymouth in early September, Bevin defended non-intervention and won the backing of Congress by the huge margin of 3 million votes to a mere 50,000.

But by the time the annual Labour Party conference gathered at Edinburgh a month later, there were growing reports that non-intervention was one-sided. While the democracies were observing the letter of the Agreement, the dictators were allegedly pouring in assistance to Franco and his rebels.

Spain was on the agenda on the first day of Labour's conference. But the headlines and photographs in the newspapers that morning showed the violent scenes over the weekend in the East End of London – the so-called Cable Street riot. They vividly reinforced fears that the Fascist threat was spreading across Europe.

The British Union of Fascists had planned a highly provocative march and series of meetings through the Jewish quarters. Between 2500 and 3000 Blackshirts paraded for an hour or so by the Tower of London, before gathering in nearby Royal Mint Street ready for the march. Between 6000 and 7000 police turned out to protect them.

Anti-Fascists mounted a determined effort to prevent the Blackshirts entering the East End. As *The Times* reported,

> Counter-demonstrations against the Fascists were so great that the narrow thoroughfares about the Aldgate were completely impassable, while attempts were made to use lorries as barriers to prevent the marchers approaching Whitechapel. 'Mosley shall not pass' and 'Bar the road to fascism' were chalked on walls and blazoned on banners. Shops were closed and many windows boarded.

The photographs in *The Times* showed the police holding back the anti-Fascist demonstrators and dismantling their road-blocks.

At the last minute, however, the police banned the march. Sir Oswald Mosley, the Fascists' leader, proclaimed that a British Government had, for the first time, surrendered to the 'Red Terror', whom he identified as 'Socialists, Communists and Jews'.

Although it was a victory for the left, it would not help calm feelings at the start of the Labour Party conference. Cable Street was unlikely to persuade many activists that non-intervention was the best way to combat Fascism.

During the conference debate, the proposal that the Party should support non-intervention was heavily criticised. Few were satisfied by the proviso that, if other powers were shown to be intervening, Britain and France should allow the sale of arms to the Spanish Government.

In his speech, the Party's deputy leader, Arthur Greenwood, accepted that, if the allegations about German and Italian intervention turned out to be true, an entirely new situation would exist. He reminded the Party that non-intervention had been an initiative of Blum, the French Prime Minister, and was supported by the Soviet Union. Moreover, if non-intervention were to end, as many hoped, Greenwood warned that, for every weapon sent to the Spanish Government, the Fascist rebels would be able to count on fifty from the Germans and Italians.

Ernest Bevin tried to hold the line for the leadership with the characteristically blunt assertion that rhetoric would not solve the Spanish problem. But on this occasion it was the leadership, not the activists, who seemed guilty of hiding behind rhetoric. Aneurin Bevan, one of the new intake of MPs on the left of the party, pointed out that everyone already knew that the Fascist powers were supplying the rebels with arms. Not all the leadership agreed with the policy: Morrison had described non-intervention as 'humbug', but did not air his views at the conference since he would have had to resign from the National Executive.

Despite the feeling in the hall, and the qualms among the leadership, the resolution was carried.

Passions were revived two days later when the delegates from Spain addressed the conference. Messages from fraternal delegates are part of the ritual of any Labour Party conference and are usually anodyne affairs, but that Wednesday morning the atmosphere was electric.

Although Señor de Asua, a Deputy Speaker in the Spanish Parliament, delivered his message in French, with Philip Noel-Baker translating, his message lost none of its force. He told delegates what most of those in the hall wanted to hear – that non-intervention was a monstrosity. Instead, it represented the most powerful form of intervention *against* the Spanish Government, since it denied them arms while the Fascist powers armed the rebels. Was it too much to ask that the democracies should allow the Spanish Government to buy arms?

But it was Señora de Palencia, a member of the Spanish Parliament, who roused the conference. She revealed that she was Scottish on her mother's side, and commented that coming to a Labour Party conference in Edinburgh was like a dream. She claimed that in the first six weeks since fighting began 70,000 men had been killed. Referring to the North Africans among Franco's troops, she proclaimed that it had taken eight centuries to free Spain from the Moors, but now they were being brought back again to kill Spanish people. Such sentiments were considered unexceptionable at the time. She was certainly effective.

As Señora de Palencia finished her speech, delegates rose to their feet and sang 'The Red Flag'. All the pent-up emotions in the hall were unleashed, a mixture of anger at what was happening in Spain and the frustration at the outcome of the debate on non-intervention two days before.

'Aren't we going to do something more than sing?' shouted a voice in the hall. There were demands that the conference should take more positive action. Some wanted to reverse Monday's vote. But the morning session was adjourned.

After lunch, the National Council for Labour announced that Attlee and Greenwood were to visit London to raise the Spanish crisis with Chamberlain, then the acting Prime Minister. Travelling overnight, they spent half an hour on Thursday morning at the Treasury talking with Chamberlain, and then returned to Edinburgh.

The following morning, Friday, 9 October, Attlee presented conference with a more strongly worded statement on Spain by the National Executive Committee. The substance of Labour's policy was unchanged, but the emphasis had shifted.

The National Executive 'emphatically' declared 'its conviction that the

Fascist powers have broken their pledges of non-intervention', and demanded an urgent inquiry. The facts were to be established without delay. If it was found that the Non-intervention Agreement was being breached, the Government should restore to the Spanish Government their right to purchase arms.

But Attlee also warned delegates, 'It has got to be made quite clear that if we demand that the Government of this country should take action to end this Agreement, we must be prepared to face any risks that may attend this action.' What Attlee had in mind was the risk of a war.

Despite their leader's warning, delegates cheered his speech to the rafters. The conference had rejected rearmament but was ready to take risks over Spain. Dalton commented, 'They were wallowing in sheer emotion, in vicarious valour. They had no clue in their mind to the risks, and the realities, for Britain of a general war.'

On the same morning, while Labour's activists were celebrating in Edinburgh, at the Foreign Office in London an important meeting was held of the International Committee for the Application of the Agreement regarding Non-intervention in Spain. The Committee had before them a note from the Soviet Government declaring that if violations of the Agreement were not stopped immediately, they would consider themselves freed from its obligations.

During October the Soviets delivered about 100 aircraft and 100 tanks, along with 500 specialist troops, to the Spanish Government. By late October, non-intervention was at best a pious hope, and in reality little more than a political convenience for the British and French Governments – a 'cruel masquerade' as Jack Jones has since dubbed it.

Labour policy was so manifestly out of touch with feeling throughout the labour movement and on the left generally that the leadership moved quickly to get themselves off the hook. At the National Council of Labour's meeting on 28 October, chaired by Bevin, Labour finally ended their support for non-intervention and pressed the Government for recognition of the Spanish Government's legal right to buy arms abroad.

But the National Government stuck resolutely to their policy of non-intervention, and the Labour leadership's opposition to non-intervention was half-hearted. In October 1937, Leonard Woolf was 'enraged with the L. [Labour] Party which sent a deputation to the F.O. [Foreign Office] and was diddled by Vansittart'. Virginia Woolf added in her diary, 'So we shan't let arms through: we shall sit on the fence: and the fighting will go on.'

In Spain itself, the image of the British labour movement had been permanently tarnished. Jack Jones had raised funds in Liverpool for the Republican cause in the early part of the Civil War, and was disappointed by the lack of financial support both from his own union, the T&G, and from the TUC. When Jones later went out to fight, he took with him a letter from his union leader, Bevin, to the new leader of the Spanish trade union organisation, the UGT, Rodriguez Vega. But Bevin's letter only 'seemed to irritate' Vega. Jones recalls that:

> he scorned the way the British labour movement had failed the Spanish socialists and trade unionists. 'Why have they not forced your Government to support us? Why have they not done more to demonstrate solidarity with us in action?' I had no answers, I felt ashamed. In my reply I spoke about the many rank-and-file activities in Britain and told him, 'I have come to fight.' He raised his eyebrows: 'One young man, well . . .'

The British labour movement had shunned their Spanish comrades in their hour of need. In his poem 'A Letter from Aragon', John Cornford revealed the depth of commitment among the Republicans:

> But when I shook hands to leave, an Anarchist worker
> Said: 'Tell the workers of England
> This was a war not of our making,
> We did not seek it.
> But if ever the Fascists again rule Barcelona
> It will be as a heap of ruins with us workers beneath it.'

The shock of Fascist intervention in Spain had a kaleidoscopic effect on the left. As the pieces began to settle, there was growing support for a 'Popular Front' in Britain.

Some of the earliest Popular Front initiatives had been inspired by Communists or Conservatives. This had done little to reduce scepticism among the leadership of the labour movement. In March 1933, Labour and the TUC rejected a call for co-operation from Harry Pollitt, General Secretary of the Communist Party.

A minority of Conservatives had been attracted to the idea of cross-party collaboration through their desire for reform to ease unemployment and poverty at home, and to prevent Britain falling prey to the ideological battles which were beginning to tear Europe apart. After the 1931 election, there were so many Conservatives in the Commons that some of the younger dissidents took to sitting on the opposition benches, facing the Government bench – a 'Tory mountain' as Harold Macmillan described it.

In February 1935, Macmillan joined forces with the former conscientious objector and pacifist, Lord Allen of Hurtwood (formerly Clifford

Allen), to set up the Next Five Years Group, which included leading people 'of all parties and of none'. That July, the Group published *The Next Five Years – An Essay in Political Agreement*, about half of which was devoted to foreign affairs and advocated a more vigorous pursuit of the 'collective peace system' through the League of Nations.

Signatories to the manifesto included Sir Norman Angell (writer and winner of the Nobel peace prize), Vernon Bartlett (journalist), Isaac Foot MP, Julian Huxley (zoologist), Eleanor Rathbone MP, Lord Elton (historian), H.A.L. Fisher (former Minister and academic), C.E.M. Joad (philosopher), David Low (cartoonist), Wickham Steed (journalist), H.G. Wells and the Archbishop of York.

Macmillan's objective was the creation of a new centre party, which would comprise people in the Next Five Years Group, plus a large part of the Labour Party. He thought that the ideal leader would be Herbert Morrison, the former Labour Minister and at the time leader of the London County Council. But these were forlorn hopes – the Group's publication in the summer of 1935 had contained the signatures of ten Conservative MPs, but not a single Labour MP.

In June 1936, Macmillan resigned the National Government whip. He devoted himself, as an Independent MP, to creating a new party. His aim was to bring together progressive opinion from all parties. But his timing was not propitious, for the very issue on which Macmillan resigned, the lifting of sanctions against Italy, sharpened the party political divide.

In the autumn of 1936, a new all-party organisation, Focus for the Defence of Freedom and Peace, was formed to help popularise the work of the Anti-Nazi Council. It marked the culmination of the efforts of Leeper and Vansittart at the Foreign Office. Focus was designed to bring together people of all political persuasions. Its launch, at which Churchill would deliver a major speech, in December 1936 was designed to rally public opinion.

In late November 1936, Captain Frederick Guest, a Conservative MP and cousin of Churchill's, informed Churchill that 'Attlee will support you on any rearmament programme. He admires & likes you. The door is open if you want to talk to him.' This information naturally remained confidential at the time, but coming in the month following Attlee's evasive speech on rearmament at the Edinburgh Party conference, it showed that attitudes were changing at the highest level in the Labour Party. Churchill told his son, Randolph, 'All the left-wing intelligentsia are coming to look to me for protection, and I will give it whole-heartedly in return for their aid in the rearmament of Britain.'

In fact, many of the 'left-wing intelligentsia' remained distinctly suspicious of Churchill. They were concerned about supporting any proposals which might place more arms at the disposal of a right-wing government. There was genuine anxiety that Fascism in Britain could be introduced in the guise of defending the country against an external threat. In particular, the strong-minded characters among the anti-appeasers on the Government benches were seen as a serious threat by some on the left – if Chamberlain and his allies could not be trusted with extra weapons, Churchill and some of his associates seemed a far worse proposition.

Nonetheless, Churchill had reason to feel encouraged at the growing cross-party support. Focus was attracting a formidable array of politicians from all sides: Conservative anti-appeasers – Sir Austen Chamberlain, Ronald Cartland, Oliver Locker-Lampson, Duncan Sandys, Paul Emrys-Evans, the Duchess of Atholl and John McEwen; Labour MPs – Arthur Henderson (the former Party leader), Seymour Cocks, Reginald Fletcher and Philip Noel-Baker; Liberals – Sir Archibald Sinclair, James de Rothschild and Dingle Foot; and Independent MPs – Sir Arthur Salter and Eleanor Rathbone.

Yet despite its impressive billing and cast-list, the launch of Focus in December had scarcely any impact. The evening before, Edward VIII had told the Prime Minister that he planned to marry Mrs Simpson, an American divorcee. Baldwin replied that this was unacceptable.

On the morning of the Focus launch, the British press finally broke their lengthy silence about the King and Mrs Simpson. Churchill, who had been one of the King's closest allies, was eclipsed. So too was Focus.

Other attempts were equally ill starred. Earlier in the autumn, the General Secretary of the left-wing Labour group, the Socialist League, J.T. Murphy, resigned to found the People's Front Propaganda Committee. Its co-founder was Allan Young, a former Mosleyite, who was helping Harold Macmillan on his book, *The Middle Way*.

The People's Front assembled an impressive company for a meeting in mid-December – the Conservative MP Robert Boothby, the Liberal MP Richard Acland, the Labour MP William Dobbie and the socialists John Strachey and G.D.H. Cole. But when Cole declared that one of the objectives must be to smash the National Government, Boothby stormed from the platform, and later told the press, 'I dissociate myself from this Movement from now on. I am through with it.'

Labour left-wingers generally opposed a broadly based Popular Front. The Socialist League, the most influential left-wing Labour grouping, advocated a 'Front' of working-class organisations.

In the summer of 1936, the Socialist League's Chairman, Sir Stafford

Cripps, initiated talks with the ILP and the Communists. But there was little progress, since the ILP maintained that any Front should be limited to socialists, while the Communists wanted all opponents of the National Government, whether socialist or not, to be included. Some Labour left-wingers agreed with the Communists. As early as September 1936, Nye Bevan was arguing that Labour should not only work with Communists, but should also work with Liberals. By doing so, he claimed, 'we shall be making the centre more solid.'

The majority of Labour supporters and trade unionists, however, were reluctant to have anything to do with the Communists. The Socialist League's proposal that the Communist Party should be affiliated to the Labour Party was rejected by 1,728,000 votes to 592,000 at the 1936 Labour conference. The conference also rejected the call for a 'United Front' of working-class organisations.

But these setbacks merely increased the Socialist League's determination to press ahead in defiance of the leadership. In January 1937, they issued their *Unity Manifesto*, a document scarcely designed to win converts. They were unconditionally opposed to rearmament and recruitment to the armed forces, called for a massive fight against Fascism, demanded the nationalisation of the arms industry and democratisation of the armed forces, and advocated a pact between Britain, France and the Soviet Union.

The upshot of the Unity Campaign was that the Socialist League were disaffiliated from the Labour Party. It was a novel way of building unity among working-class organisations.

But the Unity Campaign continued. Ted Willis (later Lord Willis, the playwright and writer), who was then on the extreme left in the Labour League of Youth, has recalled,

> We marched in demonstrations to Trafalgar Square and Whitehall to hear men like Stafford Cripps, Aneurin Bevan and the Communist leaders, Harry Pollitt and William Gallacher . . . denounce the National Government, and call for a united front, nationally and internationally, against fascism and war. . . . With clenched fists held aloft we chanted as we marched: 'Red front, red front, red united fighting front!'

In fact, support for the Unity Campaign was limited, falling well short of the numbers which the Left Book Club could command at major rallies.

In March 1937, Labour's National Executive declared that from June they would expel members remaining in the Socialist League. In May, Cripps decided to dissolve it; Cripps and other left-wingers were eventually expelled in 1939, after they had revived the Unity Campaign.

Events in Spain were also deepening the divisions between the ILP and the Communists. The ILP supported the POUM, the movement composed of revolutionary socialists and anarchists, which the Spanish Communists subjected to bloody suppression. George Orwell fought with the POUM, and wrote about the Communist attacks in *Homage to Catalonia*.

It had proved as difficult to unite left-wing socialists as it was proving to unite people from all parties. Indeed, the left wing's activities were a deterrent to an all-party Popular Front. Tory rebels and Liberals were less inclined to contemplate co-operating with Labour while some Labour members were pressing for closer ties with the Communists.

The Spanish Civil War was to have its greatest impact on the British left in a way which was quite unforeseen by most activists when the fighting first broke out.

Just three days after Franco launched his rebellion, the Parliamentary Labour Party had again voted against defence estimates in the House of Commons. Dalton, the Party's Foreign Affairs spokesman, and a small number of fellow rearmers invoked the PLP's 'conscience clause' and abstained.

There was still a very long way to go before some members of the Labour Party would accept extra defence spending, as was demonstrated on the eve of the 1936 Labour Party annual conference. In a widely publicised letter to the Glasgow *Forward*, published on 3 October, Sir Stafford Cripps urged that every effort should be made to stop recruiting for the armed forces. His aim was to force the Government to take the highly unpopular step of introducing conscription.

It was the argument which Cripps advanced for opposing the Government's policy which was most revealing:

> I think it is unlikely that, if Great Britain were conquered by Germany, Socialism would be suppressed, though that is not certain. . . .
>
> But suppose you attained your object and Great Britain won another imperial victory, what then? British Fascism would be less brutal than German, but the world situation would be no better. Another Versailles peace, another period of acute suffering for the workers, and then the next war. That's all.

Bevin's response, putting the case for supporting extra defence spending, was couched in forthright language: 'I say this to Sir Stafford Cripps. If I am asked to face the question of arming this country, I am prepared to face it. . . . which is the first institution that victorious Fascism wipes out? It is the trade union movement.' Bevin hoped that the

1936 Party conference would mark a turning point in Labour's attitude towards rearmament. He believed that the resolution on defence would finally oblige Labour MPs to stop voting against the defence estimates. But his hopes were disappointed.

Attlee maintained that since Labour could not accept that the Government was loyal to the League of Nations, there could be no suggestion that Labour would support the Government's rearmament programme.

But as 1936 drew to a close, more people on the left were coming to feel that Fascism had to be stopped, and the only way to stop it would be through war.

One of the most dramatic conversions from pacifism was Julian Bell's. In 1935, he had edited and written an introduction for a book of recollections by conscientious objectors during the 1914–18 war, *We Did Not Fight*. But by late 1936 he was arguing, 'At this moment to be anti-war means to submit to fascism, to be anti-fascist means to be prepared for war.'

The cartoonist David Low had also come to change his views by this time, and had abandoned pacifism because of the threat of Hitler. Increasingly, he found himself involved in heated discussions as he walked on Hampstead Heath, near his studio. On one occasion he was arguing with Cyril Joad, who at that stage was still a pacifist. The discussion between Low and Joad became so intense that they found themselves standing outside Hampstead Underground station, with Low gesticulating and speaking vehemently. At that time, Joad was becoming a well-known personality through his radio broadcasts. Eventually Low realised that they had attracted a small audience, and heard one of them say, 'Who does he think he is? Ought to be locked up. Dirty Nazi!'

In the Labour Party, the rearmers were well placed by the autumn of 1936 to seize the initiative. In September, Bevin was elected chairman of the TUC. A month later Dalton became chairman of Labour's National Executive Committee. Both were agreed that their most important task during their year in office was to bring the Party to take a more realistic view on defence.

The challenge of winning round their fellow socialists remained formidable. Sir Stafford Cripps was undoubtedly an extreme case, but he was a senior and influential figure in the Party. In November 1936, he told an audience in Stockport that he 'did not believe that it would be a bad thing for the British working class if Germany defeated us. It would be a disaster to the profit-makers and capitalists, but not necessarily for the working class.'

Labour supporters and trade unionists who did not subscribe to the far-fetched theories of Cripps, nonetheless had doubts about the political wisdom of trusting the Government with extra weapons. In late December 1936, Morrison voiced these fears, wondering whom the Government would select as their targets: 'But against whom? Germany or Russia? Fascism or Socialism? For peace or for war? We do not know. And the Government flatly refuses to tell us.'

In early November 1936, Bevin himself had felt it necessary to rebuff a suggestion that the TUC might support a recruiting drive for the armed forces. His reasoning indicated the extent to which the insensitive approach of the National Government alienated the labour movement and made the task of its more pragmatic members immensely difficult. As Bevin argued,

Mr Baldwin had the whole-hearted support of Labour over Abyssinia. Immediately he got that support he turned it to political account by springing an election and taking political advantage. . . . Another factor was the bitter treatment meted out to the unemployed by the Means Test and the treatment of the distressed areas. How could any Labour man, with the past ten years before him, appeal to men to join the Army?

. . . in the old days of the Liberals and the Tories, there was some consultation as to policy, but since 1931 Labour had been treated like a caste apart. It was not for us to appeal or be supplicants; it was for them to come to us and for the first time to recognise Labour as equals.

Bevin, however, was wholly convinced that Britain had to rearm. He thought Labour's total opposition was politically damaging. In March 1937, he told the Executive Committee of his union,

From the day Hitler came to power, I have felt that the democratic countries would have to face war. I believe he was taken too cheap. We have been handicapped by the very sincere pacifists in our Party who believe that the danger can be met by resolution and prayers and by turning the other cheek. While I appreciate the sincerity, I cannot understand anybody who refuses to face the facts in relation to the happenings in China, in Abyssinia, in Spain, all virtually disarmed countries. I cannot see any way of stopping Hitler and the other dictators except by force.

The rearmers eventually achieved their major breakthrough in July 1937. Dalton again queried the PLP's policy of voting against the defence estimates. He was opposed, however, by most of the PLP leadership, including Attlee, Morrison, Greenwood and Shinwell. But Dalton campaigned hard among the PLP and was supported by Transport House who reckoned that a change in approach would win votes for Labour in the country, and by the unions who saw rearmament as good for jobs.

Dalton and his allies carried the day. The PLP decided to abstain on the defence estimates, though the margin was narrow, just 45 votes to 39. When the service votes came before the House of Commons on 26 and 27 July, only six Labour MPs voted against. Labour had finally abandoned their parliamentary opposition to rearmament, though they still would not vote with the Government.

That summer, Bevin and Dalton consolidated their position. The National Council of Labour, under their joint chairmanship, published a major report, *International Policy and Defence*. The report was an unashamed rearmer tract, which declared that 'A Labour Government will unhesitatingly maintain such armed forces as are necessary to defend our country and to fulfil our obligations as a member of the British Commonwealth and the League of Nations.' When the report was presented at that autumn's Trades Union Congress and Labour Party conference, Bevin and Dalton respectively chaired the debates.

At September's annual TUC, held at Norwich, Sir Walter Citrine drew the conclusion that 'some increase of rearmament is indispensable, if this country is to face its obligations.' The report was endorsed with 3,544,000 votes in favour, and 224,000 against.

A month later, Dalton told the Labour Party at Bournemouth, 'Our country must be powerfully armed. Otherwise we run risks immediate and immeasurable. Otherwise, a British Labour Government, coming into power tomorrow, would be in danger of humiliations, intimidations and acts of foreign intervention in our national affairs.'

Earlier that summer, Morrison had still been querying whether the Government could be trusted. 'I do not take the position that my country should be disarmed, but I say, "Arms – what for?" ' But he kept quiet at the conference.

One of the most powerful speeches was made by the left-winger Aneurin Bevan, who expressed continued doubts about the wisdom of strengthening the National Government, in case 'we . . . put a sword in the hands of our enemies that may be used to cut off our heads'. Bevan agreed that it was no use thinking that Fascism could be fought 'with bladders'. But the only justification for supporting armaments would be if the Government carried out Labour policies. If the labour movement were strong enough to deny arms to a capitalist Government, that Government would fall, and Labour would win power.

Bevan's argument that the socialist way to proceed was to bring down the Government was an ingenious attempt to meet the charge that Labour could not continue opposing rearmament, year after year, only to find that when they eventually returned to office they were defenceless against the Fascist threat. The contention that Labour could hasten their return to power and pursue an acceptable rearmament programme was, frankly, incredible. But Bevan was at least recognising the urgent need to rearm, which was a big step forward from most of the speeches made at Edinburgh the previous year.

Nye Bevan's argument received short shrift from James Walker of the Iron and Steel Trades Association, who told the conference:

> Mr Bevan says that if we were to carry that vote, the vote would not matter because at 4 o'clock we would vote to have no Army, no Navy and no Air Force; we would defeat the Government and at 5 o'clock we would bring the Army, the Navy and the Air Force in again. But we could not bring the Army, the Navy and the Air Force in again if it was not there, and if those people got their way there would be no defence at all.

When the vote was finally taken, the report was endorsed by 2,169,000 votes to 262,000.

The leftist weekly the *New Statesman and Nation* saw the vote as the climax of a process which 'could be traced from the "never again" stage after the war . . . to something which in practice seems very little different from preparation for a military alliance against the Fascist powers'. It observed rather tartly that the impression on the voters would be 'that in the event of a war crisis the Labour Party would be at best as ready to co-operate with the National Government as Social Democracy everywhere proved ready to co-operate with the capitalist Governments in 1914'.

When Bevin and Dalton vacated their chairmanships in the autumn of 1937, they had achieved at least part of their objective. Labour were no longer opposed to rearmament.

# CHAPTER EIGHT

# APPEASERS IN COMMAND

He [Eden] feared that when Neville Chamberlain became Prime Minister affairs would go less smoothly in the country than with Baldwin – there would be better administration and more discipline in the Cabinet, but he would not be able to resist scoring off the Opposition.

(Oliver Harvey, Eden's Private Secretary at the Foreign Office, writing in his diary, 5 March 1937)

During 1937, the advocates of closer relations with Germany were in the ascendant.

The abdication crisis completely transformed the political fortunes of Baldwin and Churchill. The Prime Minister was widely held to have handled the crisis brilliantly, securing all-party support for the Government's line. Baldwin's reputation, which had languished since his mishandling of the Hoare–Laval Pact, was entirely restored.

For Churchill, however, the crisis proved disastrous. He was friendly with the King, and wanted him to be allowed more time to consider his position. But he had misjudged the mood of the Commons and the country. When he appeared to protest against the Government's position and attack Baldwin in the House on 7 December, he was howled down by fellow MPs. There were cries of 'Drop it!' and 'Twister!' As Harold Nicolson noted, 'Winston collapsed utterly in the House yesterday. . . . He has undone in five minutes the patient reconstruction work of two years.'

In fact, Churchill had arrived in the Commons late and had not realised that Baldwin was going some way to meet his point. But the damage was done. His stand revived all the old suspicions about his lack of judgement.

Smart political opinion moved against Churchill as strongly as it had run in his favour when the talk of a Popular Front was all the rage in the autumn of 1936. As 'Critic' now wrote in the *New Statesman and Nation*, 'people who were rallying around him are beginning to mutter about his

notorious lack of judgement.' The *Spectator* was damning: 'Mr Churchill
has hopelessly compromised not only himself but the cause for which he
has been working. . . . No one will deny Mr Churchill's gifts, but a flair
for doing the right thing at the right moment – or not doing the wrong
thing at the wrong moment – is no part of them. . . . the reputation which
he was beginning to shake off of a wayward genius unserviceable in
counsel has settled firmly on his shoulders again.'

Churchill's speech following the abdication went some way to redeem
him. But the National Government were more securely entrenched than
ever.          —

In the spring of 1937, the fates took a further hand in the destinies of the
Chamberlain family. In March, Sir Austen Chamberlain, one of the most
senior backbench critics of the Government, collapsed at his home and
died. In May, Baldwin finally retired to his beloved Worcestershire. Less
than three months after the death of Sir Austen, his younger half-brother
Neville moved into Number 10.

As Chancellor, Neville Chamberlain had been preoccupied by the
economic constraints on British rearmament and the imperative need to
avoid any 'entanglement' on the Continent of Europe. He was acutely
conscious of the revolutionary changes which massive rearmament or,
even worse, war itself would bring in British society.

Abroad, the new Prime Minister feared the spread of Soviet Communism into Central and Eastern Europe resulting from any conflict between
the European powers. And he foresaw the crippling economic and political
effects which war would bring for the British empire.

Neville Chamberlain was determined that Britain, Europe and the
empire should be spared the ravages of war. He brought to Number 10 a
new energy and single-mindedness which transformed the way policy was
made and executed. Yet he was also to introduce a new edge and harshness
into the debate, which would fuel divisions rather than heal them and
eventually create the most bitter conflict in generations.

It was ironic that Neville was the member of the Chamberlain family
who achieved the highest office. His father, Joseph, the radical Liberal
and Unionist, had groomed Austen for politics and prepared Neville for
business. Neville Chamberlain did not enter national politics until 1916, at
the age of forty-seven, when he was recruited from his position as Lord
Mayor of Birmingham to serve as Minister for National Service. The
appointment proved to be a disaster and left him with a life-long
determination never again to serve Lloyd George.

But Chamberlain was persuaded to return to national politics,
principally through the efforts of his sisters, Hilda and Ida, who were

convinced of his qualities of leadership. The death of his young cousin Norman had also affected him deeply. He described Norman as 'the most intimate friend I had' – the two men had served on Birmingham City Council together – and wrote a memoir of him, published in 1923, for private circulation. The loss of Norman helps explain Chamberlain's deep abhorrence of war and his commitment to social reform, to which his cousin had dedicated considerable effort. Chamberlain was elected to Parliament for Birmingham Ladywood in 1919 at the age of fifty, and proceeded to apply himself unstintingly to his new career.

During the 1920s, he was a highly effective, reforming Minister of Health. Throughout the 1930s he was by far the most dynamic figure in Government, serving as Chancellor of the Exchequer to two ageing Prime Ministers, Ramsay MacDonald from 1931 and Baldwin from 1935. He was also the main driving force in the Conservative Party, principally through the Conservative Research Department, the new briefing organisation and 'think-tank' which he founded in 1929 and which he chaired throughout the 1930s.

Chamberlain excluded Churchill from his Cabinet in the reshuffle following his move to Number 10. But it fell to Churchill, as the senior Conservative Privy Councillor in the Commons, to second Chamberlain's nomination as the new leader of the Conservative Party at the formal gathering of MPs, peers and prospective candidates.

Churchill's words were a warning rather than an endorsement. Emphasising the rights of dissenters within the Party, Churchill stressed that the leadership had never been interpreted 'in a dictatorial or despotic sense'. He thought the new leader's previous experience 'made it certain' that he would 'not resent the honest differences of opinion arising between those who mean the same thing, and that Party opinion will not be denied its subordinate but rightful place in his mind'.

Those who had known Neville Chamberlain on the Birmingham Council, or knew him socially, might have expected him to fulfil Churchill's hopes. Lord Home (then Lord Dunglass), who was appointed as the new Prime Minister's Parliamentary Private Secretary, recalls Chamberlain as socially charming, a man who could be marvellous company in small groups, with people whom he knew well. His wife, Anne, was an attractive woman, a good deal younger, and a perfect foil for her fastidious husband.

The young Dunglass found that, unusually for a politician, Chamberlain had a real interest in music and art. He had founded the City of Birmingham Symphony Orchestra. He loved the countryside, was an expert fisherman, and had a detailed knowledge of butterflies and of animals, birds and plants of all varieties, which he enjoyed talking about to anyone. He was privately amused by Baldwin's 'countryman' image – as Chamberlain observed, he doubted whether his predecessor at Number 10 could name half-a-dozen wild birds.

Tragically, this appealing side of Chamberlain's character rarely came across in Westminster or Whitehall. He was incapable of adopting Baldwin's emollient approach. In 1927, Baldwin had advised him to remember that his opponents were gentlemen. As Chamberlain noted in his diary, 'I always gave him the impression, he said, when I spoke in the House of Commons, that I looked on the Labour Party as dirt.'

Chamberlain seemed unable to follow Baldwin's advice – as Attlee, Labour's leader throughout Chamberlain's premiership, later recalled, Chamberlain 'always treated us like dirt'. One of Chamberlain's closest colleagues, Sir John Simon, later commented that Chamberlain had no feeling for the sensitivities of Labour politicians, and 'When Chamberlain is faced with a half-baked argument, he exposes it.'

Chamberlain's Chief Whip, Captain David Margesson, wrote later that Chamberlain:

> engendered personal dislike among his opponents to an extent almost unbelievable. I believe that the reason was that his cold intellect was too much for them, he beat them up in argument and debunked their catchphrases. Those of us who have lived in the country districts know how much a man whom they call 'sarcastic' is disliked. It's a form of mental inferiority which produces hate.

In March 1937, when still at the Treasury, Chamberlain launched an aggressive attack on the Liberal leader Sir Archibald Sinclair, which prompted the comment from Anthony Eden to his Private Secretary, quoted at the head of this chapter.

Elizabeth Harman (later Lady Longford), the daughter of Chamberlain's second cousin, had become a socialist while at Oxford. In 1931, she married Frank Pakenham (later Lord Longford), who was then working in the Conservative Research Department. But Chamberlain forbade Pakenham's work colleagues from attending the wedding – Lady Longford suspects because of a rumour about Pakenham becoming a socialist, although it also seems possible that Chamberlain may not have liked people stopping work for a wedding.

Neville Chamberlain was by temperament a 'doer', a politician who wanted to get things done rather than spend time cultivating support or smoothing the way with his opponents. He devoted himself to a dispassionate and painstaking study of the problem in hand. Once he was convinced that the right decision had been made, he tended to regard disagreement as a waste of time. He became impatient with people who obviously had not grasped the facts – if they had worked as hard at finding the solution as he had, they would obviously agree with him.

Chamberlain regarded his ministers principally as administrators who should run their departments while he dealt with the policy. His Secretary of State for War, Leslie Hore-Belisha, confided to Francis Williams, then working on the *Daily Herald*, that being a member of Chamberlain's Cabinet was 'like being a Departmental Director in a private company in which the Chairman owns all the shares. You are expected to report intelligently on departmental matters but keep quiet on everything else. It's your job to do as the Chairman tells you and keep your nose out of general policy'.

Chamberlain's preference was thus for cold, grey, frankly dull and unsympathetic figures – the likes of Sir John Simon as Chancellor, Sir Samuel Hoare at the Home Office, and Kingsley Wood as Minister for the Co-ordination of Defence.

Eden was the very antithesis, colourful, debonair, with an independent mind and a department which was not inclined to see its policy-making role entirely usurped by Chamberlain. Eden, despite his qualms about Chamberlain's impact on politics at home, saw no grounds for concern when Chamberlain told him that he would want to 'take a closer interest in foreign affairs than Stanley [Baldwin]'. It would, of course, not have been difficult to take a 'closer interest' than Baldwin, whose main preoccupation on the Continent of Europe seemed to be his holidays at Aix-les-Bains.

But once Chamberlain was firmly established in Downing Street, relations between Number 10 and the Foreign Office became increasingly acrimonious. Dunglass tried to do his best to smooth things over – he recalls trying to run his own form of appeasement between Number 10 and the Foreign Office. At times he felt he was making some progress, but then there would soon be another setback.

Dunglass's counterpart at the Foreign Office, J.P.L. (Jim) Thomas (Eden's Parliamentary Private Secretary), discovered to his surprise that he had been recommended for the job in May 1937 by Sir Horace Wilson, Chamberlain's principal adviser. Thomas and Wilson knew each other well.

Thomas was told by Wilson and Sir Warren Fisher, the then Head of the Civil Service, that he was expected to help 'build a bridge between 10 Downing Street and the Foreign Office, and to create a better understanding between the two Departments. This might lessen the damage which had been done by the Foreign Office in general and by Vansittart in particular.' But Thomas refused to play their game, and was to remain a loyal supporter of the Foreign Office and Eden.

Difficulties between Number 10 and the Foreign Office were exacer-
bated by Sir Robert Vansittart's stewardship as Permanent Secretary. The
denizens of Number 10, like the young Dunglass, sensed that they could
almost hear Vansittart's voice booming across Downing Street from the
Foreign Office opposite – what might be termed a classic case of
megaphone diplomacy.

Vansittart had his own excellent contacts in Germany, amounting to a
private intelligence system. The Foreign Office were also receiving their
own reports about the dissident elements in the German leadership.
Vansittart saw that the information from these sources was fed into the
latest intelligence reports which were sent to the Prime Minister.

Chamberlain became more and more irritated with the briefings from
the Foreign Office. Sir Frank Roberts, then a young diplomat, recalls an
incident when he was delivering the latest intelligence reports to the Prime
Minister. While he was waiting outside Chamberlain's office, he heard one
of the Private Secretaries tell the Prime Minister that a briefing from the
Foreign Office had just arrived. Roberts then heard Chamberlain
comment, 'Oh, the Foreign Office will keep on sending me this stuff to try
to make me change my mind!'

Increasingly, Chamberlain bypassed his Foreign Secretary. He turned
to an inner group of ministers comprising Sir John Simon, Sir Samuel
Hoare and Lord Halifax, all of whom favoured appeasing Hitler. Both
Simon and Hoare had served as Foreign Secretary, and Halifax had been a
successful Viceroy in India.

The Prime Minister also relied more heavily on his aide at Number 10,
Sir Horace Wilson, nominally the Government's Chief Industrial Adviser.
Wilson's office was next to the Cabinet room, and after Chamberlain's
discussions with Eden, the Prime Minister would frequently summon him
for his thoughts on foreign policy. Wilson himself later described his role
as helping remove the 'poison' of Eden's or Vansittart's views. He
provided an effective antidote, constantly bolstering Chamberlain's belief
in appeasement as the best way for the Government to deal with the
dictators.

Chamberlain was unperturbed by Wilson's total inexperience of foreign
affairs. He was someone whom Chamberlain felt he could trust. Wilson
had established a considerable reputation as a widely respected conciliator,
and Chamberlain had found him invaluable during his years at the
Treasury. He was a quietly spoken man, highly efficient, who served
Chamberlain with complete loyalty and whom the Prime Minister later
appointed Head of the Civil Service and Treasury.

Chamberlain had little time for people who wanted to debate the issues
in Whitehall. He had even less time for Parliament. Dunglass tried to keep

him in touch with the atmosphere in the Commons and with the latest gossip – vital intelligence for any Prime Minister having to cope with the press of official business while keeping in touch with the political swim. Whereas many politicians would have leapt at the chance to hear the latest from the committee rooms and lobbies of Westminster, Chamberlain regarded it as a bore. He did not like work being discarded for what he regarded as lighter-hearted diversions and made little attempt to disguise the fact. The Prime Minister worked in the Cabinet Room at Number 10 and, as a young MP, Dunglass would knock on the door and enter with some trepidation. Chamberlain's response was usually the same, 'Yes, what is it?' barely looking up from his papers, and with pen still in hand. It was a dispiriting response.

Dunglass's attempts to see that Chamberlain and backbench Conservative MPs knew each other's minds were as awkward. He would arrange for the Prime Minister to visit the tea room, and shortly beforehand would gather ten to a dozen Conservative MPs to talk with him. The Prime Minister would duly arrive, but after a few minutes would look at his watch.

Yet Chamberlain was able to achieve an extraordinary dominance in his Government, in his party and in the country during 1937 and 1938. This cannot be explained solely by his undoubted drive and determination. The key lies in his recognition of the importance of the press and broadcasting. As James Margach wrote in his classic study of the relationship between politicians and the press, *The Abuse of Power*, Chamberlain was the 'first Prime Minister to employ news management on a large scale'.

The priority which Chamberlain attached to managing the media is a key to understanding his premiership. As recent research by Anthony Adamthwaite has shown, such an appreciation puts the events and arguments of the period in an entirely new light. In particular, it gives new perspective to the repeated claims made by the appeasers that the public was not ready for war.

Chamberlain regularly had lunch with the parliamentary lobby journalists at the St Stephen's Club in Westminster. He assiduously cultivated contacts with editors and proprietors. The press office at Number 10 and the Foreign Office News Department worked to see that the Government view of foreign policy predominated, and that there was as little debate of the alternatives as possible. The Director of the Conservative Research Department, J.R. Ball, acted as a private agent for Chamberlain, keeping in contact with the Italians behind Eden's back. Cadogan, then Deputy Permanent Secretary at the Foreign Office, suggests that Ball might have inspired press articles supporting Chamberlain's policy.

The BBC had already been effectively muzzled. A major talks series during 1935–6 was banned, because the speakers included the Fascist Mosley and the Communist Pollitt. The ban was kept secret. In March 1936, a Cabinet Committee discussed a planned radio series on European issues, and decided 'to ask the BBC to refrain from arranging for independent expressions of opinion'. In early 1937, the leading Tory critic, Churchill, commented, 'If we could get access to the broadcast some progress could be made. All that is very carefully sewn up over here.' Chamberlain perpetuated the Government's control of the BBC. The Party Whips controlled which politicians were allowed to give broadcasts from the radio studios at Parliament. Churchill was effectively banned from the BBC during Chamberlain's first two years at Number 10. So much for Churchill's hope in May 1937 that the new leader would not 'resent honest differences of opinion'.

The conflict between the growing demands of the armed forces and budgetary constraint were becoming irreconcilable. In the spring of 1937, in his last Budget before he became Prime Minister, Neville Chamberlain was forced by the mounting cost of the rearmament programme to impose a tax on arms manufacturers and boost Government borrowing. Much though the Chancellor abhorred any increase in borrowing, he could see no politically acceptable alternative to raising a 'Defence Loan' of £400 million.

The manufacturers fought Chamberlain's new tax, the National Defence Contribution, tooth and nail. Ironically, they received clandestine help from J.R. Ball, the Director of the Conservative Research Department, upon whom Chamberlain could usually rely. The scheme was designed specifically to ensure that arms manufacturers were not able to make excessive profits from rearmament, thus meeting a common complaint from the left, and also helping curb inflationary pay awards. But the scheme had few friends and was unable to withstand the onslaught from industry. In its place, a more general profit tax of 5 per cent was introduced. After his defeat at the hands of the employers, Chamberlain always remained reluctant to take them on.

But it was not only the mounting financial pressures which encouraged ministers to concentrate on selected, key defence measures. Duff Cooper, a strong advocate of a Continental role for the army, had moved to the Admiralty in May 1937. In June, the Treasury had opposed the Air Ministry's demand for more bombers, and along with Inskip advocated a switch to fighters. With the top-secret development of radar, it would no longer be the case that the bomber would 'always get through'. Fighter command would be able to track down enemy aircraft far more effectively.

In early 1937, the construction of coastal radar stations was sanctioned, and in August the construction of twenty such stations was authorised. In October 1937, the first production-line Hurricane fighters took to the air. These developments all came to lend greater credibility within Whitehall to the idea of strong air defences as the key to Britain's security instead of a larger army which was able to intervene on the Continent. But there was a curious lacuna in strategic thinking, since the German bombers would be more effective if they were able to attack Britain from bases in the Low Countries and northern France. A Continental army thus had a crucial part to play in air defence by helping ensure that the Germans were unable to seize control of such strategic areas.

There was, however, a further reason why the Government did not wish to commit too many troops on the Continent. It was thought that, in the event of a massive German air attack, the Territorial Army, and possibly the Regular Army too, would be needed to preserve order in the ensuing panic. This now seems alarmist, but it was regarded as a serious risk at the time.

In fact, all decisions were based on this assumption of a massive air attack, the single knock-out blow. Yet the German air force was quite incapable of delivering such an attack. By 1937, following a period of underestimating the threat, the size and capability of the Luftwaffe was being exaggerated by the Air Ministry. This was quite unwitting, but the effects on British defence and diplomacy were profound. The Secret Service and the Foreign Office had better information, but this seems to have been ignored. The German air force was geared to supporting its army, and not enough planes would have been able to fly across the Channel with enough bombs, and return, to deliver any kind of knock-out blow. Yet Britain's defence strategy – and increasingly her foreign policy – was based on the assumption that the single, massive knock-out blow was a serious risk.

In October 1937, Chamberlain had appointed a Committee, chaired by Inskip, to try to bridge the impossible gap between the demands of the Armed Services and the strict financial regime pursued by the Treasury. Within months of forming his Government, Chamberlain had been told that only limited aircraft supplies were being produced, and Britain would remain unprepared for war until November 1939.

The Secretary of State for Air, Lord Swinton, had informed the Cabinet that the RAF was in a 'position of grave inferiority' to the Luftwaffe 'in effective air strength'. The completion of Britain's planned expansion programme would not solve the problem. Baldwin's pledge of parity would not be achieved even by 1939.

At Cabinet, shortly before Christmas 1937, Swinton told his colleagues that extra spending on more aircraft was needed if Baldwin's pledge of parity with Germany in the air was to be met. But Inskip, the Minister responsible for the Co-ordination of Defence, now argued against any increase in defence spending: 'Seen in its true perspective, the maintenance of our economic stability would more accurately be described as an essential element in our defence system; one which could properly be regarded as a fourth arm in defence, alongside the three Defence Services, without which purely military effort would be of no avail.'

The new doctrine, that the economy was the 'fourth arm of defence', had triumphed. Chamberlain rejected Swinton's call for extra spending, saying that he did not believe parity with Germany was necessary. As to the fact that this would involve breaking Baldwin's pledge, the Prime Minister told Cabinet that 'no pledge can last for ever'.

Within a month the belief in giving overriding priority to financial prudence was taken to its logical conclusion. In January 1938, the Chancellor Sir John Simon proposed cuts in defence spending plans – £6 million from the navy, £4 million from the army and £2 million from the air force. The rationing of the armed forces had begun.

Cutting back on planned defence spending put a greater premium on the need for establishing friendly relations with Germany. Chamberlain thought that one element in any package might include a transfer of the colonial territories – the Prime Minister told the Cabinet's Foreign Policy Committee that his objective was to establish Germany as 'one of the African Colonial Powers . . . by being given certain territories to administer'.

That month Chamberlain had read an anti-Nazi book by Professor Stephen Roberts, *The House that Hitler Built*. A few days after the meeting of the Cabinet's Foreign Policy Committee, he wrote to his sister,

> If I accepted the author's conclusions I should despair, but I don't and won't. Fortunately I have recently had a 'scintillation' on the subject of German negotiations. It has been accepted promptly and even enthusiastically by all to whom I have broached it and we have sent for Henderson [the British Ambassador in Berlin] to come and talk it over with us.

The need for some kind of initiative towards Germany would be welcome to Chamberlain's closest advisers. Sir Horace Wilson wrote of 'a great deal of personal depression' at this time, 'the result of war talk, and it would make a good deal of difference if the idea got about that the outlook was less dangerous. . . . We begin tomorrow [1 February 1938] a long stretch of parliamentary hard labour, with very few apples in our basket, but there is no sign of a major crisis. W.S.C. [Churchill] has been very quiet for 8 months, which is rather a long time for him.'

The response in the Eden camp to these sentiments at Number 10 was one of contempt bordering on disgust. As Oliver Harvey noted, 'The PM believes himself a man with a mission to make peace with dictators. He is both vain and obstinate and continually flattered by Simon and Hoare.'

The Cabinet battles over defence spending continued. In early February, Inskip told the Cabinet that if Swinton's demands for extra spending on the air force were met, total defence spending up to 1941 would amount to £2000 million. The level initially envisaged by the Cabinet had been £1500 million. Inskip reported the Treasury view that the extra £500 million would have to be raised from taxation, and warned that 'the effects of greatly increased taxation upon public confidence and upon the attitude of the people of this country to the defence programmes, are matters which deserve the most serious consideration.'

On Wednesday, 16 February, the Chancellor told the Cabinet that the defence budget had to be limited because of his concern about the country's future 'financial prosperity' and the ever mounting costs of the arms programmes. Swinton countered with a warning that even his proposed increase in spending 'to speak quite frankly was inadequate *vis-à-vis* Germany'.

Nonetheless, the Cabinet backed the Chancellor, and defence spending was pegged to £1570 million for the four-year period 1937–41. In consequence, little would be done to reverse the discrepancy between Britain and Germany in the resources they spent on defence – in 1935 Britain had spent 3 per cent of her Gross National Product on defence compared with Germany's 8 per cent; in 1936 the figures had been 4 per cent for Britain against 13 per cent for Germany; in 1937, 6 per cent for Britain against 13; and in 1938 they would be 7 against 17.

In early November 1937, at the start of the new session of Parliament, Neville Chamberlain had addressed Conservative backbenchers at their annual dinner at the Savoy. He took the opportunity to announce a diplomatic initiative towards Germany. No one could have imagined the shocks and surprises which were to follow over the next twelve months.

Chips Channon was at the Savoy that night and thought 'the P.M. was terrific.' Chamberlain made a statement 'that he was about to make a "gesture of friendship" to Germany. He even hinted that perhaps mandated territories might be returned, or at least that their return might be discussed. He is sending Lord Halifax. . . . The P.M. had a rapturous reception and was cheered long and loudly when he sat down. I was delighted.' Chamberlain's statement followed an invitation from Göring to attend an international hunting exhibition in Berlin. Lord Halifax seemed the ideal choice, since he frequently spoke in hunting metaphors. Such was his passion for the hunt that he had overcome a withered arm to become an accomplished horseman.

It was thought that Halifax's visit was unlikely to provoke much of a row at home. The exhibition was apparently a purely social event and, though a senior member of the Government, Halifax was not directly responsible for foreign policy. Eden was not totally against the visit, but was alarmed when he heard that Halifax might meet Hitler. The Foreign Secretary feared the effect of Britain's being seen to be running after the dictators. What conclusions would more vulnerable countries on the Continent of Europe draw? He was also angered that Chamberlain was increasingly developing an alternative foreign policy within Number 10.

Eden decided to raise the issue of Halifax's visit with Chamberlain personally, but the meeting between the two men was a disaster. Chamberlain criticised Eden, and the Foreign Secretary attacked the inadequacies of the rearmament programme. Both men lost their tempers. Eden had been recovering from influenza, and the Prime Minister's parting shot was that Eden should 'go home and take an aspirin!'

When Eden set down his thoughts in a letter to the Prime Minister later that evening, Chamberlain's reply – though intended to be friendly – attributed Eden's concern about rearmament and the general situation to the 'flu. Eden's biographer, Robert Rhodes James, relates that 'Eden's alleged infirmities were sedulously conveyed to the press by Simon and Hoare on Downing Street instructions'. Relations between Prime Minister and Foreign Secretary never recovered.

Halifax's visit went ahead. He saw Hitler, although there was almost a disastrous start to the meeting. Hitler paid Halifax the compliment of greeting him as he emerged from his car, but his lordship mistook the Führer in black trousers, silk socks and pumps for a doorman. Quick thinking by one of the German welcoming party averted a major diplomatic incident.

When Halifax reported back to Cabinet, he spoke of the 'friendliness and a desire for good relations' which he found in Germany. He saw no signs that the Germans were planning any immediate adventure. Although he expected Hitler to keep on pressing German claims in Central Europe, he did not expect that these demands would cause other countries to feel that they should intervene. During the talks, Halifax told Hitler that he saw no objection to territorial modifications in Europe, provided that they were achieved peacefully. This infuriated Eden. Hitler told Halifax that he favoured 'an advance towards disarmament'. The German Chancellor had also 'strongly criticised widespread talk of an imminent catastrophe and did not consider that the world was in a dangerous state'.

Chamberlain thought the most hopeful area for disarmament would be through some limitation on the size and power of weapons: 'That might save a great deal of expenditure.' He cited as precedent the 1935 Anglo-German Naval Treaty, an unfortunate example to choose since this had enabled Hitler to rebuild the German navy.

On the League of Nations, Chamberlain 'took the same view as Herr Hitler. At present it was largely a sham, owing more particularly to the idea that it could impose its views by force.' This put the Prime Minister totally at odds with his own Foreign Secretary. Eden believed that despite all the difficulties Britain's best hope of averting war lay in reviving the League and making a practical reality of collective security.

Later that month, Chamberlain wrote to his sister that Halifax's visit had been 'a great success', because it created 'an atmosphere in which it is possible to discuss with Germany the practical questions involved in a European settlement. . . .' The Prime Minister felt reassured by the statements that they 'had no desire or intention of making war, and I think we may take this as correct, at any rate for the present'.

What was most revealing was Chamberlain's perception of the Nazi regime's territorial ambitions, particularly as far as the German minority in Czechoslovakia (the Sudetendeutsche) was concerned. He acknowledged the Nazis' desire to dominate Eastern Europe, and thought that they wanted 'as close a union with Austria as they can get without incorporating her in the Reich'. But it was his comment that Hitler and Göring wanted 'much the same things for the Sudetendeutsche as we did for the Uitlanders in the Transvaal', which was highly significant.

*Uitlanders* was the Afrikaans term for the British settlers who moved into the Transvaal in the gold-rush of the 1890s. The clash between Boers and Britons sparked the Boer War, during which Chamberlain's father, Joe, served as Colonial Secretary. That Neville Chamberlain now equated Germany's view of a German minority with Britain's view of British settlers in a bloody conflict at the turn of the century provides a vital insight into the Prime Minister's thinking.

Chamberlain also explained to his sister that he was contemplating the possibility of appeasing Hitler by ceding territory in Africa, and was ready to negotiate German demands in Europe. The Prime Minister could not see why 'we shouldn't say to Germany "give us assurances that you won't use force to deal with the Austrians and Czechoslovakians, and we will give you similar assurances that we won't use force to prevent the changes you want, if you can get them by peaceful means" '.

There was a sinister sequel to Halifax's visit. Göbbels had told Halifax that articles in the British press and reports by the British correspondents in

Berlin were hindering better Anglo-German relations. In July 1937, the Nazi Government had expelled Norman Ebbut, Senior Correspondent of *The Times* in Berlin. Halifax agreed to do all he could to 'secure the co-operation of the British press'.

The baleful influence of the British Ambassador in Berlin, Sir Nevile Henderson, soon made itself felt. It was ironic that the choice of Henderson in the spring of 1937 was largely on the initiative of Vansittart and Eden. But the previous Ambassador, Sir Eric Phipps, a brother-in-law of Vansittart, had found the Nazis so uncongenial that he was unable to develop any kind of rapport with them.

Henderson had seemed an ideal choice. He had coped well with tough assignments in Yugoslavia and Russia. He was not the brightest but was good at social contacts, enjoyed hunting and was not likely to find Berlin as awful a place as his predecessor had. As a result, it was thought that Sir Nevile would be able to wield more influence with the German Government. For Henderson, however, it must have seemed that 'the hand of God was on him'. He had been languishing in a backwater, as Ambassador in Buenos Aires. Suddenly he was plucked from relative obscurity and given the key posting in Europe.

'I hope we are not sending another Ribbentrop to Berlin,' was Oliver Harvey's percipient comment in April 1937. After Halifax's November visit, Henderson was soon encouraging him to keep his word and was offering advice on the best way to influence the press. Halifax reassured Sir Nevile that he was having words with Lord Southwood, of Odhams Press, who owned the *Daily Herald*, Sir Walter Layton of the *News Chronicle*, Esmond Harmsworth of the *Daily Mail* and Captain Michael Wardell, chairman of the *Evening Standard*. Talks with other proprietors and editors were also on the agenda – including Lords Astor, Camrose and Kemsley, and also Geoffrey Dawson. Kemsley was particularly important because of his ownership of a large group of provincial papers.

'There are people whose tempers are inflamed more by a cartoon than by a letter-press.' That was the warning which the cartoonist David Low received from the editor of the *Evening Standard* in September 1937. Cartoons caused the Nazis great offence, and in particular Low's, which were the most powerful of the period and were syndicated around the world. Before the Halifax visit the Foreign Office Press Department had been in contact with Cudlipp, prompting his warning to the cartoonist.

After Halifax's return from Berlin, the pressure on the cartoonists increased. Halifax told old Lord Southwood that he disapproved of a cartoon published in the *Daily Herald* soon after his talks in Germany. The Prime Minister also expressed publicly his sympathy for Nazi complaints about 'bitter cartoons' in a speech to the Newspaper Society.

But the most extraordinary development was Halifax's determination to tackle David Low. Less than two weeks after returning from Germany, he had lunch with Wardell in order 'to get at Low'. Through Wardell, Halifax arranged to see the cartoonist.

The meeting was held over lunch, at Wardell's flat in Albion Gate, overlooking Hyde Park. Low later recalled that 'Lord Halifax described the Nazi point of view. . . . He drew verbally a pretty picture of Goebbles [*sic*] raging over a selection of my cartoons. . . .' When Low asked, 'Do I understand you to say that you would find it easier to promote peace if my cartoons did not irritate the Nazi leaders personally?' Halifax replied 'Yes.'

It was a very English attempt at censorship. As Low added, 'We left it at that, and sitting on Wardell's roof-garden we looked at Hyde Park below and talked about the weather.'

Although Low had little doubt about Hitler's intentions, he was prepared to accept that he might be wrong. His critical cartoons continued, although in a 'less personal key', and to replace Hitler and Mussolini Low invented the composite dictator, appropriately named Muzzler. But within weeks of Halifax's lunch with Low, events in Europe led Low to abandon his mild self-restraint.

The 'Halifax–Hitler conversations' prompted the opposition to request a debate on foreign affairs before the Christmas recess at the end of 1937. Opening the debate, Attlee declared that he saw no objection to the conversations, but wanted to know the basis on which they were held. Pinning Labour's hopes for peace on a renewed effort through the League, Attlee did not believe that 'a short-term programme of trying to get peace for a few years in exchange for a few concessions is going to get us out of the war atmosphere' (Hansard, 21 December 1937, col. 1801).

Chamberlain resented the fact that the issue had been raised in the Commons at all. He was in no mood to give much away. With his customary disregard for sensitivities at Westminster, the Prime Minister argued that 'It is so difficult to say anything that can do good, and so easy to say much that might do harm. A china shop is not the best or safest place for a fencing match . . .' (ibid., col. 1803).

Stressing the confidentiality of Halifax's talks, Chamberlain told MPs that 'a personal contact between a member of His Majesty's Government and the German Chancellor' had been established. As a result, 'we now have a fairly definite idea of the problems which, in the view of the German Government, have to be solved if we are to arrive at the condition of European affairs which we all desire . . .' (ibid., col. 1804).

The Halifax–Hitler talks were thus 'a first step towards a general effort to arrive at what has sometimes been called a general settlement . . . when reasonable grievances may be removed, when suspicions may be laid aside, and when confidence may again be restored' (ibid., cols 1804–5).

But Halifax was not the only parliamentarian who had recently talked with Hitler. Although the MP in question sat on the opposition benches, he made clear his support for the Halifax initiative. George Lansbury, the former Labour leader and pacifist, had visited Germany in response to a challenge from Churchill. His speech prompted a fresh exchange:

Lansbury:   The right hon. Member [Churchill] suggested I should
go there and preach my peace doctrines. I am glad to say that I
did so.
Churchill:   I am glad you have come back. (Ibid., col. 1822)

In contrast to his successor as Labour Party leader, Lansbury wanted to reassure the House about Hitler's intentions:

I have heard hon. Members in this House say over and over again that as the result of another war there would be neither victors nor vanquished. I do not think Herr Hitler will think I am betraying his confidence when I say that almost the first words of our conversation was [sic] on that particular point, and I have never heard it said to me more emphatically than by Herr Hitler, that another war would mean neither victors nor vanquished but the ruin of everybody. (Ibid., col. 1823)

On the persecution of the Jews in Europe, Lansbury acknowledged that they were in an 'appalling situation', but he declared that 'It has nothing to do with Hitler or Mussolini.' When this prompted other MPs to interrupt him, Lansbury retorted that he 'knew of persecutions and pogroms in Poland long before Hitler was born'. Later in his speech he added, 'the richer Jews throughout the world might have done something more to help to mitigate the situation' (ibid., col. 1827).

Speaking immediately after Lansbury, Churchill rebuked the former Labour leader for putting on 'rose-coloured spectacles when he looks at these problems', and spoke of the racial and religious persecution in Europe: 'it is a horrible thing that a race of people should be attempted to be blotted out of the society in which they have been born, that from their earliest years little children should be segregated and that they should be exposed to scorn and odium. It is very painful' (ibid., col. 1830).

Churchill thought the Prime Minister had no reason to regret that Labour had pressed for a debate. Churchill himself had been 'anxious' about Halifax's visit to Germany, reminding MPs 'how very sharp the European situation is at the present time'. The British Government's attitude was vital: 'There are at present several very important countries of second rank in size whose decision is hanging in the balance whether they should join the dictator totalitarian Powers or whether they should stand by the Covenant of the League of Nations' (ibid., cols 1832–3). Churchill emphasised that 'countries all over Europe look to Great Britain', and warned, 'If it were thought that we were making terms for ourselves at the expense of small nations or of large conceptions which are dear, not only to many nations, but to millions of people in every nation, I think a knell of despair would resound through many parts of Europe' (ibid., col. 1833). Halifax's visit had 'caused widespread commotion' throughout Europe.

Since Halifax's return, however, the French Prime Minister and Foreign Secretary had visited London. The Government had 'very wisely and promptly redressed the balance and restored the equilibrium of Europe'. Churchill hoped that the end result might thus be a closer Anglo-German understanding coupled with the 'reaffirmation of British and French solidarity'.

Referring to the specific issue of German grievances over the colonies, Churchill warned, 'though there are a very large number of people who would be willing to make sacrifices to meet German wishes about the colonies if they could be assured that it meant genuine lasting peace to Europe, none of them would yield one scrap of territory just to keep the Nazi kettle boiling' (ibid., col. 1835).

But the most striking feature of Churchill's speech was the importance he attached to the moral principles upon which the League of Nations was based. He was convinced that 'British armaments alone will never protect us in the times through which we may have to pass' (ibid., col. 1838). His own opposition to the League's sanctions against Italy eighteen months before was forgotten.

Churchill did not know when he spoke that the Prime Minister had said in Cabinet that he shared Hitler's attitude towards the League. The reasons he now gave for backing the League read like a direct reaction to Chamberlain's secret statement. Churchill maintained that:

By adhering to the Covenant of the League we secure the good will of all the nations of the world who do not seek profit by acts of wrongful and violent aggression. We secure a measure of unity at home among all classes and all parties, which is indispensable to the efficiency of our foreign policy as well as to the progress of our defensive preparations. We consecrate and legitimise every alliance and regional pact which may be formed for mutual protection. (Ibid.)

Eden, however, had heard in Cabinet what the Prime Minister really thought about the League. When the Foreign Secretary wound up the debate from the Government front bench, he began by commenting that he 'would have to be very circumspect'. It is a remark of delicious irony, since later in his speech he declared, 'I agree with every syllable which was said by my right hon. Friend the Member for Epping [Churchill] on the subject of the League' (ibid., col. 1884).

The full significance of Eden's comment would have been clear only to Chamberlain and others privy to the Prime Minister's support for Hitler's view of the League. The Foreign Secretary's coded remark was a portent of trouble ahead.

Despite the growing differences between Chamberlain and Eden over the League of Nations, over contacts with the dictators and over rearmament, there was one issue at least on which they saw eye to eye.

The New Year in 1938 heralded a dramatic change at the top of the Foreign Office. Its Permanent Secretary, the staunch anti-appeaser, Sir Robert Vansittart, was moved 'upstairs' and appointed as the Government's Chief Diplomatic Adviser. His move was welcome news at Number 10. Chamberlain had so little trust in Vansittart that for a time he had him trailed by the Security Services – an extraordinary step for a Prime Minister to take against the Permanent Secretary at the Foreign Office.

Yet the main architect of the coup was the Foreign Secretary. Although Eden and Vansittart were at one on the threat posed by Hitler, they disagreed over relations with Mussolini – Eden opposed any appeasement of the Italian regime, whereas Vansittart saw better relations with Rome as an important element in restraining Hitler. But Eden felt that a new Permanent Secretary was needed if the Foreign Office was to make a greater impact on Government policy. His action showed that he had the courage to be tough when necessary.

Vansittart was an overpowering figure, a larger-than-life character, with whom any minister would have found it hard to contend. Relations between Eden, who was then only forty, and his Permanent Secretary cannot have been helped by the fact that whenever the Foreign Secretary advocated a tougher line against Germany, other ministers would mutter, 'His master's voice' – the implication being that Sir Robert was the real boss.

Vansittart was a politician *manqué*, a trait which does not endear civil servants to their political masters at the best of times. The better the official plays the role, the more he is damned by his ministers. This was Vansittart's fate. He cut a dash in London society, with a range of impressive contacts which few politicians could ever hope to emulate. He had a way with words, which made him the envy of any politician, and he had a play performed at the Comédie Française.

Yet Vansittart was not enough of a politician to control his literary inclinations. His minutes to ministers were brilliantly written, with wonderfully constructed sentences. But they invariably ran to many pages. Sir Frank Roberts, an official in the Foreign Office during the 1930s, recalls that his contemporaries were in awe of Vansittart. They used to see his minutes and think to themselves that they would never write anything like that. Of course, Roberts and his colleagues never did write like Vansittart. This was just as well for their sakes. Hard-pressed ministers are not looking for literary gems when they start working through their red boxes last thing at night. They want their briefing on one side of paper. Vansittart's minutes, for all their brilliance, merely rankled.

Though Sir Robert's move was nominally a promotion, it was clear that his wings were being clipped. He had been robbed of his departmental power base and, although he continued to receive copies of official papers, they would inevitably filter through to his office far more slowly than when he had been Permanent Secretary.

Sir Alec Cadogan, who succeeded as head of the Foreign Office, was much more sympathetic to Chamberlain's desire to make contact with Germany. Cadogan had written in his diary in April 1937, 'If everyone in Germany is mad, and if all are bent on our destruction, disaster *must* come. Therefore, the best we can do is to *put it off*. Therefore we *must* try and talk with some of them and encourage some of them. . . . If our rearmament is backward, we must have time.'

Cadogan was the very antithesis of Vansittart, conforming to the classic image of the career civil servant, efficient and loyal. A younger son of the Earl of Cadogan, he had no pretensions to play the role of the politician. He was outwardly calm and seemingly reserved, though his diaries were subsequently to reveal him as a far more emotional character than colleagues had ever suspected. During a period of immense stress and relentless work, his diary seemed to act much as a psychiatrist's couch.

Within weeks of his appointment, Cadogan was to find himself at the heart of a row which rocked the Government. Vansittart's ominous parting words to Eden had been 'If I go, you won't last long.'

# CHAPTER NINE
# A SUDDEN DEPARTURE

Of late the conviction has steadily grown upon me that there
has been too keen a desire on our part to make terms with
others rather than that others should make terms with us.

(Anthony Eden, House of Commons, 21 February 1938,
Hansard, col. 49)

The peace of Europe must depend upon the attitude of the four
major powers – Germany, Italy, France and ourselves. . . . If
we can bring these four nations into friendly discussion, into a
settling of their differences, we shall have saved the peace of
Europe for a generation.

(Neville Chamberlain, House of Commons, 21 February 1938,
Hansard, col. 64)

In Washington on the evening of Tuesday, 11 January 1938, the United
States Secretary of State, Sumner Welles, was in touch with the British Ambassador, Sir Ronald Lindsay. His purpose was to convey a secret message
from the President, Franklin Roosevelt, to the British Prime Minister.

Roosevelt was proposing an international initiative, which he intended
to launch later that month. His plan was to urge world peace, an
international reduction in armaments, and equal access to raw materials.

Throughout the 1930s, relations between London and Washington had
been strained. After the German Government stopped paying war
reparations, the British Government thought that the United States'
demand for her war debts to be paid was unreasonable and so defaulted
after 1933. This resulted in the US banning any future loans to Britain.
The British policy of 'Imperial Preference' was regarded in America as
unfairly restricting her trade. The British were suspicious of American
isolationism, while the Americans were suspicious that Britain's imperial
interests might lead her to make an economic agreement with Germany.
Chamberlain distrusted the USA's real motives, and thought Roosevelt's
vague initiative would be counter-productive as far as his own hopes for
appeasement with the dictators were concerned.

Nonetheless, Lindsay recommended acceptance of Roosevelt's initiative 'cordially and immediately'. The new Permanent Secretary at the Foreign Office, Sir Alec Cadogan, had reservations about the initiative, but felt that it was 'important not to break with R. . .'. But when Cadogan went to Downing Street to discuss the initiative he found that Chamberlain 'hates R.'s [Roosevelt's] idea, but I tried to point out that we mustn't snub him. But he wouldn't have my addition.' As Chamberlain wrote in a memorandum:

> The [Roosevelt] plan appeared to me fantastic and likely to excite the derision of Germany and Italy. They might even use it to postpone conversations with us, and if we were associated with it they would see in it another attempt on the part of the democratic bloc to put the dictators in the wrong.

Eden was on holiday on the Riviera. Cadogan phoned him on the morning of 14 January to tell him that he should return to London immediately. Eden was met at Folkestone by Cadogan and his Private Secretary, Oliver Harvey. The Foreign Secretary privately recorded his reactions on hearing of the Roosevelt initiative, noting that there were one or two paragraphs in the message which 'are not well worded from our point of view', and there was also a 'certain vagueness about the proposals.' Yet he felt the initiative was of historic importance:

> I attach so much importance to Anglo-American co-operation that I should myself be strongly in favour of responding to Roosevelt's appeal and promising to back it. The P.M., however, did not like it because he feared it might cut across our own attempts to improve relations with the Dictator Powers.

The Prime Minister's handling of the American initiative left Eden feeling 'outraged and uneasy'. He resented the fact that Chamberlain had not consulted him before the reply was dispatched. The Prime Minister had felt that 'There was no time to consult Anthony, for in view of secrecy on which Roosevelt insisted in emphatic terms I did not dare telephone.' But Chamberlain could have reached the Foreign Secretary within hours through the British Embassy in Paris. Eden was also furious at the Prime Minister's comments in his telegram to Roosevelt, in which he mentioned his hope to grant *de jure* recognition of the Italian conquest of Abyssinia. Roosevelt was opposed to recognition at the time, although he welcomed the Anglo-Italian agreement two months later.

Eden saw the Prime Minister's initial reaction to the Roosevelt initiative as part of a whole. As he wrote in his memoirs,

He [Chamberlain] was evidently determined to see the whole American business only in the context of his impending talks with the dictators. In this sense, Roosevelt, our French allies and I were all in the same boat. We were all held to be obstructing these negotiations, in which Chamberlain had dogmatic faith.

On Sunday the 16th, the day after Eden returned to England, he visited Chamberlain at Chequers. Eden's diary reveals that both men reiterated their positions about Anglo-American relations, and their discussion turned to Italy. The Foreign Secretary made clear his opposition to any recognition of Mussolini's conquest of Abyssinia and reminded the Prime Minister that Italy had sent troops into Spain, in breach of the so-called Gentleman's Agreement. Eden argued that the less strong Mussolini was the less he appealed to Hitler. Britain's recognition of his Empire would, Eden thought, increase his authority, and, therefore, make him more attractive to Hitler.

The argument between Chamberlain and Eden lasted on and off for several days. The root of the problem remained the Prime Minister's growing determination to run his own foreign policy, but the focus for the row was to become the issue of relations with Italy.

The Prime Minister quoted letters from his sister-in-law Ivy, Sir Austen Chamberlain's widow, to the Cabinet Foreign Affairs Committee. Lady Chamberlain was in close contact with the Italian Foreign Minister Ciano, who had known her husband. The Prime Minister also went behind Eden's back by using the Director of the Conservative Research Department, J. R. Ball, as a contact with Count Grandi, the Italian Ambassador in London.

On 20 January, Chamberlain's and Eden's closest advisers became embroiled in the row. Jim Thomas warned Sir Horace Wilson that, if Eden were to resign at that stage, 'the whole of this American business might leak out from the American end and . . . the country would then know that the Prime Minister preferred to turn down the help of a democracy in order that he might pursue his flirtations with the dictators untramelled.' Wilson dismissed the Roosevelt initiative as 'woolly rubbish', and in a 'towering rage' warned Thomas that 'if America produced the facts he would use the full power of the Government machine in an attack upon AE's [Eden's] past record with the dictators and the shameful obstruction by the F.O. of the P.M.'s attempts to save the peace of the world.'

In fact, the next day Chamberlain was eventually persuaded to change his mind. His new message to the President welcomed the proposed initiative and said that recognition for Italy in Abyssinia would only be granted as part of a general settlement. Although Roosevelt's reply was friendly, the President himself had cooled on the idea, and nothing further came of the scheme.

But the incident had further soured relations between the Prime Minister and the Foreign Secretary. They were at loggerheads over an approach to Mussolini, yet Eden would not seek support for his position. As Duff Cooper, a potential Eden supporter, later wrote, 'It is much to his credit that he [Eden] abstained from all lobbying of opinion and sought to gain no adherents either in the Cabinet or the House of Commons. Had he made an effort to win my support at the time he would probably have succeeded.'

The result of Eden's abstinence was that the Cabinet were mystified when matters suddenly came to a head. In mid-February, the Cabinet were preoccupied by their acrimonious argument over Simon's demands for cuts in defence spending plans. Yet the issue of contacts with Italy was about to trigger a far more damaging political explosion.

Eden's general approach on foreign policy was receiving strong support on the backbenches, which encouraged him to stick to his guns. This was presumably Churchill's purpose when he addressed the meeting of Conservative backbenchers on 17 February. As Victor Cazalet later wrote to Stanley Baldwin, 'Winston came up to the Foreign Affairs Committee and for quarter of an hour gave us an enthusiastic eulogy of Anthony and ended by saying that we must support him. This struck me as somewhat unnecessary as we were all devoted to Anthony and no one had even faintly criticised him. I smelt, if not a rat, at any rate, a mouse.' Cazalet recalled that Eden, Churchill and Lloyd George had recently 'all been on the Riviera together'.

The upshot of Churchill's apparently spontaneous speech in favour of Eden was that a majority of the 100 or more Tory MPs at the meeting rallied to the cause. They supported a communiqué to Chamberlain calling for 'a more positive attitude by this country in Europe'. The Chief Whip, Captain Margesson, tried to prevail upon the Committee's chairman, Paul Emrys-Evans, to tone it down. But this provoked an 'indignant response' from Churchill.

The Prime Minister was due to meet the Italian Ambassador at Number 10 the next day, Friday the 18th. Eden had to insist on being there. Before the meeting, Eden read the private record of the backbenchers' Foreign Affairs Committee at which Churchill had spoken.

Chamberlain and Eden clashed openly in front of Count Grandi. After the meeting, Chamberlain and Eden had what Cadogan described as a 'set-to':

P.M. very violent – said this was last chance of getting to terms with Italy (that jackass Ivy had been telephoning him): A. [Eden] said that this was not the moment to do it. In view of Hitler's performance in Austria, and before we knew what he is going to say in his speech on Sunday, this is *not* the moment to crawl to Italy, of all countries.

Eden's own account reveals the most extraordinary scene:

N.C. [Chamberlain] became very vehement, more vehement than I have ever seen him, and strode up and down the room saying with great emphasis 'Anthony, you have missed chance after chance. You simply cannot go on like this.'

I said, 'Your methods are right if you have faith in the man you are negotiating with.'

N.C. replied, 'I have.'

The Cabinet gathered the following day, Saturday the 19th, with ministers unaware that relations between Chamberlain and Eden were at breaking point. The Prime Minister argued that there was 'an opportunity to show Signor Mussolini that he might have other friends besides Herr Hitler'. Eden was not opposed in principle to talks with the Italians. But his information was that Mussolini had already agreed to give Hitler a free hand in Austria. In return, Mussolini would be allowed freedom of action in the Mediterranean. Eden feared that without some assurance from Mussolini the result of formal talks with the Italians would be 'a panic among our friends and a rush to make a composition with Italy and Germany'.

The Cabinet backed the Prime Minister. Eden had been completely outmanoeuvred. He announced that since he could not defend the decision to seek formal talks with Mussolini, he would have to resign. As Chamberlain's account relates, 'there was a gasp of horror.'

Chamberlain's supporters spread rumours that Eden was under strain and that his judgement had gone. Sir John Simon suggested to Jim Thomas the night before Eden finally resigned that he thought the Foreign Secretary was unwell and should take a six months' holiday, adding that 'During this period he [Simon] and his Cabinet colleagues would keep his seat for him and look after foreign affairs.' Lord Halifax agreed with the comments about Eden's health. He, however, at least had the decency to confide his thoughts to his diary, adding that 'once everybody begins to feel they are being a martyr for high principle it becomes very difficult to avoid this conviction having melancholy issue.'

News of differences in the Cabinet had reached the press. Margesson, the Chief Whip, became alarmed at the likely effect of Eden's resignation on the Government. Duff Cooper noted that if Eden 'goes it will certainly be a body-blow for the National Government. There were crowds in Downing Street last night and tonight, and when he drove off there were loud cheers. This I am afraid will stiffen his attitude, he will feel that he has popular opinion behind him, which he has.'

On Sunday morning, 20 February, Eden returned to Number 10 to say that he had not changed his mind. The Cabinet, however, were determined that he should stay, and the desperate attempts to mediate between the Prime Minister and the Foreign Secretary lasted most of Sunday. But eventually, and inevitably, they failed. Eden finally tendered his resignation that Sunday evening.

Most ministers were still baffled that a difference over an approach to the Italians had provoked such deep disagreement. The Lord Chancellor, Viscount Hailsham, wrote to his son, 'I can't tell you why Anthony resigned because I couldn't make it out myself.' Victor Cazalet wrote a few days later to Baldwin that he had talked to nearly all Eden's colleagues, 'including his best friends like Shakes [Morrison], Oliver [Stanley] and Walter Elliot, and they all say they were, and still are, amazed at what happened.'

Cazalet, however, had the wit to realise that 'It was clear that something more fundamental than the Italian negotiations was at stake.' He had no inkling of the Roosevelt initiative, but commented that one of the things to emerge was that 'Anthony, consciously or unconsciously, resented the Prime Minister taking such interest – or perhaps one might even say control – in foreign affairs.'

The other aspect identified by Cazalet was that 'as long as Anthony was at the Foreign Office very little advance would be made along the lines of Anglo-Italian conversations or friendship.' But Eden's opposition to closer contacts with Italy, because of Mussolini's continued aggression in Spain, not only set him apart from Chamberlain, it also divided him from other Tory critics, notably Churchill and Leo Amery.

While Eden regarded the failure of the Roosevelt initiative as a missed opportunity, many others held precisely the same view about his refusal at the Foreign Office to accept any move towards closer relations with the Italians.

The sudden resignation of the Foreign Secretary triggered a political crisis. Although the immediate storm quickly blew over, it had a lasting impact on the Chamberlain Government. It strengthened opposition to it and sharpened the divisions over foreign policy in the country.

The Government launched an immediate propaganda offensive against

Eden. The rumours from the Whips' office about his physical and mental health were intensified. Whitehall's efforts at news management were redoubled. Oliver Harvey's diary for late February 1938 gives a graphic account from the inside:

> The Government were in a great fright at what they had done, as indeed they had every reason to be, and took every possible step to secure the London papers. *The Times*, of course, was on their side already. *Daily Telegraph* came heavily in against A. E. (Victor Gordon-Lennox [foreign correspondent] was in tears at the way his paper had behaved.) The BBC was told to say nothing that night about Germany and Italy.

The Labour leader, Attlee, was given the opportunity to voice his opinions on Eden's resignation by the newsreel company Paramount. But within hours the company was ordered to cut the item from their reports. Meanwhile at the Conservative Research Department J. R. Ball was busily ensuring that the Conservative Party faithful remained loyal to Chamberlain.

The Government's frantic efforts paid off with the press. Most papers backed Chamberlain, while Eden's principal supporters were the Labour paper, the *Daily Herald*, the Liberal-inclined *News Chronicle* and, outside London, the Tory provincial paper, the *Yorkshire Post*.

But Eden was able to attract sizeable support in the country, despite the Government's determined manipulation of the media. The cheering crowds outside Eden's London home reflected the reaction of many people. According to an opinion poll conducted that month by the British Institute of Public Opinion, fully 71 per cent thought Eden was right to resign, while only 19 per cent thought he should have stayed on. When asked whether they favoured 'Mr Chamberlain's foreign policy', only 26 per cent said that they did, against 58 per cent who did not.

The response at the Palace gratified Eden. As Harvey noted in his diary, Eden was 'delighted with his reception by the King [George VI]' when he delivered up his seals of office. The King apparently expressed 'great sympathy with his point of view and he didn't think it would be long before he saw him again'. The King's Private Secretary, Sir Alexander Hardinge, who had seen all the documents, told Eden that he thought he was right 'in all points'.

Ronald Tree, the Tory MP, was entertaining guests at his country home, Ditchley, during the weekend of Eden's resignation. The news provoked a furious row. Tree, an American by birth, was married to a niece of Nancy Astor. He was a 'confirmed believer' in Eden's approach, and later wrote that he 'could not refrain from venting my very strong feelings'. But others disagreed, particularly Nancy Astor, who happened to be one of the guests. As Tree wrote,

> We went at it hammer and tongs, Nancy Astor accusing Eden of being vain and obstinate, while I replied by telling her what I thought of Chamberlain, his policy and his attitudes. The party divided itself according to their views. Eventually the argument was settled by old Lord Ancaster who, in his distinctive Willoughby voice – no aitches but plenty of 'doncha knows' – announced that what we had better do was to have a vote and shut up about it.

Tree reckoned the vote would have been 'nearly all for Chamberlain'.

At Oxford, on the night of Eden's resignation, several undergraduates at Balliol had gathered in the room of an American Rhodes Scholar, Philip Kaiser. He was one of the few with a radio. Among the students waiting to hear the news about Eden was Edward Heath. As Kaiser has recalled,

> I remember that Ted said very little that night. It affected him. Eden was important to him. When it happened – and the resignation wasn't even reported as the first item on the news – a *gravitas*, a great thoughtfulness, settled on him, more than was the case with anybody else. He thanked me and then walked out.

The Government had lost their most popular figure, though only a few others resigned with Eden: Lord Cranborne, his deputy at the Foreign Office; Cranborne's and Eden's Parliamentary Private Secretaries, Mark Patrick and Jim Thomas; and Ronald Tree, who quit as Parliamentary Private Secretary at the Overseas Trade Department.

The failure of others to follow Eden's example angered his friends and supporters. As Oliver Harvey, Eden's Private Secretary at the Foreign Office, wrote,

> All the worst elements of the Conservative Party are loose again. . . . What is one to think of these wretched young men? Malcolm MacDonald (who could have ensured the survival for his party [National Labour] by resigning), Elliot, Shakespeare Morrison (supposed to be a future P.M.!) and Oliver Stanley ('the Stanleys have been trimmers ever since Bosworth' as Lady Cranborne said when she heard he wasn't resigning). I believe they will never live this down.

(Lady Cranborne's comment referred to the Battle of Bosworth field in 1485, when the Stanleys reputedly waited to see which way the battle was going before committing themselves for Henry Tudor and against Richard III.)

The key fact, however, was that Eden *had* gone. 'They have let our best man go, at a time like this!', Oliver Harvey confided in his diary.

Crucially, the Government could never present quite the same face to the country again. They had lost any last semblance of the broad appeal which Baldwin's team had possessed. They were unmistakably Chamberlain's men. As the *Spectator* observed, 'When the House rose on Friday of last week [18 February] it would have been true to say that the demarcation between political parties was becoming more and more blurred. Now the whole scene is transformed. The drama of the week-end has given new and vigorous life to political controversy both inside and outside the walls of Parliament.' Churchill claimed that as a result of Eden's departure, 'The Liberal, Labour and non-party voters whom Mr. Baldwin had painstakingly gathered have been summarily dismissed and will not be easy to recall. In Mr. Eden the National Government have lost their only popular figure. A fortnight ago they could have appealed to the electors with confidence. No friend would recommend them to do so now.'

In *The Gathering Storm*, Churchill's post-war account of the period, he recalled that, although he never had trouble sleeping during the darkest days of the Second World War,

> now, on the night of February 20, 1938, and on this occasion only, sleep deserted me. From midnight till dawn I lay in my bed consumed by emotions of sorrow and fear. There seemed one strong young figure standing against long, dismal, drawling tides of drift and surrender, of wrong measurements and feeble impulses. . . . I watched the daylight slowly creep in through the window, and saw before me in mental gaze the vision of Death.

Before Eden delivered his personal explanation of his resignation to the Commons the next day, Monday, 21 February, Churchill encouraged him to speak out. There was talk that up to 100 Tory MPs would back Eden. It was being said that he would make a bid for power based on his support in the country, and even that he would cross the floor of the House.

Yet Eden resisted calls to savage the Government. His own assessment was more astute. As he later revealed, he considered forming his own political party, but realised that it was impractical:

> Within the Conservative Party, I, and those who shared my views, were in a minority of about thirty members of Parliament out of nearly four hundred. Our number might be expected to grow if events proved us right, but the more complete the break, the more reluctant would the newly converted be to join us.

Eden's resignation speech was no clarion call for rebellion. But neither was it an effective rallying cry for anything else. It was no doubt difficult for Eden to judge the right tone for his speech, but he did his cause no good by seeming diffident, commenting at one point, 'In the light – my judgment may well be wrong – of the present international situation . . .' (Hansard, 21 February 1938, col. 47).

Eden played into the Prime Minister's hands by accepting that he had not resigned on an issue of principle, merely on whether 'official conversations should be opened in Rome now'. Much of his speech was devoted to Italy's flagrant intervention in the Spanish Civil War. Viewed from any objective standpoint, this was a strong point in his favour. But it won him few friends on his own side of the House, since few Conservative backbenchers cared much about events in Spain as long as the Communists were not winning.

Eden was, of course, severely limited by his self-denying ordinance on the Roosevelt initiative. He allowed himself just one, passing reference to it. In a veiled comment, he revealed that the difference over the timing of the talks with Italy was not 'an isolated issue' between him and the Prime Minister. He added, 'Within the last few weeks upon one most important decision of foreign policy which did not concern Italy at all, the difference was fundamental' (ibid., col. 48). No one picked up or queried this comment in the debate which followed.

Towards the end of his speech, however, the strength of Eden's opposition to Chamberlain's single-minded pursuit of appeasement became clear, as the quotation at the head of this chapter shows. Chamberlain's response, also cited, demonstrates the rift which had developed between Prime Minister and Foreign Secretary by the time of Eden's sudden departure from office.

Speaking again the next day, Chamberlain rubbed salt in the wound by his open dismissal of the League of Nations – of which Eden and Cranborne had been such strong supporters. The Prime Minister abandoned the position shared by every British Government since the end of the 1914–18 war. When MPs interrupted to challenge him about the Government's own fulsome endorsement of the League at the previous (1935) general election, Chamberlain retorted bluntly, 'At the last election it was still possible to hope that the League might afford collective security. I believed it myself. I do not believe it now. . . . the League as constituted to-day is unable to provide collective security for anybody . . .' (Hansard, 22 February 1938, col. 227).

Chamberlain's ready acceptance of the League's impotence, and his emphasis on the lessons which should be drawn from it, exemplified the radical shift he was bringing about in British policy. From that day on, the

Labour and Liberal Parties were able to maintain that the National Government destroyed the League, while they had sought to defend it.

The Prime Minister said he was concerned 'not to delude small weak nations'. But his preferred alternative, talks between the four major European powers, would almost certainly entail considerable sacrifices by 'small weak nations'. On the day of Eden's resignation, Hitler had announced his demand for more territories along the German borders, where there were more than ten million German-speaking people.

Eden realised when he resigned that only time and the turn of events could bring about a change in policy. He did, however, score one tactical triumph later in the debate when he established that Chamberlain had withheld from him a telegram containing information about the Italian Government's thinking.

Eden had left himself open to the charge of resigning over a mere point of detail. Chamberlain seized on this, and loyalist backbenchers echoed the charge. They needed little encouragement to give public expression to the whispering campaign about Eden's state of mind. Sir Alan Anderson commented, 'In the incident we are considering, I think the mental balance of the Foreign Secretary was wrong. I do not think he ought to have resigned' (ibid., col. 274).

But criticism of Eden did not come solely from Government loyalists. Leo Amery attacked Eden for objecting to immediate talks with Italy. It was more surprising that one of Churchill's most trusted lieutenants, Robert Boothby, should back the Prime Minister, and commend him for his 'high courage'. Boothby was relieved to see an end to the drift and muddle which had characterised British policy before Chamberlain entered Number 10. He welcomed the change in foreign policy from 'a static and negative policy . . . to a positive and dynamic one' (ibid., col. 252).

Those who spoke in the debate in support of Eden from the Government backbenches included Churchill, Vyvyan Adams, Ronald Cartland, A.C. Crossley, Paul Emrys-Evans, Major J.W. Hills, Harold Nicolson and Brigadier-General E.L. Spears. Both Adams and Cartland sought to refute the rumours about Eden's health. Cartland noted that *The Times* had reported the comments of the Chancellor of the Exchequer, Sir John Simon, in which he had claimed that Eden's resignation had been brought on by ill-health. Adams delivered a scathing attack on those who were spreading, and reporting, the rumours, declaring that 'It is not true . . . that the right hon. Gentleman [Eden] is down or ill or in any special need of rest. This miserable fiction is being repeated in that organ of cowardice and camouflage, *The Times*' (ibid., col. 297).

Cartland, who was thirty-one years old, and brother of the novelist

Barbara, suspected a generation gap in people's attitudes. He maintained that the difference between Chamberlain and Eden 'seems to run right through the country', and added,

> It exists, and deeply. It may be that sometimes the difference is a matter of age. Perhaps those who scan the horizon and have many years ahead of them look with rather different eyes at all the problems of to-day from those who have not so many years ahead. I know there are many people who sincerely say that to maintain a certain conduct in international relations at the present time is foolhardy, in face of existing dangers, but expediency in foreign policies has never been a tenet of Tory faith. (Ibid., col. 279)

Adams told MPs that 'what happened yesterday and the day before will thrill every pro-Fascist and elate every pro-Nazi in the country and throughout the world' (ibid., col. 298).

Although the opposition motion of censure was defeated by 330 votes to 168, the Government's majority was narrower than in previous foreign affairs debates. Adams was the only Government backbencher to vote with the opposition, but more than twenty others abstained. These included, in addition to Eden himself, Cranborne, Jim Thomas and Mark Patrick, and those who had spoken against the Government in the debate, Brendan Bracken and Harold Macmillan.

Eden secured a rousing public endorsement for his stand at a packed public meeting in his constituency, Leamington. But his closest supporters felt the wrath of local Conservatives, who remained loyal to their Party leader. Cranborne was in serious trouble in South Dorset, where all his prominent supporters were furious, and he sensed that he might almost be stoned. Jim Thomas likewise was in difficulty, prompting Cranborne to sympathise about the 'shortsighted and wrong-headed Tory machine'.

The Tory machine was plainly rattled, and was determined to keep tabs on the rebel MPs. A group of them began meeting at Ronald Tree's home in Queen Anne's Gate, near St James's Park, conveniently near to the House of Commons and just a stone's throw from the Conservative Research Department, then housed in Old Queen Street.

Tree was tipped off by Helen Kirkpatrick, a journalist on the *Chicago Daily News*, who worked across the street, that his telephone was being tapped. Tree had heard some 'odd clickings', but as he later wrote, 'I had not realised that the Government thought us to be so dangerous.' The instigator of the 'phone-tap later identified himself to Tree: 'during the war, I came across Sir Joseph Ball at the Ministry of Information, a dislikeable man with an unenviable reputation for doing some of

Chamberlain's "behind-the-scenes" work. . . . he had the gall to tell me that he himself had been responsible for having my telephone tapped.'

In the Commons, the loyalist Tory backbenchers had more traditional ways of venting their anger, and did so at the Government backbenchers' Foreign Affairs Committee, at the end of February. As Harold Nicolson, one of those on the receiving end of their wrath, wrote to his wife, Vita Sackville-West,

> Several people got up quite shamelessly and suggested that we should not resign at once but merely do so later when feeling had diminished. At this Winston in all his majesty rose and said that they were being mean and petty. They were not treating us fairly and he must insist on a vote, either Yes or No.
>
> They then voted. Those in favour of our not resigning were unanimous except for one little vicious hand against. That hand was the hand of Nancy Astor.

Afterwards, in the Committee corridor, a backbench friend of Nicolson's, Alan Graham, told Nancy Astor that she had not behaved very well. As Nicolson wrote, 'She turned upon him and said, "Only a Jew like you would *dare* to be rude to me." He replied, "I should like very much to smack your face." I think she is a little mad.'

Chamberlain appointed Lord Halifax, one of his trusted inner group in the Cabinet, as Eden's successor at the Foreign Office. While Halifax was still considering the offer, he told Oliver Harvey (who would serve as his Private Secretary, as he had served Eden) that he was very lazy, and asked whether he could still hunt on Saturdays.

Cranborne was replaced by R.A. ('Rab') Butler. The new Foreign Secretary was a member of the House of Lords, and Butler therefore became the principal Foreign Office spokesman in the Commons. There were no signs that the young Rab had any qualms about justifying appeasement. Indeed, Butler was more strongly committed to the policy than almost anyone else in Government – in his memoirs, Rab justified appeasement on rather different grounds to those he used at the time.

At the Foreign Office, Halifax was soon making fresh attempts to sway the media. In Berlin, on 3 March, Henderson approached Hitler with proposals for a settlement, which included colonial concessions to Germany. Two days later, Harvey noted in his diary, 'Efforts are being made to influence the Press and the BBC from anti-Italian or anti-German comment. . . .' Halifax approached the Director-General of the BBC. As Harvey again wrote, the Foreign Secretary asked Reith 'not to proceed with a series of talks on the subject of the return of the German Colonies. Reith asked pointblank whether H.M.G. wished him to stop them – to which H. replied that was so but he would deny it if challenged in public!' On 8 March, Halifax called a special meeting with the press. 'A difficult business', as Harvey recorded, 'as he appealed to them to refrain as far as possible from reporting "rumours" which might embitter relations with Germany and Italy.'

The question of news management was raised with the Prime Minister later that month. In a written parliamentary question, he was asked whether 'any instruction, request or suggestion, direct or indirect, has been made since 21 February 1938, to British newspapers to suppress or modify news or comment on the Government's foreign policy'. The Prime Minister's reply was categoric: 'No attempt has been made by instruction, request or suggestion to prevent newspapers from expressing their considered views' (Hansard, 23 March 1938, col. 1171).

Halifax and Butler had barely got their feet under their desks at the Foreign Office when Hitler launched what was then by far his most daring adventure.

Early on the morning of Saturday, 12 March 1938, German troops crossed the border into Austria. They entered as friends, and were greeted by bands and cheering crowds, who bedecked them with flowers. Later that day Hitler was given a hero's reception when he visited Linz, in Upper Austria, where as a boy he had attended school.

The newsreel footage, photographs and reports of the ecstatic welcome for the German troops served to quell the criticism of Hitler's action. From its birth in 1919, the new Austrian Republic had been uncertain of its identity. Most of its people would probably have supported union with Germany (Anschluss), but this was expressly forbidden by the Treaty of Versailles. From 1933, however, Anschluss would clearly entail Nazi rule. Although the main parties struck references to seeking union with Germany from their programmes, most Austrians remained ambivalent. The Nazis in Austria received support from across the German border. In July 1934, they had assassinated the Austrian Chancellor Dollfuss in an attempted *coup d'état*.

The new Austrian Chancellor, Schuschnigg, looked for protection of his country's independence to the south. Mussolini's role as effective guarantor of Austria reflected Italy's deep concern at the prospect of Austria becoming part of a strong, expansionist Germany. The fear of German domination ran deep, since large parts of Italy had been subjugated by the Austrian empire until the latter half of the nineteenth century.

But during 1936 and 1937 Hitler succeeded in building a new axis with Rome. As a result, Mussolini informed Schuschnigg in April 1937 that he was no longer prepared to defend Austria. And in November 1937, he told Ribbentrop, the German Foreign Minister, that Italy would accept Germany's right to settle the issue of Austria's future.

In early 1938 Schuschnigg was summoned for talks with Hitler. On 12 February, at Berchtesgaden, Hitler threatened invasion unless his demands were accepted, including the appointment of a Nazi, Seyss-Inquart, as Minister of the Interior. But on Wednesday, 9 March, Schuschnigg sought to resist and called a plebiscite on Austria's future, to be held the following Sunday. Socialists and Catholics came together to urge a vote for independence.

The news of the plebiscite took Hitler by surprise. On 10 March, he ordered his military commanders to prepare plans for an early invasion. The next day, Hitler demanded that the Austrian Government should postpone the plebiscite. When this was conceded, Göring phoned Vienna and ordered that Schuschnigg should resign and that the Nazi, Seyss-Inquart, should succeed as Chancellor.

Schuschnigg and his Cabinet resigned that evening, leaving Seyss-Inquart as the only serving minister. Göring then ordered that German troops should invade Austria. Later, an invitation was received in Berlin, allegedly from Seyss-Inquart in the name of a provisional Government. The German Government regarded this as conferring legitimacy. They crossed the border early on the Saturday morning. The Gestapo followed in their wake, to begin their persecution of Austria's minorities.

The following day, the German Chancellor was able to announce the annexation of Austria. An independent country had disappeared within a weekend, and with scarcely a shot fired.

Although both the British and French Governments went through the motions of making formal protests, London and Paris had long anticipated the Anschluss.

In mid-February, Eden had referred to the Austrian crisis in Cabinet and commented that 'He did not want to put himself in the position of suggesting a resistance which we could not, in fact, furnish.' At the time of the Austrian crisis, the French were between governments.

At the emergency Cabinet meeting after the Anschluss, Chamberlain stated that he found 'The manner in which the German action in Austria had been brought about was most distressing and shocking to the world.' It would make 'international appeasement much more difficult. . . . In spite of all, however, he felt that this thing had to come. Nothing short of an overwhelming display of force would have stopped it.'

In the country, however, many felt that Eden's decision to resign had been vindicated. In his Leicester constituency, Nicolson visited the

Newfoundlandpool Working Men's Club, where 'They are all anti-Chamberlain, saying "Eden has been proved right." ' In the very different setting of Sybil Colefax's dinner party two days later, Desmond MacCarthy, the leading literary critic of the day, commented that the Government had betrayed the country.

But the Anschluss confirmed Chamberlain in his belief that he had been right all along, and Eden wrong. On Sunday, 13 March, the day after German troops had entered Austria, he wrote, 'It is tragic to think that very possibly this might have been prevented if I had had Halifax at the Foreign Office instead of Anthony Eden at the time I wrote my letter to Mussolini.'

Victor Cazalet's blow-by-blow account caught the mood of anger and frustration felt by many:

*March 11th*: Friday – it is a real Black Letter day. The invasion of Austria – the country we all love, by those bloody Nazis. What I feel about it!

*March 12th*: Overwhelmed by news. Furious, raging, impotent. But one can't fight if the Austrians won't.

*March 13th*: All this week we have been horrified. Everyone is indignant. But it's all over, and we can't be more Austrian than the Austrians. I do think someone in Austria might have fired a shot, but I suppose it is easy to expect someone else to fight. . . . War was in the air.

*March 20th*: By Saturday things cooled down. The absorption of Austria by the Reich is complete. Austria and all we have associated with the name is gone. It's a bitter pill.

The immediate reaction from the opposition was more muted than might have been expected. Labour had little sympathy for Schuschnigg. He was, after all, the heir to Dollfuss, who had turned the artillery on the Austrian socialists only four years previously.

As with the Rhineland two years earlier, some were ready to put a comforting gloss on Hitler's action – the Austrian Republic had owed its origins to the much-maligned Versailles peace settlement. Hitler was limiting himself to his own back-yard. Austria was populated by Germans, and was a German state, to which neither Britain nor France had any commitment.

Cadogan shared these sentiments, as he revealed when he wrote to the British Ambassador in Berlin, Sir Nevile Henderson, a month after the crisis:

Thank Goodness. Austria's out of the way. I can't help thinking that we were very badly informed about feeling in that country. I've no doubt there's a section of the population hiding in cellars, and a number of those waving Swastika flags now may come to rue the day later, but we should evidently have been very wrong to try to prevent the Anschluss against the wishes of . . . a very considerable proportion of the population. After all, it wasn't our business: we had no particular feelings for the Austrians: we only forbade the Anschluss to spite Germany.

The Marquis of Lothian, whose weekend gathering at Blickling Hall at the time of the Rhineland crisis had proffered speedy advice to Baldwin, gave a wider public the benefit of his thoughts. On Monday, 14 March, *The Times* published his letter, where he argued that after the Anschluss,

The most important single aspect is that at long last it ends the disastrous period when the League of Nations Powers attempted, in the name of the Covenant, to deny to Germans, who were certainly not solely responsible for the Great War, their national unity and so drove them to accept a totalitarian regime as the one method by which they could secure their national unity and their natural rights, at a fearful price in the destruction of individual freedom at home and in the return to power politics in international affairs.

The novelist John Buchan, the then Lord Tweedsmuir, who was serving as Governor-General of Canada, wrote to his sister, 'I do not myself quite see what there is to fuss about. Austria will be much more comfortable, economically, under Germany's wing. That should have been done long ago in the Versailles Treaty. The chief trouble will be if there is any real threat to Czechoslovakia; but there again, I think, the frontier should be rectified. Surely the Versailles agreement was the most half-witted thing ever perpetrated.'

The Archbishop of Canterbury believed that despite the 'shock' of the German action, there were nonetheless 'some considerations which make for calmness and balance of judgement' (House of Lords, Hansard, 29 March 1938, col. 448). The provisions of the Treaty of Versailles were 'vindictive and arbitrary, and could not possibly be permanent'. In his view, 'The union of Germany and Austria sooner or later was inevitable,' and despite the manner in which 'the thing was done, the fact that the thing has been done, and done finally, may bring some measure of stability to Europe' (ibid., cols 448–9). The Archbishop quoted from a letter which he had received from an Austrian artist, welcoming the German annexation, and also reminded their lordships that the Roman Catholic hierarchy, 'no doubt with their own reservations, have completely and fully accepted the union.'

At the BBC there was internal criticism over their handling of the Anschluss. BBC staff were not sure whether the Foreign Office 'ban' which was imposed on the extent of news reports on the Anschluss was formal, or whether the BBC had censored itself in response to some hint. A few days before the Anschluss, the Director-General of the BBC, Lord Reith, had attended one of Ribbentrop's parties at the German Embassy, and had asked the Ambassador to tell Hitler that the BBC was not anti-Nazi. Early in 1938, the BBC cancelled a broadcast by the Labour MP Josiah Wedgwood when he refused to delete attacks on the dictators' policy as one of 'persecution, militancy and inhumanity'.

Those who did protest at the Anschluss were left in no doubt about Number 10's anger at their attitude. Lewis's department stores launched an immediate boycott of German goods, at the instigation of their head, Lord Woolton (later chairman of the Conservative Party). But Woolton was summoned to Downing Street and, as he later recalled, received a 'high-powered rocket'. Sir Horace Wilson told him that the Prime Minister strongly disapproved of his action and that he had 'no right to interfere' in the foreign policy of the country. Woolton told Wilson that he was unrepentant, and the boycott was maintained.

In the Commons emergency debate, however, the Monday after the Anschluss weekend, Chamberlain made public his anger at the German action. The 'methods adopted' called for the 'severest condemnation', and were a 'profound shock to all who are interested in the preservation of European peace'. Chamberlain also announced that the Government would consider increased rearmament in the light of events in Europe.

The Prime Minister's firmness appeared to reassure his critics in the House. The opposition parties were in the difficult position of attacking the manner in which the Anschluss was achieved, rather than the union of Austria and Germany itself – they were aware that had self-determination been applied to Austria after 1919, the Anschluss might have come a good deal sooner, before Hitler came to power. There was little that any British Government could have done to resist Hitler's swift action. Their demands for a reassertion of the principles of the League and Covenant were unlikely to make a jot of difference to the fate of Austria.

Criticism from the Government side of the House was less effective than it had been three weeks earlier in the debates following Eden's resignation. Eden himself was out of the country, having returned to the Riviera to resume his holiday. As he later recounted, it was while 'reading the French newspapers and listening to the Vienna wireless that one day

*A Class Divided*

when I tuned in, I heard Hitler's entry into Linz, the hypnotised chants of the crowd, *"Ein Volk, ein Reich, ein Führer,"* and Hitler's frenzied speech proclaiming the Anschluss.'

Churchill, however, delivered what Harold Nicolson described as 'the speech of his life'. He was in no doubt about the seriousness of the situation: 'The gravity of the event of 11 March cannot be exaggerated. Europe is confronted with a programme of aggression, nicely calculated and timed, unfolding stage by stage . . .' (Hansard, 14 March 1938, col. 95). He believed that in time the British Government and the House of Commons would come to lead the resistance to Hitler's 'overweening encroachment'. But there was no time to waste:

> If we were to delay, if we were to go on waiting upon events for a considerable period of time, how much should we throw away of resources which are now available for our security and for the maintenance of peace? How many friends would be alienated, how many potential allies should we see go, one by one, down the grisly gulf, how many times will bluff succeed, until behind bluff ever gathering forces have accumulated reality? (Ibid.)

The Anschluss represented a major strategic advance for Hitler, giving him access to a lengthy stretch of the Danube, opening up the route to south-eastern Europe, driving a wedge between the powers of the Little Entente (Yugoslavia, Rumania and Czechoslovakia), and isolating Czechoslovakia. Churchill maintained that Britain and the other democracies could not afford to accept the Anschluss, and called for urgent discussions with allies, and through the League of Nations.

Churchill's usually reliable ally, Boothby, had again spoken in support of Chamberlain, as he had in the debate on Eden's resignation. Churchill turned on Boothby for having 'jeered at the expression "collective security" ', a view shared by most Conservative backbenchers. Churchill retorted, 'What is there ridiculous about collective security? The only thing that is ridiculous about it is that we have not got it' (ibid., col. 99). The strategy which 'might even now arrest this approaching war' was a Grand Alliance, 'assembled around Great Britain and France in a solemn treaty for mutual defence'.

The Anschluss had an even more profound effect on another senior Conservative backbencher. Leo Amery had previously argued that Britain should look to its empire and avoid any European commitments, but Hitler's annexation of Austria changed his mind. His diary entry on the day that the Germans crossed the Austrian border reveals his shock:

The news of Austria's collapse came to me as a terrible blow. . . .
But what is the value of an ideal if you are not prepared to defend it,
and so Austria has fallen and with it, for a long while I fear, any idea
of European unity on free co-operative lines. . . . For us it means
facing realities and much as I dislike, from the Empire point of view,
a policy of Continental entanglements . . .

In the Commons, Amery mourned the passing of 'A small nation,
standing for something rather unique in the world, the last remnant of that
old tradition of a united Western Christendom . . .' and told MPs, 'We
have to look to those who will stand with us for the peace of Europe.' But,
unlike Churchill, he was dismissive of the League. He did, however, agree
that Britain should seek to establish better relations with Italy – a view
which he shared with Churchill, and which put both of them at odds with
Eden.

The pressing question after Anschluss was how Britain should tackle
the problem of Czechoslovakia. Chamberlain had been at pains in his
speech to reassure MPs about Germany's attitude: 'I am informed that
Field-Marshal Göring on 11th March gave a general assurance to the
Czech Minister in Berlin – an assurance which he expressly renewed later
on behalf of Herr Hitler – that it would be the earnest endeavour of
the German Government to improve German–Czech relations' (ibid.,
cols 50–1).

But few were any longer convinced by any assurances from the German
Chancellor. At the end of his Commons speech, Amery addressed the
problem of Czechoslovakia head on, and asked,

What are we going to do about that? One thing that will mean war is
for us to go on havering, half encouraging Czechoslovakia, half
encouraging France with the idea that we stand behind her, half
encouraging Germany to think that we shall run out, and then at the
last moment, in a revulsion of sentiment, coming in for what may be
the greatest disaster that Europe and the world have known. Let us
either make up our minds that we must stand out, and let everybody
concerned know it, or let us say to France, Czechoslovakia and
Germany, in language as plain and simple as we can make it, that the
first German soldier or aeroplane to cross the Czech border will bring
the whole might of this country against Germany. (Ibid., col. 86)

# CHAPTER TEN

# 'THE MICAWBER STRAIN'

We have lost our will-power, since our will-power is divided.
People of the governing classes think only of their own
fortunes, which means hatred of the Reds. This creates a
perfectly artificial but at present most effective bond between
ourselves and Hitler. Our class interests, on both sides, cut
across our national interests.

(Harold Nicolson, Diary, 6 June 1938)

In the immediate aftermath of the Anschluss, the British Foreign Office
urgently reassessed the Czech crisis. The Permanent Secretary, Sir
Alexander Cadogan, was worried about the attitude of some of his closest
colleagues, confiding in his diary on 12 March,

We are helpless as regards Austria – that is finished. We *may* be
helpless as regards Czechoslovakia, etc. *That* is what I want to get
considered. Must we have a death-struggle with Germany again? Or
can we stand aside? Former does no one any good. Will the latter be
fatal? I'm inclined to think not. But I shall have to fight Van [Sir
Robert Vansittart, former Permanent Secretary], Sargent [Assistant
Under-Secretary] and all the forces of evil. God give me courage. So
far we've not done wrong.

British perceptions of the Czech crisis were shaped before Chamberlain
became Prime Minister. From early 1937, when Eden was Foreign
Secretary, the British Government were urging Prague to meet the
grievances of the sizeable Sudeten German minority in Bohemia – the
Sudeten Germans numbered more than 3 million, in a total population of
15 million.

At the Czech parliamentary elections in May 1935, Henlein's Sudeten
German Party – Nazis by another name – had emerged as the single most
popular party, winning almost 1.25 million votes. Henlein had visited
London twice during 1935, and again in October 1937. He even impressed
arch anti-appeasers like Winston Churchill and Sir Robert Vansittart.
In May 1936 Jan Masaryk, then Czech Minister in London, said that

he regarded Henlein as 'an amiable and possibly useful person'.

By 1937, Henlein was demanding autonomy for the German areas. The Czech President, Beneš, could not concede, since Sudeten autonomy would lead to the break-up of Czechoslovakia. Nor could he be responsible for allowing a part of the country to pass under totalitarian control.

Even before the Anschluss, Prague had sought protection against the growing Nazi menace across her border. In 1935, the Czech Government had signed a defensive treaty with France, and agreed a mutual assistance pact with the Soviet Union. This committed the Russians to fight any invasion on condition that the French had rallied to Czechoslovakia's defence. The Czechs also possessed a modern armaments industry and could put thirty divisions into the field after mobilisation. From 1936, they began strengthening their border defences.

In the secret 'Hossbach memorandum' of November 1937, Hitler had set the annexation of Austria and Czechoslovakia as his prime foreign policy objectives. That same month, when the French Prime Minister and Foreign Secretary visited London, they found both Chamberlain and Eden opposed to any British commitment to defend Czechoslovakia. British opinion, they were told, would never support it. Eden suggested to his counterpart, Delbos, that Britain and France 'might concert with Germany in seeking to find a satisfactory solution to the problem'.

In the immediate wake of the Anschluss, Cadogan was disturbed to find that his political masters, Chamberlain and Halifax, had apparently undergone a *volte face*. They were 'rather on the line of Winston's "Grand Alliance",' which would commit Britain militarily on the Continent, and would inhibit her freedom to reach settlements through direct negotiation. Cadogan himself emphasised that the Sudetens were Germanic. Many Austrians, after all, had welcomed the Anschluss, and 'the same *may* be said of the Sudetendeutsch.' Annexation of the Sudeten areas therefore scarcely seemed a pretext for going to war. As Cadogan later wrote to Sir Nevile Henderson, the British Ambassador in Berlin, 'I can't view the Reich's absorption of Germans with much horror.'

Cadogan did not consider that Hitler's annexation of the Sudetenland or even the whole of Czechoslovakia would damage British interests. German political domination seemed unlikely since it would have to depend on the disparate nationalities in the region. Nor did London have any reason to worry at Germany's economic domination of Central Europe – a view which blithely ignored Germany's use of her economic and trade policies as tools of her foreign policy, and ran counter to advice from the Northern and Southern Departments in the Foreign Office.

As far as Cadogan was concerned, going to war would not solve anything – the previous war and its peace settlement had brought about Europe's present problems. He concluded, 'If we stand aside from Central Europe, we and the French may lose face, but the reverse may steel us to efforts that may make good some of the present deficiencies.'

In his diary, Cadogan became a self-confessed Micawber. 'We *must* not precipitate a conflict now – we shall be smashed. It *may* not be better later, but anything may happen (I recognise the Micawber strain). . . .'

Such was the shock of the Anschluss that it sparked rumours that the National Government was contemplating genuine coalition. Even Churchill appeared to believe the rumours. He told Nicolson on 16 March that he was biding his time, 'in the hope that the negotiations going on between Chamberlain, Attlee and Sinclair for a formula of policy that will command the assent of the whole House have either failed or come to fruition'.

On Friday, 18 March, in a speech to the Tory ladies of Stockton, Harold Macmillan stated that he favoured 'a widening of the national basis of the Government by the introduction of some of the Liberals who left it before and some of the Labour leaders'. He also wanted 'the inclusion of a great outside figure like Mr Winston Churchill'. But an indication that thinking in Whitehall was running strongly against any such change came from an unlikely source.

On 19 March, *The Times* reported a constituency speech by a junior minister, Alan Lennox-Boyd. He had stated that 'he could countenance nothing more ridiculous than a guarantee that the frontiers of Czechoslovakia should not be violated when half the people in that country could not be relied upon to be loyal to the Government of the day; and from what he knew of Mr. Chamberlain, he did not think he would make a move to give a guarantee of that kind.' The young Minister added that Germany 'could absorb Czechoslovakia, and Great Britain would remain secure'.

It was Lennox-Boyd's infelicitous choice of words and candid assessment of British self-interest, rather than the sentiments he expressed, which embarrassed the Government. In the ensuing furore, the opposition claimed that the Germans had broadcast reports of the speech to the Sudeten Germans in Czechoslovakia. Lennox-Boyd's alleged remarks even became the subject of a debate in the Commons on 21 March. The Prime Minister denied that the speech had been intended as a stalking-horse for the Government and argued that the junior Minister had been misreported. Lennox-Boyd apologised for his conduct and claimed that he had not been speaking for the Government.

On the same day that Lennox-Boyd was delivering his speech, the

Cabinet's Foreign Policy Committee met to consider the Czech crisis. The opinions expressed in private by senior ministers show that their subordinate was in fact giving his constituents a remarkable insight into Government thinking. Sir Thomas Inskip, Minister for the Co-ordination of Defence, observed that Czechoslovakia was 'an unstable unit in Central Europe' and that 'he could see no reason why we should take any steps to maintain such a unit in being.' The Chancellor of the Exchequer, Sir John Simon, thought that 'Czechoslovakia was a modern and very artificial creation with no real roots in the past.'

Although Oliver Stanley, President of the Board of Trade, favoured a commitment to Czechoslovakia, he nonetheless observed that it was 'impossible to argue that the preservation of Czechoslovakia was a vital interest of Great Britain'. And William Ormsby-Gore, the Colonial Secretary, another less than enthusiastic follower of the Prime Minister, commented that 'any specific commitment to Czechoslovakia would split public opinion from top to bottom.' The Foreign Secretary, Lord Halifax, 'could not credit' that Hitler had a 'lust for conquest on a Napoleonic scale'. Halifax also abandoned his brief flirtation with any notion of a Grand Alliance, warning that 'the more closely we associated ourselves with France and Russia the more we produced on German minds the impression that we were plotting to encircle Germany.'

Later the same day, Cadogan wrote in his diary that 'F.P.C. [Foreign Policy Committee] unanimous that Czechoslovakia is not worth the bones of a single British Grenadier. And they're quite right too!'

The day after the meeting of the Cabinet's Foreign Policy Committee, the Government received a proposal from the Soviet Foreign Minister, Litvinov. The Soviets were calling for an international conference on Czechoslovakia and 'collective actions' by all countries, 'especially the Great Powers', to preserve world peace. Yet Chamberlain was actively distrustful of Britain's potential partners in such an alliance, France and the Soviet Union, the two countries with whom Czechoslovakia had negotiated defensive pacts.

British distrust of the French was deeply ingrained. There was considerable doubt that the French would in fact be prepared to fight to defend their Czech allies. Britain should clearly be wary of committing herself to take on Hitler alone.

Nor did it help with a Conservative Prime Minister, who was almost vindictively anti-socialist, that a left-inclined government was in office in Paris. In March 1938, Chamberlain confided that he was having to deal with 'a French government in which one cannot have the slightest confidence and which I suspect to be in closish touch with our Opposition'.

Chamberlain was concerned at the capacity of any country to withstand an onslaught by the Luftwaffe. At his first meeting with the French as Prime Minister in London in November 1937, he lectured his counterpart Chautemps on the 'lamentable state' of the French Air Force. The rapid growth of the Luftwaffe alarmed British ministers and officials, since they feared its ability to deliver a knock-out blow, whereas it was principally designed to support German troops.

Above all, the Prime Minister was loath to risk sacrificing the chance of closer contacts with the Italians for the sake of a closer alliance with the French. Paris and Rome had been at loggerheads over the Spanish Civil War and were ideological enemies. But if Britain could negotiate with the Italians over Spain and the Mediterranean, both London and Paris would be free to concentrate on Central Europe, and there was the prospect that Rome would take a neutral, or possibly sympathetic, line on the Czech crisis.

Yet any doubts about the French seemed trifling by comparison with Chamberlain's reservations about the Soviet Union. Like the vast majority of Conservatives, he was deeply anti-Soviet. His rejection of Litvinov's proposed conference on Czechoslovakia ruffled few feathers on the Conservative benches.

Chamberlain felt that Moscow would welcome a conflict between Britain and Germany since the Soviet Union could only gain from war between her capitalist, imperialist enemies. As he wrote to his sister Ida the day after receiving Litvinov's proposal, the Russians were 'steadily and cunningly pulling all the strings behind the scenes to get us involved with Germany (our Secret Service doesn't spend all its time looking out the window)'.

The Prime Minister feared that any attempt to build an alliance with the Soviet Union would drive Hitler further away from Britain. Crucially in Chamberlain's view, this would scupper any hope of averting war through direct negotiation with Hitler.

There were also more practical problems militating against a closer alliance with the Soviet Union. The Red Army was being crippled by Stalin's purges, which were wiping out its most experienced and senior ranks, and was no longer capable of tipping the military balance of power against Germany. In any event, the Red Army could not come to Czechoslovakia's aid without crossing Poland or Rumania. The Poles refused to countenance Russian troops on their soil, and it was doubtful that the Rumanians would allow them to pass through.

Chamberlain gave the military considerations as his principal reasons against offering a guarantee to Czechoslovakia. In his letter to Ida on 20 March he wrote,

You have only to look at the map to see that nothing France or we could do could possibly save Czechoslovakia from being overrun by Germans, if they wanted to do it. The Austrian frontier is practically open; the great Skoda munition works are within easy bombing distance of the German aerodromes, the railways all pass through German territory, Russia is 100 miles away. Therefore we could not help Czechoslovakia – she would simply be a pretext for going to war with Germany. That we could not think of unless we had a reasonable prospect of being able to beat her to her knees in a reasonable time, and of that I see no sign. I have therefore abandoned any idea of giving guarantees to Czechoslovakia, or the French in connection with her obligations to that country.

The next day the Chiefs of Staff appeared to vindicate Chamberlain's assessment. In their study of the 'Military Implications of German Aggression against Czechoslovakia', they concluded that nothing could be done to protect Czechoslovakia from defeat. War with Germany would mean war also with Italy and Japan – in November 1936, Germany had formed an 'axis' with Italy and signed the Anti-Comintern Pact with Japan. A year later, Italy joined the Pact. Britain was 'at a stage of rearmament when we are not yet ready for war'.

As far as the majority of the Cabinet were concerned, the Chiefs of Staff report was conclusive. The politicians added their own gloss, concluding that opinion at home and among the Dominion Governments would be opposed to any British commitment. Czechoslovakia and France would have to be persuaded of the need to reach a settlement 'more acceptable to Germany'. The Foreign Secretary, Halifax, told the Cabinet, 'it was a disagreeable business which had to be done as pleasantly as possible.'

Only a few ministers queried the proposed policy. They were concerned that Hitler's intentions were not questioned. The Foreign Office proposals were 'tantamount to an invitation to Germany to take the next step in her programme'. Since 'we could not afford to stand aside and let France go under', it would be better 'to recognize the inevitable and plunge in at once to France's aid'. There was criticism of the Chiefs of Staff report (which had only been submitted on the eve of the Cabinet meeting), since the Chiefs had been 'instructed to leave Russia out of the calculation'. Germany's present military strength was possibly over-estimated, whereas in two years' time she might be better prepared for a long war. The consequences of the fall of Czechoslovakia were not considered, yet this might entail 'a year or two hence' a significant shift in the balance of power in Central and Eastern Europe. By then the other small countries in the region 'might all have collapsed before German aggression'. In short, 'disadvantageous as might be the circumstances today for intervention, they would be still more so tomorrow.' But the critics in the Cabinet were in a small minority.

Behind the scenes at the House of Commons, the younger Conservative dissidents who began to meet regularly after Eden's resignation – 'the Insurgents' as they were dubbed by the whips, and later 'the Glamour Boys' – were busily plotting wide-reaching changes in the Government.

A few weeks earlier, Chips Channon, a devoted Chamberlainite had been appointed Parliamentary Private Secretary to Rab Butler at the Foreign Office. On 17 March, he noted in his diary, 'The H. of C. is humming with intrigue today, and the so-called "Insurgents" are rushing about, very over-excited. They want to bring back Anthony Eden and their Shadow Cabinet is alleged to include Lloyd George, Winston and Eden.'

Nicolson also noted Churchill's comment that if Chamberlain's reported talks with the other party leaders did not produce 'a clear statement' he would 'refuse the whip and take about 50 people with him'. The young Tory Ronald Cartland later told Hugh Dalton that about forty Tories had been prepared to vote against the Government after the Anschluss 'in favour of some alternative combination'.

The difficulty lay in finding 'some alternative combination'. According to Claud Cockburn's satirical magazine *The Week*, the dissenters had prepared a list for an alternative Cabinet, which would comprise twelve Tories, ten Liberals and two Labour – the so-called '12–10–2 Government'.

But in the Commons the Prime Minister's skilful presentation in the debate on 24 March meant that any criticism was muted. Chamberlain exploited Conservative fears of Soviet intervention, and bluntly dismissed the Litvinov proposal for collective action. The 'inevitable result' would be 'to aggravate the tendency toward the establishment of exclusive groups of nations, which must . . . be inimical to the prospects of European peace'. Chamberlain's flirtation with a Grand Alliance had been short-lived. He spoke of Britain helping the French if France was at war, but was careful to give no formal commitment. He mollified most critics by saying that rearmament would be speeded up, along with an expansion of the air force and anti-aircraft defences.

One of the few critics to speak out during the debate was Churchill, who argued that it was no longer any use for the Government to operate on a peacetime footing: 'But is this peace in which we are living? Is it not war without cannon firing?' (Hansard, 24 March 1938, col. 1453). A much closer Anglo-French alliance was the cornerstone of any policy for countering Hitler's aggressive intentions: 'The present rulers of Germany

*Neville Chamberlain taking characteristic care to brief the press during his shuttle-diplomacy with Hitler, September 1938. Lord Halifax, the Foreign Secretary, listens anxiously.*

*Hyde Park, London, 28 September 1938. Trenches were hastily dug in parks and open spaces as rudimentary air-raid shelters in anticipation of heavy bombing by the Luftwaffe.*

(Above) *Winston Churchill with Brendan Bracken, one of his few associates on the backbenches throughout the 1930s.*

(Left) *Anthony Eden and Sir Samuel Hoare on their way to an emergency Cabinet meeting during the Abyssinian crisis, 1935. Hoare was Foreign Secretary, and Eden, Minister for League of Nations Affairs.*

*Ernest Bevin (far left) and Walter Citrine, the union leaders whose support for sanctions against Italy forced the resignation of the pacifist George Lansbury (above) as leader of the Labour Party in October 1935.*

*Buck de la Warr, leader of the National Labour Party in Chamberlain's Cabinet, with Labour Party leaders Hugh Dalton and Clem Attlee, then in opposition.*

*The Duchess of Atholl* (above, left), *nicknamed 'Red Kitty' for supporting the Republicans in the Spanish Civil War; Sir John Simon* (above, right), *one of Neville Chamberlain's most trusted colleagues; senior Tories Leo Amery* (below, left) *and Sir Austen Chamberlain* (below, right) *criticised the Government's foreign policy.*

*Sympathisers of Hitler's regime, Lord and Lady Redesdale and their daughter Unity Mitford, with Dr Fitz-Randolph of the German Embassy, at a meeting of the Anglo-German Fellowship.*

*The Cable Street riots, October 1936. Mosley's Blackshirts planned a provocative march through the Jewish quarters of London's East End, but anti-Fascist demonstrators barricaded the streets.*

PRESS CONTROL? WHY CERTAINLY, RIB, OLD BOY."

*Low's comment on the Government's efforts to prevent any criticism of the Nazi regime in the British media. The Foreign Secretary, Lord Halifax, does the goose step with Ribbentrop and the pro-German Marquis of Londonderry.*

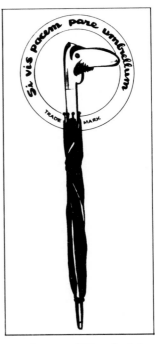

*Two images of Chamberlain: the expert angler returning from a day's fishing on Loch Ness, and Low's 'Appeasement Umbrella'.*

*Diplomats in Downing Street.* (Left) *Lord Halifax, Foreign Secretary, and Sir Robert Vansittart, Chief Diplomatic Adviser, leave after a meeting with Chamberlain as the Czech crisis flares, August 1938.*

(Below) *A year later, Sir Nevile Henderson, British Ambassador in Berlin, and Sir Alec Cadogan, Permanent Secretary at the Foreign Office, arrive for talks at Number 10 as war looms.*

*A. D. Lindsay, Master of Balliol College, Oxford, with his wife, campaigning as the anti-Munich candidate during the Oxford City by-election, October 1938.*

*Geoffrey Dawson, editor of* The Times, *with his deputy, Robert Barrington Ward, at Printing House Square. The paper's support for appeasement ended only when Hitler's troops occupied Prague in March 1939.*

will hesitate long before they attack the British Empire and the French Republic if those are woven together for defence purposes into a very powerful unit. . . .' (Ibid, col. 1445.)

As Churchill moved to the peroration of his speech, he delivered one of his most famous criticisms of appeasement:

> I have watched this famous island descending incontinently, fecklessly, the stairway which leads to a dark gulf. It is a fine broad stairway at the beginning, but after a bit the carpet ends. A little farther on there are only flagstones, and a little farther on still these break beneath your feet.
>
> . . . if mortal catastrophe should overtake the British Nation and the British Empire, historians a thousand years hence will still be baffled by the mystery of our affairs. They will never understand how it was that a victorious nation, with everything in hand, suffered themselves to be brought low, and to cast away all that they had gained by measureless sacrifice and absolute victory – gone with the wind!
>
> Now the victors are vanquished, and those who threw down their arms in the field and sued for an armistice are striding on to world mastery. . . . (Ibid., col. 1454.)

Despite these criticisms Churchill acknowledged that Chamberlain's had been 'a very fine speech'. There was no vote at the end of the debate. Talk of an immediate Tory rebellion temporarily faded away.

One of the strongest critics within the Cabinet, Duff Cooper, rated Chamberlain's speech 'a great success', on the grounds that 'Without saying so definitely, he quite clearly implied that if France went to war we should go too. That was all that I wanted.'

Chamberlain's performance won him some of his best notices from the press. Praise was not confined to the columns of Conservative-inclined papers. In the *New Statesman and Nation*, the economist John Maynard Keynes urged that Prague should 'at least attempt to negotiate with Germany a reasonable solution to the problem of the Sudeten Germans, even if this means a rectification of the Bohemian frontier. Racial frontiers are safer and better today than geophysical ones. . . .' The *Manchester Guardian* acknowledged that 'Mr. Chamberlain has overcome the enemies in his own camp', although its editorial was more critical, suggesting that 'at best Mr. Chamberlain has only half a policy.'

The Prime Minister was thus able to accompany his wife and the Cadogans for a weekend party at Cliveden in good spirits, where he would be among friends and sympathisers. His luck was in. He won the after-dinner game of musical chairs.

The twin pillars of Chamberlain's diplomacy were in place. Britain would 'keep Germany guessing', while at the same time strong pressure was exerted on the Czechs to accept a settlement. At April's Anglo-French talks in London, the French were told that they should not strengthen the Czechs' resolve to stand firm.

With an active and determined Prime Minister, Britain was taking the lead on the Czech crisis. There was to be no room for either the League of Nations, which Chamberlain had finally discounted after the Anschluss, or for international alliances. Cadogan was later to describe Chamberlain as having 'an almost instinctive contempt for the Americans and the Russians. . . . another possible drawback was that he was, in a sense, a man of one-track mind. If, after much reflection no doubt, he decided on a certain move or line of policy, nothing would affect him.'

The sharpening division in society over the Czech crisis had an immediate impact on Churchill. After Eden's resignation, the *Daily Express* accused him of promoting a 'violent, foolish and dangerous' campaign designed to take Britain into war. After the Anschluss, the editor of the *Evening Standard* terminated Churchill's contract for a regular column because his views on foreign policy were at odds with the paper's line (though this did not stop the *Standard* continuing to print Low's cartoons). Churchill negotiated a contract with Lord Camrose, owner of the more sympathetic *Daily Telegraph*.

Churchill's son, Randolph, became increasingly vituperative in his denunciations of his father's opponents. At one dinner party, his victim was Beverley Baxter, an editor of the *Daily Express* favoured by Beaverbrook. A drunken Randolph went through his repertoire of abuse about the appeasers, and then turned on Baxter. 'You wretched little Canadian piano-tuner', he mocked, continuing to repeat the gibe. Baxter's wife eventually persuaded her husband that they should leave rather than suffer the persistent insults.

At the Foreign Office there was deep concern at Churchill's proposed visit to France. The British Ambassador in Paris, Sir Eric Phipps, wrote privately to Cadogan, hoping that Churchill would not unduly excite the French. Phipps assured Cadogan that he would do his best 'to calm them down'. Some British ministers were critical of the hospitality which Churchill received from the British Embassy in Paris. But Halifax and Chamberlain had felt that it was right 'to show hospitality to him [Churchill] and generally keep an eye on his movements'.

On 28 March 1938, Henlein visited Hitler in Berlin. The Nazi press had subjected the Prague Government to increasingly hostile criticism for their alleged treatment of the Sudeten Germans and German nationals, following Czechoslovakia's pact with the Soviet Union. Henlein grasped the gist of Hitler's advice: 'We must always demand so much that we can never be satisfied.' It was a summary which earned Hitler's approval.

At Carlsbad on 24 April, Henlein made eight demands, secretly planned beforehand with the German Foreign Ministry. These included recognition of the Sudeten Germans as a distinct legal entity within the state and the right to hold and disseminate Nazi beliefs – demands which would plainly be unacceptable to Prague.

As the Czech crisis deepened, traditional party loyalties in Britain were again under stress, and society was increasingly divided. The former Foreign Secretary, Anthony Eden, was tormented by the sight of Britain being torn apart over foreign policy. He confided to Harold Nicolson, who wrote, 'He is terribly worried by the fact that Foreign Affairs are splitting the country into two hostile and even embittered groups. He is determined to do everything to prevent such a split.'

In April, the new Minister at the Foreign Office, Rab Butler, experienced the growing divide in an unexpected quarter. He and his wife were bidden to spend a Saturday night at Windsor Castle with King George VI and Queen Elizabeth. Butler's biographer, Anthony Howard, reveals that after the royal couple had gone to bed, the King's Private Secretary, Sir Alexander Hardinge, seized his chance with Butler to attack the 'lack of morality' in the Government's foreign policy. Butler responded that 'it was interesting to have such a definite criticism', and proceeded 'to answer back and to inquire whether he really felt there was anything in Labour's foreign policy'. Apparently, the next morning Butler found Hardinge 'much calmer'.

At the Palace of Westminster, Tory critics of Chamberlain found the going very rough. Government loyalists struck at the backbench Foreign Affairs Committee, open to all MPs taking the National Government whip. In early April Harold Nicolson eventually succumbed to the pressures on him to resign his post as vice-chairman. The loyalist MPs put the chairman Paul Emrys-Evans, his close ally, 'through the hoops also, asking whether he is "pro-Chamberlain" or "pro-Eden" '. New officers were elected after Easter.

During the spring and summer of 1938, the younger backbench critics lacked a leader around whom they could group. Most of them remained suspicious of Churchill's judgement, some shared the view that his time was past and others were wary of Churchill's close public association with the opposition parties.

Churchill was able, however, to evoke a unique response in the country. Following his speech the night before in Neville Chamberlain's home town, Birmingham, Churchill visited the Austin aeroplane 'Shadow' factory. He was accompanied by the young Conservative dissident and local MP, Ronnie Cartland. As Cartland told his sister Barbara:

> The men were thrilled to see him. I've never seen such enthusiasm. It's not surprising – he has such presence – such personality – also the man in the street realizes that he has been right in everything he has said since 1933. Those in high places say he's finished – I don't believe it. He has a following in the country far bigger than those in Westminster think.

Yet the pressures of Party loyalty were formidable, and were able to reassert themselves, even at the expense of old friendships. The Earl of Derby, with one son (Oliver) in the Cabinet and another (Edward) just below Cabinet rank, backed out as chairman of Churchill's Manchester meeting at the last moment. In his letter to Churchill he wrote, 'If, being head of the Conservative Party here, I intervened now, I would give the matter more prominence and more publicity than it would otherwise get.'

Eden, whose resignation in February 1938 had sparked the intensification of political infighting, represented a potential focus for the dissenters. Eden was certainly no personal admirer of Chamberlain. In April, one of Eden's closest political friends, and his former Parliamentary Private Secretary at the Foreign Office, Jim Thomas, told Harold Nicolson that Eden 'regards Chamberlain as having been definitely treacherous'.

During this period, Eden was in frequent contact with Churchill's old adversary, Baldwin. Eden's biographer, Robert Rhodes James, has revealed that 'Baldwin warned him [Eden] against getting too close to Churchill, as he would be perceived as a follower rather than a leader, to keep his own counsel, to bide his time, and to take his case to the country.' Eden not only kept his distance from Churchill, he was at pains not to be seen as the leader of any 'anti-Government cabal'.

But the dissenters not only had a leadership problem. They also faced a dilemma which was inherent in their calls for British rearmament. They argued that the Government should have done more earlier, and that more still needed to be done. But it was one thing to argue that the Government were culpable for their failure to rearm in the face of the growing Nazi menace: quite another to urge that the Government should take a tougher line with Germany.

The more the critics highlighted Britain's lack of preparedness for war and contrasted it with the military prowess of Germany, the more they helped bolster Chamberlain's case. Negotiated settlements seemed a safer bet to the international crisis than entering into commitments which, on the critics' own admission, Britain was ill equipped to undertake.

Harold Nicolson discussed the problem with his National Labour colleague, Malcolm MacDonald, one of Chamberlain's critics in the Cabinet. MacDonald told Nicolson, 'we are not really strong enough to risk a war. It would mean the massacre of women and children in the streets of London. No Government could possibly risk a war when our anti-aircraft defences are in so farcical a condition.'

The crisis caused by Eden's resignation and the annexation of Austria should have been an unqualified boon to the fortunes of the Labour Party. But they were beset by difficulties and disagreements of their own. They were conscious of the problems presented by their reliance on collective security through the League of Nations. In April 1938, Labour's National Advisory Committee on International Relations expressed doubts about 'Russia's real strength and real loyalty to the League's cause', and added that 'Without Russia's power the League's sums won't come out.'

There was a sense of despair and defeatism. Hugh Dalton noted that Kingsley Martin, the editor of the *New Statesman and Nation*, 'felt that things had gone so far that to plan armed resistance to the dictators was useless. If there was a war we should lose it. We should therefore seek for the most peaceful means of letting them gradually get what they wanted.'

Most important, the revival of the talk about a Popular Front reopened old divisions within the Party. Attlee, Greenwood and Morrison apparently showed interest in the rumours of a Churchill–Eden government, but Morrison was reported to have received a 'private snubbing' from colleagues when he hinted that Labour might join a 'Progressive Opposition' to the Government.

Many on the left were openly dismissive of the British variant of a movement which had, however briefly, given socialists a role in government in France and Spain. George Orwell wrote in February 1938 that 'In England the Popular Front is only an idea, but it has already produced the nauseous spectacle of bishops, Communists, cocoa magnates, publishers, duchesses and Labour MPs marching arm in arm to the tune of "Rule Britannia".'

The Labour Party had been uncompromising in their opposition to a Popular Front, not least because the Communist Party had campaigned strongly for the idea since 1935. The Communists were supported in their campaign by the Left Book Club, founded in 1936, and to all intents and purposes a front organisation. Any idea of a Popular Front was anathema to Transport House, which was determined to maintain Labour's hard-won and comparatively recent status as the official opposition. It did not want to see local Labour organisations, particularly in areas where they had fought to become the main challengers to the Conservatives, give any assistance to anyone other than official Labour Party candidates.

In the view of the Labour leadership, a Popular Front was both a snare and a delusion. There was virtually no chance of ousting Chamberlain's Government in the foreseeable future and certainly not before the next election. A Popular Front in the meantime could only be to the benefit of Labour's principal rivals on the left and in the centre, the Communists and the Liberals.

In April, however, the left on the National Executive, Stafford Cripps, Ellen Wilkinson, D.N. Pritt and Harold Laski, called for a special conference on the international situation and argued for a Popular Front. The Party was again deeply split. Labour's own newspaper the *Daily Herald* devoted a week of leading articles to attacks on the Popular Front idea.

Faced with this new division, the Party's line appeared to become more accommodating. A new policy document, *Labour and the Popular Front*, indicated some sympathy for the idea. Although the notion that a Popular Front might bring electoral advantage was dismissed, there was recognition that a sizeable Conservative backbench rebellion would create 'a new situation'. But little had really changed since the collapse of the earlier moves to establish a British Popular Front. The pull of party loyalties and genuine differences on other issues remained insurmountable.

Divisions in the country were made worse by both Chamberlain's policy and his style of government. As the international crisis deepened, the Prime Minister's response proved a major stumbling block to a greater sense of national unity.

Signing the Anglo-Italian accord on 16 April was regarded by Chamberlain as a significant step towards appeasing Mussolini. The Prime Minister's purpose was to split the Axis powers, ensuring that Italy would not support Germany over Czechoslovakia, and freeing both London and Paris from their worries in the Mediterranean. Under the terms of the accord, Rome agreed to reduce the number of Italian troops in Libya, who were a potential threat to Britain's position in North Africa and the Near East, and accepted a phased reduction of 'volunteers' in Spain. The *quid pro quo* was Britain's agreement to facilitate international recognition of Italian rule in Abyssinia.

The accord was not due to take immediate effect, but within weeks it became a severe embarrassment to Chamberlain. On 12 May Halifax dutifully proposed at the League of Nations that the way be cleared to grant recognition of Italian control in Abyssinia. This earned the Government opprobrium around the world and at home.

By way of returning the favour, at Genoa on 14 May, Il Duce waxed eloquent on the importance of Italy's friendship with Germany and poured scorn on the French. Italian attacks in Spain increased and British shipping came under fire. Hitler had visited Rome a week earlier, and was reassured that in the event of a German invasion of Czechoslovakia Mussolini would not involve Italy on either side.

Behind the scenes in Whitehall, a fierce argument was raging, yet again, over the level of Government defence spending. Despite Chamberlain's assurances to the Commons on 24 March of a renewed rearmament effort, at which Churchill had 'rejoiced', the Prime Minister set his face against extra defence spending – as it was, the Chancellor, Sir John Simon, increased income tax from 5 shillings to 5/6 in the pound in the 1938 Budget.

On 29 March Inskip instructed the three ministers for the armed forces that the acceleration of the rearmament programme must be achieved within the existing five-year defence budget. But the ministers for the army, navy and air force were each pressing for substantially larger estimates. Something, or someone, would have to give.

The army fared worst. The estimate of £347 million for the five-year period 1938–42 submitted by Hore-Belisha, the War Secretary, was pared by £70 million, after the Chancellor had originally sought savings of £82 million. Deep cuts were required in the sums allowed for equipment for the Territorial Army and for anti-aircraft personnel and weaponry.

The furious row over the navy estimates was unresolved for three months, and threw into sharp relief the very different assumptions on which the appeasers and the anti-appeasers based their arguments. The five-year estimate of £435 million from Duff Cooper, the First Lord of the Admiralty, had prompted Simon to suggest a cut of £80 million. In the paper which Cooper sent to Chamberlain, Simon and Inskip on 28 April, he launched a wholesale attack on the principle of 'rationing' the country's spending on defence.

Cooper argued that it was always better to err on the side of spending too much on defence, rather than too little. But his presentation was scarcely likely to appeal to the orthodox regime at Number 10 and the Treasury. Cooper maintained that if the Government misjudged what constituted an adequate level of defence spending, 'defeat in war and complete destruction' would be the result. But a mistake which led to overspending could only lead to 'severe embarrassment, heavy taxation, lowering of the standard of living, and reduction of the social services'.

Chamberlain clearly did not take the latter catalogue of risks at all lightly. He knew that he would have to face the electorate within a couple of years or so, and by the autumn of 1940 at the very latest. His foreign policy would enable his Government to square the circle – so he hoped – and thereby avoid having to choose between Cooper's two sets of risky alternatives. Agreement with the dictators would remove both the dangers of economic crisis caused by massive rearmament, and the risk of war itself. The puzzle is what Chamberlain thought would happen if, by some unhappy mischance, his policy of appeasement should fail.

During May, Cooper met Chamberlain, Simon and Inskip. As Cooper has related, this meeting 'resulted in a long and profitless argument which at moments became, on the Prime Minister's side, rather acrimonious. I cannot help irritating him.' There were further heated exchanges at Cabinet on 20 July, when Cooper lambasted the continued spending limits on the services, when there was a budget surplus of £20 million and income tax had been raised by a further sixpence. But it was Cooper's blunt political threat which won him the argument. He warned the Cabinet that if MPs thought 'all was not going well, and that, owing to financial considerations, the Government were rejecting the advice of their naval experts as to the minimum needed for security, there would be such a storm in the House of Commons that the Government could not hope to survive'. There were no prizes for guessing how MPs might find out that 'all was not going well'. After this bravura performance, the Admiralty eventually secured £410 million, only £25 million short of their original bid.

But the bloodiest battles of all were fought over the estimates for the air force. Swinton, the Minister for Air, demanded £567.5 million against the Treasury's offer of £505 million. The extra funds were deemed necessary to finance the RAF's 'Scheme L', which Swinton claimed would ensure that 'in two years' time we should be relatively stronger' and 'should not be at the mercy of Germany – as it might be said we were today – and we should possess a deterrent'. While the Cabinet sought a compromise, the RAF's Chief of Staff, Air Marshal Sir Cyril Newall, minuted Swinton that 'we are today in no position to resist any demand by Germany, and if we attempted to do so I believe we should be defeated by the knock-out blow. . . .'

The assessment of German air superiority was undoubtedly being exaggerated by this time, both by the Air Staff who had previously underestimated the threat, and outside the Government by Churchill. As we have observed, the Luftwaffe were incapable of delivering a knock-out blow. But the threat was thought to be real.

While the Cabinet were tussling over the RAF's budget, Nicolson raised the issue with Cadogan's Private Secretary at the Foreign Office, Gladwyn Jebb. Their talk, after lunch one May afternoon, occurred in the unlikely setting of the Embankment Gardens. Nicolson, Jebb and the Conservative backbencher Victor Cazalet strolled up and down, 'discussing what can possibly be done to avoid war' underneath Rodin's statue of the Burghers of Calais. 'Gladwyn feels that we must cut off any controversy at almost any price until our air-defences are in order,' Nicolson noted. 'He says that really the issue is one between losing something of our old magnificence and ceasing to be a Great Power. We have simply got to throw something to the wolves.'

Eventually the Cabinet granted Swinton extra funds for Scheme L, though only for the first two years of the five-year budget. Inskip was instrumental in 'front-loading' the programme in this way, in the hope that the policy of appeasement would work within two years' time, removing the need for any extra spending thereafter.

Providing finance for rearmament was, however, only part of the problem. Fulfilling Scheme L also depended on increasing Britain's industrial capacity. The Government was relying principally on co-operation with industry rather than compulsion.

The Government were prepared to build and equip the new 'Shadow' factories for aero-engines, which were run – at a profit – by private employers. At a time of high unemployment, there was little shortage of unskilled labour to work in them, but they were a cause of friction with the unions. As Jack Jones, then a union organiser, has commented, 'The employers were operating these ['Shadow'] factories on the basis of fat cost plus contracts, and sought to prevent the growth of trade unionism lest it rebounded on their parent factories.'

But there was a shortage of skilled labour, and this the Government made no attempt to tackle. On the union side, the AEU, the main union, steadfastly refused to accept any dilution of skilled labour, which was essential for full production.

At the time of the Anschluss Chamberlain did suggest consulting the unions. A meeting was arranged with the TUC General Council for late March 1938, and the unions' response to the Prime Minister's appeal for their goodwill at least left the door open for further talks. The AEU, however, remained intransigent in the face of any suggestion of reform. Their conservatism reflected fears about future job prospects for their members, rather than political opposition to Chamberlain. Without the prospect of sustained economic growth, they feared that their members would again face large-scale unemployment when the international crisis eased and the rearmament programme ended.

Yet Chamberlain would make no further effort to take the unions into his confidence. He would not countenance any direct Government intervention in the labour market, and feared that consulting them more fully and securing their agreement to end their restrictions on skilled labour would involve some *quid pro quo*.

Chamberlain's anxieties about the unions making demands in return for their co-operation was not far-fetched. Oliver Harvey noted in his diary in April 1938, that the former British Ambassador in France, Lord Tyrrell, was 'being very active and in touch with the union leaders . . .'. Apparently, Tyrrell advised them 'to insist on P.M. showing them rearmament figures before they consented to any agreement and these would be so damaging that they would then be able to insist on his widening the Government by taking in A.E. [Eden] again as Foreign Secretary and Winston as Defence Minister and two T.U.C. leaders.' Harvey added, 'These should in fact be the conditions of their co-operation in the rearmament campaign.'

In mid-May, Chamberlain informed the Cabinet that aircraft production would continue to lag behind Germany's 'unless we were prepared to undertake the tremendous measures of control over skilled labour as in Germany. . . . He doubted whether the nation would be prepared to go as far as that at the present time.'

The TUC's General Council saw Chamberlain again in late May, but by then it was clear that the Prime Minister was not prepared to do anything more than rely on exhortation. The engineering unions also met their employers in late May. The bosses immediately demanded greater interchange of workers between skilled trades, a dilution of skilled labour, the recruitment of women and increased overtime working. Inevitably, a fearful and suspicious union like the AEU would make no concessions.

Although the recession of 1938 largely enabled employers to overcome the skill shortage, there were again acute shortages when the economy revived in 1939. Eventually the AEU was forced to accept dilution, but only after valuable time had been wasted and much output had been lost.

As far as Chamberlain was concerned, the political price of any significant increase in consultation or state intervention was simply too high to contemplate. His critics, however, were in no doubt that the price had to be paid. At the time of Chamberlain's second round of talks with the union leaders, Oliver Harvey discussed the issue with Eden. As Harvey wrote,

Only an All-Party Government will be able to put across the drastic regimentation of industry and labour which is essential if we are to equal the Totalitarians without ceasing to be a Democracy. . . . He [Eden] heard however that the Government are completely defeatist and hold that a Democracy can never compete with the Dictators –

which, as A.E. [Eden] said, is all rot: we won the [1914–18] War
without ceasing to be a Democracy.

On 16 May, Chamberlain, aided by David Margesson, his loyal Chief
Whip, took a further step in refashioning the Cabinet in his own image.
The Minister for Air, Viscount Swinton, was sacked following a singularly
inept performance by the Ministry's spokesman in the Commons, Lord
Winterton. Although the onslaught on the Air Ministry's performance was
a political embarrassment to Chamberlain, the incident provided a
convenient pretext for Swinton's dismissal.

The Air Ministry's failings were attributable to the shortage of funds,
which was not Swinton's doing. Swinton, however, was a longstanding
critic of the Prime Minister. He had annoyed Chamberlain by his fight for
extra resources, and was advocating the need for the state to take
compulsory powers to overcome skill shortages. Chamberlain was strongly
opposed to Swinton's plan, since he thought it would antagonise business
and labour, and cause economic chaos. The Prime Minister offered him
the post of Lord President of the Council in an attempt to keep a
potentially awkward critic within the confines of Whitehall, but Swinton
refused.

Swinton's successor as Minister for Air, Kingsley Wood, had served as
Minister for Health since 1935. His other ministerial experience was
limited to Education and the Post Office. He was joined at the Air
Ministry by the young Captain Harold Balfour, who had no previous
ministerial experience but could justifiably claim some knowledge of
aircraft from his days as a fighter pilot in the 1914–18 war. Balfour,
commenting on Wood, unkindly said that he was 'a splendid little man but
he admitted not knowing one end of an aeroplane from another.' In fact,
Wood was not as pliant as has sometimes been suggested, and began
demanding more funds.

The reshuffle spread gloom among the backbench dissidents. Harold
Nicolson wrote of his feeling of despair to his wife Vita Sackville-West:

> Here we are at the gravest crisis in our history, with a genius like
> Winston doing nothing and Kingsley Wood as our Minister for Air
> with Harold Balfour as his Number Two. It is all due to David
> Margesson. I admire David, since he is strong and efficient and
> kind. But I do not believe that he is a good Cabinet-maker. Much
> sickness left behind.

At the same time, Chamberlain seized an opportunity to remove from
the Cabinet the Colonial Secretary William Ormsby-Gore, who had
succeeded his father as Lord Harlech. According to Oliver Harvey, 'the

P.M. . . . hates him [Ormsby-Gore] and the whole Cecil connection.'
Ormsby-Gore was married to Lady Beatrice Cecil, and had been a close
associate of Eden's. Two members of the Cecil 'connection' had left the
Government within less than three months, Lord Cranborne having
resigned from the Foreign Office with Eden.

On 18 May, Nicolson had reason to feel even more despondent,
following a scene he witnessed at his gentleman's club: 'On my way home
I stop at Pratt's where I find three young Peers who state that they would
prefer to see Hitler in London than a Socialist administration. I go to bed
slowly, pondering upon the Decline and Fall of the British Empire.'

A far more public demonstration of the readiness in some circles to
appease Hitler had occurred a few days earlier in Germany. Before the
kick-off in the soccer match between Germany and England, the teams
lined up facing the Führer's box, which contained Göbbels, Göring, Hess
and Ribbentrop, as well as the British Ambassador, Sir Nevile Henderson.
The German team included several former Austrian international players.
When the German national anthem was played both teams gave the Nazi
salute.

There had been much soul-searching among the English team when the
Football Association's officials told them that they should make this
gesture. The instruction reflected Henderson's concern that everything
should be done to secure German sympathy, and a recognition of Nazi
sensitivities by the Secretary of the Football Association, Stanley Rous,
who had observed the 1936 Olympic Games.

Before the match, the anti-appeaser Sir Robert Vansittart had contacted
Rous to emphasise that it was 'really important for our prestige that the
British team should put up a really first class performance'. England won
6–3. In Berlin, Henderson believed that the spirit in which the match had
been played gave the 'promise of cordial relations in future insofar as
sporting fixtures are concerned'.

On 19 and 20 May, a week after the soccer international, London, Paris
and Prague received reports of German troop movements near the Czech
border. Reassurances from Berlin that these were merely training
exercises rang hollow as similar disclaimers had preceded the occupation
of Austria. The Czechs ordered a partial mobilisation. The British
Government warned Germany that in the event of an invasion, the French
were bound by treaty to support Czechoslovakia, and Britain would
almost certainly support France. The Chamberlain Administration thus
found themselves in the unaccustomed position of receiving plaudits for
taking a firm stand against a potential aggressor from the usually critical

*News Chronicle* and the *Daily Herald*. When no invasion occurred, it appeared that Hitler had backed down.

Hitler was furious. He had no intention of invading as early as May, yet he had been seen to retreat. The 'May crisis' strengthened his resolve to seize control of Czechoslovakia, and to do so more quickly than he had originally envisaged. On 30 May, he signed a secret directive updating the plans ('Operation Green') for the invasion. This death warrant on Czechoslovakia was to be executed by 1 October 1938, at the latest.

Chamberlain had been deeply disturbed by the 'May crisis'. Following the Anschluss he had been determined to avert war over the Czech crisis, yet a couple of months later Europe had drifted to the brink. Memories of 1914 were reawakened. As Virginia Woolf noted, 'One shot at a policeman, and the Germans, Czechs, French will begin the old horror. The 4th of August may come next week.' For Chamberlain, the moral was clear. Efforts should be redoubled to settle the Czech crisis before it embroiled the rest of Europe in war. The role which the French played would clearly be crucial, since they were bound by treaty to defend Czechoslovakia against invasion. And if the French became involved in a war, it would be practically impossible for Britain to stand aside.

But how could the crisis be resolved? To those who listened that spring to the American air ace, Charles Lindbergh, there seemed little choice. The Lindberghs were again in the country during the 'May crisis', with Charles reiterating his message – as Nicolson summarised it, 'we cannot possibly fight since we should certainly be beaten. The German Air Force is ten times superior to that of Russia, France and Great Britain put together.'

Of Chamberlain's critics, Eden was probably the best placed to appreciate both the purpose of, and the limits on, Britain's foreign policy. He was, after all, one of the architects of the general policy of appeasement. His comments shortly after the crisis are illuminating:

Nobody will quarrel with the Government's wish to bring about appeasement in Europe. Any other intention would be as foolish as it would be wrong. But if appeasement is to mean what it says, it must not be at the expense either of our vital interests, or of our national reputation or our sense of fair dealing. Appeasement will be neither real nor lasting at such a price. It would merely make real appeasement more difficult at a later stage. There must be a point at which we, as a nation, must make a stand and we must clearly make a stand when not to do so would forfeit our self-respect and the respect of others.

But Nicolson discovered at lunch with Halifax that the new Foreign Secretary's mind was heading in a quite different direction:

> We discuss the question of conciliating Goering. Halifax says that he would be pleased by an invitation to Sandringham. Ronnie [Cartland] and I say that we would resent any such thing. It would affect American opinion. It would lower our dignity. No, ask Goering to Nepal as much as you like, but do not expect the Queen to shake hands with him. Halifax is rather startled by our vehemence.

But how would the Prime Minister's mind be working? The previous November, as has already been noted, he referred to the Sudeten German minority as Germany's *uitlanders*, the name given by the Boers to British settlers in the Transvaal. It was a telling indication of how Chamberlain was likely to approach the issue. In May, at a lunch given by Nancy Astor at her London house, 4 St James's Square, Chamberlain suggested to American correspondents that Czechoslovakia should cede the Sudetenland to Germany.

During the summer of 1938, the farce of the talks in Czechoslovakia between the Czech Government and Henlein ran and ran. Henlein was bound to reject whatever concessions Beneš offered him. As the weeks passed, the British Government became increasingly perturbed at the lack of progress. Their overriding desire to avoid being drawn into war with Germany, while preserving an apparently honourable position, prompted Halifax to take a unilateral initiative. In July, during King George VI's visit to France, the Foreign Secretary informed Daladier and Bonnet of his plan to intervene directly by sending a mission to Prague.

When Beneš heard of the plan, he was incensed. But the French Government urged him to accede to the initiative. Bonnet privately informed the Czech Ambassador in Paris that Prague could not count on French support in the event of war.

Before Halifax could secure the approval of the Sudeten Germans, however, news of his proposed initiative was leaked in the *News Chronicle*. The British Government's only choice was to abandon the idea, or press ahead regardless. On 26 July, Chamberlain announced the details of the plan, such as they were, to the House of Commons.

The mission was to be led by Viscount Runciman, aged sixty-eight, a year younger than the Prime Minister, and a fellow devotee of the winged collar. Runciman lacked any previous experience as a diplomat and, like Chamberlain, had a business background, in Runciman's case as a shipbuilding magnate in the north-east of England. He was a former

Liberal minister in the Campbell-Bannerman and Asquith Governments, and a National Liberal who had served from 1931 in the Cabinet as President of the Board of Trade. His resignation in June 1937 occurred amongst much recrimination when Chamberlain succeeded Baldwin as Prime Minister and had excluded Runciman from his inner councils.

The Runciman mission bore all the hallmarks of a face-saver. The terms of reference were disturbingly vague. Runciman's status and his remit were clothed in ambiguity. Chamberlain's version, given to the Commons, was that Runciman 'would not be an arbitrator but investigator and mediator . . . independent of His Majesty's Government and of all Governments. He would act only in a personal capacity and it would be necessary that he should have all the facilities and information placed at his disposal'.

Opposition reaction to the Runciman mission was critical. The Labour MP Morgan Jones thought it savoured 'too much of the squeezes which the Government have applied to various other countries in the interest of peace'. The Liberal leader, Sinclair, warned that conceding to dictators would result in war. Czechoslovakia had to be supported against excessive demands. Among the Conservative dissidents, A.C. Crossley approved sending the mission, but foresaw disaster in any weakening of the resolute attitude towards German aggression which the Government had adopted during the 'May crisis'.

Press reaction was sceptical, including even the pro-appeasement *Evening Standard*, which wondered 'whether the British Government should ever have persuaded the Czech Government to assent to the appointment – on terms so capable of being misunderstood, and for a purpose so fraught with complications'. And the *News Chronicle* was more caustic, commenting on Runciman's fate that 'No-one – certainly no Czech and no German – is going to accept Mr. Chamberlain's bland assurances that the British Government has really nothing to do with his success or failure'.

In fact, the British and French were unwilling to fight for the Czechs, and therefore all the pressure was being put on Beneš to make yet more concessions. On the same day that Chamberlain announced the Runciman mission in the Commons, Sir Nevile Henderson was telling the Foreign Office in London, 'The Czechs are a pig-headed race and Beneš not the least pig-headed among them. . . .' Henderson thought that 'so long as the Germans trust us', all was not lost, and 'we shall have at long last to put our feet down very firmly and say to Beneš "you must" '.

Against this inauspicious background, Runciman arrived in Prague on 3 August. Henlein was still as adept as ever at preserving his public image of reasonableness. After dealing with his intermediaries, Runciman's deputy, the Foreign Office civil servant Frank Ashton-Gwatkin, was received by Henlein on 22 August. Ashton-Gwatkin later said of the Sudeten Nazi, 'I like him. He is, I am sure an absolutely honest fellow'.

The Sudeten Nazis summed up their view of Runciman in the song quoted by Roy Douglas:

> *Wir brauchen keinen Weihnachtsman,*
> *Wir haben unseren Runciman!*

> We need no Father Christmas,
> We have our Runciman!

During August, the Government in London began receiving messages that, unless rapid progress was made, Hitler would make clear his own views at the Nazi Party Rally starting at Nuremberg on 5 September.

The time was fast approaching when Chamberlain's personal foreign policy would be taken to its logical conclusion.

# CHAPTER ELEVEN

# 'THE BLEAK CHOICE'

We seem to be very near the bleak choice between War and Shame. My feeling is that we shall choose Shame, and then have War thrown in a little later on even more adverse terms than at present.

(Winston Churchill, in a letter to Lord Moyne, early September 1938)

For the best part of August and September each year during the 1930s, there was a sense that Britain was once again being ruled from her country houses and landed estates. Whitehall became a deserted village. Ministers of the Crown rarely saw each other, except possibly on the grouse moors from the 'Glorious Twelfth'. The business of governing the country reverted to the more leisurely pace of a bygone age.

Nineteen-thirty-eight was different. On 30 August, ministers gathered at Number 10 for an urgent meeting. They had been summoned by the Prime Minister because of reports that Hitler was planning to attack Czechoslovakia. Although the meeting was not a formal Cabinet, only four ministers were absent. The hastily arranged *ad hoc* discussion was also attended by Sir Nevile Henderson, the British Ambassador in Berlin, whose recall was in itself a signal to the German Government of London's extreme concern.

Yet this sudden flurry of activity was, in a sense, misleading. Nothing changed as a result of the ministers' meeting. It failed to produce a single new initiative. Chamberlain's action was not motivated by any desire for fresh thinking by ministers. Far from it. His real purpose was to reaffirm that at this critical juncture he retained the collective confidence of his Cabinet.

The ploy worked brilliantly. There was overwhelming support for the approach outlined by the Foreign Secretary Lord Halifax and endorsed by Chamberlain. The gist of their case was unaltered since the Cabinet discussions of the spring. Opinion in the country and the empire would be seriously divided by any declaration that Britain would fight if Germany invaded Czechoslovakia.

It was doubtful whether Britain was in a position to carry out any commitment to fight if Hitler invaded Czechoslovakia. Churchill's proposal that Britain, France and Russia should send a joint note to Berlin might prompt Britain's co-signatories to ask 'embarrassing questions as to our attitude in the event of Germany invading Czechoslovakia'. Reports received during the summer that moderate opinion in Germany was urging Britain to issue a warning were dismissed. Britain's hope was that Runciman could achieve a settlement and meanwhile 'keep Germany guessing as to our intentions'. Duff Cooper's call for a show of force by the navy was vetoed.

Chamberlain's arguments were reinforced by the editorial which Kingsley Martin had written in the left-wing weekly, the *New Statesman and Nation*, published the Saturday (27 August) before the ministers met. Martin had argued that if Runciman failed to reach a settlement 'the question of frontier revision, difficult though it is, should at once be tackled. The strategical value of the Bohemian frontier should not be made the occasion of a world war. We should not guarantee the status quo.'

In practical terms, the result of the ministers' meeting was entirely negative. No new warnings were to be issued, no measures taken which Hitler might regard as provocative. Nor was there any decision on what Britain would do in the event of a German attack on Czechoslovakia. The political outcome, however, was crucial. Chamberlain had won the backing he sought for his attempts to avert war at almost any cost. It did not matter a jot that the principal reasons advanced by the Prime Minister and Foreign Secretary reflected upon the British Government's own lack of resolve over a period of years.

As far as the majority of ministers present on 30 August were concerned, the arguments put forward by Halifax and Chamberlain were compelling. They were hardly inclined to raise queries about the assumptions on which Government policy had been based for several years – after all, some had helped shape those assumptions and others were appointed because they were known to share them.

If any ministers harboured doubts about the direction of policy over recent years, this was scarcely the moment to raise them. The country was facing an international crisis. Their task, as they sat round the Cabinet table listening to the Foreign Secretary and Prime Minister, was not to conduct an inquest into how Britain had found herself in such a predicament but to consider the options now open to the Government. Faced with the situation as they saw it in the late summer of 1938, most ministers felt they had no choice but to support Chamberlain in his efforts to avert war.

Chamberlain, however, had concealed one vital piece of information from his ministers. Privately, he was already working on a plan which could be put into effect if a German attack seemed imminent. On the previous Sunday evening, 28 August, less than forty-eight hours before the ministers' meeting, he had discussed the crisis with his trusted adviser at Number 10, Sir Horace Wilson. They considered what could be done if a German invasion was about to be launched. Between them, they developed 'Plan Z', which would entail Chamberlain visiting Hitler uninvited and without any preliminary talks, and seeking to resolve the crisis face to face before the invasion could begin.

A few days after the ministers' meeting, members of the Cabinet had resumed their traditional pursuits and duties, many miles from Whitehall. Chamberlain departed for Balmoral as the guest of the Royal Family. Inskip, Duff Cooper and Sir Samuel Hoare, the Home Secretary, also headed for Scotland. Cooper spent three days 'grouse-driving every day'. Hoare relieved Chamberlain as 'Minister in Attendance' at Balmoral, and had to stay an extra day when the King required him to join the shoot.

Events would not wait on Britain's country-house government. On 31 August, Winston Churchill wrote to Halifax. Unaware of the outcome of the ministers' meeting, he proposed two initiatives, neither of which would commit Britain to the 'dread guarantee'. In the first, he took further his idea of drafting a joint note with the French and Soviet Governments, and urged that the note should be shown to President Roosevelt. He also urged that there should be a show of force by the Royal Navy, as Cooper had advocated, of the kind he had initiated when First Lord of the Admiralty during the international crisis of 1914.

Churchill was deliberately seeking to encourage Hitler's opponents within the German leadership to take a stand. He had been visited at Chartwell on 19 August by Major von Kleist, of the German Army. Von Kleist had warned that Hitler would attack Czechoslovakia during the second half of September. But he claimed that the German generals were for peace, and 'if only they could receive a little encouragement they might refuse to march'.

While Churchill took the reports about opponents to Hitler within the German regime seriously, Chamberlain was sceptical. Vansittart also met von Kleist, but when Chamberlain read a note of their meeting, he commented that von Kleist 'reminds me of the Jacobites at the Court of France in King William's time and I think we must discount a good deal of what he says.'

A rift began to develop between Chamberlain and Halifax, only days after their impressive double act. Halifax drafted a speech on 1 September which he planned to deliver as the Nazis gathered for their Nuremberg Rally. Its aim was to urge the Czechs to reach a negotiated settlement, while warning the Germans against resorting to force, even referring to the progress of British rearmament and the resolve of the British people.

But Halifax was dissuaded from delivering the speech by Chamberlain's objections. Chamberlain attributed Halifax's sudden divergence to Cadogan's absence from the Foreign Office on a golfing holiday at Le Touquet. The Prime Minister told Inskip that he thought Halifax had become unsettled under Vansittart's influence.

While Chamberlain thought his Foreign Secretary was 'unsettled', Halifax had cause to wonder at his Prime Minister's judgement. Chamberlain himself referred to Halifax's shocked reaction when he first told him about Plan Z. On 3 September, the Prime Minister wrote to his sister:

> is it not positively horrible to think that the fate of hundreds of millions depends on one man, and he is half mad? I keep racking my brains to try and devise some means of averting catastrophe, if it should seem to be upon us. I thought of one so unconventional and daring that it rather took Halifax's breath away. But since Henderson thought it might save the situation at the 11th hour, I haven't abandoned it, though I hope all the time that it won't be necessary to try.

The casual description of Hitler as 'half mad' is extraordinary when Chamberlain was increasingly inclined to place his faith in a face-to-face approach. At this stage, the Prime Minister appears to have been less naive than some other appeasers. On Sunday, 4 September, the leader in the *Observer*, then under the editorship of J.L. Garvin, declared,

> We have utterly and absolutely declined to believe that Herr Hitler is a melodramatic monster with a deficiency of brains – that he is either mad or bad to the degree of precipitating an unnecessary world-war with open eyes, by a violent onslaught on Czechoslovakia.

Halifax believed in traditional diplomacy more strongly than his self-confident Prime Minister, and was certainly a good deal less sanguine than Garvin. The Foreign Secretary was still inclined to explore the scope for Britain making some kind of effort to deter Hitler. At a meeting later that Sunday, Halifax considered, along with Cadogan (back from holiday), Vansittart and Wilson, 'the idea of a private warning to Hitler'. Cadogan 'gave some support' to the idea, but according to Oliver Harvey's diary Halifax finally decided against it the next day, Monday, 5 September.

On Monday the 5th Halifax appeared to be back in line with his Prime

Minister's thinking, encouraged by some optimistic news from Prague. He wrote to Winston Churchill saying that he thought it better to wait on developments in Central Europe. He did not think that the suggestion of collective action, which the Soviet Ambassador Maisky had put to Churchill, 'would be helpful'. Halifax confided to Churchill that Lord Runciman's deputy, Frank Ashton-Gwatkin, had 'telegraphed last night [4 September] to say that on the whole it was satisfactory'.

That Monday evening, Harold Nicolson was due to broadcast one of his regular talks on BBC radio. But the BBC was being closely monitored and effectively controlled in what was broadcast on the international crisis. It received warnings about the opinions expressed in current affairs programmes from both the Foreign Office and Sir Horace Wilson at Number 10. The latter suggested that an eye be kept on talks such as *The Past Week*, a regular series which Harold Nicolson had started broadcasting during the summer.

Nicolson's script for his talk on 5 September was sent to the Foreign Office, who said they would prefer that no talk should be given about the international crisis. The BBC told Nicolson to rewrite his script, and vetoed a second version in which he planned to talk about the Nazis' brutal beating-up of a bishop. Eventually, a script about the rise in the price of milk was accepted, and the broadcast went ahead. During the September crisis, two of Vernon Bartlett's talks on international affairs in Children's Hour were cancelled at the request of the Foreign Office.

In Prague on Tuesday the 6th, Beneš made more concessions, in the so-called 'Fourth Plan'. The net effect was to grant Henlein virtually everything he had demanded in his speech at Carlsbad the previous April. Beneš had been under continued pressure from the British and French Governments, and when he delivered a copy of the Fourth Plan to Runciman, he warned that it 'amounted to a capitulation and would in future years be regretted by Britain and France'.

Despite that grim prophecy, this represented the major breakthrough which London and Paris had been seeking for months.

Any grounds for sustaining some shred of optimism were soon shattered. In London, on the evening of Tuesday the 6th, Theodor Kordt, Chargé d'Affaires at the German Embassy, secretly called on Sir Horace Wilson at Number 10. He was acting in an entirely private capacity. Kordt's message was that a German invasion of Czechoslovakia was imminent: Hitler would 'march in' on the 19th or 20th. The next morning, Kordt repeated his message to Halifax and urged that the British Government should warn Germany of the likely consequences.

Yet any warning from the British Government would have been

seriously undermined by the time that Kordt returned, the next morning, to see Halifax. In an editorial on Wednesday, 7 September, *The Times* argued:

> If the Sudetens now ask for more than the Czech Government are ready to give in their latest set of proposals, it can only be inferred that the Germans are going beyond the mere removal of disabilities for those who do not find themselves at ease within the Czechoslovak Republic. In that case it might be worth while for the Czechoslovak Government to consider whether they should exclude altogether the project, which has found favour in some quarters, of making Czechoslovakia a more homogeneous state by the cession of that fringe of alien populations who are contiguous to the nation to which they are united by race.

*The Times* was, in effect, inciting the Sudeten Germans to reject the Czech Government's capitulation to their demands, and at the same time was egging on the Nazis to press for the outright cession of the Sudetenland to the Reich. An editorial along these lines in any other newspaper would have been of little consequence, but *The Times* was still widely regarded as the Government's unofficial mouthpiece.

Geoffrey Dawson had written the leader on 6 September, on his return from a month's holiday. Across Europe it was assumed that its message, at such a critical hour, must have been the result of a deliberate initiative by the British Government. The signal was clear – Britain was not prepared to stand by Czechoslovakia.

The Foreign Office issued a statement dissociating itself from the leader, but by then it was too late. Any official protest needed to come from Number 10 if it was to carry weight.

Although Halifax criticised the editorial in his talks with Corbin, Maisky and Masaryk, the representatives of the French, Soviet and Czech Governments in London, he was not as angry with *The Times* as the Foreign Office would have people believe. Indeed, Rab Butler, Halifax's deputy at the Foreign Office, suggested in his memoirs that Halifax knew about the editorial in advance: 'I am myself convinced that Halifax knew this article was to be written: the two Yorkshiremen were very close and I saw Dawson leaving the Office on 6th September after a long interview with the Foreign Secretary.'

The following day, after the editorial had appeared, Halifax joined Dawson for an amicable lunch at the latter's London club, a stone's throw from the Foreign Office across St James's Park. Dawson wrote in his diary,

There was a hubbub, as I fully expected, over the morning's leader –
reactions in Prague and Berlin, and the Foreign Office went through
the roof – Not so, however, the Foreign Secretary, who came and
lunched with me at the Travellers', and had a long talk. He is as
much in the dark as everyone else, as to what is likely to happen
next. . . .

Halifax was making little secret of his uncertainty at this time. Only a day
earlier, he had written to Runciman: 'The principal trouble, of course,
remains that we cannot possibly tell . . . what is going on inside the brains
of the one man who matters.'

In Prague on the morning of the 7th, the Czech Government's Fourth
Plan was formally presented to the Sudeten German negotiators. The fact
that it granted virtually all Henlein's demands put them in an awkward
position. Hitler was due to deliver his own pronouncement on the Sudeten
problem within a matter of days (on Monday the 12th) at the Nuremberg
Rally. It seemed that Hitler had been robbed of any pretext for direct
intervention in Czechoslovakia.

But within hours Henlein's followers manufactured an incident, which
culminated in the arrest of two Sudeten German Party parliamentary
deputies. The Sudeten German representatives cited this as their reason
for deferring the negotiations. They and the rest of Europe were waiting
on the German Chancellor.

In London, the Prime Minister seized personal control of the Government's handling of the Czech crisis. Chamberlain had returned from
Scotland late on 7 September and the following morning set up his own *ad
hoc* inner group of ministers and officials. The Cabinet was subordinated.
Remarkably, during this period of international tension, there was no
meeting of the Cabinet's Foreign Policy Committee, which had last met on
16 June. It would not meet again until November.

On Thursday, 8 September, *The Times* reiterated its call for the transfer of the Sudetenland to Germany. That morning's first meeting of
Chamberlain's inner group was attended by Halifax and Sir John Simon,
the Chancellor of the Exchequer, with three officials, Sir Horace Wilson,
Cadogan and Vansittart. Chamberlain was against sending any private
warning to Hitler, and wanted instead to activate Plan Z. This was the
first that Vansittart had heard of the scheme. He was totally opposed to the
idea.

The pressure on the Government to issue some kind of warning to
Germany was intensifying. The Labour Party National Executive,
meeting at Blackpool, urged ministers to declare that 'The British

Government must leave no doubt in the mind of the German Government that they will unite with the French and Soviet Governments to resist any attack on Czechoslovakia.'

The next day, Friday the 9th, Vansittart's call brought Sir Anthony Eden back from holiday in Ireland to see Halifax. Eden advised that Hitler should be made fully aware that, if France were involved in conflict, Britain would be too. According to Eden, Halifax agreed, and commented, 'my mind is moving on just such a project and indeed I was going to speak to Neville about a draft today.'

Later that day, it was decided both to send a warning and to prepare for Chamberlain to make a visit to Germany to see Hitler. Over the next few days, Plan Z increasingly occupied the minds of the inner group of ministers and their closest official advisers. Henderson, who was in Nuremberg to observe the Nazi rally, advised against the original plan that Chamberlain should arrive in Germany uninvited – Henderson's quarters were in a railway carriage, while the Redesdales and Lord Brocket were entertained in some splendour by their Nazi hosts.

As the preparations for implementing Plan Z proceeded, the potential benefits of a face-to-face meeting with Hitler began to magnify in Chamberlain's mind. As he wrote to his sister, 'I do not want to do anything which would destroy its chances of success because, if it came off, it would go far beyond the present crisis, and might prove the opportunity for bringing about a complete change in the international situation.'

The content of Chamberlain's warning to Hitler is remarkable, considering Chamberlain's resistance to any European commitment, his deep suspicion of the French and Soviet Governments and his antipathy towards Labour. The warning stated that, in the Government's view, the latest Czech proposals went a long way to meeting the claims of the Sudeten Germans. In the event of force being used against Czechoslovakia, France would honour her treaty obligations and:

> the sequence of events must result in a general conflict from which Great Britain could not stand aside. In this connection the recent declaration made on behalf of the British Labour movement, in which they call upon the British Government to state that 'they will unite with the French and Soviet Governments to resist any attack upon Czechoslovakia', shows how opinion in responsible Labour circles is moving. Whatever might be the issue of such a struggle, no one can doubt that the end must be disastrous to all concerned – victors and vanquished alike.

Halifax instructed Sir Nevile Henderson to deliver the message while he was in Nuremberg. On Saturday, 10 September, however, news of the instruction was leaked in the *Daily Mail*. Number 10 denied the report.

Later that day, Henderson informed London that he strongly opposed the warning. He had already made the British Government's position clear, a claim which had more than a touch of the implausible about it. Less than a week earlier, he had written to Cadogan, the Permanent Secretary at the Foreign Office, 'I do wish it might be possible to get at any rate *The Times*, Camrose, Beaverbrook Press, etc., to write up H. [Hitler] as the apostle of peace. It will be terribly short sighted if this is not done.' Henderson now counselled that the proposed warning would 'drive Herr Hitler straight off the deep end'.

Chamberlain's inner group met that Saturday afternoon. It was brought to full complement with the return to London of Sir Samuel Hoare, the Home Secretary, finally released by the King from his duties on the shoot. Henderson's advice was accepted. Only Vansittart objected. He later told the Labour politician Hugh Dalton that it was a disaster that he had been usurped by Horace Wilson.

Halifax emphasised in his telegram to Henderson that he accepted the Ambassador's advice on condition that Henderson had already made clear the substance of the Government's message, and that he was sure the Foreign Minister Ribbentrop had understood it. Reports of Henderson's behaviour at the Nazi rally, where he reportedly spoke about his aversion to the Czechs and Britain's guilty part at Versailles, show that there was no chance of Halifax's message getting through. The surprise is that he ever expected that it would, given the strength of Henderson's personal convictions about appeasing the Nazis.

So much for Britain's warning to Hitler.

Chamberlain's inner group were greeted by the forbidding sight of Churchill waiting in the hall at Number 10 as they emerged from their conclave on the afternoon of Saturday the 12th. As Hoare noted in his diary, 'He had come to demand an immediate ultimatum to Hitler,' which he believed 'was our last chance of stopping a landslide'. Churchill also apparently claimed, contrary to the Government's information, that 'both the French and the Russians were ready for an offensive against Germany.' But Churchill's plea made no impression on the Government, and he wrote to his friend Lord Moyne expressing the gloomy sentiments quoted at the head of this chapter.

Eden had made similar comments. Oliver Harvey noted in his diary that weekend, 'I have a feeling that A.E. [Eden] is right when he says that the present Government will run away if it comes to a show-down. . . .' Harvey himself was 'not reassured' with the membership of the inner group, 'especially Simon and Hoare', which was 'taking all the decisions. None of the younger generation there.'

Eden's judgement seemed to have been vindicated on the evening of 10 September. The Dominion Governments were informed that Halifax had told Corbin, the French Ambassador, that 'although Great Britain might feel obliged to support France in a conflict . . . it did not mean that we should be willing automatically to find ourselves at war with Germany. . . .'

The Government were at sixes and sevens. Twenty-four hours earlier, Chamberlain had been prepared to issue a warning to Hitler citing the movement of opinion in 'responsible Labour circles'. When Halifax spoke with Corbin, he was still expecting Henderson to pass on the gist of the warning. Yet there was no mention to the French of any pressures on the British Government to take a firm stand – suddenly all the pressures were pushing in the opposite direction. It is not difficult to see who Halifax was trying to bluff. Nor is it difficult to see that Hitler would not fall for it.

One of the most revealing insights into ministerial thinking was unwittingly provided by Oliver Stanley, the Colonial Secretary. The younger of the Stanley brothers tended to be one of the Cabinet's more critical members. Harold Nicolson dined late with him on Sunday the 11th, and noted in his diary, 'His point of view is, I suppose, typical of the better type of Cabinet opinion. What the worst type of opinion may be passes my comprehension.'

Stanley was longing to 'get out of' any conflict, and thus lost 'no opportunity of reviling the Czechs'. But it was the reasoning behind Stanley's fear of Britain's being drawn into war which acts as the searchlight, suddenly illuminating the appeasers' rationale. As Nicolson recalled, 'any reference to Russian assistance makes him wince, and at one moment he sighed deeply and said, "You see, whether we win or lose, it will be the end of everything we stand for." By "we" he means obviously the capitalist classes.' Oliver Stanley's fear was echoed by J.L. Garvin, the pro-appeasement editor of the *Observer*, who wrote to a fellow appeaser, Lord Astor, during the Czech crisis: 'If war comes . . . all forms of property will be taxed nigh to extinction under the delusive name of "Conscription of Wealth".'

The Prime Minister shared similar sentiments. Chamberlain had relied on the co-operation of business, and had eschewed intervention on any truly significant scale. His diplomacy was influenced by a deep suspicion of the Soviet Union, and the fear that Bolshevism would spread into Central and Eastern Europe.

Viewed from this perspective, the Churchillian view of Czechoslovakia as a small, independent democracy being threatened by a totalitarian neighbour was turned on its head. Instead, to quote J.L. Garvin, 'At present Czechoslovakia is a corridor for Russia against Germany.'

There was a strong sense among the governing class that war would inevitably bring with it a social revolution at home and a political revolution abroad, in addition to all the other costs – economic, physical, psychological. The old order would be swept away.

Chamberlain was determined to see through his strategy, and was not going to let the niceties of Cabinet government stop him.

The Cabinet meeting on 12 September, held only hours before Hitler delivered his speech at the Nuremberg Rally, was the first formal meeting since the summer holidays, and the first sizeable meeting of Cabinet ministers since 30 August. As Duff Cooper noted, 'The Cabinet was called at the worst possible moment – too late to take any action before Hitler's speech, too soon to consider the new situation which that speech might create.'

The Cabinet was not informed of the existence of Plan Z. Halifax reported that he and Chamberlain had seen Churchill again the previous day, who urged them to warn that if Germany 'set foot in Czechoslovakia we should at once be at war with her'.

The Foreign Secretary also claimed that Eden, in contrast, 'had expressed complete agreement with the line taken'. This was seriously misleading. Harvey's diary reveals that on the 10th Eden was 'very worried at the decision not to send a warning', and that on the 11th Eden had told Halifax that 'he saw the point of not sending warning in view of Henderson's advice but he mistrusted the man's judgement: he urged that the Government should announce further naval movements.'

Eden was actually backing Duff Cooper's line, not the Government's. Indeed, on the morning the Cabinet met, Eden had effectively issued his own warning. In a letter to *The Times*, Eden wrote, 'In any international emergency that threatened the security of France this country would be found at the side of the French Republic, whatever the consequences.'

The Cabinet, however, approved Halifax's proposal that he should give only a non-committal reply to his French counterpart, Bonnet, about Britain's exact intentions if France marched.

Halifax had done an about-turn on the Czech crisis. Five days earlier, the Foreign Office had publicly repudiated the call by *The Times* that the Sudetenland should be ceded to Germany. Yet by 12 September, as Oliver Harvey's diary reveals, Halifax felt that any deal between the Czechs and the Sudetens simply would not last.

The Foreign Secretary had come to the conclusion that separating the Sudetenland from Czechoslovakia was the only solution. A plebiscite should be held, and all Czech territory which voted to join the Third Reich should be transferred. According to Harvey, Halifax believed that 'In order to enforce such a plebiscite, the idea would be to summon a Four-Power Conference – Great Britain, France, Germany and Italy.' The Government of Czechoslovakia would thus be excluded from any say in their own future.

Before the Cabinet adjourned, there was approval for Kingsley Wood's proposal that the Chiefs of Staff should present a new assessment of the military position in the event of war with Germany. Amazingly, their gloomy report in the spring had not taken into account the most crucial question in 1938 – what would be the situation if Germany was able to annex Czechoslovakia? Oliver Stanley asked that this consideration should be included.

At Nuremberg on 12 September, Hitler hurled insults at the Czechoslovakian state, demanded self-determination for the Sudeten Germans and proclaimed that if no one else would go to their defence Germany would not stand idly by.

In Sussex, at their country home, Harold Macmillan and his wife, Lady Dorothy, listened to a broadcast of Hitler's speech. They were joined by their near neighbour, Viscount Cecil of Chelwood, who did not own a radio. Macmillan later recalled the spectacle of Cecil 'lying at full length, almost flat, on the sofa . . . with his long, emaciated body, his splendid head, and the great beak-like nose – like a modern Savonarola'. Lady Dorothy translated, calling on what she had learned from a succession of German governesses. 'At the end, Lord Cecil, who had not moved throughout, slowly uncoiled from his recumbent position. He said, gravely and slowly, "This means war." '

Hitler's outburst, less than 100 miles from the Czech border, provoked riots that evening by the Sudeten Germans. The Czech Army restored order, and the following day Prague imposed martial law.

On Tuesday the 13th, ministers in London and Paris were running scared. Intelligence reports suggested that a German invasion was planned on 25 September. Chamberlain's inner group discussed the possibility of a plebiscite in the Sudetenland and concluded that despite the practical difficulties it was preferable to war. Thus ministers were actively considering the mechanism for the cession of the Sudetenland to Germany less than a week after they had repudiated *The Times* editorial suggesting the same idea.

When the inner group met the service ministers that evening, Duff Cooper called for the mobilisation of the fleet and an immediate meeting of the Cabinet. Both suggestions were rejected.

Duff Cooper had been joined at dinner at the Admiralty the night before by Churchill. Cooper's fraternising with critics irritated Chamberlain's closest colleagues. Sir Samuel Hoare, the Home Secretary, essayed in his diary a rationalisation for Chamberlain's readiness to sidestep the convention and protocol of Cabinet government: 'The trouble was the anti-Chamberlain clique. They dine together at Admiralty House [i.e. Cooper's HQ] and Winston was usually there. Everything said in the Cabinet repeated. They all regard war as inevitable. Intrigue with dissident French Ministers in Paris. . . . difficulty in speaking freely to the Cabinet in these conditions. . . .'

In the French Cabinet, the Foreign Minister Bonnet eventually carried the day for the appeasers. French ministers were alarmed to hear Lindbergh's assessment of the Luftwaffe's strength and his view that it was geared to launch bombing offensives, which was misleading since it was principally geared to support the Wehrmacht, the German Army. Bonnet informed Phipps, the British Ambassador, that 'no further military measures were contemplated, and peace must be maintained at any price.' When Phipps had confirmed that this was indeed the French Government's position, he noted, 'I fear French have been bluffing, although I have continually pointed out to them that one cannot bluff Hitler. . . .'

Chamberlain was now determined to proceed with his visit to Hitler, although there was as yet no Cabinet authorisation for the plan. On the night of Tuesday, 13 September, Chamberlain's telegram was dispatched to Hitler:

> In view of the increasingly critical situation I propose to come over at once to see you with a view to trying to find a peaceful solution. I propose to come across by air and am ready to start tomorrow.
>
> Please indicate earliest time at which you can see me and suggest place of meeting. Should be grateful for your early reply.

Chamberlain was flouting the conventions of government on two counts. Not only did he lack Cabinet approval, he was proposing to leave the country yet had not informed the monarch, who, even today, must grant permission for the Prime Minister to go abroad.

On the morning of Wednesday the 14th, the Cabinet were finally informed of the telegram to Hitler. Chamberlain told his colleagues that he did not see how any democracy could refuse a plebiscite. As for the rest of Czechoslovakia, Harvey noted in his diary the Prime Minister's view that 'it might be necessary to neutralise it under guarantee of Great Britain, Russia, France and Germany.'

The news of the proposed visit was enthusiastically endorsed. Duff Cooper said that he had come to Cabinet prepared to recommend a mobilisation of the fleet, but much preferred Plan Z. He warned, however, that 'the choice is not between war and a plebiscite, but between war now and war later'. Welcoming Chamberlain's 'brilliant proposal' Sir John Simon was prophetic: 'if he comes back with the seeds of peace with honour, he will be immediately acclaimed as having carried out the greatest achievement of the last twenty years.'

The King's formal approval was received at Number 10 that afternoon.

Chamberlain and Halifax had, on various occasions, both referred to Hitler as being 'half-mad', 'mad' or 'lunatic', yet the Prime Minister was hoping not only to agree a settlement of the Sudeten problem, but also to reach some much wider understanding with the Führer.

Direct talks between Chamberlain and Hitler, without colleagues or aides present, represented an incredibly high-risk strategy. It could backfire all too easily. Hitler would be in a strong position. The British Prime Minister had a patent desire to avert war at almost any price and was under a political imperative to return with a settlement.

The impact of Chamberlain's surprise initiative shook the political landscape. On Thursday, 15 September, the morning of his departure for Germany, Chamberlain received a good press. Even the papers which were usually hostile praised his initiative. 'Good luck, Chamberlain!' was the headline in Labour's *Daily Herald*, which maintained that his 'bold course . . . will receive general support'. In the Liberal *News Chronicle* the Prime Minister was applauded for 'one of the boldest and most dramatic strokes in modern diplomatic history'. The critical Tory *Daily Telegraph*, referring to appeasement in its correct, non-pejorative sense, observed that 'the good wishes of everybody who has the appeasement of Europe at heart will accompany Mr. Neville Chamberlain on his mission.'

These sentiments, from some of Chamberlain's traditional critics, reflected the widespread support for his action throughout the country. To many people it seemed absurd that Europe was on the brink of war over the Sudetenland – though this partly reflected the British Government's determined efforts to ensure that there was little discussion about the international crisis.

Chamberlain had emerged as a decisive man. He was making a supreme effort to chart a way through the morass of claim and counterclaim between Czechs and Sudeten Germans. His approach was worth a try, though few had given any thought to what Chamberlain might be able to do in order to avert war. It was enough for most people that he was going to talk to Hitler.

Even the Labour leadership felt reassured. Immediately before Chamberlain left for Berchtesgaden, Hugh Dalton told Douglas Jay that 'Chamberlain had assured him that he was going to Germany to inform Hitler that if he made any more aggressive moves, we should be ready to fight.' It was clear to Jay that Dalton, 'who was nothing if not sceptical', believed this, and Jay naturally felt 'somewhat reassured'. When Jay was warned by the economist Tommy Balogh 'in characteristically lurid terms that a ghastly sell-out was impending', Jay still thought Dalton 'must be a better judge than the shrewd but erratic Balogh'.

But Vansittart, the lone anti-appeaser on Chamberlain's inner group, believed that Chamberlain's shuttle diplomacy was fatally flawed. The day after Hitler's abusive Nuremberg speech, Vansittart wrote: 'every hour that we live demonstrates more clearly that it is Germany, not Russia, that threatens the physical existence of every country. . . . So long as this is the case it would surely be an unpardonable folly to assist Germany in driving off the map an associate whose weight we may need.'

Churchill shared Vansittart's perspective. In Oliver Harvey's words, Churchill regarded Chamberlain's initiative as 'the stupidest thing that has ever been done'. He argued in his column in the *Daily Telegraph*, published on the 15th, that if, despite the pressures on them, the Czechs fought, they could resist for three or four weeks and inflict heavy losses on the Germans: 'from the moment that the first shot is fired . . . the whole scene will be transformed and a roar of fury will arise from the free peoples of the world, which will proclaim nothing less than a crusade against the aggressor.' Churchill maintained: 'This is no time for bluff.'

Chamberlain's proposed trip created a new bitterness in political debate. Churchill had been in regular contact with Chamberlain and Halifax, but his son Randolph wrote to warn him that Chamberlain's coterie could not be trusted. 'When they are with you they are careful to talk in honourable terms; if I have read them more truly it is because their underlings are less discreet with me.'

The shock of Chamberlain's dramatic initiative divided people who had previously agreed. On the day of Chamberlain's departure, Harold Nicolson wrote about his disagreement with his wife Vita Sackville-West:

How difficult it is to decide! Vita takes the line that the Sudeten Germans are justified in claiming self-determination and the Czechs would be happier without them in any case. But if we give way on this, then the Hungarians and Poles will also claim self-determination, and the result will be that Czechoslovakia will cease to exist as an independent State. Vita says that if it is as artificial as all that, then it should never have been created. That may be true, although God knows how we could have refused to recognise her existence in 1918. It all seemed such a reality in those days. Hitler has all the arguments on his side, but essentially they are false arguments. And we, who have right on our side, cannot say that our real right is to resist German hegemony. That is 'imperialistic'. Never have the conflicting theories become so charged with illusions.

Some appeasers also had their doubts. Lord Lothian explained to Nancy Astor that although Chamberlain's initiative was 'noble and heroic', he feared that the Prime Minister would probably be forced to make concessions:

> having gone as far as we have I'm inclined to think that rather than split the country and the democratic world by immediate concessions we ought to say that if Hitler invades Czechoslovakia it means war. . . . We have, I think, strong cards in the long run and I think Hitler would hesitate. But if, having gone as far as we have in the last three weeks, we run away now and do something which is tantamount to 'selling the pass' the prestige of the totalitarian methods and powers will be such, and the derision and depression of the democracies so acute, that it will go hard with the old British Empire.

Chamberlain arrived in Germany on Thursday, 15 September. Henlein, the leader of the Sudeten German Party, arrived the same day. This self-imposed exile declared that 'We want to go over to Germany.' This really meant that he wanted Germany 'to go over' to Bohemia and annex the Sudetenland.

At the Berghof early that evening, Hitler and Chamberlain talked alone for three hours, accompanied only by Hitler's interpreter. Hitler convinced Chamberlain that German troops could invade Czechoslovakia at any moment. In fact, no invasion could be launched for another two weeks.

Chamberlain told Hitler that he was not authorised to give any commitment about the Sudetenland without prior Cabinet approval. But in his personal opinion, 'on principle I had nothing to say against the separation of the Sudeten Germans from the rest of Czechoslovakia, provided that the practical difficulties could be overcome.'

The two leaders agreed to meet again shortly to discuss the practicalities. Chamberlain later wrote to his sister, 'I had established a certain confidence, which was my aim, and on my side, in spite of the hardness and ruthlessness I thought I saw in his face, I got the impression that here was a man who could be relied upon when he had given his word.'

On Friday, 16 September, Chamberlain left Germany, and Runciman also left Prague to return home to London. In some quarters, the Prime Minister was assuming hero status. That morning, in place of a leading article, *The Times* printed the poem by the Poet Laureate, John Masefield, quoted at the head of Chapter One (see p. 1).

Harold Nicolson encountered Vincent Massey, the Canadian High Commissioner, at his club:

I say, 'Well, are the Government going to give way?'
He says, 'It is better to have smallpox three years from now than at once.'
I say, 'Yes, but if we have it now, we shall recover; if in three years, we shall die.'

The Government's efforts to see that the press published the right message were stepped up at this time. Halifax was keen that proprietors and editors were seen instead of the parliamentary lobby and diplomatic correspondents. Hoare, a member of the inner group, began giving daily press briefings on the crisis, and saw the 'opposition' papers, including the editor of the pro-Labour *Daily Herald* and the chairman of the Liberal-inclined *News Chronicle*. A few days later, Duff Cooper was surprised that the *Daily Herald* joined other papers in their favourable comments on Chamberlain's initiative. Layton later censored his foreign correspondent's reports on Chamberlain's shuttle diplomacy in the *News Chronicle*.

On Saturday the 17th, Chamberlain began the task of selling the fruits of his labours at the Berghof. The Prime Minister could normally rely upon the majority of his Cabinet colleagues for their compliance, but he soon found himself in some difficulty.

Duff Cooper's account, though it comes from one of the Prime Minister's most vehement critics, conveys the atmosphere in the Cabinet room. The 'curious' feature was that Chamberlain 'recounted his experiences with some satisfaction'. The Prime Minister said that Hitler 'struck him as "the commonest little dog" he had ever seen', yet he was obviously pleased to hear that Hitler thought he 'was a "man" '. But 'the bare facts of the interview were frightful.' The Prime Minister had not even mentioned any of the schemes prepared in London before he left, and 'From the beginning to the end Hitler had not shown the slightest sign of yielding on a single point.'

This impression was confirmed by one of Chamberlain's loyalest supporters, Sir Thomas Inskip, who recalled that 'The P.M. was astonishingly fresh and alert. . . .' Chamberlain apparently reported that

'Hitler became excitable as he talked, but no signs of insanity were shown. While he talked his common appearance was forgotten, and the P.M. was impressed with his power.' On the substance of the talks, 'The P.M. had come to the conclusion that though Hitler was determined, his objectives were strictly limited. . . .' The meeting was 'too heated and electric' to raise any of the plans discussed beforehand in London. 'The impression made by the P.M.'s story was a little painful. . . . The P.M. said more than once to us he was just in time. It was plain that H. had made all the running: he had in fact blackmailed the P.M.'

Chamberlain made it clear to his colleagues that he wanted to press on at full speed with his personal diplomacy. There was no time to be lost. He had established a rapport with Hitler, whom he thought 'would not be too difficult'. In the meantime, he argued against recalling Parliament until it would be helpful to do so.

The Cabinet were divided. Discussion lasted for five hours, with a break for lunch. Duff Cooper, Oliver Stanley, Walter Elliot and Lord Winterton voiced their dissent, although only Buck de la Warr, leader of the National Labour Party, was prepared to go as far as saying that he was prepared to face war rather than make concessions to Hitler. But the majority backed Chamberlain, though Hoare and MacDonald spoke respectively of the need for a *quid pro quo* from Hitler and 'reasonable' conditions.

The Foreign Secretary had invited the French Government for consultations on the talks, and warned his colleagues that 'it was very important that we should avoid allowing the French to say that they had come to London and found that we had decided to give the show away.'

In his summing up, Chamberlain 'rather deprecated any attempt to tie his hands too closely by fixing precise limits beyond which he should not go, when the negotiations resumed'. He later wrote to his sister, 'We had two Cabinets lasting five hours and finally overcame all critics, some of whom had been concerting beforehand.'

Buck de la Warr later saw his political colleague, Blanche ('Baffy') Dugdale, and told her of the dilemmas facing critics in the Cabinet. Dugdale was the niece of the former Conservative Prime Minister, A.J. Balfour (whose biography she wrote), but she had left the Party in 1937 because of her opposition to the Government's foreign policy. She had joined the National Labour Party, and became the parliamentary candidate in Central Southwark.

The Czech crisis was to renew Dugdale's crisis of conscience. She was scornful of the critics in the Cabinet for their private complaints about Chamberlain, while being prepared to go part of the way with him. As she noted in her diary after her talk with Buck de la Warr:

But what a position! They are going to resign if 'the terms' are not to their liking – e.g. they would sell the Egerland, but no more. I told Buck then, and I told Walter [Elliot] later this is a hopelessly weak position. Buck said to me: 'Tell Walter that if he goes I will.' I replied I would give no such message. Later he modified it to 'Tell Walter that if he goes he will not go alone.' I urged Buck all I could to *go*. For one thing (though I did not say this) he will count for nothing if he stays; if he resigns, he may help make a nucleus.

After Cabinet on Saturday evening, Chamberlain, Halifax and Sir Horace Wilson received a delegation at Number 10 from the Labour leadership – Herbert Morrison, Hugh Dalton and Walter Citrine. It was bound to be a difficult meeting because the National Labour Council had given its strong backing to Czechoslovakia.

Citrine opened by commenting that many in the Labour movement 'thought that British prestige had been gravely lowered by Chamberlain going to see Hitler'. Chamberlain sought to demolish Labour's position by emphasising the weakness of the French Air Force and the unreliability of the Russians.

Anti-appeasers on the Government benches were equally perturbed. That same day, the Conservative MP, Vyvyan Adams, wrote to Churchill urging him to give a lead: 'The dismemberment of Czechoslovakia would mean another trench lost to decency. I beg you to use your immense prestige to impress this palpable fact on the Government and the public.'

Division was not limited to the political world. According to Harvey, the Royal Household was split. King George VI's Private Secretary, Sir Alexander Hardinge – who had clashed with Rab Butler over the Government's foreign policy months earlier – was 'horrified', but the King himself was more sympathetic to the Government's predicament, writing to his Assistant Private Secretary, Sir Alan Lascelles, that 'The French arrive tomorrow and if they won't stand up to Hitler how can we and the world must be told it is their fault and not ours.'

Chamberlain's next challenge was to convince the French Government that the only hope of averting war was the effective dismemberment of Czechoslovakia. Yet he also had to ensure that the French did not blame the British for such a settlement – after all, the French Government were undoubtedly as keen as the British to avoid going to war with Germany.

The two Governments would then face the formidable obstacle of persuading the Czechs. This might require that London and Paris guarantee the remaining parts of Czechoslovakia, although Chamberlain and Halifax wanted to avoid any such commitment. And to add to

Chamberlain's task, he needed to secure the agreement of the French and the compliance of the Czechs within a matter of days, before his next meeting with Hitler.

At their talks in Downing Street, the British and French agreed that Prague should be urged to accept the transfer of the Sudetenland to Germany. The pill would at least be sweetened for the Czechs by a requirement that the transfer must be put into effect by an International Commission. The British Government also reluctantly agreed to act as co-guarantors of the new Czech borders, though this was unlikely to thrill the Czechs – as Vansittart pointed out, they would 'only be getting a British guarantee in place of a Russian one'.

But there was still some opposition to the proposed deal within the British Cabinet. At its meeting the next day, Monday the 19th, Leslie Hore-Belisha, the Secretary for War, could not see how the new, reduced Czechoslovakia could survive. It would be economically and strategically unsound. Britain was incapable of implementing the guarantee, which Hore-Belisha argued was merely 'a postponement of the evil day', and he warned that 'there was a risk that we were putting our signature to something which might involve us in dishonour'. The canard of British public opinion was produced to counter Hore-Belisha's doubts – while a section were vocal for war, the majority were said to be opposed to a war resulting from the Czech crisis.

The Cabinet had again been presented with a *fait accompli*. It was vital that the British and French Governments were united, and a speedy answer of some sort was needed for the Prime Minister's next meeting with Hitler. Even Duff Cooper felt bound to concede that the 'prospect of war was so appalling that "postponement of the evil day" was the best course'.

The day after the Cabinet's decision, Inskip and Sir Horace Wilson received the latest military assessment from General Ismay, Secretary to the Committee of Imperial Defence and the Chiefs of Staff sub-committee. It appeared to vindicate Chamberlain's policy. Ismay concluded that 'If war with Germany has to come, it would be better to fight them in say six or twelve months' time, than to accept the present challenge'.

Ismay recognised the Allied superiority at sea and on land. He also acknowledged that over the coming months German air superiority would actually increase still further. But his analysis was based on the Luftwaffe's supposed ability to inflict a speedy knock-out blow. Britain therefore needed time to improve her air defences. The possibility of an early defeat had to be averted, although during any postponement of conflict the *overall* military balance would continue to shift in Germany's favour.

In fact, the Chiefs of Staff subsequently discovered that the Wehrmacht was maintaining only eight or nine divisions on the western front, far fewer than they had thought. Ismay also changed his mind much later, arguing that it would have been better to fight in 1938 rather than 1939. But those were not the assessments made at the time, and the politicians had to reach judgements on the basis of the advice they were given.

One of the most effective critics of Ismay's view was the military strategist, Basil Liddell Hart. This was ironic, since earlier Liddell Hart had himself been strongly opposed to any Continental commitment for the British Army. He had been a strong influence on Hore-Belisha at the War Office, and also on Chamberlain – although as Chancellor the latter had conveniently ignored the other key element in Liddell Hart's strategy, which was the need for a fully modernised, mechanised army.

Liddell Hart was now in close touch with the Conservative critics Churchill and Eden and with the Labour leadership. He argued that 'although the strategic ground for a stand was much less favourable than over Abyssinia in 1935, over the Rhineland in 1936, or over Spain in the last two years, it was better to make a stand now than to postpone it – as the situation was likely to be worse the following year if Czechoslovakia was abandoned.'

But events were now set in train, and in Prague the British and French Ministers, Newton and Lacroix, had called on Beneš to inform him of the Anglo-French proposals. Harvey noted in his diary on 19 September that 'every pressure is being applied to Beneš to accept and to accept quickly. Poor Masaryk has taken to his bed with grief. . . .' That evening, Halifax told Churchill that it was the French who were reluctant to go to war to defend the new Czech frontiers.

On Tuesday the 20th, Churchill flew to Paris and talked with Mandel and Reynaud, ministers in the French Government who shared his view of the Anglo-French approach. But like the dissident ministers in the British Cabinet, they were in a minority. Churchill sought to dissuade Mandel and Reynaud from resigning, since if they were to do so they would lose any ability to influence policy.

Reports were circulating that the Czech Government might be minded to refuse the Anglo-French proposals, and while in Paris Churchill contemplated sending a telegram to Beneš telling him to stand firm. But he decided against, because he felt that he had no authority to advise the Government in Prague.

In Prague, Newton and Lacroix were once more dispatched to see Beneš. The British Ambassador in Paris, Phipps, observed to Bonnet that the time seemed to have come when Beneš should be told that unless he accepted the proposals Britain and France would 'wash their hands' of Czechoslovakia if Germany attacked.

When Phipps's colleagues at the Foreign Office heard of the Ambassador's reflections, there was near panic. The cause of anxiety was not the sentiments expressed, but the fear that Britain would be held responsible for abandoning the Czechs. As Oliver Harvey noted, the fear was that Phipps's comment 'would be used as evidence that we had pressed the French Government to evade their treaty obligations'.

In the early hours of Wednesday the 21st, Newton and Lacroix delivered Phipps's formula to Beneš. Later that day in London the Cabinet met at Number 10 amid ominous reports that Hungary and Poland were preparing to advance their own claims on Czechoslovakia. As Ministers pondered these reports and discussed Germany's intentions, the news came through that the Czechs had finally acceded to the terms.

Chamberlain would, after all, be able to pay his return visit to Hitler on Thursday the 22nd, only a week after his first meeting. He would be returning with his Cabinet's backing. Most remarkable of all, however, he had secured the agreement of the French and Czech Governments to negotiate the transfer of part of Czechoslovakia to Nazi Germany.

# CHAPTER TWELVE

# 'FLY, FLY, FLY AGAIN'

If at first you don't concede,
Fly, fly, fly again.

(Maxim whispered by officials in the Foreign Office who were
critical of Chamberlain's personal diplomacy, September 1938)

Chamberlain had won over his Cabinet and the French and Czech
Governments. But he had squandered the goodwill which existed
throughout the country at the time of his first visit.

In the few days before Chamberlain's second flight, the unease felt
across all shades of opinion in Britain was given focus by the leak in
Paris of the Anglo-French proposals. On the morning of Monday,
19 September, the French press published the gist of the supposedly
confidential talks between the British and French Governments in London
the previous day.

On Monday the 19th Harold Nicolson visited Eden and found him 'in
despair'. Their conversation captured the feeling of many critics – that it
was hard to see an alternative, but the Government should never have
allowed themselves to be put in that position in the first place. Eden
admitted that if he had been in Halifax's position 'he might have done the
same as he did'. But Nicolson noted, 'Only he adds with a smile, "But I do
not think I should have put myself in Halifax's place." He says it is very
difficult to criticise one link in the chain of events, when the whole chain is
in itself vicious.'

It is almost impossible to appreciate the depth of many people's
pessimism at the time. Nicolson and Eden discussed 'the effect of our
surrender. He [Eden] takes the very gloomiest view, feeling that
leadership in Europe has now passed completely from our hands into those
of Germany.' As their conversation drew to a close, 'we talk of what small
comfort it is to have been proved right, and how terrible has been the
influence of the Cliveden set. As I leave him he says, "Well, we shall not
be able to avert war now." '

Later the same day, before recording one of his regular talks for the
radio, Nicolson dined with de la Warr and Elliot, Cabinet ministers who

had both criticised Chamberlain following the Berghof talks. Despite any natural inclination to sympathise with Nicolson, they devoutly upheld the principle of collective responsibility. This was notably true of Walter Elliot, who was unable to shake Nicolson from his sense of impending doom: 'He [Elliot] is very charming and plausible, but my heart is no lighter and my anger in no way undiminished as I make my way to the B.B.C.' At the BBC, he was met by the young radio producer, Guy Burgess. Nicolson proceeded to 'deliver my talk in a voice of ironic gloom. I then go to the Café Royal with Guy, where we meet James Pope-Hennessy who is almost in tears over England's shame.'

The following morning, Tuesday the 20th, the British press reported and commented upon the Anglo-French proposal. The criticism from the anti-appeasement press was bitter, even by their standards, and was in complete contrast to their readiness less than a week earlier to give Chamberlain the benefit of the doubt. Their worst fears had been realised.

Reflecting the surge of anger across the political spectrum, the Tory *Daily Telegraph* opined that 'a policy which does not command general approval is worse than useless.' The more popular and independent-minded *News Chronicle* commented that 'bewilderment is giving place to a feeling of indignation.' The *Daily Herald* argued that the Czechs had been 'betrayed and deserted by those who had given every assurance that there should be no dismemberment of their country'.

The pro-appeasement press rallied to defend Chamberlain. With stunning understatement, *The Times* observed that 'The general character of the terms submitted to the Czechoslovak Government could not, in the nature of things, be expected to make a strong *prima facie* appeal to them.'

Harold Nicolson's morning on Tuesday the 20th began with a 'phone call from Baffy Dugdale: 'She said she had been sick twice in the night over England's shame, and that at breakfast she had read *The Times* leader. . . . Having read these words she dashed to the lavatory and was sick for a third time. She then returned and wrote a letter to Buck [de la Warr] saying that she must resign from the National Labour Party.'

Baffy Dugdale desperately tried to organise some opposition to the proposals. When she spoke with the Liberal leader Sir Archibald Sinclair, he told her to 'Try to get Anthony [Eden] into the open – he is the only leader for the former Government supporters.' But she did not know Eden well enough. She urged Sinclair 'to press for a meeting of Parliament – even if it does give Neville a majority; their plan of making all this a *fait accompli* without summoning Parliament is an abrogation of Parliamentary Government, as well as all else.'

Nicolson dictated a letter to his Party leader, in which he warned de la Warr that 'if the terms being imposed on the Czechs were such as given in the Press, I might have to consider opposing the Government and resigning from a Party which had not said one word against them.'

At lunch, Nicolson was involved in an incident which revealed the deepening division within the political establishment. It was of the kind which were to become more frequent and more bitter over the next few weeks. Nicolson was at the Beefsteak with a group who were all busily attacking *The Times* for its leader. As they spoke, Robert Barrington-Ward, Deputy Editor of *The Times*, entered the room. But one of the members did not know Barrington-Ward and, as Nicolson recalled, calmly proceeded to ask of Nicolson:

'What was it, Harold, that you said about *The Times* leader just now?' Considering that Barrington-Ward wrote that leader, the situation is awkward. I replied, 'I said it was a masterpiece of unctuous ambiguity, and I do not mind in the least repeating that in the presence of its author.' General embarrassment. Barrington-Ward gets very red, and I fear I do also.

While at the Beefsteak, Nicolson also talked with Vernon Bartlett, who had reported the Berghof talks for the *News Chronicle*. He informed Nicolson that a German general had told him that a plot to launch a military coup against Hitler had been abandoned. As Nicolson noted, the reason for its abandonment was that 'now that Chamberlain has capitulated, the stock of Hitler and Ribbentrop has soared to such a point that there was nothing more to be done.'

The Government came under a hail of criticism from the opposition parties. Speaking at Limehouse Town Hall, on Sunday the 18th, the Labour leader, Attlee argued:

It is a very melancholy thing to find that one is a true prophet. The labour movement has warned the country ever since 1932 that yielding to aggression in one part of the world meant an increase of aggression in another. We are now paying in anxiety for a wrong foreign policy assumed since Labour was thrown out of office. I pray heaven that we may not have to pay in blood.

Two days later, following the publication of the Anglo-French proposals, the National Labour Council passed a resolution declaring 'that this is a shameful betrayal of a peaceful and democratic people and constitutes a dangerous precedent for the future'. The labour movement also set about planning a great campaign of public meetings.

On 21 September, Attlee saw Chamberlain and told him, 'You have abandoned these people completely. You have made an absolute surrender. All Eastern Europe will now fall under Hitler's sway. We are full of the most profound disgust. This is one of the biggest disasters in British history.'

The Government's policy awakened patriotism as well as internationalism on the left. Dalton noted in his diary that when a Labour deputation met Halifax, George Dallas, leader of the agricultural workers and chairman of the 1938 Labour Party conference, half rose from his seat and declaimed at the Foreign Secretary, 'Lord Halifax, after listening to you, we are ashamed to be Britishers.'

Sir Archibald Sinclair, in one of the most telling criticisms of Chamberlain's actions, proclaimed that 'we have merely submitted to Herr Hitler's demands and our submission has been extracted, not by a sudden conversion to the justice of his case, but by the threat of war.'

From the Government's own side, there was strong criticism from Viscount Cecil, Anthony Eden and Vyvyan Adams. Eden told his constituents that 'The British people know that a stand must be made. They pray that it will not be made too late.' Adams wrote to the *Daily Telegraph*, arguing that 'the betrayal of Czechoslovakia will . . . stimulate the Nazi Government to such arrogance that it will some day commit an act of aggression which even France or Great Britain or both will deem intolerable, and it will make abundantly more probable our defeat in isolation.'

On his return from France on Wednesday the 21st, Churchill strongly condemned Chamberlain's policy and argued that 'The partition of Czechoslovakia under pressure from England and France amounts to the complete surrender of the Western Democracies to the Nazi threat of force.' Stressing that such a settlement would free 'twenty-five German divisions' for the western front, Churchill declared that 'The belief that security can be obtained by throwing a small State to the wolves is a fatal delusion.'

The anger at Chamberlain's personal diplomacy revived the prospect of some all-party alliance. There was closer agreement on foreign policy and defence between Tory dissidents and the opposition parties than at any previous time.

Churchill was impressed with the line which the National Council of Labour had taken, and had phoned Attlee on Tuesday the 20th, telling him 'Your declaration does honour to the British nation.' Attlee responded, 'I am glad you think so.' Dalton learned later in the day that Churchill's call had been intended as 'an overture for some kind of concerted action', and that Churchill was 'huffed that Attlee did not make a warmer response'.

Some Labour leaders wanted to develop closer contacts with the Tory rebels. Yet Dalton felt that it would not help either Labour or the rebels:

'It would not strengthen any appeal of ours if it were associated with Winston or Eden or the Liberals, even if they would join, and I doubt whether it would strengthen any appeal of theirs for us to be associated with it.' Indeed, Dalton feared that any such move 'might upset a large number of our own Party and destroy our credit in the home market'.

The battle in the press became increasingly bitter. The pro-appeasement *Evening Standard* commented in its leader on Wednesday the 21st that 'With every step taken by Mr. Chamberlain to preserve the peace the moral idealists in the community become more bellicose. As the danger of war recedes they insist loudly that we should have been willing to fight.'

On Thursday the 22nd, the morning of Chamberlain's second flight to Germany, the anti-appeasement *News Chronicle* published a page of letters from readers criticising the Government's policy, commenting, 'They are but a small fraction of the mass of correspondence almost unprecedented in volume and overwhelmingly opposed to the Anglo-French plan to partition Czechoslovakia.'

The next day, the *Daily Herald* reported that on Thursday evening 'ten thousand people massed in Whitehall . . . shouting "Stand by the Czechs!" "Chamberlain must go!" ' A poll conducted by Mass Observation showed that 40 per cent regarded Chamberlain's policy as wrong, with only 22 per cent in favour, and 28 per cent undecided. The mood as Chamberlain returned for his second round of talks with Hitler was markedly different from the atmosphere only a week earlier.

The Government's anxiety prompted one of the most startling incidents in their long campaign of news manipulation. On 22 September, Paramount issued a newsreel about the forthcoming talks, which included comments by two senior journalists, Wickham Steed, a former editor of *The Times*, and A.J. Cummings of the *News Chronicle*. The newsreel contained comments such as 'Germany is marching to a diplomatic triumph. . . . Our people have not been told the truth.' It was shown in over 100 cinemas, and audiences applauded.

Research by Anthony Adamthwaite now reveals that an official at Conservative Central Office immediately complained about the newsreel. Halifax took up the issue with the American Ambassador, Joseph Kennedy, who contacted the American parent company. The Home Secretary, Sam Hoare, was consulted, and although he claimed that he did not favour censorship, nonetheless felt that the speeches in the newsreel should not be included while Chamberlain's talks with Hitler were in progress. Kennedy contacted the company, and the offending newsreel was withdrawn.

Chamberlain was in a distinctly vulnerable position. He desperately needed to reach a settlement, politically and militarily. The mounting political pressure on him at home was acknowledged in a conversation at the airport between two of the dignitaries who had come to bid the Prime Minister *bon voyage*. The editor of *The Times* and Kordt, the German Chargé d'Affaires in London, acknowledged that 'opposition to Chamberlain's policy is increasing'. Dawson commented, 'If Chamberlain were to return without an understanding based on the Anglo-French plan, public opinion would turn against him.'

But Chamberlain had allowed Hitler to wrest the initiative from him at their first meeting. The Anglo-French plans had subsequently been published. British diplomats now feared that Hitler would make further demands. The interception by German intelligence of the Czech Government's 'phone calls to its embassies in London, Paris and Berlin meant that Hitler already knew Chamberlain's thinking on the possible arrangements for transferring the Sudeten areas.

The second round of talks were held at the Hotel Dreesen, on the banks of the River Rhine in Bad Godesberg, a small town to the north of Bonn. Hitler and Chamberlain resumed their face-to-face discussion after lunch on Thursday, 22 September, accompanied by a British interpreter and recorder, Ivone Kirkpatrick, in addition to Paul Otto Schmidt, who had performed the role alone at the Berghof.

Hitler allowed Chamberlain to outline the Anglo-French proposals in some detail. The British Prime Minister suggested that areas with a Sudeten German population of 80 per cent should be transferred automatically, and those with 65 per cent could be taken as a guide for an international commission to arbitrate. Hitler then delivered his bombshell. He told Chamberlain, 'I am very sorry, but all this is no longer any use.'

Hitler demanded the immediate cession of the Sudetenland, with the new frontier running 'along the language frontier'. The issue had to be resolved by 1 October at the latest. The Czech authorities should therefore withdraw and be replaced immediately by German troops to maintain order. The plebiscite could be conducted by an international commission later. That evening, after the talks were adjourned, Chamberlain telephoned Halifax in London to tell him of Hitler's new demands.

The next morning, Friday the 23rd, Chamberlain sent a letter to Hitler, objecting to an immediate occupation of Sudeten areas by German troops. Chamberlain drew specific attention to the problems that such a proposal would cause with public opinion in Britain and France, and also with the Czechs themselves. There was rich irony in Chamberlain citing these particular problems. The Prime Minister had been none too pleased with criticism of the Anglo-French proposals, yet the fact that they had attracted such heavy flak gave him at least one bargaining counter when he had left himself precious few others.

Hitler and Chamberlain met again later on Friday evening, after a further exchange of letters, this time in the presence of their close advisers. When the Germans presented their demands, the deadline for evacuation of the Sudeten areas by the Czech authorities had been brought forward to 26 September, a mere three days ahead. Neither Hitler nor Chamberlain wanted to break off the talks. But all that Chamberlain could secure were minor changes in the German text, and a postponement of the deadline to 1 October.

The Godesberg meeting ended in the early hours of Saturday, 24 September. Later that day Chamberlain returned to London to try, yet again, to persuade his colleagues that he was near to a settlement with Hitler.

Chamberlain's Cabinet colleagues in London became increasingly restive during the negotiations in Bad Godesberg. Halifax and the inner group of ministers were unable to have any regular, direct contact with the Prime Minister. Chamberlain had entrusted liaison between Bad Godesberg and Whitehall to Sir Horace Wilson, who adopted an impossibly off-hand manner.

A few hours after Chamberlain's departure for Godesberg, news reached London that Henlein's paramilitary Freikorps had seized control of the Sudeten towns of Eger and Asch. After consultation with the French Government, the inner group of ministers felt that they could no longer advise the Czechs against mobilisation.

But Chamberlain was anxious that the Czechs should not take any action which might upset his talks with Hitler. The inner group therefore withdrew their message before it was communicated to the Czech Government. Apart from Chamberlain's telegram on the morning of Friday the 23rd, saying that the Czechs should be discouraged from mobilising, ministers in London had to rely for news on the sketchy information provided by Wilson.

On the Friday afternoon, Halifax and his close colleagues finally took matters into their own hands. The Foreign Secretary dispatched a telegram to Chamberlain, advising that the Government's attitude towards mobilisation by the Czechs had to be changed. Halifax also told the Prime Minister, 'you should not leave without making it plain to the Chancellor if possible by special interview that, after great concessions made by Czechoslovak Government, for him to reject opportunity of peaceful solution in favour of one that must involve war would be an unpardonable crime against humanity.'

This remarkable assertion of Cabinet government was quite at odds with the usual tenor of Chamberlain's Administration. The Prime Minister responded, rather weakly, that the Czechs should at least be made aware of the possible ramifications of mobilising. Later that day, the Czech Government called up all men up to the age of forty.

The rest of the Cabinet were having an even more frustrating time. On the first day of the talks, Halifax received anxious letters from two Cabinet dissidents, Duff Cooper and Oliver Stanley, urging that German troops should not be allowed to enter Czechoslovakia under any circumstances until the frontier had been settled. The frustration of the dissidents only intensified as events unfolded and they found themselves reduced to the role of spectators.

Most ministers heard enough to sense that the talks were not going well, yet they were barred from even the limited contact with Godesberg available to the inner group. With no formal Cabinet meetings during the Prime Minister's absence, they were unable to take any of the executive decisions needed to prepare the country in case the talks collapsed.

A vivid portrayal of the depth of frustration can be gleaned from Duff Cooper's experience during those anxious few days. His recollections begin on the evening of Thursday the 22nd:

> We went to a cinema after dinner, but before going I rang up the Resident Clerk to know if there was any news. He told me that they had sent a telegram to Prague to the effect that we could no longer be responsible for advising the Czechs not to mobilise. I couldn't stay at the cinema for more than a quarter of an hour as the inanity of it got on my nerves. I walked home and sent for the latest telegrams. . . . I rang up the Private Secretaries at Downing Street; nobody was there. I rang up the Foreign Office and learnt that Halifax, Simon, Hoare, MacDonald and Inskip [the inner group] were in conference and that there had been a message to the effect that we Service Ministers were being put in a very difficult position. The country might be within twenty-four hours of war and we were not being given the latest information which was available to some of our colleagues.
>
> After half an hour, having received no reply, I rang up again and learnt that the Ministers had dispersed. With some difficulty, I got on to the Cabinet Officers and spoke to Ismay [Secretary of the CID]. He told me that he himself had given the message to Tom Inskip, who had immediately got up and gone home to bed.

As First Lord of the Admiralty, Duff Cooper possessed at least some scope for action, and off his own bat he authorised the navy to make preliminary preparations for war.

Outside the Cabinet Chamberlain's critics were beset by a cruel combination of emotions – besides their anger that Chamberlain was attempting to negotiate with Hitler and their complete lack of confidence in his inclination to drive a hard bargain, they had to endure the frustration which came from their complete impotence.

After Chamberlain's departure for Germany on Thursday the 22nd, Churchill summoned a small number of fellow critics to his London flat. Shortly before the meeting, Churchill had called at Number 10 and was told that the Government were 'at last taking a firm stand'. The critics began assembling at 11 Morpeth Mansions while Halifax and the inner group were pondering the news of the seizure of Eger and Asch by the Freikorps.

The conspiratorial scene that afternoon in Morpeth Terrace, was recorded by Nicolson: 'As I approach the door, I see the vulture form of Bob Cecil slipping into the flat. While I wait for the lift to descend, Winston appears from a taxi. We go up together. "This", I say, "is hell." ' Churchill replied, 'It is the end of the British empire.'

Churchill's eight fellow dissidents were Nicolson, Brendan Bracken and Sir Archibald Sinclair (the Liberal leader); and from the Lords, Robert Cecil, Horne (the former Conservative MP and Chancellor), Lloyd, Lytton and Wolmer. According to Nicolson, who wrote up his summary of the meeting the same evening, Churchill spoke about his briefing at Number 10:

> Chamberlain is to demand from Hitler (a) early demobilisation; (b) agreement that the transfer of the Sudeten territories should be undertaken gradually by an international commission; (c) that there must be no nonsense about Polish or Hungarian claims; (d) that what remains of the Czechs shall be guaranteed.

Churchill's audience was shocked. 'We say at once: "But Hitler will never accept such terms." "In that case", says Winston, "Chamberlain will return tonight and we shall have war." '

As the meeting continued, Jan Masaryk phoned to say that the Germans had occupied Asch. There was also a call from Attlee, the Leader of the Opposition, to say that they would 'come in with us if we like'.

Despite the worsening crisis and the talk from Number 10 of Chamberlain's tough line, the dissidents remained distinctly sceptical. As Churchill stood 'behind the fire-screen, waving a whisky-and-soda', they eventually agreed their position, which Nicolson summarised: 'Either

Chamberlain comes back with peace with honour or he breaks it off. In either case we shall support him. But if he comes back with peace with dishonour, we shall go against him. "Let us form the focus," says Winston. We say that indeed we will. But that it would be better to wait until we hear what has really happened at Godesberg.'

Nicolson drew his colleagues' attention to a more worrying aspect of the Government's communiqué on the Godesberg talks, namely the reference to a 'general agreement'. The dissidents were alarmed. 'They all agree that this is a terrifying prospect. It may mean surrender on fronts far more extended than the Czech front, and in return for such quite valueless concessions as "a fifty years' peace", "no bombing of open towns".' And Nicolson added, 'We all feel that it is terrifying that a man like Chamberlain should be exposed to such terrors and temptations.'

After the meeting, Nicolson walked through the London streets 'feeling that we are very near to war'. His thoughts highlight vividly the dilemmas which faced everyone. 'When war comes it will be a terrible shock to the country. The bombing of London by itself will provoke panic and perhaps riots. All those of us who said "We must make a stand" will be branded as murderers. I know that.'

Neville Chamberlain returned to London on Saturday, 24 September. He lunched with Halifax, and in the afternoon briefed his inner group on the outcome of his talks.

Six months earlier, Cadogan had referred to his anti-appeaser colleagues in Whitehall as the 'forces of evil', but he was deeply shocked when he saw Hitler's Godesberg memorandum:

Hitler's memo. now in. It's awful. A week ago when we moved from 'autonomy' to cession, many of us found great difficulty in the idea of ceding people to Nazi Germany. We salved our consciences (at least I did) by stipulating it must be an 'orderly' cession – i.e. under international supervision, with safeguards for exchange of populations, compensation, etc. Now Hitler says he must march into the whole area *at once* (to keep order!) and the safeguards – and plebiscites! – can be held *after*! This is throwing away every last safeguard that we had. The P.M. is transmitting this 'proposal' to Prague. Thank God he hasn't yet recommended it for acceptance.

But Chamberlain's main concern was the political difficulty of selling the latest demands. He rationalised his cavalier abandonment of safeguards for the Czech people – safeguards which he and the Cabinet had regarded as vital before Godesberg – by arguing that since the principle of cession had now been accepted, it was better for the transfer to take place as quickly as possible.

Even more remarkable was Chamberlain's impression of the relationship which he felt he had established with Hitler. 'He thought he had established some degree of personal influence over Herr Hitler. The latter had said to him: "You are the first man in many years who has got any concessions out of me." '

Chamberlain also told the inner group that 'Herr Hitler had said that if we got this question out of the way without conflict, it would be a turning point in Anglo-German relations. That, to the Prime Minister, was the big thing of the present issue. He was also satisfied that Herr Hitler would not go back on his word once he had given it.'

Halifax, Hoare and Simon accepted Chamberlain's argument. But Cadogan's scathing comments about his political masters would make any Whitehall mandarin blanch.

> I was completely horrified – he [the Prime Minister] was quite calmly for total surrender. More horrified still to find that Hitler has evidently hypnotized him to a point. Still more to find P.M. has hypnotized H. [Halifax] who capitulates totally. P.M. took nearly an hour to make his report, and there was practically no discussion. J.S. [Simon] – seeing which way the cat was jumping – said after all it was a question of 'modalities', whether the Germans went in now or later! Ye Gods! And during Thursday and Friday J.S. was as bellicose as the Duke of Plaza Toro. . . . I gave H. a note of what I thought, but it had no effect. . . . I told J.S. and Sam Hoare what I thought: I think the latter shares my view, but he's a puny creature. . . .

The full Cabinet met at 5.30 p.m. Chamberlain urged acceptance of Hitler's terms, arguing that Hitler would keep his word, that he would not seek further territorial expansion once the Sudetenland was transferred, and that there was a prospect of a wider Anglo-German agreement.

Chamberlain sought to impress upon the Cabinet his experience earlier that day:

> That morning he had flown up the river over London. He had imagined a German bomber flying the same course. He had asked himself what degree of protection we could afford to the thousands of homes he had seen stretched out below him, and he felt that we were in no position to justify waging a war today in order to prevent a war hereafter.

Chamberlain's Cabinet colleagues were less compliant than the inner group. Oliver Stanley argued that 'If these terms were accepted, Herr Hitler's price would only rise again and we should then find that we had bartered away many of the strong points in our position.' For Duff Cooper, 'The future of Europe, of this country and of democracy was at stake.' He protested that Hitler could not be trusted and believed that the British public would not accept his demands. He maintained that the Czechs would fight, and asserted that Britain should mobilise to support them. The Cabinet was adjourned until Sunday morning, without any decisions being made.

Cadogan was still seething with rage. That night, he drove Halifax home 'and gave him a piece of my mind but didn't shake him'. His diary gives eloquent testimony to the likely nature of this enraged public servant's highly political lecture to his political boss, captive in the passenger seat:

> I know we and they [the French] are in no condition to fight: but I'd rather be beat than dishonoured. How can we look any foreigner in the face after this? How can we hold Egypt, India and the rest? Above all, *if* we have to capitulate, let's be honest. Let's say we've been caught napping: that we can't fight now, but that we remain true to all our principles, put ourselves straight into war conditions and *rearm. Don't* – above all – let us pretend we think Hitler's plan is a *good* one. I've never had such a shattering day, or been so depressed and dispirited. I can only hope for a revolt in the Cabinet and Parliament.

There were signs that Cadogan's wish for a political revolt might be granted. On Saturday the 24th, the senior Conservative backbencher Leo Amery wrote to Chamberlain, 'Are we not bound to tell Hitler that the demand is in our opinion unreasonable?' Amery's action was an important storm signal of likely trouble in the Conservative Party, since he was an imperialist, whose views had been strongly influenced by Chamberlain's father. Amery had never wanted the Government to assume commitments on the Continent of Europe, but, as he pointed out, the Prime Minister's intervention had inevitably involved Britain in the Czech crisis:

> War is an awful thing, and there might have been much to be said for keeping out of this business altogether on the grounds of our weakness. But after the line you took up in May, after Runciman's mission, and, above all, after your own personal intervention, we have assumed a responsibility which we cannot now shirk without putting ourselves in an impossible position.

That weekend, Sheila Grant Duff, the journalist with many friends in

Czechoslovakia, was anxiously trying to find out what was happening at Bad Godesberg. Douglas Jay and his wife were staying with her in Kent. Grant Duff was a relative of Clementine Churchill's, and as Jay has recalled, 'Sheila rang up the Churchills at neighbouring Chartwell, and boldly from a telephone kiosk in the lane asked Churchill what he thought was going on in Germany. He replied down the telephone: "I don't know, but I suspect it is something shameful." '

Next morning, Sunday, 25 September, it became clear that appeasers were shaken by what had happened at Bad Godesberg. The *Observer*, usually sympathetic to Chamberlain, sounded as vehemently anti-Hitler as any anti-appeaser: 'The Nazi power last week threw off the mask before the British Prime Minister and demanded in effect his total capitulation on their soil. They counted that their armed advantage had made them already the masters of the earth. Not yet.'

Halifax too had been having second thoughts, spending a sleepless night – which was, perhaps, not all that surprising after his lift home from Cadogan. It seemed that Cadogan did 'shake him'.

At Sunday's special Cabinet, Halifax shocked his colleagues. Without any prior warning, the Foreign Secretary confessed that overnight he had had second thoughts about accepting the new terms; 'he could not rid his mind of the fact that Herr Hitler had given us nothing and that he was dictating terms, just as though he had won a war but without having to fight. . . .' Halifax concluded that he had worked 'most closely with the Prime Minister throughout the long crisis. He was not quite sure that their minds were still altogether at one.'

Chamberlain was mortified, but said nothing. There followed a bizarre exchange of notes between Prime Minister and Foreign Secretary, as the Cabinet discussion continued.

Chamberlain:   Your complete change of view since I last saw you
      last night is a horrible blow to me, but of course you must form
      your opinions for yourself. However, it remains to be seen what
      the French say.
          If they say they will go in, thereby dragging us in I do not think
      I could accept responsibility for the decision. But I don't want to
      anticipate what has not yet arisen.
Halifax:   I feel a brute – but I lay awake most of the night,
      tormenting myself and do not feel I could reach any other
      conclusion at this moment, on the point of coercing CZ
      [Czechoslovakia].
Chamberlain:   Night conclusions are seldom taken in the right
      perspective.

Halifax:   I hope you don't think I agree with Buck [de la Warr]! I
should like the Czechs to agree on the facts – but I do not feel
entitled to coerce them into it.

Chamberlain:   I can't help feeling that there is some confusion.
What pressure *can* we put on the Czechs except the negative one
of saying that we are not coming in unless the French are in it?
What we should do is to discuss frankly with the French the
position. If in the end they do go in we must still be in Mar. 24
position [i.e. Chamberlain's Commons speech of that date, stating
that there was no fixed commitment to join France in a war].

What D.C. [Duff Cooper] and O.S. [Oliver Stanley] want us to
do is to *encourage* French and Czechs to resist and *promise* them
our help. That I will not myself consent to.

Bad Godesberg had proved a turning point for Halifax. During
Chamberlain's absence, he had borne the brunt of the criticism of
Government policy. While Chamberlain excluded the Foreign Office and
talked daily to Wilson, Halifax was talking with Cadogan and Orme
Sargent. After his initially favourable impression of the Hitler regime, the
Foreign Secretary had, as Maurice Cowling puts it, come 'to loathe
Nazism' and regarded Hitler as 'a criminal lunatic'.

The Cabinet meeting on Sunday the 25th lasted for the best part of the
day, but was unable to reach any clear conclusion. Simon, Maugham
(Lord Chancellor), Kingsley Wood, Stanhope (President of the Board of
Education) and Burgin (Minister for Transport) supported Chamberlain.
Halifax was now firmly among the critics, who included Hailsham, Duff
Cooper, Oliver Stanley, de la Warr, Winterton, Hore-Belisha and Elliot.

That evening, as she awaited news of the outcome of the Cabinet, Baffy
Dugdale felt that 'an awful retribution is preparing for the Cabinet'. If
they were to stand firm, and war was prevented, 'then *what* an indictment
of the policy of surrender, and the rage and the humiliation of the nation
will vent itself (and rightly) upon them.' But if, 'as seems likely, there is
war, Neville could no longer unite the nation.'

She spoke with Viscount Cecil (Bob Cecil), who 'Thinks that the War
Prime Minister would and should be Winston. Bob wants a predominantly
Conservative Government, and would therefore include some Rubber
Stampers [members of the Chamberlain Cabinet], but of course none of
the Old Brutes [Chamberlain, Hoare, Simon] nor Halifax.' When Baffy
Dugdale retorted that '*none* of the present Cabinet have shown themselves
fit to govern in peace or war,' Cecil replied that she should not judge them
too harshly: 'resignations are difficult and unpleasant things to carry
through.' And as Bob Cecil stood on the doorstep to bid her goodbye, she

thought, 'What splendour, what courage, what nobility of soul! If he were only twenty years younger!'

By the evening of Sunday the 25th, both the Czech and French Governments had rejected Hitler's terms. Chamberlain prevented publication of Jan Masaryk's letter, which informed the Government of Prague's rejection, for fear that it would trigger an immediate German invasion.

But on Sunday evening Masaryk gave a press conference, and on the morning of Monday the 26th details of the Godesberg terms appeared in both *The Times* and the *New York Times*. Chamberlain had been tipped off about the publication the evening before, and immediately sent a message to Hitler telling him that the leak was the work of the Czechoslovak Legation in London, and assuring him that this was not the 'last word'. It does not seem to have crossed his mind that the Czechs might have been indignant at the proposed transfer of their territory without having had any say.

In Chamberlain's talks with the French on Sunday evening, it emerged that they were unable to give any clear outline of their military plans in the event of a German invasion of Czechoslovakia. The Cabinet met at midnight. The Prime Minister outlined a new initiative. He suggested that he should write to Hitler, recommending that a Joint Commission be set up, with German and Czech members and a British representative. This Commission would consider how to give effect to the proposals currently agreed by the Czech Government (i.e. the Berchtesgaden, or Anglo-French, proposals). Chamberlain felt that there was a chance this might work. If it did not, at least Britain could show that she had made every effort.

The bearer of the new message to Berlin was to be Sir Horace Wilson. If Hitler rejected the plan, Wilson was authorised to say on Chamberlain's behalf that 'France would go to war, and that if that happened it seemed certain that we should be drawn in.'

Chamberlain had conceded what his critics had urged on him since the German annexation of Austria six months earlier – a commitment to support the French if they went to the aid of Czechoslovakia. Duff Cooper left the Cabinet room that night feeling pleased, and amazed.

# CHAPTER THIRTEEN

# MUNICH WEEK

How horrible, how fantastic, incredible it is that we should be digging trenches and trying on gas masks here because of a quarrel in a faraway country between people of whom we know nothing. It seems still more impossible that a quarrel which has already been settled in principle should be the subject of war.

(The Prime Minister, Neville Chamberlain, speaking during his radio broadcast, 27 September 1938)

London awoke on the morning of Monday, 26 September, to the threat of imminent war. Chamberlain's envoy, Sir Horace Wilson, left for Berlin, but even the Prime Minister did not expect the mission to succeed. Hitler was highly unlikely to relinquish the demands he had made at Godesberg.

Despite Chamberlain's efforts, the demands had proved unacceptable to the British Cabinet. *The Times* described them as 'quite incapable of fulfilment'. On the letters page, Leo Amery took pride of place on the issue: 'Are we to surrender to ruthless brutality a free people whose cause we have espoused, but are now to throw to the wolves to save our own skins, or are we still able to stand up to a bully? It is not Czechoslovakia but our own soul that is at stake.'

The country was hurriedly preparing for war. At noon, the Cabinet met and discussed the necessary emergency defence measures at home. The Colonial Secretary reported that he had seen the High Commissioners. They had all said 'in the strongest possible terms' that no opportunity for peace by negotiation should be missed: 'acceptance of Herr Hitler's terms was better than war.' The Secretary for India, Lord Zetland, had already warned his Cabinet colleagues that war against Germany would provoke trouble in India and the Middle East from those who opposed British rule. Most ministers, conscious of the constraints on imperial Britain, were still anxious to avoid any European entanglement.

Ministers agreed that Chamberlain should make a radio broadcast to the nation and the empire the following evening. Prodded by a letter from Churchill, Chamberlain reluctantly agreed that Parliament should be recalled from recess to debate the crisis the following day, Wednesday, 28 September.

That Monday, there were at least two meetings of anti-appeasers. At the first, held in the morning in the office of Brigadier-General Sir Edward Spears in St Stephen's House, across Bridge Street from the House of Commons, Leo Amery found half-a-dozen young Conservative dissidents. The Spears group planned to issue a public statement, as Conservatives, calling for co-operation with Russia. But Amery was strongly opposed, fearing its effect on the rest of the Party: 'At the moment it would only put off many of our people, while once war is declared they will only too readily welcome help from the Devil himself.' And he doubted that it would have much effect on Germany.

During the afternoon, another meeting was held at Churchill's flat, near Victoria Station. Churchill's guests included Leo Amery, Robert Boothby, Robert Cecil, Sir Edward Grigg, Lord Lloyd, Lord Lytton, Harold Macmillan, Harold Nicolson, Sir Archibald Sinclair and Edward Spears.

Churchill's guests were already discussing 'whether National Service should be proclaimed at once', when he burst in, straight from seeing Chamberlain at Number 10. According to Nicolson, Churchill said, 'The Cabinet were in a blue funk last night.' Simon had apparently urged 'further retreat'. But 'the younger people revolted', the Simon faction lost ground, and then the French arrived, 'all brave and solid this time, plus Gamelin [Chief of the French General Staff], who restored confidence. In the end the Cabinet were all united in feeling how brave, how strong, how resolute they had always been.'

Churchill reported the gist of Chamberlain's message to Hitler: 'it is not in the least a retreat. It is merely an attempt to save Hitler's face if he wants to climb down. . . .' Churchill 'had urged the P.M. to mobilise the Fleet at once and call up all reserves. He [Chamberlain] says he will do so at 9 p.m. this evening if Hitler's speech at 8 p.m. is not conciliatory.'

The dissidents then discussed their own plans. Nicolson summarised their position:

> If Chamberlain rats we shall form a united block against him. We do not think he will rat, and therefore we shall then rally behind him (poor man). We shall press for a Coalition Government and the immediate application of war measures. Above all, the blockade must be put into force at once. Then national service, even if it entails conscription of capital. Then at once we must get in touch with Russia.

It seems remarkable that a gathering composed predominantly of Conservatives contemplated 'conscription of capital' and getting 'in touch with Russia'. Chamberlain's determination to appease Germany was largely rooted in his opposition and the opposition of the vast bulk of Conservatives to radical proposals of this kind, since they would entail a transformation of British society and a revolution in Britain's attitude towards the Soviet state.

After leaving Churchill's flat and making his way back to his Inner Temple apartment, Harold Nicolson caught his 'first sight of the War of 1938'. This was a poster in the Strand:

> 'City of Westminster: Air Raid Precautions: Gas Masks' Notice', followed by instructions where to get yourself fitted for masks. My second sight was workmen digging trenches feverishly in Green Park.

The dissidents' desire for an immediate initiative had a quicker impact than they could have dared hope. They had judged that the Germans would be deterred only if it was clear that the British Government would be prepared to fight alongside the Russians. Churchill went straight to see Halifax, to urge the Foreign Secretary that he should issue a statement before Hitler's speech.

That evening, Halifax issued the following statement from the Foreign Office:

> During the last week Mr. Chamberlain has tried with the German Chancellor to find the way of settling peacefully the Czechoslovak question. It is still possible to do so by peaceful negotiations.
>
> The German claim to the Sudeten areas has clearly been conceded by the French, British and Czechoslovak Governments, but if in spite of all efforts made by the British Prime Minister a German attack is made upon Czechoslovakia the immediate result must be that France will be bound to come to her assistance, and Great Britain and Russia will certainly stand by France.
>
> It is still not too late to stop this great tragedy, and for the peoples of all nations to insist on settlement by free negotiations.

Chamberlain was furious. He feared that the statement would provoke Hitler. Unusually, the Foreign Office had not cleared the text with Number 10. The statement had been drafted by Rex Leeper, Head of the Foreign Office's Information Department.

Leeper was as strongly opposed to appeasing Hitler as his former boss, Vansittart, and had become irritated by Number 10's hijacking of foreign policy. But Leeper was penalised for the part he had played and soon found himself moved to another post and the following summer was appointed Minister in Bucharest.

On the Monday, Attlee wrote to Chamberlain. The opposition's strategy bore a striking resemblance to the Foreign Office statement.

Labour's leader declared that the Bad Godesberg terms had 'profoundly shocked British opinion'. The only means by which peace could be preserved was through a joint declaration by Britain, France and Russia 'to resist any attack upon Czechoslovakia'. That evening, a huge Labour Party rally at the Albert Hall pledged resistance to the latest German demands.

The evening of Monday the 26th at Cliveden must have been a singularly depressing affair. The appeasers' cause seemed lost. War looked unavoidable, unless Britain was prepared to accept total humiliation.

Joining the Astors were various relatives, Tom Jones and the Lindberghs. The party listened to Hitler's speech, which was translated for them by two German boys who had spent the summer in England. Lord Astor and Jones were arguing that Britain would have no choice but to fight if the Germans invaded Czechoslovakia, but were countered by Nancy, her son William and Lindbergh. Eventually, Jones was won round, and later wrote, 'Since my talk with Lindbergh on Monday I've sided with those working for peace at any cost in humiliation, because of the picture of our relative unpreparedness in the air and on the ground which Lindbergh painted, and because of his belief that the democracies would be crushed absolutely and finally.'

The influence of Charles Lindbergh has been attested to by A.L. Rowse, one of the younger generation of anti-appeasement fellows of All Souls. 'Great play in those days, I remember, was made of Lindbergh as omniscient in air matters, who was able to assure us that the Russians couldn't fight anyway. Dawson [editor of *The Times*] quoted Lindbergh to me: he was made much of by the Cliveden set.'

Lindbergh's message had in fact already got through to the Cabinet. At their meeting the day before, Kingsley Wood had referred to the American's depressing assessment of relative air strengths. Although the Minister warned that Lindbergh 'had perhaps become an unwitting tool of the Germans', he nevertheless accepted that his analysis was 'fair, if somewhat superficial'.

After the evening at Cliveden, Tom Jones sought to impress Lindbergh's message on the great and the good. He contacted his former political masters. He tried, unsuccessfully, to persuade Baldwin to speak in the Lords. He was no more successful with Lloyd George – there was no meeting of minds between the old Liberal and the American pilot. Jones made no headway at all with Labour, since Hugh Dalton rejected a suggestion that Lindbergh should appear before the Party's National Executive on the grounds that 'we knew exactly what he would say, and did not wish to hear this pro-Hitler and anti-Russian story once again.'

Hitler's wrath in his speech on the Monday evening had been directed at Beneš rather than Chamberlain. This raised slender hopes among the remaining optimists in the Government.

Amery, however, found that Hitler's speech was 'the most horrible thing I have ever heard, more like the snarling of a wild animal than the utterance of a human being, and the venom and vulgarity of his personal vilification of "Beneš the liar" almost made me feel sick.'

Tuesday the 27th was another day of mounting tension. Vita Sackville-West wrote from Sissinghurst to her husband in London:

> I do not at all like the prospect of you staying Friday night in London. If Saturday is really to be the *giorno fatale*, the first raids on London will be launched directly after midnight on Saturday, I mean 1 a.m. on Sunday morning.
>
> In the meantime we are going on with preparations here, as though war were certain. We have all been fitted for gas-masks, and a trench has been dug in the calf-orchard. Everyone is calm, resolute and cheerful. One hears more jokes than ever, although they all realise quite well what it means. I do respect the English for all their faults!

As war loomed, *The Times* asserted that 'The Godesberg Note reverts to the worst form of Prussianism in using the language of a bully, fixing a time limit of a few days.' So much for the 'Spirit of Potsdam', of which *The Times* had held such high hopes shortly after Hitler's accession to power, five years earlier.

At the Foreign Office, Cadogan was having 'A frightful afternoon, the worst I have ever spent'.

A few hundred yards away, in St Stephen's House overlooking Parliament Square, there was a further meeting of dissident Conservative MPs, in Spears's office. Amery again attended, and found that feelings were running high, 'particularly Harold Macmillan, very wild, clamouring for an immediate pogrom to get rid of Neville and make Winston P.M. before the House met [on the following day]. I poured cold water on that sort of talk.'

The exodus from London to the provinces, the 'safe areas', was gathering momentum. The London Underground was temporarily closed for special structural work, to make it suitable for shelter during air-raids.

In Paris, the French Cabinet decided against a general mobilisation for the time being. In the streets outside and at the railway stations, the mass flight from the capital was well under way.

In Berlin, Chamberlain's emissary, Wilson, saw Hitler. In a vain effort to strike a deal with the Führer, Wilson had sought to reassure him, saying that 'A catastrophe must be prevented at all costs. . . . I will try and make these Czechs sensible.' Wilson saw Hitler twice, but got nowhere. At their second meeting, Wilson read out the Prime Minister's declaration, agreed by the Cabinet at midnight on Sunday – Britain would support the French in the event of their going to the aid of the Czechs.

On Tuesday evening, Duff Cooper convinced his colleagues on the inner group (with Inskip, MacDonald and the service ministers also in attendance) that the fleet should mobilise on the following morning, Wednesday the 28th.

Before the inner group met, Cadogan and Halifax had drawn up a new plan, in a last-ditch effort to preserve peace. Essentially the 'time-table' plan, as Cadogan dubbed it, envisaged German occupation of Sudeten areas in stages, from 1 to 31 October. The precise details would be settled by Czech and German plenipotentiaries and an International Boundary Commission. There would also be a joint international guarantee of the new borders. The ministers gave the go-ahead for the new time-table plan to be submitted immediately to Hitler and Beneš.

Late on Tuesday, Hitler wrote to Chamberlain, urging that he should try to persuade the Czechs to change their mind and accept the Godesberg proposals. Halifax had already ordered that the heavy hand should be used to persuade the Czechs to agree to the new time-table plan. They should realise that this was their last chance to escape invasion, and that if they failed to take this opportunity the rest of Europe would become embroiled in a disastrous conflict. After a general European war, Czechoslovakia would be obliterated.

Chamberlain was anxious to conceal from Parliament the degree of pressure which London had exerted on the Czechs to bow to Hitler's demands. He had promised Attlee that a White Paper would be published in time for the emergency debate when Parliament resumed the following afternoon, Wednesday the 28th. But ministers agreed that when the White Paper was printed it should omit the message sent by the Czech Government accepting the Franco-British proposals. This document referred to the strong and continuous pressure put upon the Czech Government by the French and British representatives.

At eight o'clock in the evening of Tuesday, 27 September, the Prime Minister Neville Chamberlain delivered his broadcast to the British nation and empire. It was one of the most remarkable occasions in the history of broadcasting.

The events which prompted the broadcast were extraordinary in themselves. But what makes the occasion so striking are the Prime Minister's comments and the clandestine 'political warfare' which Chamberlain personally authorised during Munich week.

Shortly before Chamberlain was due to make his broadcast, he left a discussion in Wilson's room with Cadogan, Halifax and Wilson. The pressure on Chamberlain showed as he returned to the Cabinet room, where the microphone was installed. Cadogan noted in his diary, 'Poor P.M. (quite exhausted) said "I'm wobbling all over the place" and went in to broadcast.'

Characteristically, Chamberlain began by saying how grateful he was to everyone who had written to him. He then uttered those few, astonishing words, which encapsulated his view of the entire crisis (see the quotation at the head of this chapter).

It seems almost inconceivable that a British Prime Minister should talk in those terms, using the phrase, 'in a faraway country between people of whom we know nothing'. Yet all Chamberlain's actions and earlier statements during the Sudeten crisis are consistent with the phrase. He saw the issues in precisely those terms. He was adamant that Britain and her empire should not be on the brink of war because of events in Central Europe. As far as Chamberlain was concerned, the strategic interests of Britain and her empire did not lie anywhere near Czechoslovakia.

The Prime Minister was still anxious to keep the door open for a peaceful settlement. The last thing that he wanted was to tie Britain's fate to that of the Czechs. He was certainly not going to talk about them in heroic terms.

Yet, when all is said and done, Britain was on the brink of war. The Prime Minister must have known that he would probably be faced, in a few days' time, with the awesome responsibility of asking for an extraordinary effort from British subjects all round the globe. Some would be required to make the supreme sacrifice. But his only justification was Hitler's unreasonable behaviour at Bad Godesberg.

Chamberlain quite deliberately sought to dismiss any idea that major issues of values or interests were at stake:

> However much we may sympathise with a small nation confronted by a big and powerful neighbour, we cannot in all circumstances undertake to involve the whole British Empire in war simply on her account. If we have to fight it must be on larger issues than that. . . .
> Armed conflict between nations is a nightmare to me, but if I were convinced that any nation had made up its mind to dominate the world by fear of its force, I should believe it must be resisted. Under such domination life for people who believe in liberty would not be worth living. . . .

Clearly, Chamberlain did not yet believe that Germany 'had made up its mind to dominate the world'.

Leo Amery's reaction to the broadcast was scathing. He wrote in his diary, 'If ever there was an essential civilian, a citizen accustomed to deal with fellow citizens on City Council or in Cabinet, and a man quite incapable of thinking in terms of force, or strategy, or diplomacy, it is Neville.'

Baffy Dugdale heard the repetition of the broadcast later that evening: '*most* lamentable in tone. I only hope it may complete the conversion of my friends to my point of view! . . . Is the man mad? And then it was translated into German, so that Hitler would be sure to understand that Chamberlain had said tonight that he would not fight for a small nation. Good God!'

The Prime Minister's statement was no great rallying cry to arms. But that was not Chamberlain's purpose. He was still bent on preserving peace, even at this eleventh hour. That was the message he wanted Germany to receive, as well as Britain and the empire. And he wanted that message to get to the German people, not merely their Government.

Chamberlain was fully aware of Hitler's sensitivity to propaganda and its effectiveness. The Nazi Governmen . took great care to see that only its censored and doctored versions of what foreign Governments were saying reached the German people. The impact of messages which were received from outside Germany, by Germans in their own homes, was therefore likely to be all the greater. Hitler would pay more regard to the effect of any foreign broadcast which penetrated his wall of censorship.

The BBC's broadcasts were transmitted to Germany on the medium wave. Later on the Monday evening, a German translation of the Prime Minister's speech was broadcast on BBC transmitters, much to the surprise of listeners in Britain. But there was concern about poor reception in Germany.

Chamberlain was leaving nothing to chance. He personally authorised an intensive propaganda offensive, designed to reach as many ordinary German listeners as possible. The unlikely launch-pad was the commercial station, Radio Luxemburg. By 1938, it was attracting mass audiences throughout Britain and Europe – in Britain, its peak audiences totalled four million listeners, approaching almost half the comparable figures for the BBC.

Yet behind this innocuous façade, Radio Luxemburg was a tool of the British Government's propaganda machine. The front organisation was a company, Wireless Publicity Ltd, set up in 1936. This meant that the Government had a stake in Radio Luxemburg and was able to use the station for 'cultural propaganda'.

Radio Luxemburg was particularly useful because it supplemented the more 'high-brow' efforts of the British Council, and was located only ten

miles from the German border. The British Government were undeterred
by the fact that they were breaking international law. The station provided
the crucial link in Chamberlain's strategy to see that his message was
beamed directly into German living rooms, as a recent study by Nicholas
Pronay and Philip Taylor has revealed.

Chamberlain's speech was relayed live by Radio Luxemburg, although
it was a close-run thing. The BBC and the Post Office engineers only
succeeded in making the connection with Luxemburg – for the first time
ever – with five minutes to spare before the Prime Minister began
speaking. A translation in German was also broadcast.

During the night of the 27th/28th, six messages from the allied leaders,
including Chamberlain, were translated into German and recorded on
discs, for broadcast on Radio Luxemburg – an appeal for a peaceful
settlement from President Roosevelt; the replies to the American
President from Chamberlain, Daladier and Beneš; Chamberlain's message
to Hitler of 1 a.m. on the morning of the 27th; and Chamberlain's radio
broadcast of 8 p.m. that evening.

At 7.45 a.m. on Wednesday the 28th, the company's plane left for
Luxemburg with the discs, which were later played at intervals throughout the day. As the British fleet mobilised, as trenches were being dug
and anti-aircraft guns erected in London, Germans tuning in to Radio
Luxemburg heard Chamberlain's speech and those of the other allied
leaders. The operation continued over the next day, with recordings of
Roosevelt's second appeal and Chamberlain's speech in the House of
Commons on the afternoon of Wednesday the 28th also being translated,
recorded and flown out to Luxemburg for transmission at frequent
intervals.

Chamberlain's unremitting propaganda campaign and his readiness to
use covert methods, in breach of international law, are remarkable. They
belie totally the image of Chamberlain as a naive, old-fashioned, provincial
politician who was completely out of his depth. They show him as a leader
of immense determination, energy and single-mindedness.

On the evening of Chamberlain's broadcast, Sheila Grant Duff received a
'phone call from Hubert Ripka, a Czech journalist and academic, in
Prague, saying that Britain was again putting great pressure on the Czechs
to concede Hitler's demands. When she called Churchill to pass on this
information, he was angry with her. 'He had only the previous day himself
seen the Prime Minister and Foreign Secretary and they had assured him
that all this was at an end.' Churchill wondered if he, personally, had to
draw the Czechs' attention to the firm statement from Halifax at the
Foreign Office (this was the statement which had angered Chamberlain

and led to Leeper being moved to other duties). 'What more', Churchill shouted down the 'phone, 'did the Czechs want. They were having me on and I better take care and he all but slammed down the receiver.'

Unbeknown to Churchill, the Foreign Office statement had been disowned by Number 10. Despite what had been said in Churchill's own talk with Chamberlain and Halifax, the Prime Minister was still seeking a deal with Hitler.

The British Cabinet met shortly after Chamberlain's broadcast on Tuesday evening. The pull of the empire on British policy was felt ever more powerfully. The High Commissioners from the Dominions 'had all visited Downing Street that afternoon and had all represented that in their view further pressure should be put upon the Czechoslovak Government to accept Herr Hitler's terms'.

The Prime Minister's adviser, Wilson, had returned from his talks with Hitler and told ministers that the only way to prevent the Germans taking to arms was for the Czechs to concede the Bad Godesberg demands. Duff Cooper, who had entertained Churchill to dinner at the Admiralty that night, attacked Wilson's plan. Halifax said that he could not back the idea, because he would be unable to assure the Czechs that the Germans would stop at the points indicated on Hitler's map as the limits of the German occupation. This was decisive, and Wilson's case was lost.

Hopes for peace were fading fast. Cooper was calling for the immediate mobilisation of the fleet, a demand which he had confided to Churchill over dinner and which had prompted the latter to recall his own 'experiences a quarter of a century before . . .'. Cooper's demand was eventually granted, and all ships were sent the warning telegram shortly before midnight.

Chamberlain was still desperately hoping that something would turn up. He told ministers that he would avoid giving any commitment to Czechoslovakia in his Commons speech the following day.

During Tuesday the 27th, Roosevelt had written to Hitler suggesting an immediate conference 'of all the nations directly interested' in the Czech crisis, to be held 'in some neutral spot in Europe'. The next day, Chamberlain echoed the American appeal, proposing that a five-power conference be convened. He wrote to Hitler, 'I cannot believe that you will take the responsibility of starting a world war which may end civilisation for the sake of a few days' delay in settling this long-standing problem.' Chamberlain also sent a message to Mussolini, urging him to use his influence with Hitler.

On Wednesday the 28th, Chips Channon flew back from France, in time to hear Chamberlain's speech in the Commons. When he arrived at Heston airport, 'there was war atmosphere, with young airmen lounging about, smoking; we heard the word "Boche" again, and someone said "mufti". It was 1914 all over again.'

By midday, crowds were gathering around the Palace of Westminster, where MPs were beginning to arrive for the afternoon's debate. Yet the crowds were eerily quiet as they watched and waited in Parliament Square.

At lunchtime, shortly before leaving Number 10 for the Commons, Chamberlain heard that Hitler had been persuaded to postpone military action for twenty-four hours. Mussolini was in touch with Hitler and had suggested that he should accept the calls for an international conference. The French Government had also informed Hitler that they were prepared to make more concessions.

The Commons was packed, as were the galleries for distinguished visitors. There to hear the Prime Minister were his wife, Anne, Queen Mary and the Duke and Duchess of Kent. Among the contingent of foreign observers was the son of the American Ambassador, the young John F. Kennedy, then in his early twenties.

When Chamberlain entered the Chamber of the House of Commons that afternoon, Harold Nicolson was already in his seat on the back-benches. The Prime Minister 'was greeted with wild applause by his supporters, many of whom rose in their seats and waved their order-papers. The Labour Opposition, the Liberal Opposition and certain of the National supporters [including Nicolson] remained seated.'

A little while later, shortly before three o'clock, the Prime Minister 'rose slowly in his place' from the green leather Treasury bench, 'spread the manuscript of his speech upon the box in front of him' and opened the emergency debate. In front of him on the table of the Commons was a microphone, installed so that Peers who could not find a seat on the benches reserved for them at the front of the public gallery could listen to the speech, specially relayed to the House of Lords library.

Within minutes, the Prime Minister was warning the House that 'Today we are faced with a situation which has had no parallel since 1914.' He outlined the three options open to the Government in the summer, when negotiations between the Czech Government and the Sudeten Germans became deadlocked. 'Either we could have threatened to go to war with Germany if she attacked Czechoslovakia, or we could have stood aside and allowed matters to take their course, or, finally, we could attempt to find a peaceful solution by way of mediation' (Hansard, 28 September 1938, cols 5–6).

Chamberlain again cited the mood of the country as a major reason for the Government's rejecton of war with Germany. 'Indeed, this country, which does not readily resort to war, would not have followed us if we had tried to lead it into war to prevent a minority from obtaining autonomy, or even from choosing to pass under some other Government' (ibid., col. 6).

What the Prime Minister did not say was that the Government had made little effort to explain the issues involved, or give any kind of lead to the country. Every effort had been made to prevent alternative points of view being expressed – Churchill was still effectively banned from broadcasting on the BBC, Nicolson's talks had been restricted to non-controversial topics, and even Vernon Bartlett's news programme for children had been censored.

As the *Listener* had commented at the time, people were listening to the radio for news and information 'as never before'. But apart from the recorded statements of the Prime Minister, 'what else are we being given? . . . Surely, though, it should be possible to broadcast even one talk explaining, as simply as possible, the facts about the Czechoslovak problem.'

In his speech, Chamberlain referred only to the rights of one minority, the Sudeten Germans, with no mention either of the sovereign rights of the majority, the people of Czechoslovakia, or of the rights of minorities within the Sudetenland who were opposed to Nazi rule. There were shades of his reference in his broadcast the night before to 'a faraway country', as he told MPs, 'However remote this territory may be, we knew, of course, that a spark once lighted there might give rise to a general conflagration, and we felt it our duty to do anything in our power to help the contending parties to find agreement' (ibid.).

Yet the Prime Minister was deliberately concealing a crucial part of the story from Parliament. Most MPs were unaware of the scale of the pressure which the British Government had exerted on the Czech Government to concede to Hitler's demands. Had they known, they would have better appreciated the grim irony in Chamberlain's reference to doing 'anything in our power to help the contending parties to find agreement'.

Nicolson gave his own eye-witness account of the events in the Commons, in one of his series of regular talks on BBC radio, broadcast that night. He described how the Prime Minister 'spoke in calm and measured tones and the House listened to him in dead silence. . . .' The only interruptions came from the Commons' messengers bringing in their pink message slips and telegrams to MPs. Churchill, 'who sits at the end of my row, received so many telegrams that they were clipped together by an elastic band'.

As Nicolson recounted,

The first burst of applause occurred when Mr Chamberlain mentioned Lord Runciman's great services, and as he did so, he removed his pince-nez between his finger and thumb, raised his face to the skylight and spoke with friendly conviction. Being an experienced Parliamentarian, he would abandon his manuscript at moments and speak extempore.

While Chamberlain was speaking, Hitler had set in train the events which were suddenly to transform the whole situation. The Führer's message was transmitted via Henderson and Cadogan at the Foreign Office to the Palace of Westminster. It was rushed across the few hundred yards from the Foreign Office to the Commons and handed in to the officials' box at the back of the Speaker's chair on the Government side of the Chamber, and was then hurriedly passed to Chamberlain's Parliamentary Private Secretary, Lord Dunglass, sitting on the bench directly behind the Prime Minister. Since Chamberlain was speaking, Dunglass passed it forward to Sir John Simon, sitting next to the Prime Minister. But Simon did not appreciate the urgency of the message, and made no immediate effort to hand it to Chamberlain. An anxious Dunglass realised that the Prime Minister was nearing the end of his speech, and felt that he should see the message before sitting down. After an agonising delay, Simon eventually realised that he should attract Chamberlain's attention and hand him the note.

Chamberlain had been speaking for over an hour. He had just revealed Hitler's agreement to postpone sending in his troops for twenty-four hours. When Simon showed him the note, the Prime Minister paused for a moment to study it. Although MPs did not hear his comment to Simon, the microphone picked it up, and Peers listening to the relay of the speech distinctly heard Chamberlain ask, 'Shall I tell them now?' They also heard Simon's whispered reply, 'Yes.'

As Nicolson related, the Prime Minister 'adjusted his pince-nez and read the document that had been handed to him. His whole face, his whole body, seemed to change. He raised his face so that the light from the ceiling fell full upon it. All the lines of anxiety and weariness seemed suddenly to have been smoothed out; he appeared ten years younger and triumphant.'

Chamberlain then delivered the dramatic news:

I have something further to say to the House yet. I have now been informed by Herr Hitler that he invites me to meet him at Munich tomorrow morning. He has also invited Signor Mussolini and M. Daladier. Signor Mussolini has accepted and I have no doubt M. Daladier will also accept. I need not say what my answer will be. [An hon. Member: 'Thank God for the Prime Minister!'] (Ibid., col. 26)

Channon was almost overcome with emotion: 'every heart throbbed and there was born in many, in me, at least, a gratitude, an admiration for the PM which will be eternal. I felt sick with enthusiasm, longed to clutch him. . . .'

Nicolson vividly captured the scene:

That, I think, was one of the most dramatic moments which I have ever witnessed. For a second, the House was hushed in absolute silence. And then the whole House burst into a roar of cheering, since they knew that this might mean peace. That was the end of the Prime Minister's speech, and when he sat down the whole House rose as a man to pay tribute to his achievement.

Nicolson's broadcast ended at that point. Yet he had not told his listeners of the real reaction of some anti-appeasers to the dramatic news, and the trouble which this caused them. As Nigel Nicolson's footnote to his father's diary entry reveals, Harold typed some additional words on his carbon copy, at the end of the transcript. These read as follows: 'I remained seated. Liddall [the Conservative Member for Lincoln] behind me, hisses out, "Stand up, you brute!" '

Others who remained seated included Churchill, Eden and Amery. Their reaction was noted by another spectator of the scene in the Commons, who referred to 'the grim, set faces of three men'. Lennox-Boyd recalled that Members near Churchill were shouting, 'Get up! Get up!' The only vocal protest against the news of the Four-Power Conference was uttered by the Communist MP, William Gallagher.

In the circumstances, the emergency debate was adjourned, the House rising far earlier than expected shortly before 4.30 p.m. Churchill approached Chamberlain to wish him 'God speed'. But according to Nicolson, there was an edge in their exchange. 'When all his supporters crowded round him to congratulate him afterwards, he showed great satisfaction and even greater self-satisfaction. Winston came up: "I congratulate you on your good fortune. You were very lucky." The P.M. didn't like that at all.'

In the smoking room afterwards, Amery found Conservative MPs feeling that 'Hitler having once consented to confer could be persuaded by Mussolini to be reasonable, especially if Mussolini joined in the guarantee for the fulfilment of terms.'

Baffy Dugdale had been unable to get a seat in the visitors' galleries at the Commons, and had listened to the reports of the Prime Minister's speech being carried on the radio as Chamberlain spoke. Her first reaction at the news was 'incredible, almost stunning, relief'. She quickly began to have doubts, but within ten minutes Walter Elliot was telephoning her from the Commons, 'still under the intoxication of the House of Commons scene'. She understood from 'that contact with one person over the telephone . . . why no voice of criticism, or even question of policy could conceivably have been raised in the House of Commons *today*'.

In Downing Street, the crowd who rushed to surround Chamberlain's car as it returned from the Commons found the Prime Minister 'a changed man'. Smiling and waving his hat, he commented, 'It's all right this time,' and took his wife affectionately by the arm as they turned to enter Number 10.

Although few of the crowd could yet have been aware of exactly what had happened in the Commons, *The Times* reported: 'There was none the less a remarkable change in atmosphere. A great load seemed to have been lifted from their minds. . . . The change in public demeanour was as plain as the difference between "before" and "after" in a pictorial advertisement.'

Churchill later issued a statement to the press, making it clear that he had 'wished the Prime Minister "God-speed" in his mission, from the bottom of my heart'. He added that Chamberlain's 'indomitable exertions . . . to preserve peace' made it certain that, should he be forced to declare war, 'his signal will be obeyed by a united nation and accepted by a united Empire. . . .'

Leo Amery walked home from the Commons with the Conservative backbencher Godfrey Nicholson and Labour's Hugh Dalton. He found them 'very pessimistic both about the betrayal of the Czechs and about Russia being left out of the picture'.

At a meeting of the League of Nations Union later that day, Baffy Dugdale saw opposition MPs 'who had not been enthusiastic themselves, but had met the impact of the enthusiasm. They were like men who had been bruised.' Violet Bonham Carter, 'hard as steel, took Archie Sinclair, her leader, to task, in front of us all for having said nothing. He and Philip [Noel-Baker] both assured us that it would have been *physically* impossible, but Violet was implacable.'

That afternoon in the City, Douglas Jay happened to meet two friends, Paul Einzig and 'Otto' Clarke (later Sir Richard Clarke, Permanent Secretary to the Treasury in the 1960s). As they stood on the traffic island at the junction of Threadneedle Street and Bishopsgate, Einzig told Jay that 'Chamberlain had surrendered and announced in Parliament he was going to Munich.' As Jay has recalled, 'Clarke asked me: "Which is worse, fear or shame?" We all three answered: "Shame".'

That night, Nicolson wrote in his diary, 'I find an immense sense of *physical* relief, in that I shall not be afraid tonight of the German bombs. But my moral anxieties are in no way diminished.'

★

In a blaze of congratulation and publicity, Chamberlain left for the Four-Power Conference at Munich early in the morning of Thursday the 29th. The Cabinet turned out to wish him well, with the sole exception of the dissident Lord Winterton.

The morning's press was 'ecstatic', although in the case of the *Daily Telegraph*, criticism of the impending talks had been stifled. Its draft leader on Munich was dropped after the editor, Seymour Berry (son of Lord Camrose), was warned by Sir Samuel Hoare, the Home Secretary, not to be critical.

Nicolson's friends telephoned to say how awful they thought the outcome of the talks would be, but there was also a call from an old adversary, 'Margot Oxford [Asquith's second wife] rings me up and says, "Now Harold, you must agree that he is a great man." I say, "Not at all." "You are as bad as Violet [Bonham Carter, her stepdaughter]", she snaps; "he [Chamberlain] is the greatest Englishman that ever lived." '

Chamberlain's arrival in Munich fell short of the heroic. According to Vernon Bartlett, who was reporting the conference for the *News Chronicle*, the Prime Minister was about to review the SS guard of honour when he realised that he had left his umbrella on the plane, and sent his Private Secretary to retrieve it.

The talks between the four powers' leaders at the Führerhaus in Munich were surprisingly informal and perfunctory. This reflected the desire held by all four powers to reach a settlement. The British, the French and the Italians did not want a war. Within the Nazi leadership, there were those who wanted a peaceful settlement. Hitler himself was acutely aware that he had lost any element of surprise in his planned occupation of Czechoslovakia. He could no longer secure the annexation of the Sudetenland without precipitating a general European conflict.

There was little sign of enthusiasm for such a war among the German people. Privately, the Luftwaffe were far more sceptical than Lindbergh or the British Air Staff about their ability to bomb targets in Britain. Hitler was cutting his losses for the time being, and getting as much as he could from an international agreement. In any event, it seemed that London and Paris were desperately anxious to concede a good part of what he wanted, and were ready to see that the terms were imposed on the Czech Government.

Although Hitler was annoyed at having backed down, he was still in a stronger position than Chamberlain, who was desperate for the conference to succeed. Hitler had little trouble in rejecting the British Prime Minister's suggestion that the Czechs should be included as participants at the talks.

★

In London, there was deep apprehension among anti-appeasers as the news from Munich was awaited. Their headquarters was the Savoy Hotel, in the Strand. They gathered in a private room for a lunch planned weeks before by the Freedom and Peace group. Their numbers included Churchill, Sinclair, Arthur Henderson, the Tory rebel peers Cecil, Lloyd and Lytton, Harold Nicolson, Arthur Salter (the Independent MP, representing one of the Oxford University seats), the Liberals Megan Lloyd George and Violet Bonham Carter, and the journalists Wickham Steed, Walter Layton and Liddell Hart, and the author Norman Angell.

Most of the afternoon was spent drafting a telegram to send Chamberlain telling him that if he sought to impose further onerous terms on the Czechs the signatories would oppose him in Parliament. The intention was that Churchill, Cecil, Attlee, Eden, Sinclair and Lloyd should sign. But the plan foundered. According to Nicolson, 'Anthony Eden refused to sign on the grounds that it would be interpreted as a vendetta against Chamberlain' (Eden himself later had no recollection of this incident, and could find no mention of it in his diary or papers). Attlee refused to sign without the approval of his Party.

'There was thus no time,' wrote Nicolson. 'We sat there gloomily realising that nothing could be done. Even Winston seemed to have lost his fighting spirit.' Violet Bonham Carter recalled that 'Leaden despair descended upon us as we realised our helplessness; and when we parted there were tears in Winston Churchill's eyes.'

Churchill stayed on at the Savoy for a dinner of the Other Club, an all-party, non-political group which he and the late F.E. Smith (Lord Birkenhead) had established nearly thirty years earlier. Those attending included two Government ministers, Duff Cooper and Walter Elliot, the peers Horne and Moyne, the MPs Bracken, Boothby, Richard Law, David Lloyd George and Archibald Sinclair, the journalists J.L. Garvin, Walter Layton and Colin Coote, and 'the Prof', Lindemann.

The atmosphere of 'Munich night' instantly pervaded the gathering. Coote later wrote that following the earlier failure of the Freedom and Peace meeting,

> Churchill was in a towering rage and a deepening gloom. . . . he turned savagely upon the two Ministers present, Duff Cooper and Walter Elliot. One could always tell when he was deeply moved, because a minor defect in his palate gave an echoing timbre to his voice. On this occasion it was not an echo, but a supersonic boom. How, he asked, could honourable men with wide experience and fine records in the Great War condone a policy so cowardly? It was sordid, sub-human, and suicidal.

Duff Cooper sought to defend the actions of the Government of which he was a member, but with which he had such little sympathy. The argument raged. Cooper wrote in his diary, 'I insulted Prof. Lindemann, Bob Boothby *and* I insulted Garvin, so that he left in a rage. Then everyone insulted everybody else and Winston ended by saying that at the next General Election he would speak on every Socialist platform in the country against the Government.'

As the acrimonious evening wore on at the Savoy, across the West End, in St James's Street, Nicolson had been waiting to hear the news from Munich. He had left following the abortive attempt to send a telegram to Chamberlain: 'Afterwards I go to Brooks' [gentleman's club] to look at the tape. So far as one can see, Hitler gets everything he wants.'

Outside the Savoy, newsboys began announcing that agreement had been reached at Munich. Coote rushed out to buy a paper. When he returned, Duff Cooper seized it and read out the terms. As Coote later recalled, 'There was a silence as if all had been stricken dumb. Duff rose, and exited without a word.' But according to Boothby, who was also at the dinner, as Cooper left he whispered that he would resign.

As the remaining members of the Other Club left the Savoy, Churchill paused at the door of a packed restaurant and muttered to Richard Law, 'Those poor people! They little know what they will have to face.'

The Munich terms, agreed in the early hours of Friday, 30 September, marked little more than a minor retreat by Hitler from the demands he had made at Bad Godesberg. The Munich Agreement was only marginally nearer to the Anglo-French proposals.

Under the terms of Munich, German troops would occupy heavily German areas in the Sudetenland between 1 and 10 October. The extent of any further German occupation would be settled by an international commission, which would include representatives from the German and Czech Governments and would oversee plebiscites in any areas which might subsequently be ceded to Germany. In addition, Britain and France guaranteed Czechoslovakia's new borders. When the terms were relayed to Prague, the Czech Government felt they were left with no realistic alternative but to accept the outcome.

At breakfast at their hotel on Friday morning, Chamberlain discussed with Dunglass his plan to return to see Hitler and persuade him to sign a general agreement between Britain and Germany. The Prime Minister was particularly concerned that he should be able to demonstrate to the Americans who was in the right and who was in the wrong in any subsequent conflict. If Hitler signed, and honoured it, that was all well and good. If, however, Hitler breached the agreement, he would plainly be seen as the guilty party, and it would be easier to rally opinion against him, particularly in America.

Home has recalled that when they returned to the Führerhaus later on the Friday morning, they found Hitler in a foul mood. Nonetheless, Chamberlain suggested that he and the Führer should agree a statement of general understanding between their two Governments. Hitler concurred. As Chamberlain read out the short proposed draft, the Führer repeatedly shouted '*Ja!*' Both leaders signed the Anglo-German Agreement, pledging that the two countries would attempt to resolve any future differences through discussion and not force.

After Chamberlain left Munich, Hitler was reported to have commented, 'If ever that silly old man comes here again with his umbrella, I'll kick him downstairs and jump on his stomach in front of photographers.'

# CHAPTER FOURTEEN
# 'SHAME AND RELIEF'

He [Halifax] told me he thought it was a horrid business and
humiliating, no use blinking the fact, but yet better than a
European war.

(Oliver Harvey, diary entry, 1 October 1938)

'Shame and relief.' That was the reaction which Sir Isaiah Berlin recalls
his father giving at the news of Munich, echoing the former French
Premier, Léon Blum.

'Came down to breakfast to read that in Munich honour died,' observed
Baffy Dugdale.

'Meanwhile the paeans of hysterical praise are almost nauseating,'
wrote Oliver Harvey. 'Not a word about the Czechs and poor Beneš, at
whose expense and by whose consent peace had been achieved.'

'But what one hates is the terrible ghastly farce of that "victory drive",'
Ronnie Cartland told his sister Barbara, 'that "triumphant" appearance on
the balcony of Buckingham Palace when in the streets of Prague the
people wept openly at being forsaken.'

Churchill's wife, Clementine, and Lord Cecil 'solemnly discussed
marching themselves with a select band to Downing Street and hurling
a brick through the windows at Number 10.' This was Churchill's
recollection of the mood after Munich, written in a private note some years
later, and revealed by his biographer Martin Gilbert.

The Foreign Office 'was unenthusiastic, and within the bounds of
propriety, positively hostile.' But John Colville, then a Third Secretary
(later Private Secretary at Number 10), shared the enthusiasm of the
crowds greeting Chamberlain. 'So for some minutes I stood alone on the
first-floor balcony facing Number 10, while my colleagues buried their
recalcitrant heads in their work.' Colville was soon joined by one of the
leading anti-appeasers:

While the returning Prime Minister's car was surging through
hysterical crowds, a french window opened beside me and the
Deputy Under Secretary, Sir Orme Sargent, stepped on to the
balcony. He surveyed the scene below with dislike and disdain. 'You

might think', he said to me, 'that we had won a major victory instead
of betraying a minor country.' Then, after a pause, as the window
opposite opened and it was clear that Chamberlain was expected to
say a few words, Sargent added: 'I can bear almost anything
provided he doesn't say it is Peace with Honour.'

As the crowd cheered, Sargent 'turned on his heel, closed the french
window behind him', and left Colville alone on the balcony.

One diplomat resigned his post at the British Embassy in Berlin in
protest over Munich. He was Con O'Neill (later Sir Con O'Neill, the
distinguished diplomat), then twenty-six years old, a fellow of All Souls,
and the son of the Unionist MP, Sir Hugh O'Neill, then chairman of the
Conservative 1922 backbench committee and one of the most senior
loyalists on the Government backbenches. Roger Makins (later Permanent
Secretary at the Foreign Office, subsequently Lord Sherfield) recalls
spending an evening over a bottle of vodka in Berlin, trying to persuade
O'Neill to change his mind.

O'Neill wrote to his friend Jo Grimond saying that he was 'disgusted
with the attitude and arguments of most of my Embassy colleagues and
particularly with the behaviour of our notorious Ambassador'. Unfortunately, he was required to stay on for three months before his resignation
took effect – 'It is harder, if you will permit me a gruesome image, to
drown oneself in cold blood,' he wrote to Grimond. O'Neill's father
appealed to Sir Horace Wilson to persuade his son to reverse his decision
and stay on. Wilson replied that not only would he refuse to do so, he
would insist that he should go.

When Walter Elliot told Baffy Dugdale that he would accept the
Munich terms and not resign from the Cabinet over them, she retorted
that 'for both our sakes, and the sake of our past and our future, we had
better pull down the shutters between us for the present, and would he let
me decide when we might pull them up again. . . . He agreed to all this –
much moved. . . .'

At first, the sentiments of the anti-appeasers were drowned in a flood-
tide of emotion. Chamberlain was receiving strong support across the
political spectrum. Before Munich, the veteran trade unionist Ben Tillett
wrote to him, 'Some day the wonderful part you have played with patience
to avert the degradation and brutality, will be estimated for its worth and
meaning.'

The former Liberal Party leader, Viscount Samuel, himself a Jew,
wrote to the Prime Minister on the Friday immediately after Munich, 'I
would offer you my warmest congratulations. I have followed the course of
the negotiations, not only with full sympathy for the object in view but

with complete agreement with the course you have taken at every stage. Any fool can go to war, but it needs the highest qualities of statesmanship to keep the peace. These you have shown in full measure. . . .'

The Conservative MP Victor Cazalet heard the news when he arrived in Auckland, New Zealand. He was to become highly critical of Munich, but when he first heard of the settlement he wrote in his journal, 'War over. What a relief! Out in these parts universal support for Chamberlain.' Cazalet was later killed during the war, in the plane crash that killed the Polish leader General Sikorski – Cazalet was serving as liaison officer between the Free Poles and the British Government.

Harold Macmillan later observed of the period immediately following Munich, 'The whole world seemed united in gratitude to the man who had prevented war. No wonder the Prime Minister lived in an exalted, almost intoxicated mood. To question his authority was treason; to deny his inspiration almost blasphemy.'

At the Friday evening Cabinet, only Duff Cooper voiced any uneasiness. Although he conceded that the Munich terms were an improvement on the Bad Godesberg demands 'he was afraid that we might get into the position in which we were drawn into making further concessions.'

Afterwards, the National Labour leader, Buck de la Warr, told Nicolson that Munich was 'not quite as bad' as he (Nicolson) had thought. Even Vansittart, the leading anti-appeaser in Whitehall, urged Nicolson not to attack Chamberlain. 'If we start recriminations we shall create splits. What we have got to do is to come together for the next danger.' In Vansittart's view, Chamberlain would be forced to form a coalition government, and the likes of Nicolson would rule themselves out if they were to attack Munich.

Leo Amery was due to fulfil a long-standing constituency engagement in Birmingham Sparkbrook, Chamberlain's home city. Before he left, Baffy Dugdale had seen him. Although he would not sign her petition from the League of Nations Union, she noted: 'I did not realise quite what courage it takes for a Conservative M.P. to go against the tide *tonight*. The scenes of the P.M.'s return . . . seem to have beggared description.'

Amery found his constituents 'delirious with enthusiasm', but nonetheless voiced his 'misgivings'. In due course, he warned, 'the question of what kind of peace we have secured, and the price we have paid for it' would need to be examined, 'We shall have to consider whether it has been altogether a triumph for reason and settlement by conciliation or a barely veiled acceptance of the victory of fear and of naked force. I fear that the latter conclusion is the moral which Germany, and other nations for that matter, are likely to draw.'

Nicolson attended a meeting of Tories at the home of one of the leading dissidents, Brigadier-General Spears. His intention was to gain signatures to a letter to the press, protesting at the Munich terms. To Nicolson's dismay, 'The Tories there agree with the terms of the letter, but feel it might do them harm in their constituencies.'

The weekend press was almost entirely favourable to Chamberlain. The *Manchester Guardian*, despite its natural abhorrence of Nazism, summed up the feelings of all those who did not want a war, particularly a war over Czechoslovakia: 'great as are the injustices that Czechoslovakia suffers under the Munich Agreement, and they are for her calamitous, they cannot be measured against the horrors that might have extinguished not only Czechoslovakia but the whole of Western civilization.'

The *Daily Telegraph* commented, 'Peace, even at a price, is a blessing so inestimable that the first and predominant reaction to our release from the torturing fears of the past few days is one of profound thankfulness.'

*The Times* eulogised Chamberlain's achievement: 'No conqueror returned from a victory on the battlefield has come home adorned with nobler laurels than MR. CHAMBERLAIN from Munich yesterday; and KING and people have shown alike by the nature of their reception their sense of his achievement. . . .'

Sunday's papers were among Chamberlain's strongest supporters. Chamberlain's closest press confidant, W.W. Hadley, editor of the *Sunday Times*, provided the most uncritical reception for Munich. Neither France nor Britain had been ready to fight. Chamberlain had heralded in a new dawn in Europe, in which fighting might never again be necessary. And tribute was paid to Hitler: 'we must acknowledge the courage that dared go back on an ultimatum – a very difficult step, and not least so for a dictator.' In the same paper, 'Atticus' wrote, 'And now I am going home to take all my books on Europe, place them in my garden trench and have it filled in.'

The *Observer*, edited by J.L. Garvin, like Dawson one of the Milnerite appeasers, wondered what the opposition parties would have done. The Munich settlement was the only possible option, given the circumstances.

But the most fulsome praise came from the Conservative-inclined *Sunday Graphic*, where the columnist Beverley Baxter wrote, 'because of Neville Chamberlain the world my son will live in will be a vastly different place. . . . In our time we shall not see again the armed forces of Europe gathering to strike at each other like savage beasts.'

On Saturday morning, Virginia Woolf's postman told her, 'How all will worship C[hamberlai]n now: but in 5 years' time we may be saying we ought to have put him, Hitler, down now. These dictators and their lust for power – they can't stop. He'll get stronger and stronger. Then . . . But now we can't help being glad of peace. It's human nature. We're made that way. . . .'

Later that morning, Duff Cooper saw Chamberlain at Number 10 and tendered his resignation. Walter Elliot had told Cooper that if he (Cooper) resigned, he would go too. Cooper dissuaded him, saying it would be better for him to go alone, since he did not want to injure the Government.

Cadogan commented in his diary, 'Good riddance of bad rubbish.' Channon wrote, 'I am sorry for Diana; they give up £5,000 per annum, a lovely house – and for what? Does Duff think he will make any money at literature?'

But Cooper received a letter from Louis Mountbatten, who wrote:

I expect it is highly irregular of me, a serving naval officer, writing to you on relinquishing your position as First Lord, but I cannot stand by and see someone whom I admire behave in exactly the way I hope I should have the courage to behave if I had been in his shoes, without saying 'Well done'.

Saturday's issue of *The Times* included the large photograph of the Chamberlains on the balcony of Buckingham Palace, with the King and Queen. Lady Diana Cooper saw the photograph 'torn and burnt in the fireplace by a man of principle'.

Vansittart's advice was disregarded by Nicolson, who attacked Munich in his speech in Manchester. He depressed his audience, who 'had all hoped against hope that the Prime Minister was right'. But they subsequently confessed their own doubts about what had been done: 'Many of them said to me afterwards, "You have put into words the feeling which we woke up with this morning and which we at once suppressed." '

The staunchly anti-appeasement *News Chronicle* first raised the critics' standard in the press, suggesting that there was a price to pay for the Munich settlement. Relief was natural, but 'for all that, we may already begin to ask what is the price we have had to pay. That price is the sacrifice of a small and noble people; a people that have borne themselves throughout this crisis with a courage, a nerve and a restraint which have been an example to all democracies.'

Press criticism of Munich sharpened. The Conservative *Daily Telegraph* qualified its initial welcome with a warning that Hitler's assurances could not always be trusted, and it soon moved to share the ground occupied by the Tory rebels. The *Manchester Guardian* and the *News Chronicle* attacked Chamberlain for the plight of a much weakened Czechoslovakia and the reduced prospects for democracy in Europe. Labour's *Daily*

*Herald* argued that Chamberlain should have involved other powers, not least the Czechs themselves, and the Russians. In similar vein, the pro-Labour *Reynold's News* criticised Chamberlain for destroying what remained of collective security.

As the debate was hotting up in the press, so the rows were starting in the country. On the night of Duff Cooper's resignation, Lady Willingdon, 'an ex-Vicereine' (wife of a former Viceroy of India), commented to Kenneth Clark, 'I should like to crush his head to a jelly.' As Clark observed, 'It showed how rapidly civilised modes of thought and behaviour can vanish under the pressure of bad conscience and the threat of danger.'

A short while after Munich, Lady Diana Cooper was visiting Conrad Russell. He wrote to Fiona, his sister, that Lady Diana 'talked "crisis" the whole evening. Lady Horner and Katharine [Asquith] listened in hostile silence, being very strong Chamberlainites. They think Duff mad or inexplicably silly.'

Friendships were strained. C.P. Snow, the novelist, and then a scholar at Cambridge University, argued bitterly with his close friend, Charles Allberry – on whom Snow later based the character of Roy Calvert in *The Light and the Dark*. Allberry was then an Oriental scholar, and he and a German professor were the world experts on Coptic scripts. As Philip Snow has written, 'The two Charleses argued endlessly as Munich came and went – Allberry trying to hide from the inevitable, Charles [C.P. Snow] maintaining that war had to come if civilization was to survive.' Allberry later volunteered, 'in utter despair', as a bomber pilot: 'C.R.C. Allberry is now merely a name on the War Memorial plaque in Christ's Chapel.'

Hugh Gaitskell's vehement opposition to Munich led to a temporary breach with his friend Robert Fraser, leader writer on the *Daily Herald*, who was passionately pro-Chamberlain. It also severely strained Gaitskell's relations with the economist Evan Durbin, who felt that there was no case, whether diplomatic, moral or strategic, for war with Germany over the Sudetenland. Gaitskell wrote to Durbin, 'I suppose you just don't realise how deeply some of us feel this business or how helpless we feel about the future. . . .' Although he did not agree with them, he could at least understand the argument that said strategically Britain was in no state to fight, or even the pacifist view, 'But I cannot understand those who thought it *morally* right. . . . I do not often cry – but I did after Berchtesgaden – the last time was on February 14th 1934 [the defeat of the Austrian socialists].'

Social occasions were wrecked. At a luncheon party, Barbara Cartland was told that 'those traitors – Winston Churchill, your brother [Ronald Cartland] and his like should be shot.'

At a dinner party at Kenneth Clark's country home at Lympne, in Kent, Maurice Bowra clashed with an acquaintance of Robert Boothby's, a pro-Nazi, called Eckersley. When Eckersley delivered a ferocious attack on bourgeois society, Bowra 'suddenly let out a stream of abuse in sergeant-major language'. The clash culminated when Bowra told Eckersley, 'I look forward to using your skull as an inkpot.' Clark ordered them both to leave.

Violet Bonham Carter spent 'all dinner' arguing politics with William Jolliffe some weeks later. But according to Conrad Russell, their debate was 'sotto voce for fear of an explosion. I could just hear "League of Nations" and "Appeasement" faintly whispered as if they were the kinds of buggery which they feared might be overheard. I think a flare up and wigs on the green would have been preferable. Billy is for Chamberlain out and out.'

Families were divided. Often it was a generation difference, the parents for Munich, the children against. Partly this reflected the parents' recollections of the 1914–18 war – in many cases the fathers had served, and many people in their forties and fifties had lost brothers or close friends. The historian Robert Blake recalls arguing about Munich with his parents. He thought it was a disaster, but to his parents Munich meant that the horrors of the Great War would not be visited upon their son's generation.

'Feelings were divided' in Harold Macmillan's family and his wife's, the Cavendishes (family name of the Dukes of Devonshire) who 'were slower to move' over Munich than the Cecils. Macmillan's gesture of defiance on Guy Fawkes night caused trouble:

> It was our custom every year, on 5th November, to have a fine bonfire at home and to crown it with a straw figure, wearing an old hat or cast-off suit. . . . This year we had a splendid representation, of Chamberlain, and sacrificed for the purpose a black Homburg hat in quite good repair, as well as a rolled umbrella. Some of my relations were staying with us at the time and this caused a deep feud. What made the scene more dramatic was the presence of some forty or fifty Czech refugees to whom I had been able to give shelter and hospitality in various houses and cottages on our estate.

In some cases Munich literally split families. Christopher Cadogan, an undergraduate at Oxford University and a Liberal, was strongly opposed to Munich. But his father Commander Cadogan thought Munich was excellent and ordered the family butler to bring the best champagne from the cellar to toast Chamberlain's success. Christopher refused to join in the toast. Commander Cadogan immediately ordered his son from the house.

They were finally reconciled after war had broken out. Not long afterwards Christopher was killed in the Mediterranean.

The weekend after Munich, both Chamberlain and Churchill repaired to the country to prepare their speeches for the Commons debate. Lady Diana Cooper telephoned Churchill to tell him herself of her husband's resignation. She later recalled his reaction: 'His voice was broken with emotion. I could hear him cry.'

During Saturday morning, Churchill's sole visitor at Chartwell was the young BBC radio producer Guy Burgess, who was a Soviet agent at this time and who had also been recruited by the British Secret Service.

Churchill was worried that he had received a request for 'advice and assistance' from President Beneš – 'Herr Beans' as he called him – yet did not know how he could reply. According to Burgess's biographer Tom Driberg, Churchill then asked Burgess, ' "What advice can I return, what assistance can I proffer? Here am I" – Churchill added, rising from his seat and thumping his chest – "here am I, an old man, without power and without party. What advice can I give, what assistance can I proffer?" ' When Burgess suggested that Churchill could offer 'his eloquence', Churchill seemed pleased. ' "My eloquence!" Ah, yes, that . . . that Herr Beans can rely on in full and indeed" – he seemed to turn aside and wink at himself – "some would say, in overbounding measure. That I can offer him. . . ." '

As Burgess left to return to London, Churchill handed him a copy of *Arms and the Covenant*, which he inscribed: 'To Guy Burgess, from Winston S. Churchill, to confirm his admirable sentiments'. That evening, after Burgess had returned to London, he wrote to Churchill, attacking Chamberlain and the Munich settlement. He added that he had heard the news of Duff Cooper's resignation, and he urged Churchill, 'You alone have the force & authority to galvanise the potential allies into action.'

That Saturday lunchtime, Chamberlain, by then exhausted, travelled down to Chequers. He wrote to his sister: 'We came here immediately after lunch, and walked up through Crow's Close to the Chequers church way. I came nearer there to a nervous breakdown than I have ever been in my life. I have pulled myself together, for there is a fresh ordeal to go through in the House'.

The Prime Minister also wrote to the Archbishop of Canterbury, telling him that he was 'sure that some day the Czechs will see that what we did was to save them for a happier future'. He also felt that 'we have at last opened the way to that general appeasement' which he was convinced could alone preserve peace.

But drafting his speech would be no easy task. Even during his triumphal reception, the Prime Minister had been aware that the euphoria would quickly fade. As he was driven through the streets of cheering crowds on Friday evening, he remarked to Lord Halifax that 'This will all be over in three months.'

Churchill, in his own account of the war years suggested that Chamberlain was talking about the European crisis itself being over in three months, but this was mistaken. Chamberlain was aware that immense dangers still lay ahead. He also commented to his Foreign Secretary, 'We must hope for the best, but prepare for the worst.'

These admissions by the Prime Minister reveal him to be less naive than the anti-appeasers thought at the time and than many have thought since. But they indicate too the difficult position in which he found himself as a result of his personal diplomacy with Hitler.

Chamberlain had to present a convincing case both for the settlement with Hitler and for the continuation, even acceleration, of British rearmament. Nicolson neatly summed up the quandary in which Chamberlain and his supporters found themselves, when he wrote: 'It is difficult to say, "This is the greatest diplomatic achievement in history: therefore we must redouble our armaments in order never again to be exposed to such humiliation." '

The four-day debate was followed closely. Chamberlain's repetition of Disraeli's claim of 'Peace with Honour' prompted others to do their own historical research. Before Churchill's speech, Conrad Russell wrote to Lady Diana Cooper,

> I've spoken to Katharine [Asquith] on the telephone. I think she's going to remain loyal to the Coroner [Chamberlain]. He's her King and he can do no wrong. When Dizzy said he had brought back Peace with Honour, Mr Herbert Paul said it was the Peace which passeth all understanding and the Honour was that kind of Honour which we are told exists among thieves.

When MPs assembled in the Commons shortly before three o'clock on Monday, 3 October, to debate Munich, they first heard Duff Cooper's resignation speech. Although Cooper spoke for forty minutes, he held the full attention of the House in one of the most powerful speeches of its kind.

Cooper recounted his experience of the previous Friday, as he made his way to attend what turned out to be his last Cabinet meeting, on the evening of Chamberlain's return from Munich: 'I was caught up in the large crowds that were demonstrating their enthusiasm and were cheering, laughing, and singing; and there is no greater feeling of loneliness than to be in a crowd of happy, cheerful people and to feel that there is no occasion for oneself for gaiety or for cheering' (Hansard, 3 October 1938, col. 29).

Cooper believed that the 'great defect in our foreign policy during recent months and recent weeks' had been that Britain had failed to make clear her position. 'During the last four weeks we have been drifting, day by day, nearer into war with Germany, and we have never said, until the last minute, and then in the most uncertain terms, that we were prepared to fight' (ibid., col. 31).

After the 'rape of Austria', Cooper had urged a clear statement of British foreign policy, but his former Cabinet colleagues had told him that the country was 'not prepared to fight for Czechoslovakia'. Yet Cooper argued,

> it was not for Czechoslovakia that we should have been fighting if we had gone to war last week. . . . It was not for Serbia that we fought in 1914. It was not even for Belgium, although it occasionally suited some people to say so. We were fighting then, as we should have been fighting last week, in order that one great Power should not be allowed, in disregard of Treaty obligations, of the laws of nations, and the decrees of morality to dominate by brutal force the Continent of Europe. For that principle we fought against Napoleon Bonaparte, and against Louis XIV of France and Philip II of Spain. For that principle we must ever be prepared to fight, for on the day when we are not prepared to fight for it we forfeit our Empire, our liberties and our independence. (Ibid., cols 31–2)

Chamberlain's continual fear of 'irritating' Hitler was mocked by Cooper, as was the notion that Sir Horace Wilson's mission to Berlin might have some effect on the German Führer: 'We know that a message delivered strictly according to instructions with at least three qualifying clauses was not likely to produce upon him on the morning after his great oration the effect that was desired' (ibid., cols 33–4). This incident pointed up 'the deep difference' between Chamberlain and his former First Lord. 'The Prime Minister has believed in addressing Herr Hitler through the language of sweet reasonableness. I have believed that he was more open to the language of the mailed fist' (ibid., col. 34).

Cooper conceded that the Munich terms were an improvement on Hitler's Bad Godesberg ultimatum, and confessed that he 'spent the greater part of Friday trying to persuade myself that those terms were good enough for me'. But in the end, 'they stuck in my throat'. Although the Prime Minister had won important modifications, 'still there remained the fact that the country [Czechoslovakia] was to be invaded' (ibid., cols 36–7).

The wrench of resigning, but also the reward, can rarely have been better expressed than in Cooper's peroration:

I have forfeited a great deal. I have given up an office that I loved, work in which I was deeply interested and a staff of which any man might be proud. . . . I have ruined, perhaps, my political career. But that is a little matter; I have retained something which is of great value – I can walk about the world with my head erect. (Ibid., col. 40)

Brilliant though the speech was – and maybe because of its brilliance – its immediate impact is now the subject of myth. In his memoirs, *Old Men Forget*, Duff Cooper relates that the speech was reported for *The Times* by its young parliamentary correspondent, Anthony Winn. According to Cooper, the editor Dawson tampered with Winn's copy, playing down the impact of the speech in the House and inserting a description of the speech as a 'damp squib'. Despite Dawson's interference, Winn's by-line still appeared on the report in the following day's editions. Winn was furious and resigned.

Duff Cooper's version of events has generally been accepted. In fact, *The Times* devoted two columns to a full report of Cooper's speech, and the phrase 'damp squib' did not appear. The report was attributed to the paper's staff in the Press Gallery, not to Winn himself – in any case, in those days *The Times* did not use the attribution 'Lobby Correspondent', as Cooper suggested.

Although some clash with Dawson over the reporting of Duff Cooper's speech finally prompted Winn's resignation, the historian Franklin Gannon has revealed that the underlying reason was Winn's growing disillusionment with the paper's editorial stance. In his letter of resignation Winn wrote:

The Duff Cooper episode apart, my distaste for what I frankly regard as a silly and dangerous policy has been hardening for many weeks. . . .

Since, rightly or wrongly, I hold these views it is impracticable for me to be the Parliamentary Correspondent of a paper which was the first responsible advocate of secession, and which still has hopes of a genuine friendship with the Nazi regime.

The standard of rebellion had been run up by Duff Cooper's speech. But the Tory rebels were besieged. The party leadership and many local associations regarded the days after their leader's great triumph as 'open season' for attacks on any rebels.

Harold Nicolson was soon in trouble in his Leicester constituency following his critical speech on the Saturday after Munich. He was attacked in the letters columns of the local press, and discovered that his constituency agent was 'really rattled'.

The rebels' immediate fear was that Chamberlain would call a snap election to cash in on his popularity. A general election was due within the next two years, before the autumn of 1940, and elements within the Government and at Conservative Central Office were urging the Prime Minister to go to the country early.

This advice was supported by the Party's own private analysis. The Conservative Research Department had suggested that on the basis of by-elections during 1938, up to the end of the summer, the Government could expect to be returned at a general election with about the same huge majority in the Commons (around 250). The prospect of another landslide would obviously have been tempting to senior Conservatives. And there was the added attraction for Party loyalists that it might offer an opportunity to silence the critics on their own side.

The vote at the end of the four-day debate on Munich assumed a new significance. Harold Macmillan told Labour's Hugh Dalton of rumours that the vote on the Government's motion would be treated as a test of loyalty: 'Those who abstained this week, as well as any who voted against the Government, would be marked down for destruction and official Tory candidates run against them.'

It was in this highly charged atmosphere that Chamberlain and Attlee opened the first day's debate.

Despite the force of Duff Cooper's speech, Chamberlain refused to respond when he rose to speak immediately afterwards. But it would have taken more than Cooper's speech – however exceptional – to deflect the Prime Minister from his prepared defence of Munich.

Chamberlain argued that the Four-Power Agreement was justified because the Czechs had already accepted the principle of ceding the predominantly German areas of the Sudetenland when they agreed to the Anglo-French proposals. All that remained to be settled were the conditions, method and timing of the transfer. Unless the transfer was settled quickly, there was every chance of a 'conflict which might have precipitated the catastrophe' (ibid., col. 42).

In Chamberlain's view, the terms which Hitler accepted at Munich were a significant improvement on the Bad Godesberg demands. He did not, of course, reveal that it had taken a Cabinet rebellion to prevent his conceding the Bad Godesberg demands. Instead, the House was regaled with a point-by-point account of the gains he had secured from the German Führer on his last visit.

Munich was presented as a reversion to the Anglo-French proposals. Instead of an immediate occupation on 1 October, the Munich terms involved an occupation in five stages over ten days. The details of the German occupation of parts of the Sudetenland, including the drawing of Czechoslovakia's new boundaries, would be set by an international commission. There would also be provision for internationally supervised plebiscites in areas which were not overwhelmingly German. In addition, the Prime Minister proudly proclaimed that Britain would be a guarantor of the new Czech frontiers – though privately Chamberlain had been most reluctant to give any such guarantee.

But Chamberlain's speech was interrupted, and there were cries of 'Shame!' as he continued to recite the list of gains which he claimed to have won from Hitler. The Prime Minister persisted, 'It is my hope and my belief that under the new system of guarantees the new Czechoslovakia will find a greater security than she has ever enjoyed in the past' (ibid., col. 45).

The Prime Minister paid handsome tributes to Daladier and Mussolini, and called for a wider appreciation of Hitler's role: 'After everything that has been said about the German Chancellor to-day and in the past, I do feel that the House ought to recognise the difficulty for a man in that position to take back such emphatic declarations as he had already made amidst the enthusiastic cheers of his supporters . . .' (ibid., col. 47).

As to the General Agreement which he and Hitler had signed, this had 'laid the foundations of peace', and reflected 'sincerity and good will on both sides'. It reflected the objective which Chamberlain had set when he entered Number 10: 'Ever since I assumed my present office my main purpose has been to work for the pacification of Europe . . .' (ibid., col. 48).

But the Prime Minister's argument soon ran into trouble. Following his litany of diplomatic achievements, he somehow had to justify the need for continued rearmament. He cautioned, 'Let no one think that because we have signed this agreement between these four Powers at Munich we can afford to relax our efforts in regard to that programme at this moment' (ibid., cols 49–50). Chamberlain was unable to resolve the contradiction at the heart of his speech and concluded in some confusion,

While we must renew our determination to fill up the deficiencies that yet remain in our defensive precautions, so that we may be ready to defend ourselves and make our diplomacy effective – [Interruption] – yes I am a realist – nevertheless I say with an equal sense of reality that I do see fresh opportunities of approaching this subject of disarmament opening up before us. . . . (Ibid., col. 50)

Attlee, replying as Leader of the Opposition, seized immediately upon the Prime Minister's confusion with a characteristically spare, but telling, observation: 'The Prime Minister at the end of his speech said that we must continue to arm. It was a comment on his other statement that we have peace for our generation' (ibid., col. 51). Attlee had the sense from the outset to recognise that Munich had prompted unrelieved rejoicing and was hailed by many as a great triumph. But he turned this to his advantage, highlighting the fact that 'in the mind of every thoughtful person in this country when he heard that this settlement had been arrived at Munich, there was a conflict. On the one hand there was enormous relief that war had been averted, at all events for the time being; on the other, there was a sense of humiliation and foreboding for the future' (ibid., col. 51).

Munich was 'one of the greatest diplomatic defeats' ever suffered by Britain and France and was a 'tremendous victory' for Hitler. The Labour leader recognised the 'great exertions' made by the Prime Minister in the cause of peace, but added,

When the captain of a ship by disregarding all rules of navigation has gone right off his course and run the ship into great danger, watchers from the shore, naturally impressed with the captain's frantic efforts to try to save something from the shipwreck, cheer him when he comes ashore and even want to give him a testimonial, but there follows an inquiry, an inquest, on the victims, and the question will be asked how the vessel got so far off its course, how and why it was so hazarded? (Ibid., col. 52)

Although Chamberlain was greeted 'as the man who saved peace', he was in fact 'the man who brought us into danger of war'. The cause of the immediate crisis was not the existence of minorities in Czechoslovakia, or the 'wonderful principle of self-determination', but 'because Herr Hitler had decided that the time was ripe for another step forward in his design to dominate Europe' (ibid., col. 54).

Attlee questioned the value of the protection which would be afforded to the minorities in the Sudetenland, now swallowed up within the Third Reich. He also seriously queried the validity of the British guarantee of the new Czechoslovakia, which had been deprived of a defensible frontier.

Chamberlain's policy had been to abandon collective security and the League. Tragically, 'instead of strengthening the people whose natural interests were with ours, we have had nothing but constant flirtations with this and that dictator' (ibid., col. 63). Attlee wondered,

And what have we got in place of the alliances and covenants and collective security and all the rest of it which buttressed this country in the past? We are left with two promises, one from Signor Mussolini and one from Herr Hitler. That is really all we have got. We have to walk by faith – the faith of the Prime Minister in Signor Mussolini and his faith in Herr Hitler. (Ibid., col. 64)

The alternative prescribed by Attlee was the summoning of an international peace conference, which would include the USA and the Soviet Union. It would tackle the 'causes of war that are afflicting this world', including 'the wrongs of the Versailles Treaty', 'the wrongs of minorities', 'the colonial question', 'the question of raw materials' and 'the great economic question'.

Though Attlee had exposed the crucial weaknesses in Chamberlain's argument, his own case was constrained by the need to maintain unity within his own Party.

Throughout the four-day debate, many speeches reflected the strains on traditional party loyalties. On the opposition benches, Chamberlain won praise from the pacifist rump, although the out-and-out pacifists now represented only a small minority on the Labour benches. But there was also a strong sense of relief felt among working-class communities that they might be spared another world war.

Within little more than an hour of Attlee's speech, George Lansbury was challenging the line taken by his successor as Labour leader: 'It is all very well to talk of the price that is being paid to-day in what is called humiliation and degradation and power politics . . .' (ibid., col. 89). Lansbury reminded MPs of the much greater price which had been paid by the many millions who lost their lives in the 1914–18 war.

Later in the debate Chamberlain received support from an even more unlikely quarter. James Maxton, the ILP leader, praised the Prime Minister for what he had done for working people in all countries. 'With all my political antagonisms, with all my antagonisms to the political philosophy of the people who stand beside him, I am not going to stand here and lie. Last week he did something which the common people of the world wanted done . . .' (Hansard, 4 October 1938, col. 195).

This prompted Conrad Russell, in his letter to Lady Diana Cooper, to comment on the uncomfortable political alliances created by Munich – Conservative and ILP, Tory and Liberal: 'The poor old Coroner [Chamberlain] – he really has been pretty bad. Mr Maxton extols him to the skies – he must mind that as much as Duffy [Cooper] minds Violet B.C.'s [Bonham Carter] patting him on the back.'

Yet perhaps the most moving and effective expression of support for
the Munich Agreement from the Labour benches came from Ernest
Thurtle, who, like Lansbury, represented a constituency in the East End
of London (he had also married one of Lansbury's daughters). But
Thurtle was no pacifist. He was, however, concerned at the plight of his
own working-class constituents in the event of war:

> Having got to the position at Munich where the question was
> whether it was to be the Munich Agreement or war, if that issue was
> put to me, I say the Munich Agreement before war. . . . I speak here
> as representing the feelings of the people I represent. They live in a
> very vulnerable area, the East End of London. They certainly are
> not cowards – far from it. They are good English men and women
> and they hate international bullying. They hate seeing small nations
> suffer, but I am bound to say that, even so, such is their horror of
> war, such is their sense of utter helplessness – no air-raid shelters for
> them against the known and unknown terrors which seemed to be
> coming to them – that I should be a hypocrite if I denied that when
> the news came that this agreement was reached they did heave a deep
> and general sigh of thankfulness. I would like to ask my colleagues
> who may differ from this attitude, who is going to sit in judgement
> on them? Who would dare take the responsibility for seeing death
> and destruction rained down upon these helpless people if by any
> means it could be avoided? (Hansard, 5 October 1938, col. 425)

By far the most striking feature of the debate was the extent of criticism of
Munich from the Government's own side of the House. Despite enormous
pressure from the Whips to toe the line, on the grounds of Party loyalty
and personal loyalty to the Prime Minister, each day of the debate was
marked by powerful contributions from the Tory rebels. But the question
remained how effective their rebellion would be, and whether they would
form any new alliance with the opposition parties.

The reality of Munich had come as a profound shock to Chamberlain's
opponents in the Conservative Party and throughout the rest of the
political spectrum. Their disunity had given him a free hand. Now, there
was a new recognition by anti-appeasers that they should co-operate. As
Dalton later wrote, 'Thus, for a fleeting moment, it seemed possible that
a large-scale Tory revolt against Chamberlain might change the whole
scene.'

The former Foreign Secretary, Anthony Eden, speaking on the first day
of the debate, gave short shrift to the kind of approach favoured by Attlee
– more international conferences were not the answer. But Eden offered

other common ground, on which anti-appeasers could meet: 'by a revival of our national spirit, by a determined effort to conduct a foreign policy upon which the nation can unite – I am convinced that such a policy can be found – and by a national effort in the sphere of defence very much greater than anything that has been accepted hitherto' (ibid., col. 88).

At the end of the first day's debate, the rebels still had to resolve what they should do in the critical vote in three days' time. Their political careers might well depend on their decision.

Boothby told Baffy Dugdale that 'threats were used' against him and others at the end of the first night's debate that 'if they vote against Government . . . the Whip will be withdrawn, and candidates run against them. This shows the Government was frightened . . . but the men are both angry and shaken.'

That night, Macmillan attempted to bring Labour and the Tory rebels together. He approached Dalton and suggested that he and Attlee might meet Churchill and some of his group to discuss the terms of the amendment which the opposition would table. Dalton declined on Attlee's behalf, but was himself prepared to go back to Brendan Bracken's house. There he found Churchill with Bracken, Eden, J.P.L. (Jim) Thomas and other Tory rebels, trying to organise the maximum possible revolt. They impressed upon Dalton the need for Labour to avoid an amendment which would, in effect, amount to a Vote of Censure on the Government, since that would frighten off too many Tories and send them back into the arms of the Whips.

Dalton found himself discussing the detailed wording of Labour's amendment with Government backbenchers. One draft included a reference to 'national unity and strength', but Dalton told Churchill, 'That is not our jargon.' Churchill replied, 'It is a jargon we may all soon have to learn.' When Dalton warned that some Labour MPs would press for a toughly worded amendment because they 'were anxious to be brave and uncompromising', Churchill retorted, 'It is not enough to be brave. We must also be victorious.'

Dalton also learned that night of the rebels' fears that between twenty and thirty of them would be victimised by the Whips, and was asked about the possibility of mutual support from Labour in their constituencies, in the event of an election being called. Although Dalton recalled giving only a cautious response, Macmillan thought his reaction more favourable.

That same night, Churchill and his group told Leo Amery that if Chamberlain decided to call an early election, they intended splitting from the Conservatives to form their own distinctive party. Churchill had also telephoned Roy Harrod, the Oxford economist and a Liberal, about the possibility of building up a united front. Harrod suggested making contact with trade union leaders. 'I have done that already', replied Churchill, 'they are worse than Chamberlain.'

The next day, the second day of the debate, Labour tabled their amendment. It largely met the Tory rebels' concerns. Viscount Cranborne spoke, and as one of the Cecil family it was almost *de rigueur* that he should reiterate the anti-appeasers' call for a much greater national effort to rearm. The day before in the Lords, his cousin Viscount Cecil of Chelwood had delivered a swingeing attack on the Government for their abandonment of the League of Nations and their policy of appeasement.

The most telling speech that second evening came from Sir Sidney Herbert, who rarely spoke in the Commons and needed encouragement from Churchill to catch the Speaker's eye. Herbert later thanked Churchill for his support, and for allowing him to speak from Churchill's usual seat. He confessed to Churchill that before he went to the Commons, 'I lay in bed from 2 to 4 p.m. in a mixture of coma & terror – I could write no further notes, nor arrange my speech – & had it not been for you, I think I should have "run out".'

Herbert issued a public warning against the use of strong-arm tactics by the Party's Whips,

> We can be led but we cannot be bullied. . . . if it is a case of going into the Lobbies [i.e. voting in the Commons], and if we are told that only those who vote straight are to get the coupon [i.e. be allowed to stand again as Conservatives], then I can say, quite honestly, that there will be a great many people in the Conservative party who will not vote straight. (Ibid., col. 243)

But it was his concern about the rumours of a 'Munich' election which hit home:

> there are also rumours going round to the effect that if things go smoothly, and favourably, there will be a General Election. Now I do not care at this time about my own party, or any other party, but there could be no greater iniquity in the world than to force a General Election on the people of the country at this moment. . . .
>
> Does anyone think that such a solution, whatever way the election goes, will be to the advantage of our country; does anyone think that in such circumstances this respite will have helped us to rearm, and does anyone in this House believe that there is anything except rearmament that can help us? I ask him [Chamberlain] to make his Government really national, to broaden its basis, to invite the Labour Party into it, to invite, above all, the trade union leaders into it. (Ibid., cols 243–4)

Besides these blunt warnings and unequivocal advice, Herbert delivered one of the most effective jibes at the inadequacy of the Government's efforts to rearm. 'We have talked long enough about "the years which the locusts have eaten". I was led to believe that the locusts had stopped nibbling about two years ago, but I can hear their little jowls creaking yet under the Front Bench' (ibid., col. 245).

Churchill later wrote to Herbert, 'You stopped the General Election by your speech; and as you spoke I seemed to hear the voice of that old Conservative Party I once honoured and not of this over-whipped crowd of poor "whites".'

Although the anti-appeasers were in a small minority, there was deep unease not far below the surface of the parliamentary Party. As a dissident, Nicolson would have looked for signs of disquiet, and his judgement was likely to be coloured by his own prejudice. But his diary entry for Tuesday the 4th reads: 'Baldwin in the Lords backs Chamberlain and will thereby rally Tory opinion, which was becoming very wobbly, to his side. But there is no doubt that the mass of Tory Members feel Chamberlain was too weak at Munich and that we have been humiliated unnecessarily.'

Churchill did not speak until the third day of the Munich debate, on Wednesday the 5th. Because of his close contacts with Czech sympathisers and the Czech Government, he knew something of the real story behind Czechoslovakia's capitulation, and was far better placed than the vast majority of MPs whom Chamberlain had kept in the dark. Churchill pulled no punches in talking about the 'unbearable pressure' which the British and French Governments had brought to bear on Prague.

In the Commons, Churchill customarily occupied a seat on the front bench, separated from the Treasury bench used by ministers only by a narrow gangway. Thus, when he rose to speak, he stood within a few feet of ministers sitting at the Dispatch box.

When the Speaker called Churchill at 5.10 p.m., the Commons was packed and the atmosphere electric. Churchill hoped that it would be possible 'for the most severe expressions of honest opinion' to be exchanged in the House, 'without rupturing personal relations'. He began 'by saying what everybody would like to ignore or forget but which must nevertheless be stated, namely that we have suffered a total and unmitigated defeat, and that France has suffered even more than we have' (Hansard, 5 October 1938, col. 360). At this, Nancy Astor cried out, 'Nonsense!' Churchill met her cry with the crushing observation that the Chancellor of the Exchequer, Sir John Simon, had admitted in his speech at the start of the day's debate that Hitler had gained all he sought at Munich.

The achievements claimed for the Prime Minister's shuttle diplomacy were dismissed: 'the German dictator, instead of snatching his victuals from the table, has been content to have them served to him course by course' (ibid., col. 361).

The difference between the positions reached at Berchtesgaden, Bad Godesberg and Munich could 'be very simply epitomised' as follows: '£1 was demanded at the pistol's point. When it was given, £2 were demanded at the pistol's point. Finally, the dictator consented to take £1 17s 6d [£1.87½p] and the rest in promises of good will for the future' (ibid., col. 361).

He regarded it as a 'fraud and a farce' to invoke the name of 'self-determination' for the terms agreed at Munich. Hitler's expansionist designs could have been checked if Britain and France had stood together in the summer and 'maintained a close contact with Russia'. He attacked the lack of any British commitment to defend the Czechs, arguing that:

such a policy in order to succeed demanded that Britain should declare straight out and a long time beforehand that she would, with others, join to defend Czechoslovakia against an unprovoked aggression. His Majesty's Government refused to give that guarantee when it would have saved the situation, yet in the end they gave when it was too late, and now, for the future, they renew it when they have not the slightest power to make it good. (Ibid., col. 364)

On Czechoslovakia's plight, Churchill observed, 'All is over. Silent, mournful, abandoned, broken, Czechoslovakia recedes into the darkness. She has suffered in every respect by her association with the Western democracies and with the League of Nations, of which she has always been an obedient servant' (ibid.). No matter what Chamberlain claimed for Munich, Prague's fate was sealed. 'You will find that in a period of time which may be measured by years, but may be measured only by months, Czechoslovakia will be engulfed in the Nazi regime' (ibid., cols 365–6).

The prospect was unrelievedly bleak. A 'disaster of the first magnitude' had befallen Britain and France. All the countries of Central and Eastern Europe 'will make the best terms they can with the triumphant Nazi Power' (ibid., cols 367–8). Hitler might well look westward and then, Churchill warned, 'bitterly will France and England regret the loss of that fine army of ancient Bohemia which was estimated last week to require not fewer than 30 German divisions for its destruction' (ibid., col. 369). In addition, Germany had gained a further twelve divisions through the annexation of Austria. Yet Britain was in the process of adding, in four years, a mere four battalions to the British Army.

Churchill reiterated the arguments of Herbert, warning Chamberlain against 'the constitutional indecency' of calling 'a sort of inverted khaki election' (ibid., col. 371). Instead, Churchill demanded, 'An effort at rearmament the like of which has not been seen ought to be made forthwith, and all the resources of this country and its united strength should be bent to that task' (ibid., col. 372).

In conclusion, Churchill addressed the problem which had to be faced by all Chamberlain's critics – the euphoric response to Munich, the hero's welcome which greeted the Prime Minister:

> I do not grudge our loyal, brave people, who were ready to do their duty no matter what the cost, who never flinched under the strain of last week – I do not grudge them the natural, spontaneous outburst of joy and relief when they learned that the hard ordeal would no longer be required of them at the moment; but they should know the truth. They should know that there has been gross neglect and deficiency in our defences; they should know that we have sustained a defeat without a war, the consequences of which will travel far with us along our road; they should know that we have passed an awful milestone in our history, when the whole equilibrium of Europe has been deranged, and that the terrible words have for the time being been pronounced against the Western democracies: 'Thou art weighed in the balance and found wanting.'
>
> And do not suppose that this is the end. This is only the beginning of the reckoning. This is only the first sip, the first foretaste of a bitter cup which will be proffered to us year by year unless by a supreme recovery of moral health and martial vigour, we arise again and take our stand for freedom as in the olden time. (Ibid., col. 373)

'A great and *terrible* speech,' observed Baffy Dugdale, who was watching that day's debate from the visitors' gallery with Violet Bonham Carter.

Churchill had spoken for forty minutes, and immediately after his speech, just before six o'clock, he left the Chamber for a further meeting of dissident Conservative and National Labour MPs at Brendan Bracken's house. Its purpose was to decide how they should vote the following day, at the end of the Munich debate.

As Nicolson noted, 'It would be a pity if some of us voted against, and some abstained. It would be far more effective (since there is little hope of many voting against) if we all abstained.' Yet Churchill said at the meeting that he refused to abstain, since – to quote Nicolson – 'that would mean that he half agreed with the Government'.

Nicolson himself spoke later that evening – having tried to catch the Speaker's eye since three o'clock he was eventually called at 9.25 p.m. But his continual bobbing up and down had given him 'a prominence in the House' which, Nicolson confessed privately, 'was unjustified by my juniority'. MPs flocked in to hear him speak, and Nicolson felt that his speech 'made its effect'.

Like other anti-appeasers, he referred to the pressures which had been brought to bear on him not to rock the boat: 'I know that in these days of realism those of us who try to keep our election pledges are told that we are disloyal to the party. The actual expression used to me was "You must not bat against your own side." As if it were a game of cricket that was being played in this most revered Assembly' (ibid., cols 433–4). Nicolson recounted the variety of insults being hurled at the anti-appeasers – that they had 'one-track minds', that they were 'eccentric', that they were suffering from 'hysteria'. Adding that he knew that he and those who thought like him were accused of 'possessing the Foreign Office mind', he concluded, 'I thank God that I possess the Foreign Office mind.'

But the Foreign Office's principal spokesman in the Commons spoke last for the Government that night, and he certainly did not possess what Nicolson would have regarded as 'the Foreign Office mind'. Rab Butler could more accurately be described at this time as possessing a Number 10 mind – he was a committed appeaser, and gave an unqualified endorsement of Munich: 'I must emphatically give my opinion as one of the younger generation. War settles nothing and I can see no alternative to the policy upon which the Prime Minister has so courageously set himself' (ibid., col. 453). Butler's biographer, Anthony Howard, has pointed out that there was no indication in Butler's private papers to suggest that he harboured any doubts about appeasement at the time.

Nicolson had a drink, after his own speech, with Rob Bernays, a National Liberal and junior Minister. Bernays was disenchanted with appeasement but had decided not to resign. As Nicolson wrote, Bernays 'is miserable because Violet Bonham Carter cut him in the lobby. He puts up all the usual stuff about it being far easier to resign than not to resign. But he knows that I feel less about him. He ought to have resigned.'

The following morning, Thursday, 6 October, the House met at 11.00 a.m. MPs first discussed the motion in the Prime Minister's name that Parliament should adjourn later that afternoon, until 1 November. This provoked an acrimonious series of exchanges. Harold Macmillan, who did not speak in the main debate, now spoke against such a long adjournment:

'We are being treated more and more as a kind of Reichstag to meet only to hear the orations and register the decrees of the government of the day' (Hansard, 6 October 1938, col. 488). He was worried that a lengthy adjournment would 'increase the dangerous feeling that the whole thing is over, that we have "peace for our time", that we need not bother any more . . .' (ibid., col. 489). Macmillan, however, was convinced 'from the bottom of my heart' that 'the situation . . . is more dangerous and more formidable, more terrible than at any time since the beginning of Christian civilisation' (ibid.).

Some minutes later, Churchill took up Macmillan's reference to the alleged disregard for Parliament:

I know that there is a certain under-current of derision of Parliament even among its own Members, and a feeling no doubt among Ministers, 'What relief it will be when we have got them sent about their business and we can get on with our work.' That is exactly the idea which in other countries has led to the institution of dictatorships, the same process of impatience with the parliamentary machine which has swept it away and has led to its replacement by one-man rule. (Ibid., col. 493)

This rankled Chamberlain. As he replied to the objections Churchill again intervened. The Prime Minister's temper snapped. He rounded on Churchill and accused him of being 'unworthy', and adding for good measure, 'A repetition of tittle-tattle about the way in which Cabinet business is conducted is not doing justice to the sincerity and to the sense of responsibility of Cabinet Ministers' (ibid., col. 495). Chamberlain's comment recalls Hoare's reference to the irritation among the Prime Minister's closest colleagues at the way Duff Cooper had been telling the anti-appeasers what was being said in Cabinet.

Yet when Chamberlain spoke later that day, at the conclusion of the Munich debate, he was much more emollient. He at last responded to fears that he might call a 'snap' general election. Attributing rumours of an early election to 'a portion of the Press' the Prime Minister said that he did not wish to 'capitalise' on the widespread feeling of relief for narrow party advantage, and added, 'It is possible that we may want great efforts from the nation in the months that are to come, and if that be so, the smaller our differences the better' (ibid., col. 548).

The Conservative Party managers had considered an early election, but had been forced to accept that, despite Munich, the country was about to embark on a much larger rearmament programme and might well be at war in the imminent future. One of the underlying appeals of appeasement for many Conservatives had been that it would avert the social changes which would flow from large-scale rearmament or war. Now the country was about to rearm on a massive scale.

The chairman of the Conservative Party, Douglas Hacking, confided to a journalist that rearmament was impossible without the co-operation of the trade unions. This might require bringing some leaders of the labour movement into the Government. An election would stir up conflict, and ruin any prospect of co-operation.

In the closing moments of the Munich debate, Chamberlain also sought to deal with one of the central criticisms levelled at him – that he had spoken about 'peace for our time' on his return from Munich, yet had also argued the need for continued rearmament. He asked that too much should not be read into his phrase about 'peace for our time', which he had used 'in a moment of some emotion, after a long and exhausting day, after I had driven through miles of excited, enthusiastic, cheering people' (ibid., col. 551).

At four o'clock that afternoon, as the division bells rang around the Palace of Westminster and the lobbies were cleared, it soon became apparent that a number of MPs on the Government benches were staying seated in their places instead of filing out to vote.

Dalton saw Macmillan before the vote and suggested a meeting between the Labour leaders – Attlee, Morrison and Dalton himself – and three or four of the rebels. But the Tories held back. Their immediate fears had been eased by Chamberlain's ruling out an early election, and they did not want to risk further trouble with their constituency associations.

So, despite Churchill's reservations, the Tory rebels abstained. As Nicolson noted, 'Our group decide that it is better for us all to abstain than for some to abstain and some to vote against.' In all, thirty to forty Government backbenchers abstained, twenty-two of them ostentatiously remaining seated throughout the division.

There were splits in the other parties too. About eighteen Labour MPs apparently abstained, and the ILP formally did not vote. The Liberals were split, fourteen voting against the Government and four supporting Chamberlain.

There were many doubts among those voting with the Government. Shortly before the division, Walter Elliot wrote to Baffy Dugdale – he had not resigned from the Cabinet over Munich, and as we have seen she had told him that she did not want to see him for a while. Elliot wrote, 'I shall have to do what I think I ought,' and went on to explain, 'My responsibility for this is very simple. I did not know enough or work hard enough, three years ago, or even two, at the problem of armaments. . . . It is no use resigning – that does not get me out of my responsibility. The

Munich terms stick in my throat as much as ever they stuck in Duff's.'

The greatest embarrassment for the Government was not the total of their backbenchers who rebelled, but their 'reputation'. Those abstaining included Churchill, Eden, Duff Cooper, 'Bobbety' Cranborne, Leo Amery, Vyvyan Adams, Robert Boothby, Brendan Bracken, Ronald Cartland, Anthony Crossley, Paul Emrys-Evans, Sidney Herbert, Sir Roger Keyes, Richard Law, Harold Macmillan, Harold Nicolson, Duncan Sandys, Louis Spears, Jim Thomas and Lord Wolmer. In Nicolson's words, 'The House knows that most of the above people know far more about the real issue than they do.'

'It was clear that the Government was rattled by this', Nicolson concluded. 'The House breaks up with the Tories yelling to keep their spirits up. But they well know that Chamberlain has put us in a ghastly position and that we ought to have been prepared to go to war and smash Hitler. Next time he will be far too strong for us.'

Yet Leo Amery, another rebel, wrote to Chamberlain after the vote, praising the Prime Minister's concluding speech, which 'moved me very deeply, and very, very nearly persuaded both myself and Anthony Eden to vote. I only hope, most sincerely, that the misgivings which even you could not dispel to-day, will be disproved by the events of the near future.'

Churchill was angered that some of his friends and erstwhile supporters had voted with the Government. Alan Lennox-Boyd, a junior minister at the time, later recalled that as a result Churchill 'regarded me as a renegade'. The young backbencher Patrick Donner later told Churchill's biographer Martin Gilbert:

After the debate Churchill came up to me in the corridor and abused me like a Billingsgate fishwife. I was no longer 'Patrick' after ten years, and the intimacy was never recreated. It was the underlying principle for him. You must have principles. He was right in his way. It was very sad for me. I adored him. . . .

If you voted against what he regarded as the national interest that was that – he was prosecution counsel and judge combined.

Chamberlain reflected on the Munich debate in a letter to his sister the following Sunday, 9 October: 'I must say that I found the 4 days' debate in the Commons a pretty trying ordeal, especially as I had to fight all the time against the defection of weaker brethren & Winston was carrying on a regular campaign against me with the aid of Masaryk the Czech Minister. They, of course, are totally unaware of my knowledge of their proceedings: I had continual information of their doings and sayings. . . .' Chamberlain had found the debate deeply wounding. He had tried to counter what he termed (rather unfortunately) 'the poison gas' in the

Commons by reading the many letters and messages he had received praising his efforts. 'All the world seemed to be full of my praises except the House of Commons. . . .'

Chamberlain's feelings at the criticism of Munich in the Commons were shared by Queen Mary. She wrote to her son, George VI, 'I am sure you feel as angry as I do at people croaking as they do at the P.M.'s action, for once I agree with Ly. Oxford [Margot, Asquith's second wife] who is said to have exclaimed as she left the House of Commons yesterday, "He brought home Peace, why can't they be grateful". . .'

The weeks following Munich were an 'anxious and depressing' time for Churchill and the other Tory rebels. 'Each of us was attacked in his constituency by the Conservative Party machine, and many there were who a year later were our ardent supporters who agitated against us.' Churchill himself survived the threat of censure from his Epping constituency association only by threatening to resign his seat and fight a by-election. At the association's decisive meeting, he won a vote of confidence, though only by three to two.

Yet no sooner was the immediate crisis over than the differences between the rebels began to reappear. As Dalton later wrote, 'Eden and some others were very moderate and wanted "national unity" with everybody, while Churchill and Duff Cooper were out for Chamberlain's blood and inclined to join with anyone else to get it.'

Macmillan saw Dalton again the week after the Commons debate and tried to revive the idea of unity against Chamberlain. Tory rebels, Labour and Liberal MPs should join forces to form a new National Government. The idea was gaining support on the left of the Labour Party, who had previously set their faces against any kind of co-operation with Tories – Cripps suggested to Dalton launching a national appeal against the Government jointly with the Liberal leader Sinclair and the Tory rebels. Despite this, Dalton still thought the chances of any cross-party alliance were remote, and urged Macmillan that the Tories should start voting against the Government instead of abstaining.

Dalton and Macmillan did try to organise a meeting between Attlee and Morrison and Churchill and Cooper to co-ordinate their tactics against the Government. Macmillan wanted to concentrate on specific points including the humbug of Munich and the deficiencies in arms and ARP. But Cooper would not attend the proposed meeting without Eden, and Eden would not attend at all.

Some weeks later, Viscount Cecil and Baffy Dugdale lunched together and discussed 'the lamentable failure of the opponents of H[is] M[ajesty's] G[overnment] to cohere'. Eden had accepted an invitation to speak to the

League of Nations Union, but would not appear on the same platform as the leaders of the opposition parties, Attlee and Sinclair.

Contacts between Labour and some Tory rebels continued. On 17 October, Duncan Sandys, one of Churchill's closest aides, spent an hour with Dalton, who recalled, 'He tackled me . . . on the possibilities of co-operation between anti-Chamberlainite Conservatives and our Party. Could propaganda based on a common platform be started?'

But it was not only the differences between the Tory rebels which would cause problems with any cross-party alliance. There were divisions in the other parties about how to combine against Chamberlain. When Viscount Cecil suggested to the Liberal, Violet Bonham Carter, a Lib–Lab pact in the constituencies, 'she nearly bit his head off.'

Labour were also split. The day after seeing Duncan Sandys, Dalton held a meeting at his flat to discuss Labour's policy after Munich. Among those attending were Evan Durbin, Robert Fraser of the *Daily Herald*, Hugh Gaitskell (then a parliamentary candidate), Douglas Jay, Kingsley Martin (editor of the *New Statesman and Nation*), Philip Noel-Baker, John Wilmot (who had won the East Fulham by-election in 1933) and Leonard Woolf.

When Dalton argued for a policy of all-out resistance to Hitler, even if it meant war, Jay has recalled that only he, Gaitskell and Noel-Baker agreed with Dalton. The majority still did not believe that war was inevitable. After Munich, Robert Fraser wrote to Dalton, warning him that the real danger of Fascism came from within – from the very people in the Tory Party with whom Dalton had been in close contact. Fraser feared that if Chamberlain was overthrown by Churchill, the latter would run the country on Fascist lines and prepare for a war to settle old debts with Hitler. Jay remembers that after the meeting at Dalton's flat, he was utterly depressed at the 'demoralized mood of the non-pacifist wing of the Labour Party'. There seemed no hope of the opposition stiffening Chamberlain, or Chamberlain stiffening the French.

Gaitskell and Jay talked about the meeting on the Underground from Victoria to Charing Cross, only a few stops. During that short journey, as Jay later recalled, Gaitskell argued 'with the utmost confidence' that Dalton and his supporters 'would soon convert the Labour Party, that they and Churchill would overturn and supplant Chamberlain, and that in the end Roosevelt would be drawn in to help us'.

After the Munich debate, Parliament adjourned for almost a month, until 1 November. The complaints which Macmillan and Churchill had raised about the adjournment at such a critical period were taken up by the historian R.H. Tawney, who also expressed the deeper criticism about the lack of effective debate before Munich. As he wrote to the *Manchester Guardian* in mid-October,

> The Führer Prinzip is not yet part of the British Constitution. If the Prime Minister of a Parliamentary State has not time for Parliament . . . he is not fit to be Prime Minister. . . . a revolution in foreign policy has been effected . . . without the nation's representatives being heard . . . till things had gone so far that debate was almost useless.

Within the BBC there was a similar feeling that debate had been stifled. A former chief news editor conducted a post-mortem on Munich, and concluded, 'To my mind one of the serious features of . . . the crisis . . . was the ignorance of the people of this country . . . of much of the essential knowledge they should have had. . . . We have, in fact, taken part in a conspiracy of silence. . . .'

Churchill was still effectively banned from the BBC. In an effort to get his message across to the American public, he went to the extraordinary length of hiring a slot on commercial radio on 16 October.

Yet the Commons had helped shift the onus of the debate over Munich. The Government were no longer able to assume that Chamberlain's deal with Hitler received automatic approval, as the Prime Minister's own cautious speech at the end of the Munich debate had demonstrated.

In part, the effectiveness of the Commons debate was an accident of timing. The weekend break between Chamberlain's triumphant return and the opening of the debate allowed the immediate euphoria to fade, giving MPs time to reflect and reach a more balanced judgement.

Parliament had acted as the grand inquest for the nation. The Government survived, but did not emerge unscathed. Soon, the debate would return to the people.

# CHAPTER FIFTEEN
# 'A VOTE FOR HITLER!'

There are only too many who say 'What difference does it make
  One way or the other?
To turn the stream of history will take
  More than a by-election.'

(Louis MacNiece, extract from *Autumn Journal*, 1939)

In October 1938 the eyes of the world were again turned towards Oxford, as they had been five years earlier when the 'King and Country' debate caused a sensation. The Oxford City by-election became a referendum on Munich.

Oxford City was one of five by-elections pending at the time of Munich. The Government 'chose to start with Oxford. That was the ideal constituency in which to get a vote of confidence for Mr. Chamberlain's policy,' wrote Tom Harrisson in the popular weekly news magazine *Picture Post*, which had been launched the day after Munich. 'So the Oxford City by-election became at once a focus of world interest. Roosevelt watched it. Mussolini watched it. Especially, Hitler watched it.'

The Oxford by-election was entirely dominated by Munich. The formal announcement of the sitting MP's death had been delivered to a packed House of Commons immediately before Chamberlain began his historic speech on the eve of Munich. The writ was moved on Friday, 7 October, the day after the vote at the end of the Munich debate.

The University reassembled for the new academic year on the same day that the writ was moved – the peace bought at Munich seemed to have removed any risk that the undergraduates would suddenly be called up for military service. The arguments which divided Parliament were to reverberate in the colleges and common rooms of the University, and throughout Oxford.

That autumn's events were never forgotten by the three young dons at the centre of the controversy which raged in the Oxford City Labour Party. R.H.S. (Dick) Crossman was then thirty, Patrick Gordon Walker thirty-one and Frank Pakenham thirty-two. They were each to hold Cabinet office in post-war Labour Governments, but at the time of the by-election they were ambitious young men, making their way in academic and political life.

These dramatic events were set in train on Sunday, 7 August, when the fifty-year-old Conservative MP for Oxford City and Deputy Speaker in the Commons, Captain R.C. ('Bobby') Bourne died suddenly during a family holiday in Argyllshire.

Quintin McGarel Hogg (later Lord Hailsham, the Conservative Lord Chancellor) was selected by the local Conservatives as their candidate. Hogg was the thirty-one-year-old son of the senior Cabinet Minister, Viscount Hailsham, Lord President of the Council and until March 1938 Lord Chancellor. Hogg had strong links with Oxford. He had been an undergraduate at Christ Church, was a former President of the Union and had spoken against the motion in the 'King and Country' debate. He continued to visit the University as a fellow of All Souls, although he was having to work hard establishing himself as a barrister in London. He made a reputation as a 'poor man's lawyer', and in the process gained an insight into working-class life.

Among Hogg's contemporaries at All Souls – 'the world's most exclusive brain-club' as *Picture Post* described the college – were Isaiah Berlin, Douglas Jay and A.L. Rowse. Although the appeasers were strongly represented among the senior fellows, Hogg was one of the few younger fellows of All Souls who supported Chamberlain. Hogg made no bones about his views, and was reckoned to be virtually incapable of entering a room without finding himself in a debate. But Hogg's combative personality was to stand him in good stead for a tough campaign. He was to reflect in later life, 'As a baptism of political fire for a young man, the Oxford by-election was extremely rough stuff.'

The prospects looked good for Hogg. The Conservatives had held Oxford for all but two of the previous fifty years. At the previous general election in 1935, Bourne had won almost two-thirds of the vote in a straight contest with Labour, giving him a majority of 6645. The City was changing rapidly with the development of Morris's Cowley motor works and working-class housing to the east, but they lay beyond the constituency boundary.

The opposition vote seemed certain to be split, since the Liberals were planning to field a candidate for the first time since 1924. They had selected a candidate after the 1935 election, although he withdrew a few months before the by-election. Following Captain Bourne's death, however, the City Liberals quickly set about finding a replacement, and turned to Ivor Davies, in his mid-twenties and already selected as a Liberal candidate in Scotland.

But the choice of Davies immediately sparked off a dispute among

Oxford Liberals. Most local Liberals wanted their own candidate to stand. But leading University Liberals, including the President of the Union Alan Wood and the young economics don at Christ Church, Roy Harrod, disagreed. They believed that the only realistic chance of defeating the Conservatives in Oxford lay in an electoral pact, which would enable all shades of opposition to rally behind a single candidate.

On 12 September Ivor Davies himself offered to stand down, though only on condition that the Labour candidate did likewise. Davies later confessed that his action had merely been a 'gimmick'. But it annoyed many City Liberals, and was to cause mayhem in the Labour camp.

Patrick Gordon Walker had fought the seat for Labour in 1935. He was a young politics don at Christ Church, and was then on the left of the party. He was remembered by those he taught for his sartorial style, as well as his politics – he wore canary yellow pullovers and sandals, which was not at all typical of Oxford dons in the 1930s, and followed a Marxist line.

Gordon Walker had supported the left's Unity Campaign, launched by Sir Stafford Cripps in 1937, which advocated joint action by Labour, the ILP and the Communists. But by the time of the by-election, he had drifted away from the Communists, and felt that loyalty to the Labour Party provided the most effective defence against Fascism in Britain. He was worried that electoral pacts would undermine local Labour parties where Labour candidates were required to step down – Oxford being a case in point – and did not want to see socialist domestic policies abandoned for the sake of an alliance on the single issue of foreign policy.

In addition, Gordon Walker was also deeply suspicious of the anti-Chamberlain Conservatives, and could not see how anyone could seriously regard Churchill as less of a threat than Chamberlain. Like many on the left, Gordon Walker feared that Fascism in Britain might march under an anti-Fascist banner.

The upshot was that this unlikely proletarian rejected Davies's offer. There the matter seemed destined to rest. But this was to reckon without the influence of Oxford's radical dons and the Communist sympathisers in the local Labour Party.

The University played a much stronger role in the local Labour Party than in the local Liberal Association. Two young dons, Dick Crossman of New College and Frank Pakenham (later Lord Longford) of Christ Church, both City councillors, were particularly prominent. Crossman had previously opposed Popular Front campaigns. But as leader of the Labour Group on the City Council his conversion to the idea of an electoral pact at the by-election was to carry considerable weight with loyalist, middle-of-the-road opinion in the local party.

Pakenham had worked in the Conservative Research Department until

1932, and became a socialist following the fight with Oswald Mosley's Blackshirts at Oxford Town Hall only a couple of years earlier. As Pakenham has since written, 'I was in the position of a convert, anxious subconsciously to make up for lost time, to get on with the job, even to prove himself (though in my case there was no conscious thought of this) as good a Socialist as any.'

By the late 1930s, in Pakenham's words, 'the local Labour Party and I were very far to the left. We were prepared to join each and every movement intended to ginger up our national leadership. At one moment it was the United Front – Labour, ILP and Communists. At the next the Popular Front – Labour, Liberal and Communists.'

Pakenham did not realise at the time how many members of the local Party were Communists or were 'as near as makes no difference of "the Party" '. The line from Moscow urging Popular Fronts received strong support within the Oxford Party from sympathisers among the busmen, railway workers and Morris car workers at Cowley, some of whom lived within the City boundary.

On the morning of Saturday, 8 October, the day after the writ for the by-election was moved, Dick Crossman visited Gordon Walker in his room at Christ Church and told him of a new proposal: that he (Gordon Walker) and Davies should stand down to make way for a single, independent candidate. A.D. ('Sandie') Lindsay, the Master of Balliol and recently retired Vice-Chancellor of the University, was ready to consider standing. Gordon Walker gained the impression that if he himself was against it, nothing more would come of the idea.

At dinner in Christ Church on Saturday evening Gordon Walker was shocked to hear from Pakenham that Lindsay's supporters understood that he was willing to stand down. On Sunday, Gordon Walker called on Lindsay, to tell him that while he could see something in the proposal, there were nonetheless serious objections. He did not think that Transport House would agree, he was frightened of the effects on the local Labour Party and he doubted that Lindsay would win the working-class vote.

But the moves for Oxford's own Popular Front were fast gathering pace. Monday's *Oxford Mail* carried an 'Appeal for Liberal–Labour Agreement at Oxford: Mr R.F. Harrod, the Christ Church Economist, on the Need for Electoral Pact'. Roy Harrod argued that the 'issue of foreign policy . . . transcends all others in importance', and therefore the Labour and Liberal candidates should get together and agree that one or the other withdraw. Opposition to Chamberlain's approach would then be united behind one candidate. After all, 'Oxford . . . is the home of compromise and sweet reasonableness.' But this cut no ice with Gordon Walker.

The next morning, Tuesday the 11th, Lindsay telephoned Gordon Walker. Lindsay had spent Monday in London at Labour headquarters testing the likely reaction of the Labour leadership to his candidature. He had seen Attlee, the Party leader, Arthur Greenwood and the National Agent, George Shepherd. Lindsay told Gordon Walker that 'they would like to do it if they could.' According to Gordon Walker, Lindsay apparently spoke as if the whole business was settled and urged him to get in touch with Davies, saying 'You must do it, if the thing is to be done.'

Gordon Walker was increasingly embattled. 'Oxford Labour In Favour of Pact', was the front-page headline in Tuesday evening's *Oxford Mail*, referring to a statement from the local Labour Party Chairman, H.S. Richardson – one of the local Party officers whom Gordon Walker suspected of being under Communist Party influence.

On Wednesday the 12th, Gordon Walker visited Transport House to put his case to the by-elections sub-committee, which included Attlee and Hugh Dalton. He felt reassured and, confident of success, hurried back to Oxford in time to catch the deadline for the *Oxford Mail*. The evening issue duly carried his statement under the headline 'Master of Balliol's Candidature Wrecked'.

But his hopes were short-lived. At about noon on Thursday, after a morning's teaching, he was told by an *Oxford Mail* reporter that a deputation of Popular Fronters from the constituency Party was already on its way to Transport House. They had quickly turned Shepherd's agreement to receive them to their advantage. The *Oxford Mail* reported 'New Moves in the Oxford By-election'.

After their meeting with Shepherd, the deputation again demonstrated their sure touch with the press. Their statement that 'the matter was in suspense till the members' meeting this evening' appeared in the *Mail*'s stop-press. They had achieved a remarkable coup. Only hours before the crucial meeting, they created the impression that Transport House was having second thoughts.

About 140 people turned up for the evening meeting at St Michael's Hall, mainly Labour Party members but also undergraduates, a few Liberals and some Communists. Labour's Assistant National Agent T.H. Windle attended, although Gordon Walker had earlier declined an offer that a Transport House official should be present. Gordon Walker later felt aggrieved that Windle did nothing to allay doubts about the national leadership's position, apparently giving the impression that as far as Transport House were concerned, the matter rested entirely with Gordon Walker.

When the vote was taken, there was apparently no attempt to check that only *bona fide* Labour Party members took part. The result was a shattering defeat for Gordon Walker: 109 voted in favour of Labour withdrawing its official candidate, and only 30 against.

With Gordon Walker out of the running, there was unlikely to be any serious problem about Davies's withdrawal. The Liberals' expenses of between £200 and £300 were met, and the way was cleared for Lindsay to stand as an Independent Progressive. Davies welcomed Lindsay's candidature, but Gordon Walker's offer of help to Lindsay left no one in doubt about his real feelings: 'I am not standing down. The local Labour Party is withdrawing the Labour candidate.'

Gordon Walker suspected that jealousy, possibly subconscious, of his position as the official Labour candidate might have influenced Crossman to support a Popular Front candidate. Yet Gordon Walker's own reluctance to relinquish the Labour candidature is equally open to question. In fact, both men's views on who should stand against Hogg seem to have been quite genuine.

Pakenham was the major beneficiary. Within weeks of the by-election, he was selected by the Oxford City Labour Party to succeed Gordon Walker as the prospective parliamentary candidate. Yet it is hard to see Pakenham having conceived the Machiavellian plot required to oust Gordon Walker and bring about his own succession.

Referring to 'the strange forces at work during this period', in his autobiography *Born to Believe*, Pakenham has written that: 'They threw together, not only extreme realists and idealists, pure patriots and pure pacifists, but also totalitarian Communists. The main purpose of these last was separate and hidden, but they were united with the others by perfectly genuine hatred and fear of Fascism.'

Pakenham himself denies consciously acting out of any sense of personal ambition, but later confessed, 'Opening as it did (though this was in no sense its motivation) the way for me to become Parliamentary Labour candidate for Oxford myself, it represents the political step which I would most prefer to "have back" if I could have my time again.'


On the evening of Sunday, 16 October, A.D. Lindsay, the Master of Balliol, announced to a packed meeting of the college in the junior common room his intention to fight the by-election as an Independent Progressive. It was an emotional occasion, which inspired Balliol's undergraduates – they included Edward Heath, Denis Healey and Roy Jenkins.

Lindsay's decision to stand immediately transformed the by-election into a referendum on Munich. His contest with Hogg generated enormous excitement. As the *Oxford Mail* commented, following a clash one night outside the Town Hall between the two sets of supporters, 'Oxford has seen nothing like this demonstration for years. All the spirit of old-time electioneering campaigns were [*sic*] recalled and spectators began to recall the scenes in 1922 when Frank Gray won the constituency for Liberalism.'

The by-election generated much noise throughout the day-time too, setting a precedent which many dons deplored. It was one of the first British elections in which loud-speaker vans were used extensively, piercing the quietude of college quads and disrupting tutorials.

Yet many dons and students were actively involved in the campaign. 'Although this is a City by-election,' the *Oxford Mail* reported, 'its outstanding feature is the open ranging of rival forces in the University.' Dons bombarded the local press and *The Times* with a barrage of Hogg and Lindsay manifestos and letters of support. Some were concerned at the propriety of a recently retired Vice-Chancellor standing for Parliament. It would never do to give people the wrong idea. Eighteen assorted bursars, censors, deans, fellows, masters, principals, professors, provosts, treasurers and wardens complained to *The Times* (where else?) of 'the danger' that Lindsay's 'opposition to the Government may be thought to command wider influence among senior members of the University than in fact it does . . .'. But this fig-leaf of neutrality soon slipped to reveal something rather less academic and altogether more partisan (their equanimity could not have been helped by those loud-speaker vans passing the college walls): 'Mr. Lindsay is unlikely to speak for the University as a whole if he challenges the Prime Minister's determination to use every means at his disposal in an attempt to confirm and extend the peace which he and his collaborators lately saved from destruction.'

In true academic fashion, a rejoinder was dispatched from the Lindsay camp. Fourteen assorted fellows, masters, presidents, principals, professors, provosts, rectors, students and wardens proclaimed their champion's 'courage, independence and practical capacity'.

Undergraduates were the most enthusiastic campaigners. As *Picture Post* reported, 'Oxford term was in full swing, and being October term a third of the university's undergraduates had arrived for the first time. They had no vote or proper part in the affair; they had plenty of fun though.' The magazine's on-the-spot account of one of the election meetings conveys the atmosphere:

Meeting at Town Hall – 700 present. Suddenly Chairman announces that 'The Conservative party with their usual diabolical cunning, I'm sorry, I should say with their usual technique, are outside with a poster display. So you know what to expect.'

Immediately many, especially undergraduates, troop out.

Outside the Town Hall steps is a scene of confusion, terrific shouting; police in force, but they cannot keep the crowd from extending on to the centre of the road from both pavements. The centre of the uproar is eleven undergraduates, each of whom holds over his head a large piece of cardboard with a letter on it. Standing in line, these letters read VOTE FOR HOGG. As the crowd streams out of the meeting, they surround the Hogg supporters. Holding up Lindsay posters, HITLER SAYS DON'T YOU DARE, they defy the attempts of the police. Within three minutes they have swamped the Conservatives, split them up so that the letters still read OT FROG. Then the crowd starts roaring in gathering momentum . . . 'HITLER WANTS HOGG'. One of the best brains in the world, a Fellow of the Royal Society, stands on the Town Hall steps and roars out: 'A vote for Hogg is a vote for Hitler.' And a laboratory assistant starts another slogan, at once taken up amidst tremendous laughter: HITLER WANTS HOGG FOR CHRISTMAS. Then they grab the remaining Conservatives, pull down their cards, tear them up and form into a procession which goes roaring down Carfax towards Balliol, shouting for Lindsay. So what professors lack in pep, students more than make up for. . . .

Lindsay had a lot of time to make up. Hogg had already been campaigning for over a week, and polling day was a mere ten days away. Lindsay had to steal Hogg's thunder. He had to get across a simple message, and fast. To win, he needed to secure the full Labour and Liberal vote, and also had to convert a significant share of the Conservative support.

'Sandie' Lindsay certainly won respect for his sincerity. But whether he was the right person for the hurly-burly of one of the most contentious by-elections of the century is more doubtful. He had an impressive radical and intellectual pedigree, but would he appeal to ordinary voters? He was the presbyterian son of a theology professor and was active in the Workers' Educational Association. His religion and interest in public affairs were intensely important to him. He had fostered Balliol's radical tradition. In 1926 he expressly forbade Balliol students from acting as blacklegs during the General Strike. When Gandhi visited England in the early 1930s, Lindsay was his host in Oxford and befriended him.

He had no lack of conviction in his own beliefs. Though a passionate democrat, he was determined to have his own way on causes to which he was committed. Legend has it that he would adjourn University meetings if the decision went against him.

Although he was a long-standing member of the Labour Party, his politics seemed closer to Harold Macmillan's description of his own political beliefs while at Balliol, a quarter of a century earlier, 'I was a Liberal–Radical, a Tory Democrat, and a Fabian Socialist.'

Lindsay's strongest supporter was his enthusiastic wife, Erica. His right-hand man during the campaign was a young Balliol don, John Fulton (later Lord Fulton). Other active supporters included Frank Pakenham, the historian Christopher Hill and undergraduates of all political persuasions, including Ted Heath, then a leading figure in University Conservative politics, and Denis Healey, then a member of the Communist Party and an officer in the University Labour Club.

In his election address, Lindsay explained that he was standing 'In protest against the foreign policy of the Government, in response to the request of a committee representing Liberals and Labour, and assured of support by many Conservatives . . .'. His opposition to Munich was eloquent:

> I shared the universal relief when, in a desperate situation, war was for a time averted; shared the admiration felt for the determination which Mr Chamberlain showed in that desperate situation; rejoiced at the spontaneous outburst of enthusiasm for peace which was evoked among all the people in Germany and Italy as well as in other countries. Yet along with men and women of all parties I deplored the irresolution and tardiness of a Government which never made clear to Germany where this country was prepared to take a stand. I am unable to forget the intolerable harshness of the terms imposed on Czechoslovakia. I am dismayed by the evidence accruing every day that our Government is not seeing to it that even this humiliating settlement is respected. I look with deep misgiving at the prospect before us.

Lindsay's policy for rearmament included those aspects to which Chamberlain and most Conservatives were most deeply opposed: 'we must insist that rearmament be tackled as a truly national effort; it must not be scamped for private profit, or thwarted through private control. It must make defence against air attack fundamental, and it must be used to abolish unemployment.' He recognised that this would entail 'a profound change in the industrial structure of the country', involving more state control. 'State control with us will be democratic if the trade unions and local authorities of this country are taken into co-operation and into the full confidence of the Government.'

The only Conservative MP to back Lindsay publicly was Harold Macmillan, himself a Balliol scholar until his studies were disrupted by the outbreak of war in 1914. Not only had Macmillan rebelled over Munich, his views on economic policy in his book *The Middle Way*, published earlier that year, were similar to Lindsay's. In his letter of support to Lindsay, quoted in *The Times* on 24 October, the Monday before polling day, Macmillan argued:

> The times are too grave and the issue is too vital for progressive Conservative opinion to allow itself to be influenced by party loyalties, or to tolerate the present uncertainty regarding the principles governing foreign policy. We are faced with the urgent need for a vital effort to ensure the safety of our country and Empire, and to preserve our conception of freedom and civilisation. I hope, therefore, that progressive opinion in Oxford, whether Liberal, Labour or Conservative, will seize the opportunity of returning you to Parliament next Thursday.

Macmillan visited Oxford and spoke for Lindsay. He told a packed meeting at the Town Hall that they could always appease lions by throwing Christians to them, but the Christians had another name for it. 'England should herself be united upon a foreign policy that is common to the great mass of people. . . . If all Conservatives will search their hearts they will find it is their duty at this election to make it by its result a dramatic and striking testimony to that tremendous need for real unity which our people passionately desire.'

But Macmillan's participation angered many Conservatives. He heard that the question of his ejection from the Carlton Club was being considered by the committee. As he later wrote, 'It was apparently a rule of the Club that one member was not to oppose another in any election.' But Macmillan heard nothing, either from the Government Chief Whip or from the club secretary.

During the Oxford campaign other leading Conservative rebels were conspicuous by their absence. It really was a case of the dog that didn't bark. The Conservative rebellion over Munich had created high hopes of a new Popular Front movement. But neither Churchill nor Eden intervened. Privately they wanted Lindsay to win, but they were not prepared to speak publicly against an official Conservative candidate and for a member of the Labour Party.

Churchill's previous experience of intervening in an Oxford by-election, in one of the University seats, had not been a success. He had publicly backed one of the candidates, the controversial Professor Lindemann (later Lord Cherwell), who was one of his closest associates. But Churchill's attempt to influence opinion backfired, and the rival candidate, Sir Arthur Salter, was elected.

Although Eden was apparently 'tempted' to give Lindsay his public backing, he decided not to speak or send a message of support. His biographer, Robert Rhodes James, has commented, 'it would have been very remarkable for a former Foreign Secretary to go so far so soon after his resignation.'

Churchill refused Lindsay public support. He did, however, communicate his private support to Lindsay's followers in an unorthodox way. During the campaign his son Randolph, who openly backed Lindsay, visited Oxford to see how the by-election was going. With Solly Zuckerman (later Lord Zuckerman), he attended one of Hogg's public meetings at the Town Hall. Characteristically, Randolph was unable to resist heckling and was ejected by the stewards.

Afterwards they repaired to Zuckerman's North Oxford home, where a number of Lindsay supporters had gathered. Randolph telephoned his father to tell him the news, while Zuckerman worried about the mounting cost of the trunk call. After some discussion on the telephone, Randolph held the instrument towards the others in the room saying that his father had a message for them. As they listened, Churchill's voice could be heard booming down the line: 'Lindsay must win!'

Apart from Macmillan, who was scarcely a household name at the time, other Conservatives prepared to back Lindsay publicly came principally from the University. Ted Heath and like-minded colleagues in the Oxford University Conservative Association had backed Eden at the time of his resignation, and now opposed Munich.

At the Oxford Union debate on Thursday the 13th, before Gordon Walker and Davies had withdrawn, Heath proposed the motion that 'This House deplores the Government's policy of peace without honour', and was supported by Christopher Mayhew, a former President of the Union. According to the report in *Isis*, Heath 'attacked the muddled policy of the Government, which had been largely responsible for bringing us to the verge of disaster'. He argued, in the report's summary, that 'it was certainly not self-determination which resulted from Munich. He had no faith in a lasting peace, but foresaw further trouble. . . . Hitler could not be trusted: that was clear to everyone save Mr Chamberlain.' And, as the report concluded, 'as a Conservative, Mr Heath must have astonished some of his confrères by his bitter attack.' In the Union a month later, Heath was attacking the Government as 'nothing more or less than an organised hypocrisy, composed of Conservatives with nothing to conserve and Liberals with a hatred of liberty'.

Roy Jenkins had arrived at Balliol only the week before, and the post-Munich debate was the first he attended at the Union. He thought Heath's speech 'was highly polished and very effective . . . a very good speech'. Yet Jenkins felt that Mayhew's had the edge. Heath himself reported on the debate, describing Mayhew's performance as 'brilliant', and omitting any reference to his own. Mayhew argued that 'never again would our military position be so strong compared to that of Germany. We should have made a firm stand with the other countries which had been with us.' And according to Heath, Mayhew 'taunted the Tories with having lost their patriotism when there was a job worth doing to be done'. The motion was carried by 320 votes to 266.

A group of former officers of the Oxford University Carlton Club and University Conservative Association published a manifesto urging their friends to vote for Lindsay. Yet there was no ill-feeling between the Chamberlainite Conservatives and the pro-Lindsay Tories. One Balliol Tory who was against Lindsay and for Hogg was Hugh Fraser (later a Tory MP and late husband of Antonia Fraser, daughter of Lord and Lady Longford). Fraser later recalled that he was just 'rather anti-Lindsay – it was more that than policy with me.'

During the campaign, both groups would lunch at the [Oxford] Carlton Club, the Chamberlainites sitting on one long table, the pro-Lindsay Tories on another. Then they would disperse for an afternoon's canvassing.

The Liberals gave the strongest public support for Lindsay. His Liberal supporters read like a roll-call of the great and the good – the Party leader Sir Archibald Sinclair, Isaac Foot and his son Dingle Foot, Richard Acland, Megan Lloyd George, Lady Violet Bonham Carter, Lady Gladstone, Sir William Beveridge and Professor J.B.S. Haldane.

Labour's public support was limited by the rumpus over the candidature. None of the party's senior leaders visited Oxford. But among the Labour politicians who appeared on Lindsay's platform during the campaign were Lord Strabolgi, John Parker MP and the left-winger Ellen Wilkinson. The writer H.G. Wells, a Fabian socialist, also gave his public backing to Lindsay.

But cross-party support and switching across traditional political loyalties was by no means entirely in Lindsay's favour. National Liberals, whose senior ranks included the Cabinet ministers Sir John Simon and Leslie Hore-Belisha, naturally supported Hogg. So did some National Labour politicians, including Lord Sanderson, a former Principal of Ruskin College, and Kenneth Lindsay, who stood at Oxford as the Labour candidate in 1924.

Gordon Walker's fear all along had been that the Lindsay campaign would not reach the working class. The row which had split the City Labour Party was denying Lindsay support from traditional, right-wing Labour leaders. Lindsay was helped by the three Liberal agents who had been assisting Davies, but Labour provided no outside help. The *Daily Express* characterised Lindsay's predicament as 'a very odd "Popular

Front" in which the biggest partner does not show his shirt front'.

Tom Harrisson's on-the-spot report for *Picture Post* suggested that Lindsay and his advisers had little idea how to communicate either their message or their candidate to the voters:

> One of the reasons for adopting Lindsay to represent a sort of anti-Government Popular Front was that 'everyone knew him'. Because he was a great University figure, his donnish advisers took it for granted that everyone in the town knew him as well as they did. They were wrong. Over half the Oxford electorate didn't know Lindsay from Adam. And so, with only ten days to go, they wasted three assuming that it wasn't necessary to tackle the vital job of making the candidate mean something to the voters. The very idea of doing that was repugnant to a lot of the dons, who have lived all their lives without speaking Oxford Town English. Said one – a famous philosopher – 'If he can't win on his own merits, without being vulgar, better to lose.'

Lindsay hated the vulgarities of electioneering. He was shocked by the slogan, 'A Vote for Hogg is a Vote for Hitler!' The authorship of this slogan has subsequently been attributed to various people, including Julian Amery (later a Conservative MP and minister), Dick Crossman, the Communists and the philosophy don John Austin, who pursued Hogg throughout the campaign and heckled at every opportunity.

It was an uphill struggle for Lindsay's supporters to see that the voters got to know him. In Ivor Davies's view, he was 'the worst Parliamentary candidate I have ever encountered'. Another leading Liberal used the damning words, 'magnificent but inaudible'. Although Lindsay mixed happily with people outside the University through his role in the Workers' Educational Association, he clearly went through agonies seeking votes on the doorstep or in the street.

Some of Lindsay's supporters were less fastidious. For Lindsay's sake, that was probably just as well. By the last few days of the campaign, the popularising of Lindsay was proceeding apace. Lindsay the candidate was being dragged from the college cloisters – not quite literally in person, but in publicity hand-outs – and portrayed as the kind of man to whom anyone would warm. The voters were told that he played moderate tennis and bad golf, that he had a country cottage in the Lake District, that his hobby was cooking and that he grew potatoes. *The Times* observed, with a touch of condescension, that some of the publicity for Lindsay 'could be described as popular rather than academic'.

In contrast Hogg was a formidable candidate, who had been putting his message across from day one of the campaign. He was more at ease canvassing, and met various groups, from women working in a laundry to the printers at the Oxford University Press. Tom Harrisson's thumb-nail sketch is enlightening on the choice before the electors: 'Young, dynamic, keen on mountain climbing, he has been described in the Press as "a blue-eyed boy with a Cupid's bow of a mouth".'

In the first week of the campaign, Hogg's father, Viscount Hailsham, Lord President of the Council, spoke for his son at Oxford Town Hall – the meeting was taking place while local Labour Party members were at St Michael's Hall debating whether Gordon Walker should withdraw. Viscount Hailsham's speech was a more significant event than might be supposed today. In the 1930s, convention decreed that Cabinet ministers and former Cabinet ministers did not participate in parliamentary by-election campaigns. Hailsham argued, however, that the Labour Party had been disregarding the convention, and therefore his public act of filial support was quite permissible.

Writing about the campaign some thirty years later, in an article entitled 'Hindsight', Hogg claimed,

> I never defended Munich as just. I never defended Mr. Chamberlain's rather emotional outburst on his return, which I always recognised as the natural revulsion of an exhausted man who has succeeded beyond his expectations. My interpretation of 'peace with honour' was that Munich represented the last chance of the dictators to prove their good faith, and a final opportunity for the democracies, while keeping the agreement, to make preparation for the conflict there might be.

But Hogg was naturally less prone to qualify his statements during the hectic campaign. His appeal to the voters was a call for unity, an occasion for the people of Oxford to demonstrate that the country was solidly behind the Prime Minister: 'Mr. Chamberlain came back amidst the applause of the entire British Public. And the people of this country will vote for him. It is not enough that we should win. Of course we are going to win. We must win by a vast, an overwhelming majority.'

In his election address, Hogg went as far as to claim that ' "Peace with Honour" is a watchword of the Party of which I am a member.' In exuberant mood, he told a noisy open meeting at St Giles on the last Saturday evening of the campaign, 'The issue in this election is going to be very clear. I am standing for a definite policy. Peace by negotiation. Mr. Lindsay is standing for no definite policy he can name. He stands for national division against national unity. His policy is a policy of two left feet walking backward.'

The count took place at the Town Hall immediately after the polls closed on Thursday, 27 October. As the time of the declaration approached, the roads around the Town Hall were impassable and the City centre was packed.

Shortly after eleven o'clock the Lord Mayor emerged on to the Town Hall balcony to declare the result. There was much cheering, barracking and egg-throwing from the crowded streets below. Hogg stood to the Lord Mayor's right, Lindsay to his left. Standing at the front of the crowd below was Mrs Bourne, the mother of the deceased MP, who had bravely supported Hogg during the campaign.

Eventually the crowd quietened down enough for the Lord Mayor to declare the result. Hogg, the National Conservative, won 15,797 votes. Lindsay, the Independent Progressive, 12,363. Hogg's majority was 3434.

The cheering and jeering reached a new crescendo. Some of Lindsay's supporters were in tears. Hogg was eventually able to make himself heard: 'It is not my victory. It is Mr Chamberlain's victory. It is a victory for democracy, for peace by negotiation, and it is a victory for a united Britain. It is a victory above all for the ordinary man and woman, who have shown again the common sense and judgement of the British elector.'

Lindsay countered with his own claim, 'I feel that we have started a movement. . . . there is a spirit in Oxford which nothing will stop.'

'Wild Scenes after Declaration of Poll' was the front-page headline in the next day's *Oxford Mail*. It took Hogg more than twenty minutes before he was able to make his way through the crush to his car. And before he could leave for a tour of his committee rooms, a gang gathered round and rocked his car. Eventually he was able to make good his escape. But long after midnight the crowds were still milling around the streets of Oxford.

The girl students had to be back in their colleges by midnight. They arranged to hear who had won by asking the boys to cycle past and shout out the result. In due course, they heard the cries from the street, 'The Hogg's in! The Hogg's in!' Interviewed for Channel Four, Edna Healey, then at St Hugh's, recalls that a philosophy don had asked the girls to let her know the result. When the students told her, she was distressed, commenting that she had wanted Lindsay to win – although, of course, she had voted for Hogg.

The halving of the Conservative majority since the 1935 general election gave some comfort and encouragement to Lindsay and his supporters. Perhaps Oxford really had 'started a movement' of opinion against the Government. Yet Hogg had held the seat and given a creditable performance.

Lindsay and his supporters had succeeded in making Oxford a single-issue election, transforming the by-election into a referendum. But the upshot was that Hogg's victory was bound to be seen as a demonstration of public support for Chamberlain. This criticism was aired, predictably, by Gordon Walker the day after the declaration: 'The immediate result of narrowing down the whole election to the single issue of foreign policy has been to give Mr. Chamberlain a gratuitous and unmerited vote of confidence on this issue.'

He had a point. If Labour had fought the campaign on its full domestic and foreign programme, 'an increase in the anti-Government vote would have been of far greater significance, and a Conservative victory would never have been interpreted – as this one will be – as a vote of confidence on the single issue of foreign policy.'

But Gordon Walker was not giving sufficient credit to Lindsay's achievements. Lindsay had in fact polled 2702 votes more than Gordon Walker in 1935 and had boosted the anti-Government share of the vote from 37 to 44 per cent.

What is more, fears that Lindsay would not reach the working-class vote were ill founded. As research shows, a rudimentary opinion poll conducted during the Oxford by-election reveals that Lindsay retained the bulk of Gordon Walker's support in 1935. Lindsay was also far more successful than Hogg (by almost two to one) in attracting support from people who did not vote at the 1935 general election – these may well have included many Liberals, who did not have a Liberal candidate to vote for in 1935, along with other abstainers, newcomers to the constituency and those who had previously been too young to vote.

The excitement of the by-election was not restricted merely to the University, but spread to capture interest throughout the City. Significantly, the turn-out was substantially higher at the by-election, 76 per cent in October 1938 compared with 67 per cent at the general election. It seems unlikely that that would have been possible without the dramatic intervention of an Independent Progressive. Lindsay's candidature focused people's greater interest in foreign policy. He provided a clear choice, for or against the Government, on that single issue.

As *Picture Post* concluded, 'Oxford, the first of a whole chain of by-elections, has shown new tensions and tendencies in the party system, new loyalties and disloyalties cutting across the old and rather care-worn traditions.' There was great optimism about the prospects for a new Popular Front campaign:

> However much the leaders try to squash (as they are doing) the
> increasing wish for one opposition party, all the indications are that
> if they persist in that attitude, local parties will revolt, as they did in
> Oxford. Many Opposition politicians now think that to face the call

for 'Unity behind Chamberlain', there should be 'Unity against Chamberlain'.

'German View of Oxford Election Result' ran the front-page headline in the *Oxford Mail* on the Saturday after polling. The German press were reported to be taking the Oxford result 'as a sign that the Munich Agreement may become the permanent basis for British foreign policy'. There were also some choice comments on Lindsay and his supporters. According to the *Boersen Zeitung*,

> Those who had an opportunity of making contact with the younger and older academic set at Oxford would have been frightened by the wanton arrogance with which these quarters condemned the National Socialist Germany's domestic and foreign policy, had it not been evident that this academic set merely represented that kind of parlour Bolshevism which exists in all those countries of post-War Europe where there are young people without a real task in life.

Labour did win the next parliamentary by-election at Dartford on 7 November, but it was a highly marginal constituency which had changed hands six times between 1920 and 1931, and the swing to Labour was comparatively small. *The Times* reported, 'The principal issue in the campaign was the foreign policy of the Government,' but there was no substantial increase in turn-out as had been the case at Oxford.

Taken together, Oxford and Dartford showed that Munich was not proving an election-winner for the Government. But neither was there much sign of 'the start of a movement' which Lindsay had envisaged. This conclusion was apparently borne out at the by-elections at Walsall and Doncaster on 16 and 17 November. In straight contests, the National Liberals held Walsall and Labour held Doncaster. Unemployment and social problems played a greater role than at Oxford or Dartford. As at Dartford, the swing against the Government in both seats was small, and there was little increase in turn-out.

On the same day that polling took place in Doncaster, the voters also went to the polls in the very different seat of Bridgwater in Somerset. In 1935, the Conservative, Reginald Croom-Johnson, had won a majority of 11,699 over the Liberal, with Labour trailing third. It seemed that the new Conservative candidate, the twenty-six-year-old Patrick Heathcoat-Amory, had booked himself a safe passage to the Commons.

But long before there was any prospect of a by-election, Popular Front supporters had been active in Bridgwater, notably in Minehead, where the Left Book Club had an active local branch. When the by-election was called, it was suggested that the broadcaster and journalist Vernon

Bartlett might be a suitable Popular Front candidate. Some years earlier, Bartlett had been a staunch disarmer, and had lost his staff job at the BBC in 1933 over his criticism of Simon's mishandling of the Disarmament Conference. He remained a controversial figure, and became a committed opponent of Chamberlain's foreign policy. He covered the Prime Minister's three visits to Hitler as foreign correspondent for the *News Chronicle*, and as we have seen during the Munich crisis his news programmes for children were censored. Bartlett agreed to stand, on condition that both the Liberal and Labour parties backed him, which they eventually did.

Lindsay and many others who had supported him at Oxford went to Bridgwater and spoke for Bartlett. But most Tory dissidents were still reluctant to give public support to anyone standing against an official Conservative candidate. Bartlett later revealed that 'Mr Churchill, who so obviously shared my distrust of Hitler, wrote privately that for political reasons he could not send me a message of good wishes.'

Unlike Oxford City, Bridgwater was a large, sprawling, rural constituency. In an attempt to overcome the problem, Bartlett found an ingenious way of putting his broadcasting background to good use. He recorded a speech on a gramophone disc, and arranged for it to be broadcast from a loud-speaker. On one occasion, however, it became stuck, and the puzzled voters merely heard Bartlett's voice repeating 'Bridgwater' over and over again.

Bartlett's campaign concentrated on meetings in villages. Over 150 such gatherings were held, and although Bartlett took care to cover other issues, the campaign was fought on the single issue of foreign policy. Left Book Club members from Bath, Cleveden, Glastonbury, North Somerset and Taunton canvassed for Bartlett.

A week before polling, the news was dominated by reports from Germany of a wave of fresh attacks on Jews, the so-called 'Krystallnacht' riots, in which their windows were smashed and their shops looted. The sequence of events had begun on Monday the 7th, when a junior German diplomat at the Embassy in Paris was shot by a young Polish Jew. The German's death on the 10th was the pretext for an outbreak of vicious Nazi attacks on the Jewish community.

On Friday the 11th the headlines in the British press read 'Synagogues in Flames', 'Orgy of Hitler Youth', 'Thousands Arrested', 'Wave of Suicides'. This new wave of anti-Jewish persecution undermined the assumptions behind Chamberlain's diplomatic efforts in Europe. Hitler scarcely seemed the sort of leader who would be persuaded by rational argument, let alone one who could be trusted.

The Bridgwater declaration came early on the afternoon of Friday,

18 November. A large crowd, estimated at around 6000, gathered for the result. Heathcoat-Amory polled 17,208 votes, Bartlett 19,540. A five-figure Conservative majority had been turned into a 2332 majority for the Independent Progressive. It was a sensational result, and a profound shock to Chamberlainite Conservatives. 'We have been beaten by Hitler and the BBC' declared an understandably shaken Heathcoat-Amory. He was later killed during the war.

Bartlett was carried shoulder-high round the streets of Bridgwater. Commenting on the lessons of his own sensational victory for the rest of the country, he said that he had 'quite deliberately accepted to stand in an agricultural constituency where I was told that the chances of winning were practically nil, and I have been most encouraged by the way in which even in the remotest villages, audiences have listened to and discussed questions of foreign policy.'

Not only was there a large swing against the Government, the numbers voting also increased dramatically. The proportion turning out to vote leapt from a respectable 73 per cent in 1935 to a remarkable 82 per cent in the by-election, a fractionally larger increase in turn-out than at Oxford City three weeks earlier. At Bridgwater, as at Oxford, the heightened public interest in foreign policy had been fostered, and then expressed itself in what became a referendum.

The result at Bridgwater seemed to confirm Lindsay's hope that 'a movement' had been started at Oxford. The movement of 'Unity against Chamberlain' which *Picture Post* envisaged and believed was widely desired by many opposition politicians appeared to be up and running.

Within a fortnight of the Bridgwater result, however, Conservative candidates were returned at by-elections in two safe seats – West Lewisham in suburban South London and the Fylde in rural Lancashire. Yet these had been straight contests with Labour, and not with Independent Progressives. Also in both cases the numbers voting had fallen compared with 1935, and only 58 per cent of the electorate turned out in West Lewisham. The difference with Oxford and Bridgwater, where Popular-Front-style campaigns were mounted, is striking.

By late November 1938, an eighth by-election was in the offing in the rural Scottish constituency of Kinross and West Perthshire. The Conservative MP, Katharine, Duchess of Atholl, 'Red Kitty', had long been a critic of the Government, and was already seriously at odds with her constituency association before Munich. In April 1938 she had resigned the Government whip in protest at Chamberlain's foreign policy. The following month her local association declared that they backed Chamberlain.

The Duchess of Atholl's opposition to Munich was the last straw for her local party. Undeterred by the fact that the Duke was presiding over their meeting on 20 November, they voted by 273 votes to 167 to seek another candidate for the next election, 'who will support the Prime Minister's policy of peaceful understanding in Europe'. The Duke immediately resigned his position, and the Duchess, against the advice of Churchill and other friends, resigned her seat by applying for the Chiltern Hundreds.

The ensuing by-election, held on 21 December, was a straight contest between the Duchess and an official Unionist candidate, a farmer who was well known locally. In contrast to Lindsay at Oxford, Churchill readily granted the Duchess a statement of public support. He referred to her adherence 'to the first principles of the Conservative Party', his fulsome backing no doubt reflecting the earlier support which the Duchess had given him over the India Bill in the early 1930s.

But the Duchess was seriously handicapped by the lack of support from other parties. Labour lacked an effective organisation in the constituency, and the Liberals disliked what they regarded as her reactionary approach on domestic policy. This cost her dear on polling day, when heavy snow put a premium on providing cars to get the voters to the polling booths.

The Duchess's defeat by 1313 votes came as a deep shock to her. She cancelled a tour of her committee rooms, and 'celebrated' her defeat by playing Beethoven's Waldstein and Appassionata Sonatas. She consoled herself by saying that she would have more time to devote to her husband and her music.

Her staunch public support for a Popular Front was exceptional among Conservative politicians. It is ironic that her defeat should have been partly attributable to lack of support from the opposition parties.

Yet the Duchess's demise demonstrated one of the great flaws in the Popular Front idea. No matter how much its more ardent advocates might have wished it were otherwise, politicians who agreed on foreign policy, and who even agreed that foreign policy was the pre-eminent issue of the day, still could not wish away every other difference. Apart from the minority of fervent Popular-Fronters, Labour politicians in the main were equivocal, Liberals suspicious and Conservatives cautious.

At the time of the Munich crisis, the Conservative Research Department advised that on the basis of the by-elections held up to the summer 'a General Election held then would have made very little difference to the Government's majority.' But after the Munich by-elections, the Research Department hurriedly revised their advice, with David Clarke (later a distinguished director of the Department) preparing an urgent note that on no account should the Government risk an election during the winter of 1938–9.

Doubts and confusion in the public mind had set in very soon after the near-hysterical relief displayed at Chamberlain's homecoming. Oxford and Bridgwater demonstrated that there was a substantial body of opinion in the country which opposed Munich, and which cut across traditional party loyalties. This opposition to appeasement could be mobilised, if given a clear lead.

Within weeks of Munich, external events were to exert an even stronger influence on political opinion in Britain. They would finally shatter the illusions of the previous decade.

# CHAPTER SIXTEEN

# END OF ILLUSION

> What was to be the value of the long looked forward to,
> Long hoped for calm, the autumnal serenity
> And the wisdom of age? Had they deceived us
> Or deceived themselves, the quiet-voiced elders,
> Bequeathing us merely a receipt for deceit?
>
> (T.S. Eliot, extract from *East Coker*, 1940)

The details of the transfer of the Sudetenland to the Third Reich had been finalised while the House of Commons was still midway through its debate on the Munich Agreement.

In Berlin on Wednesday, 5 October 1938, the International Commission, established under the terms of the Munich Agreement, granted Hitler virtually all the territory he had demanded in his Bad Godesberg ultimatum. The German occupation was to be completed by the following Monday, 10 October.

Later on Wednesday the 5th, Churchill and Nicolson savaged the Government in the Munich debate, and Rab Butler delivered his fulsome defence of appeasement. Yet, incredibly, the news from Berlin was little remarked in London. The immediate euphoria of Munich was beginning to fade, but the International Commission had an air of respectability about it. After all, the Czechs were represented on it, having been excluded from the Munich conference itself. The democracies (Britain, France, Czechoslovakia) outnumbered the dictator powers (Germany and Italy) on the Commission by three to two.

Yet the International Commission was a sham. It met in Berlin, and consisted of the diplomats of the Munich powers in the German capital, plus a representative from the Czech Government – Britain was represented by Sir Nevile Henderson, who had once described the Czechs as a 'pig-headed race'. The Commission met under the chairmanship of the Secretary of State in the German Foreign Office, Weizsäcker. In reality, the line-up was not three against two, but four against one – the four Munich powers were determined that the Czechs should concede as quickly as possible.

Roger Makins (later Lord Sherfield) served on the Commission's sub-committee on frontiers. He has recalled that after three days a colonel from the German staff appeared, told the committee it was not making satisfactory progress, and adjourned the session. The sub-committee did not meet again.

At the Foreign Office in London, Frank Roberts had been told to 'bone up' on Poland before the ink was barely dry on the Munich Agreement. This indicated a recognition that Hitler's ambitions in Eastern Europe had not been satisfied. At this stage it did not necessarily presage war, but indicated that Munich was likely to be regarded as only one element – albeit a crucial one – in the appeasement of Nazi Germany.

In early November 1938, Chamberlain took the opportunity of the Prime Minister's annual speech at the Mansion House to reassure the country: 'We can all look forward to a happy Christmas.' There was, however, 'a disastrous *fond* of naïveté in Mr Chamberlain's character', as Kenneth Clark discovered shortly after the Munich Agreement.

Clark and his wife were lunching at Number 10. When Clark displayed his habitual wariness of Government entertainment wines he noticed his wife at the other end of the table 'making violent signs of assent'. As Clark later recalled,

> It was the best Hock I have ever drunk. Mr Chamberlain, who had observed our pantomime, was delighted. 'It was given me', he said, 'by the wine growers of Germany for having saved the peace of the world.' After lunch he led us to a small showcase containing various trinkets and charms. 'All these', he said, 'were sent me in gratitude for the Munich Agreement.'

Within days of Chamberlain's Mansion House speech, anti-Jewish disturbances had swept across Germany – the Krystallnacht riots. Chips Channon's reaction revealed his misplaced sympathies: 'I must say Hitler never helps, and always makes Chamberlain's task more difficult.' Yet even Chamberlain's loyalest and most sycophantic supporter was now forced to conclude that he could 'no longer cope with the present [German] regime which seems to have lost all sense and reason'.

Oliver Harvey, Halifax's Private Secretary at the Foreign Office (and formerly Eden's), considered that 'The Jewish pogroms have shaken up world opinion – even the City – as to the character of the criminal regime we are up against in Germany.' He sensed that as a result, the country was 'beginning to stir': 'On all sides you hear of uneasiness and dissatisfaction, especially among the people in the provinces – working classes, etc., also among all the intelligent classes in London, journalists, writers, artists, civil servants, professionals generally.'

A few days later, following Vernon Bartlett's by-election triumph at Bridgwater, Harvey was discussing 'Munich and after' with his Foreign Office colleague, William Strang. They agreed that 'any war, whether we win or not, would destroy the rich idle classes and so they are for peace at any price.' In Harvey's view, 'The smug ones are the rich, the industrialists, the landowners, the idle, the party hacks – these still do not see that the Nazis will not save their dividends and their estates.'

The bulk of the Conservative Party stayed loyal to their leader and his policy. But the minority of dissidents were permanently disaffected, and others who had reluctantly supported the Government in the lobbies at the end of the Munich debate remained uneasy. Soon after that debate, Chips Channon had sensed a 'wave of anti-Chamberlain feeling' and wrote of a 'cleavage in London society about Chamberlain', observations which were in part prompted by Noël Coward's cocktail party for the 'opposition', attended by Eden and other anti-appeasers. At around the same time Cazalet noted, 'People do seem disquieted about the sort of paralysis which seems to have seized everyone in Government. Is Chamberlain (*J'aime Berlin*) afraid to do anything in case it irritates Hitler? Is he [chasing] a will-of-the-wisp in trying to come to terms with Germany?'

But the Tory dissidents were in a precarious position. The Prime Minister dominated the Party and commanded its loyalty. A general election was due within two years, and was probably only a year to eighteen months away. Tory Party activists find it almost impossible to stomach any sign of disloyalty to the leader at the best of times. But the dissidents had not only rocked the boat when the Party was increasingly preoccupied with the next election, they had compounded their sin by rebelling against the man who had single-handedly saved the country from war.

Inevitably, Chamberlain's critics came under heavy fire from their local Conservative Associations. Even Churchill, an established parliamentarian, had great trouble fending off a determined attempt by a section of his Epping constituency party to drop him as the official Conservative candidate at the next election.

In the Commons, many Tory MPs were still deeply sceptical of Churchill. Their doubts about his judgement persisted, and his readiness to collude with opposition politicians frightened away others who were more sympathetic. As the winter of 1938–9 drew in, he remained an isolated figure.

Eden was in a 'difficult position' according to Victor Cazalet, because 'he does not wish to be disloyal to the Conservative Party. He will not serve under Chamberlain, and at the same time is not prepared to strike out on his own. . . .' In fact, as Robert Rhodes James makes clear in his biography, Eden was seriously discussing with Leo Amery, Lord Cranborne and Jim Thomas the possibility of not standing again as Conservatives. And in speeches Eden was arguing for economic and social reform to go hand-in-hand with a commitment to rearmament, since England must be a country worth fighting for.

At this time, Eden was also urging that a truly National Government should be formed. He found that Halifax was in substantial agreement – indeed, the Foreign Secretary had advised Chamberlain to broaden the Government after Munich. But the Prime Minister was opposed, telling Halifax that Eden ignored the fact that the 'conciliatory part of the policy', appeasing Germany, was as important as rearmament.

Eden though was not prepared to denounce his own Government, an attitude which disappointed many when he addressed a League of Nations rally in November 1938. Violet Bonham Carter, who had shared the platform, subsequently commented that she felt more like moving a Vote of Censure than a Vote of Thanks for Eden.

Within the Government, the events of the autumn and the Prime Minister's approach had done nothing to dispel the anxieties of a small number of discontented ministers. By December, five ministers just below Cabinet rank were actively considering resignation. But the ministerial plotters were deterred by the fear that the Prime Minister would recommend an early dissolution of Parliament. They were afraid that an election in the wake of their resignation would expose them to the risk of being dropped as official Conservative candidates.

On Monday, 2 January 1939, the headline in the *Daily Express* proclaimed, 'This is why you can sleep soundly in 1939'. The article went on to say: 'There will be no great war in Europe in 1939. . . .'

Behind the scenes in Whitehall, however, reports had been received since mid-December that Hitler's first move might be not the 'eastward drive', but a surprise attack in Western Europe. In fact, the reports were false. They had been planted by Hitler's opponents in an effort to stiffen British resistance. Their effect on British strategy certainly turned out to be decisive.

Since the autumn, the French had been pressing the British for a stronger military commitment – in November, Chamberlain and Halifax had received a cool reception in Paris, where they were met with cries of *'Vive Eden!'* and *'À bas Munich!'* Chamberlain still opposed any Continental commitment. In January 1939 he sacked Inskip when he learnt that the Minister for the Co-ordination of Defence was preparing a paper which advocated the establishment of a Ministry of Supply.

But Halifax increasingly felt that Britain should support France. His change of mind was to prove decisive. When the War Secretary, Hore-Belisha, presented demands for an extra £81 million on the army's budget, Halifax argued that Britain should support France, otherwise the French might stand aside while Germany fought Britain. At the end of January 1939, the Cabinet's Foreign Policy Committee recommended joint staff talks with France and Belgium, and an Anglo-French undertaking to resist any German attack on Holland or Switzerland. In February, Chamberlain finally accepted that Britain should develop the military capability required to give a stronger commitment to the French.

Hore-Belisha's presentation of the new army estimates in early March 1939 clearly demonstrated that Britain had finally abandoned the concept of 'limited liability' – the notion that Britain should avoid any Continental commitment and concentrate on self-defence against a knock-out blow from the air. The Government was embarked upon full-scale rearmament. In 1938, Britain had spent 7 per cent of her Gross National Product on military expenditure, but during 1939 this soared to 18 per cent (Germany's military spending was running at 17 and 23 per cent of its GNP in the same two years).

In one sense, Chamberlain was proved right. Massive rearmament and war were ruinous economically. Within a couple of years, Britain was bankrupt and had to rely on the United States to bale her out. But this also made nonsense of Chamberlain's view, which had prevailed as Government policy up to 1939, that sound finance was vital if Britain was to withstand a long war. Despite years of appeasement and financial rectitude, Britain found herself at war and broke.

In early 1939, however, Chamberlain seemed increasingly confident that he could save the peace. In the New Year, he had revived his efforts to win over Italy to Britain's side. Accompanied by Halifax, he visited Rome for talks with Mussolini. The initiative failed, not least because Mussolini regarded Chamberlain's hesitation and tentativeness as a sign of weakness.

Yet at home the visit marked an improvement in Chamberlain's standing. According to Channon, 'Old Brolly got back from Rome – his stature enhanced, his prestige increased. He is winning through and will probably be Premier for years to come. He was well received in London.'

Chamberlain told the American Ambassador, Joseph Kennedy, that the combination of British and American rearmament, coupled with the warning against the dictators recently issued by Roosevelt, 'may do the trick'. Kennedy, however, found it difficult to reconcile the Prime Minister's 'hope that appeasement will still be worked out and his fear that

Hitler has in his hands, and is quite likely to use them, the means of causing a world war'.

So confident had Chamberlain become that on 9 March he gave the lobby correspondents an extremely optimistic briefing on the European outlook. The Prime Minister had not thought to inform, let alone consult, his Foreign Secretary. The next day at the Foreign Office, Cadogan noted that 'All the press carries a ridiculous "rainbow" story. Much too optimistic.'

A few days later, Chamberlain wrote to his sister: 'Like Chatham [the elder Pitt] I know that I can save this country and I do not believe that anyone else can. . . . I ought to be good for at least one more Parliament after this. . . .'

But the Czech crisis was again dominating the headlines. On 10 March, the Czech President, Hacha, declared martial law in an attempt to preserve the unity of the remaining parts of his state. Hitler responded by inviting the deposed Slovak leader, Tiso, for talks in Berlin.

In London, the renewed crisis stirred all the antagonisms of Munich. On Monday, 13 March, Harold Nicolson found the Commons 'in a dreadful state': 'most people really believed that Munich settled the Czech question and are deeply disturbed. For instance Charles Waterhouse [a Tory MP] (who is usually friendly in personal contact) gets up and leaves when I inadvertently sit next to him in the smoking-room.'

On the morning of Wednesday 15 March, the shattering news reached London that German troops had occupied Prague. British foreign policy was in tatters. The Government's military advisers had urged them to reduce their enemies and increase their friends. But for most of the 1930s, the emphasis had been placed on the former at the expense of the latter. They had pinned their hopes on appeasement. It was a tragic mis-judgement. As the fall of Prague finally demonstrated, their enemies were implacable.

Yet the British Cabinet decided that there was nothing they could immediately do. Chamberlain attempted to justify their failure to act on the ground that the Government were no longer bound by the guarantee made to the Czechs at Munich, because the state of Czechoslovakia had ceased to exist – the day before the German occupation, the leaders of the eastern province of Slovakia (under duress from Hitler) had unilaterally declared their independence from Prague.

Cazalet felt that the fall of Prague was 'just so appalling as to be unspeakable. It has roused the ordinary "man in the street" as nothing else has. We seem very near war. It looks as though Hitler is determined to dominate Europe.' On 16 March, the new Duke of Devonshire (a brother-in-law of Harold Macmillan), a minister just below Cabinet rank, took the remarkable step of explaining in public that the Government's policy was not 'bearing fruit'.

That morning, *The Times* had declared that the 'invasion, occupation and annexation of Bohemia and Moravia, are notice to the world that German policy no longer seeks the protection of a moral case'. In each of the previous instances of German intervention – the Rhineland, Austria and the Sudetenland – 'it has been difficult not to allow some extenuation for it in the Allied blunders of the past, and not to see in it some substance of justice.' But Prague was different. *The Times* had abandoned the line it had held throughout Hitler's first six years as German Chancellor.

In the Commons, Eden urged that the democracies should take collective action to defend themselves against German aggression. Sir John Simon's dismissive response infuriated the younger Tory dissidents, who now began working closely with Churchill.

On Thursday, 17 March, Chamberlain was due to deliver a major speech in Birmingham. As Nicolson noted, 'The feeling in the lobbies is that Chamberlain will either have to go or completely reverse his policy. Unless in his speech tonight he admits that he was wrong, they feel that resignation is the only alternative.'

Chamberlain was addressing the Party faithful in his native city, on the eve of his seventieth birthday. The major statement on social reform which he had planned was jettisoned. In his speech, Chamberlain defended Munich and the idea that differences between states were best settled through discussion. But he echoed *The Times* in his argument that until Prague 'there was something to be said' for every German intervention, 'whether on account of racial affinity or of just claims too long resisted'. The latest episode, however, seemed 'to fall into a different category':

> Is this the end of an old adventure, or the beginning of a new? . . . is this, in fact, a step in the direction of an attempt to dominate the world by force? . . . No greater mistake could be made than to suppose that, because it believes war to be a senseless and cruel thing, this nation has so lost its fibre that it will not take part to the utmost of its power in resisting such a challenge if it were ever made.

Harold Macmillan was 'enraged that Chamberlain should remain on'. According to Nicolson, Macmillan was convinced that 'all the Edenites have been too soft and gentlemanlike'. In fact, Eden and the younger Tory MPs who associated with him were now so disaffected that they were talking of resigning the Conservative whip and standing as Independents. Only a radical change of policy would dissuade them.

In late March, a motion in Eden's name was supported by forty MPs, including Churchill, Amery and Duff Cooper. The dissident Tories were calling for:

a National Government . . . formed on the widest possible basis, and . . . such a Government should be entrusted with full power over the nation's industry, wealth and man-power, to enable this country to put forward its maximum military effort in the shortest possible time.

After Prague, Chamberlain was no longer confident that he had the right answer for dealing with the dictators. As a result Halifax, who had already changed his mind about the best approach, was able to exercise much greater influence. This was to lead to a significant shift in British policy.

'I must say it is turning out – at present – as Van[sittart] predicted and as I never believed it would', wrote Sir Alec Cadogan after the fall of Prague.

Britain now set about trying to encourage a diplomatic grouping of the independent states in South-eastern and Eastern Europe, or a 'dam', as Cadogan described it, which would check any further advances by Hitler. But events overtook the British Government, and led them to take a series of decisions which finally spelt the end of appeasement and made war virtually inevitable.

A little over a week after the fall of Prague, Hitler's troops struck to the east of Poland, seizing the Baltic territory of Memel, which Lithuania had annexed from Germany in 1923. There were reports that Hitler's troops would strike yet again to fulfil German claims on Danzig (Gdansk) and the Polish corridor, a strip of territory which provided Poland's access to the Baltic, but which was formerly German and which cut off East Prussia from the rest of Germany. In fact the rumours of the planned German attack were again instigated by dissident elements within Germany, and turned out to be untrue.

The British Government responded by declaring that they would guarantee Poland's independence (though not Poland's territorial integrity), persuading the French to join them as co-guarantors. The key figures in pushing the Polish guarantee were Halifax and his Permanent Secretary, Cadogan, as the historian D.C. Watt has revealed. Their motivation seems to have been a mistrust of the Polish leader, Colonel Beck, whom they feared might reach an agreement with Hitler which would scupper any hope of building a bloc of states to restrain German expansion. It was clear too that if Hitler were to launch a coup against the

Poles, and nothing had been done to deter him, the British and French would lose all credibility throughout Europe.

The Polish guarantee would also bring a political benefit to the Conservatives. With a general election drawing near, it would help reunite the Conservative Party. The dissidents would be reassured that at last a stand was being taken against Hitler. Yet it was also acceptable to Chamberlain, because it allowed enough flexibility for a negotiated settlement of Germany's territorial claims.

The guarantee, however, was opposed by Halifax's deputy at the Foreign Office, the arch-appeaser Rab Butler. It was also opposed on grounds of military strategy by the dissident Liddell Hart, who had been critical of appeasement and Munich.

In early April 1939, Mussolini invaded Albania, in flagrant breach of the Anglo-Italian Agreement. Mussolini's action sparked Nicolson into a private rage at the 'defeatist and pampered group in London' who had long been assuring the dictators that 'the capitalists of England' were on their side. Surely, as intelligent a man as the Italian Ambassador, Grandi, would not leave Mussolini 'under any illusion that the will-power of the country is concentrated in Mrs Ronald Greville. . . . He must know that in the last resort our decision is embodied, not in Mayfair or Cliveden, but in the provinces. . . .'

Also in April, Hitler denounced the 1935 Anglo-German Naval Agreement, and a month later, Germany and Italy signed their 'Pact of Steel', which effectively gave Berlin a free hand to launch any offensive they chose. The growing threat from the dictator powers in the Balkans led the British and French Governments to extend guarantees of independence to Rumania and Greece. In May, a further guarantee was extended to Turkey.

The spring 1939 crisis had triggered a major diplomatic offensive by London and Paris. Yet their guarantees of independence were intended as a transitional move until a bloc of East European states was built up which could resist German expansion. Issuing the guarantees, however, proved counter-productive, since the incentive for Poland and Rumania to develop their own alliance was removed, and London and Paris lost any leverage over them.

The Marquis of Lothian, though an appeaser for most of the period, had opposed Munich. He had recently been appointed British Ambassador to the United States, and when he met Cazalet in the spring of 1939 they 'went over the whole ground of world affairs.' As Cazalet noted, 'We are all agreed now. "No concessions" – nothing to violence and blackmail.'

But not everyone was agreed. Harold Nicolson was told of a conversation overheard in the Chamber of the Commons between two

Conservative backbenchers. 'I suppose', one of them had remarked, 'we *shall* be able to get out of this beastly guarantee business?' To which the other MP replied, 'Oh, of course. Thank God we have Neville.'

Despite the shift in policy, the bitterness over appeasement persisted in Britain during the summer of 1939. The divisions had run too deep over previous years to be quickly forgotten. Besides, some appeasers were still searching for any opportunity to resurrect their doctrine.

Harold Nicolson was bitter about one person in particular: 'I should be most unhappy if I were Lady Astor. She must realise that her parrot cries have done much damage to what (to do her justice) she must dimly realise is the essence of her adopted class and country.' Nancy Astor, however, was among those who began urging that Churchill should be brought into the Government. In Channon's view, she was 'frightened by anonymous letters and gossip about the so-called "Clieveden Set" ', and as a result had 'thrown over her principles and is urging Chamberlain against his better judgment, to take the plunge'.

The healing process was hindered because Chamberlain was palpably unable to inspire a sense of national unity. He remained deeply suspicious of critics within his own Party, let alone in the opposition parties. Chips Channon observed a telling episode:

> Neville was in a rage yesterday and in the morning whilst he was going over questions he delivered himself of an angry tirade against the 'Glamour Boys'. More particularly Bobbety Cranborne, who is the most dangerous of the lot. 'Beware' he said 'of rampant idealists. All Cecils are that.'

The result was that Tories with wider appeal were left out of the Government and had little enthusiasm to return under Chamberlain's stewardship. As Eden later wrote, he was undecided what his own course of action should be: 'Even if asked to go back into the Government as it was at that time, I did not want to accept. I knew that my return would not be welcome to the Prime Minister and most of his senior colleagues; they would only tolerate it in response to public demand.'

Chamberlain was quite incapable of winning the confidence of any other group apart from his own devoted loyalists within the Conservative Party. As Oliver Harvey commented to Halifax, 'the P.M. was not trusted by the Opposition whatever he did and they still did not trust his foreign policy.'

Although the unions and the Government were beginning to work more closely together, their relationship remained patchy and uneasy. The unions had co-operated in the Government's national service campaign from early 1939. Talks were also held with the Ministry of Labour about the organisation of industrial relations in wartime. Yet when a Ministry of Supply was finally established in July 1939, only businessmen were appointed to its industrial advisory panel.

Chamberlain had mishandled the introduction of conscription in April by promising to consult the unions but then summoning them to hear his plans. The Prime Minister had recognised, however, that there was a need to assuage their fears that the arms manufacturers would make fat profits during any war, as they had in 1914–18, and announced the Government's commitment to 'taking the profit out of war', through the imposition of an excess-profits tax in wartime. In May, Chamberlain also acceded to demands for a Ministry of Supply to be set up, authorising the necessary legislation.

Although Citrine, the TUC's General Secretary, was more conciliatory towards Chamberlain and was usually ready to give him reassuring advice, the labour movement remained deeply antagonistic. Chamberlain still represented the most narrow and unappealing brand of Conservatism. At Labour's annual Party conference in May, Bevin warned delegates:

> Behind Chamberlain are the bankers; they are the principal supporters of appeasement for Germany. They do not want justice for the German masses – that is a quite different thing. I am anxious to prevent this movement fighting for the preservation of the Paris Bourse, the London Stock Exchange, the Amsterdam Exchange and Wall Street.

The suspicions that the appeasers were still at work behind the scenes lingered on among Tory dissidents and within Whitehall. In April, in a speech in the Commons, Churchill made a veiled reference to Sir Horace Wilson's continuing influence when he wondered aloud 'whether there is not some hand which intervenes and filters down or withholds intelligence from Ministers' (Hansard, 13 April 1939, col. 34). Wilson had become notorious among anti-appeasers for his part in Munich. 'There goes the man who betrayed his country', a senior MP commented when he saw Wilson crossing the lobby of his London club.

In May, Oliver Harvey had noted that ' "Appeasement" is raising its ugly head again. I keep hearing indirect reports that Number 10 is at it again behind our backs.' Harvey's fears were prompted by a leader in *The Times* which argued that Danzig was not worth a war, and by a contribution from Lord Rushcliffe in the letters column suggesting 'a general negotiation' with Germany, 'covering all matters in dispute'. Chamberlain had stayed as Rushcliffe's guest on the shores of Loch Ness while fishing in Scotland. The letter was reckoned to be the handiwork of Sir Horace Wilson.

But the scope for the appeasers to revive their policy was seriously reduced during the summer. Polish resistance to German claims on Danzig convinced Hitler that there was no alternative to an invasion. But he first needed to isolate Poland, and realised that a deal with his ideological enemy, Stalin, would best suit his purpose.

Hitler, however, was not alone in looking to Moscow. In London and Paris, the creation of a Grand Alliance, long since advocated by Churchill, seemed to offer the only prospect of deterring further German aggression. Churchill reiterated his call for an alliance with the Soviet Union. By July 1939, the press campaign for his return to Government had reached a crescendo.

Eden hoped that it might still be possible to deter Hitler and avert a war, but this could only be done through a determined stand by Britain and France, in alliance with the Soviet Union. Eden even offered to go to Moscow himself and negotiate the agreement.

Chamberlain, however, was strongly opposed to any deal with the Russians. As Cadogan noted, 'In his present mood, P.M. will resign rather than sign alliance with Soviet. So have to go warily. I am, on balance, in favour of it. So, I think, is H. [Halifax].' Eventually, Chamberlain did sanction talks with the Russians, but the subsequent Anglo-French efforts to build closer links with the Soviet Union were half-hearted and lacked authority – a senior official from the Foreign Office, William Strang, visited Moscow, not a minister. The desultory talks dragged on through the summer, and were doomed to almost certain failure, unless the Russians felt they had absolutely no alternative. During what proved to be the final round of talks in Moscow, the then leader of the British mission, the improbably named Admiral Sir Reginald Aylmer Ranfurly Plunkett-Ernle-Erle-Drax, was told by Chamberlain in London that 'the House of Commons had pushed him further than he wished to go.' The message from Number 10 was unlikely to galvanise the mission.

The Germans, however, were in a position to promise Stalin more than the British and the French could ever hope to offer. The Russians were deeply concerned at the threat from Japan in the east, and were desperate to avoid any trouble on their western flank. An alliance with Britain and France carried a serious risk of involving them in an early conflict against Germany. Only an agreement with Hitler himself would avert the danger of a war in the west. A deal which provided extra territory on Russia's western borders would strengthen the Soviet Union's sense of security.

The summer had also brought fresh conversations between the British and German Governments. These had been initiated by Göring's right-

hand man, Helmut Wohltat, with a view to averting a war. As D.C. Watt
has pointed out, Wohltat later gave the impression that the British
Government had started the talks – presumably because Ribbentrop, by
then Hitler's Foreign Minister, was denying that there was any alternative
to war with Britain.

Wohltat's initiative was principally concerned with improving trade
relations between Britain and Germany, with a view to economic
appeasement. Halifax, Sir Horace Wilson and a junior minister at the
Department of Overseas Trade, Robert Hudson, were involved in the
talks at various stages. On 22 July, the details were leaked in the *News
Chronicle* in an article by Vernon Bartlett, and the contacts ended
immediately.

The revelation had far greater impact than the talks themselves were
ever likely to have had. The Soviets were convinced that Chamberlain's
Government were preparing for a new round of appeasing Hitler at
Poland's expense. Hitler concluded that the will to appease still flourished
within the British Cabinet. And suspicions about Chamberlain's true
intentions were renewed among Britain's allies – France, Poland and the
United States.

Those suspicions were shared in Westminster and Whitehall. The Tory
dissidents were already brooding about their position at the next general
election, which had to be held within little over a year. Eden and his group
were considering whether they could stand as Conservatives.

But they might not be given that choice. There were fears of a second
Munich, this time to grant Hitler territory in Poland, after which
Chamberlain would castigate the dissidents as warmongers and force them
out of the party at the election. In early August, the Prime Minister again
demonstrated his inability to unite the country. His proposal that
Parliament should adjourn until October provoked a storm of criticism.
Churchill argued that the Government were wrong to tell MPs

'Begone! Run off and play. Take your gas masks with you. Do not
worry about public affairs.' Leave them to the gifted and experienced Ministers, who, after all, so far as our defences are concerned,
landed us where we landed in September of last year, and who, after
all – I make allowances for the many difficulties – have brought us in
foreign policy at this moment to the point where we have guaranteed
Poland and Rumania, after having lost Czecho-slovakia and not
having gained Russia (Hansard, 2 August 1939, cols 2441–2).

The Prime Minister ignored Churchill's advice not to push through the
adjournment on party lines. Chamberlain retaliated against his critics by

making the vote one of confidence in the Government and in his leadership.

Chamberlain's vindictiveness provoked an outspoken attack on his leader from Ronald Cartland, who declared that it was much more important 'to get the whole country behind you than make jeering, pettifogging party speeches which divide the nation'. As he told the House, 'We are in a situation that within a month we may be going to fight, and we may be going to die' (ibid., col. 2495).

After Cartland's outburst, Chamberlain was apparently involved in an attempt to have the young MP dropped as the official Conservative candidate in his seat of Birmingham, King's Norton. Cartland was later killed in the retreat from Dunkirk.

On 23 August, the Nazi–Soviet Non-aggression Pact was signed, and Hitler was poised to attack Poland. Yet at the Foreign Office Oliver Harvey was 'terrified of another attempt at a Munich and selling out the Poles. Horace Wilson and R.A. Butler are working like beavers for this.'

In the event, Britain signed a formal treaty of alliance with Poland. Hitler postponed his planned invasion, and in Downing Street there were brief hopes that a settlement to the Polish question might be negotiated. But early in the morning of Friday, 1 September 1939, German troops invaded Poland.

In London, later that day, over dinner at the Savoy Grill, Churchill confided to Duff Cooper and his wife Lady Diana that Chamberlain had invited him to join the Government. After leaving the restaurant in the total darkness of a black-out, Lady Diana later recalled that she and Duff 'were nearly run down and kindly succoured by an outsize car in which sat the Duke of Westminster, the "Bendor" I had once loved.' It was an 'uncomfortable salvation'. The Duke began by 'abusing the Jewish race', adding his praise for the Germans and 'rejoicing that we were not yet at war'. As Lady Diana recounted,

> when he added that Hitler knew after all that we were his best friends, he set off the powder-magazine. 'I hope', Duff spat, 'that by tomorrow he will know that we are his most implacable and remorseless enemies.' Next day 'Bendor', telephoning to a friend, said that if there was a war it would be entirely due to the Jews and Duff Cooper.

The coming of war was to cause further division within the Mitford family. Lord Redesdale reverted to his original feelings about Germany, and joined the rest of the country in the war effort. But his wife Sydney, Lady Redesdale, had been so impressed by what she had seen in Germany that she stuck to her pro-Nazi views for the rest of her life. In the end the disagreement became so sharp that the Redesdales were forced to live apart.

The British Government postponed any immediate declaration of war. Chamberlain's motive appears to have been a desire to keep in step with the French, who were anxious to implement their evacuation and mobilisation before declaring war. Nonetheless, the delay revived suspicions that he was seeking another Munich.

When the Prime Minister addressed the Commons on the evening of Saturday, 2 September, he failed to mention any British ultimatum and spoke about the scope for a negotiated settlement if German troops would withdraw from Poland. His prevarication lost him support on all sides. Some of the younger Tory dissidents urged Eden to intervene, but Duff Cooper realised that even some Tory loyalists were perturbed, and he persuaded the Chamberlainite chairman of the Conservative backbench Foreign Affairs Committee, Sir John Wardlaw-Milne, to speak. Ironically, Channon had engineered Wardlaw-Milne's election to the post the previous May, in order to keep the Edenites quiet.

In Attlee's absence through ill-health, Labour's deputy leader, Arthur Greenwood, rose to speak for the opposition. 'Speak for England!' came the cry from the Tory benches, variously attributed to Leo Amery and Robert Boothby. The dissidents were by no means the only Conservatives who cheered Greenwood as he pressed Chamberlain to delay no longer and declare war on Hitler. The Labour Party had become the hawks: a Conservative Prime Minister and his closest acolytes had been the doves.

After the debate on Saturday night, as a violent thunderstorm raged over London, a number of ministers, including Oliver Stanley, Walter Elliot and Buck de la Warr, gathered together to discuss Chamberlain's performance. They resolved not to be cheated again, as they had been by Munich, and agreed that there should be a further meeting of the Cabinet.

Although Churchill had been told privately by Chamberlain that he would soon be invited to join the Government, he had not heard from the Prime Minister throughout the entire day. Churchill felt very badly treated. He had wanted to intervene in the Commons that evening, but had felt constrained by Chamberlain's approach. Churchill discussed what he should do into the early hours with colleagues, including Eden, Duff Cooper, Robert Boothby, Brendan Bracken and Duncan Sandys. As Duff Cooper noted in his diary,

Bob [Boothby] was convinced that Chamberlain had lost the Conservative Party forever and that it was in Winston's power to go to the House of Commons tomorrow and break him and take his place. He felt very strongly that in no circumstances should Winston consent to serve under him. Was it better to split the country at such a moment or bolster up Chamberlain? That seemed at one time the decision that Winston had to take.

The British ultimatum was sent to Berlin early the next morning, Sunday, 3 September. It lapsed at 11.00 a.m. Cazalet had come up to London to hear war declared. As he arrived in London, 'a false air raid was heralded. Very dramatic. People running to shelters.'

At 11.15 a.m., Chamberlain broadcast to the nation. He left no one in doubt about his own feelings that despite all his efforts he had been unable to stave off war any longer:

> You can imagine what a bitter blow it is to me that all my long struggle to win peace has failed. Yet I cannot believe that there is anything more, or anything different, that I could have done, and that would have been more successful. . . .

Cazalet wrote, 'No overstatement, no appeal to emotion or sentiment. Just a heartfelt cry against the stupidity of it all.'

When the Prime Minister spoke to the Commons, he made no attempt to disguise his feelings: 'everything that I have worked for, everything that I have hoped for, everything that I have believed in during my public life, has crashed into ruins . . .' (Hansard, 3 September 1939, col. 292). Churchill referred to the many efforts Britain had made for peace, adding that 'in our own hearts this Sunday morning there is peace. Our hands may be active, but our consciences are at rest' (ibid., col. 295).

A couple of hours later, Cazalet was leaving London with Nicolson, who described their eventful exodus to the Kent countryside:

> At 1.50 I motor down with Victor Cazalet to Sissinghurst. There are many army lorries passing along the road and a few pathetic trucks evacuating East End refugees. In one of those there is an elderly woman who shakes her fist at us and shouts that it is all the fault of the rich. The Labour Party will be hard put to it to prevent this war degenerating into class warfare. When I reach Sissinghurst I find that the flag has been pulled down.

It speaks volumes for Chamberlain's tenacity that despite the shattering impact of leading his country into war, he persisted as Prime Minister and was determined to see the war through.

But he hated war, and it soon began to take its toll. Within two days of its start, he was writing to the Archbishop of Canterbury,

> you will understand how hateful I find my personal position. I simply can't bear to think of those gallant fellows who lost their lives

last night in the R.A.F. attack, and of their families who have first been called upon to pay the price. Indeed, I must put such thoughts out of my mind if I am not to be unnerved altogether.

Chamberlain was able to draw some strength from the morality of Britain's position, which he felt his policies had helped create. As he wrote in the early days of the war, 'It was of course a grievous disappointment that peace could not be saved, but I know that my persistent efforts have convinced the world that no part of the blame can lie here. The consciousness of moral right, which it is impossible for the Germans to feel, must be a tremendous force on our side.'

Chamberlain accepted that war required that he should seek to build a more broadly based government. He therefore recalled Churchill and Eden to the Government on the day war was declared. Churchill had suggested Eden's appointment, pointing out to Chamberlain that in the absence of Labour politicians he would be a necessary reinforcement.

Churchill returned to the Admiralty, where he had served during the First World War, and was appointed to the War Cabinet. He again occupied the wood-panelled office, with its view across Horse Guards Parade to Number 10 and its maps showing the disposition of the fleet. A senior officer who was present at Churchill's return, later recalled,

As he once again took the First Lord's chair in the famous Board Room, Churchill was filled with emotion. To a few words of welcome from the First Sea Lord he replied by saying what a privilege and honour it was to be again in that chair, that there were many difficulties ahead but together we would overcome them.

Eden had been in two minds about returning to government, because it would not be the truly National Government he considered necessary in wartime. But Churchill had told him that his place was in the Government, with him. Eden was offered only the Dominions Office, without a seat in the War Cabinet. He accepted, but later wrote,

Two years before, I had been a principal figure in the Cabinet, now I was back again, not because my former colleagues wanted me to join them, but because the country had judged me to be right and them to be wrong in the controversy over my resignation. I was there on condition that I took no effective part in anything outside the work of my department.

Chamberlain offered posts to the Labour and Liberal leadership. But the opposition parties could not accept working in a Government in which Chamberlain and his close associates, Simon and Hoare, would continue to wield the real power. Such was the antagonism felt towards Chamberlain throughout the labour movement that had any Labour politicians accepted the offer they would have split their party.

War demanded a national effort, but Chamberlain's Government still had trouble coming to terms with their old adversaries in the unions. The Ministries of Supply and Food had been set up without trade union representation, at either national or local level. In early October, however, a TUC deputation to Number 10 finally succeeded in persuading Chamberlain to adopt a radical change within Whitehall. As a result, the new ministries introduced arrangements for union representation, and the Prime Minister issued a circular to all Government departments requiring their maximum co-operation with the TUC.

Yet for months following the declaration of war, the worldwide war which many had expected simply failed to materialise. After Germany's rapid conquest of Poland, Hitler's plans to attack on the western front were repeatedly thwarted by the weather. Lansbury and other pacifists on the left, and pro-Nazis and others on the far right, including Lord Brocket and the Duke of Buccleuch, all persisted in urging a negotiated peace.

Throughout the winter of 1939–40 Chamberlain continued to delude himself that the conflict would remain limited – even Hitler would shrink from inflicting the horrors of another world war on the German people. Leo Amery, who was chairing the group of Edenite Tories now that their leader had returned to Government, said of Chamberlain, 'Loathing war passionately he was determined to wage as little of it as possible.'

Chamberlain's utter abhorrence of war had not grown any weaker as the time passed. After six weeks, his comments were as anguished as they had been at the outset. On 14 October, a German submarine penetrated the defences at Scapa Flow and torpedoed the battleship *Royal Oak*. The Admiral and more than 800 officers and men were drowned. The disaster profoundly shocked Chamberlain: 'How I do hate and loathe this war. I was never meant to be a war Minister, and the thought of all those homes wrecked with the *Royal Oak* makes me want to hand over my responsibilities to someone else.'

In December 1939, the Commons went into secret session to discuss the war effort. Amery recalled that the Prime Minister,

> With unconscious naïveté explained that it was absurd to complain of inadequacy of supplies when we had only *begun to think* of having an army on the Continent, even of five divisions, as late as March [1939], of anything more *after we had guaranteed Poland,* of anything required to equip a substantial force *after we had accepted universal*

*service.* . . . In a quick-witted assembly like the French he would have been howled down, but the House found the explanation profoundly reasonable. [Amery's emphasis]

Chamberlain seemed to act on the assumption that the Conservatives would be able to continue running the country through a limited war, without major upheavals in the pre-war *status quo*. Major differences with the unions on the question of wages, as inflation increased, and the severe shortages of skilled labour were left unresolved for months.

Other members of Chamberlain's Government were under no illusion that the war would intensify, and what this would involve on the 'home front'. Greenwood's comment in the Commons in December 1939 to the effect that the war would shake many strongly held views led Eden to respond, 'I fear that this war will do very much more than that. The war will bring about changes which may be fundamental and revolutionary in the economic and social life of this country. On that we are all agreed.' (Hansard, 6 December 1939, col. 756.)

The 'phoney war' ended on 9 April 1940, when Hitler's troops invaded Norway. The invasion took Whitehall by surprise – Chamberlain had just declared that Hitler had 'missed the bus'. The British troops sent to Norway were left without adequate air or naval support. The fiasco of Britain's response, which, ironically, was in large part Churchill's responsibility, brought to a head the growing criticism of Chamberlain's handling of the war.

Some, at least, sympathised with the Prime Minister's position. King George VI, who had been as disappointed as Chamberlain at the failure of Munich, confided, 'I did not like the way in which, with all the worries and responsibilities he had to bear in the conduct of the war, he was always subject to a stab in the back from both the House of Commons and the Press.'

At Westminster, in addition to the two main opposition parties, there were three groups who were generating growing criticism of Chamberlain's conduct of the war. One was the group of young Tories who had been meeting since 1938 and who were chaired by Leo Amery now that Eden was back in Government. Another group was a cross-party gathering led by the Liberal Clement Davies and including the Tory Robert Boothby and the National Labour MP Harold Nicolson.

The third group was set up during the early months of 1940 around the nucleus of the Cecil family. This was the 'Watching Committee', formed by the Marquis of Salisbury and Lord Cranborne, and specifically set up 'to watch administration of the war and to harass Ministers where they ought to be harassed'. Other members included the former Lord

Chancellor Viscount Hailsham, the former pro-German the Marquis of Londonderry, the former appeaser Nancy Astor and the former Minister for Air whom Chamberlain had sacked, Viscount Swinton.

The Marquis of Salisbury had been a contemporary of Austen Chamberlain, whom he had come to respect, but he had never taken to Neville. Salisbury had approved of Eden's and Cranborne's resignations in February 1938, had taken offence at Chamberlain's dismissal of Ormsby-Gore (a member of the Cecil family through marriage) a few months later, and was unhappy about Munich. Like many other Cecils, Salisbury looked forward to an inevitable battle between the ideals of Christianity and the forces of evil.

The young Tory, Cecil and Davies groups met continuously during the last week of April and the first week of May. The climax to their criticisms came in the tense and bitter two-day debate on the Norway fiasco in the Commons on Tuesday 7 and Wednesday 8 May.

On Tuesday the 7th, Channon had noted, 'The "glamour boys" [the young Tories] are smacking their lips but their full strength is not yet known.' There was one person, however, who had a pretty shrewd idea. That morning, Alec Dunglass, the Prime Minister's Parliamentary Private Secretary, went to see Channon's boss, Rab Butler, in his room at the Foreign Office. Dunglass warned Rab that he thought things would go badly for Chamberlain, adding that there was a strong feeling in the country which was not reflected in the Whips' Office.

According to Dunglass, it was increasingly probable that the opposition would force a vote. Although Chamberlain was talking about staying on if the majority was above sixty, this depended on the extent to which the Labour leaders were encouraged to enter the Government. Dunglass urged Butler to talk to Halifax and persuade him to become Prime Minister.

During the two days of the Norway debate, there were many moments of drama and tension. But an incident before the start of the second day's debate symbolised the passing of one era and the start of another. The House paid its last respects to the former Labour leader, George Lansbury, who had died the previous day, yet many of the MPs remembering the old pacifist were wearing military uniforms, having returned from war service for the debate.

Memorable speeches attacking the Government's handling of the war were made by Duff Cooper and Sir Roger Keyes, in full uniform as Admiral of the Fleet. Lloyd George gave his famous advice to Churchill, who was to close the debate from the front bench, not to act as 'an air-raid shelter' for his colleagues. The most telling contribution came from Leo Amery, who turned on his Party leader and repeated Cromwell's declaration:

You have been here too long for any good you have been doing.
Depart, I say, and let us have done with you! In the name of God,
go! (Hansard, 7 May 1940, col. 1150)

At the end of the first day's debate, Attlee realised the extent of the
unease on the Conservative benches. The next day, the opposition
declared their intention to divide the House, prompting an ill-judged
comment from Chamberlain: 'I accept the challenge. I ask my friends, and
I still have some friends in this House, to support the Government tonight
in the lobby' (Hansard, 8 May 1940, col. 1266).

Lloyd George, in his last intervention in the Commons, retorted,

It is not a question of who are the Prime Minister's friends. It is a far
bigger issue. He has appealed for sacrifice. . . . I say solemnly that
the Prime Minister should give an example of sacrifice because there
is nothing which can contribute more to victory in the war than that
he should sacrifice the seals of office. (Ibid., col. 1283)

When the division was called, there were incredible scenes of anger and
emotion. Chips Channon and the other loyalists 'watched the insurgents
[rebels] file out of the Opposition Lobby (Teenie Cazalet could not make
up his mind and abstained). "Quislings," we shouted at them, "Rats."
"Yes-men," they replied. I saw all the expected ones, and many more –
Hubert [Duggan] among them and my heart snapped against him for ever.'

The result revealed that the Government's majority had been cut from
over 200 to 81. It was a shattering blow to Chamberlain.

In all, more than forty supporters of the Government (including more
than thirty Tories) had voted with the Opposition, among them Quintin
Hogg, the Chamberlainite candidate at the Oxford City by-election,
and Nancy Astor, the former appeaser. Among the rebels were Leo
Amery, two former Secretaries for War, Duff Cooper and Leslie Hore-
Belisha (sacked by Chamberlain only four months earlier), and also Robert
Boothby, Harold Macmillan, Harold Nicolson and Ronald Tree.

A further sixty Government backbenchers abstained. Many of them
ostentatiously remained in their seats in the Chamber – as *The Times*
commented, 'among whom young service members in uniform were
conspicuous'.

One of Chamberlain's most loyal acolytes, Rab Butler, wrote of his
feelings immediately after the division:

The final scene in the House was very distasteful. It reminded me of
certain scenes in the history of Peel. The singing of 'Rule Britannia'
by Harold Macmillan was much resented by Neville who rose

looking old and white-haired, as he has become, and marched out realising, as he did, that he could not go on.

As Channon recalled, 'Neville appeared bowled over by the figures, and was the first to rise. He looked grave and thoughtful and sad: as he walked calmly to the door, his supporters rose and cheered him lustily and he disappeared. No crowds to cheer him, as there were before and after Munich – only a solitary little man, who had done his best for England.' Ronald Tree, who had voted against the Government, later recalled the 'tremendous' bitterness displayed by Chamberlain's supporters after the vote. Several approached him in the lobby afterwards, making hostile remarks. One of the loyalists told him, 'You've got what you've been working for – I only hope you will regret it for the rest of your life.'

Not only Chamberlain's political allies were upset at his treatment. King George VI felt that it was 'most unfair on Chamberlain to be treated like this after all his good work. The Conservative rebels like Duff Cooper ought to be ashamed of themselves for deserting him at this moment.'

Over the next day or two, Chamberlain tried various manoeuvres to retain the premiership. He let it be known that he was prepared to sacrifice Hoare and Simon, and he tried to persuade the Labour Party to enter a coalition.

On the afternoon of Thursday, 9 May, Chamberlain saw Halifax and Churchill at Number 10 and told them that Labour must enter the Government. The Labour leaders, Attlee and Greenwood, then joined the meeting. As Attlee later recalled, 'It is not pleasant to have to tell a Prime Minister to his face that he must go, but I thought it the only thing to do.' The Leader of the Opposition told Chamberlain: 'Mr Prime Minister, the fact is our Party won't come in under you. Our Party won't have you and I think I am right in saying that the country won't have you either.'

Attlee and Greenwood then departed to consult their Party, in conference at Bournemouth, saying that they would ask two questions: '1) Are you prepared to serve under Chamberlain? 2) Are you prepared to serve under someone else?'

After they had left, Churchill kept quiet. Halifax immediately ruled himself out as Chamberlain's successor on the grounds that the country could not be led from the House of Lords in wartime. As Halifax later told Cadogan, 'I thought Winston was a better choice. Winston did *not* demur. Was very kind and polite but showed that he thought this was the right solution.'

On Friday, 10 May 1940, Britain awoke to the news of the German invasion of the Low Countries. As Channon commented, Hitler had 'seized on the psychological moment when England is politically divided, and the ruling caste riddled with dissension and anger'.

The War Cabinet met before eight o'clock that morning. It seemed that Chamberlain thought the crisis would make it impossible for him to leave Number 10. But he had lost too much support. Attlee had been contacted at Bournemouth, and over the telephone gave the replies to the two questions he had put to his Labour colleagues: 'The answer to the first question is, no. To the second, yes.'

Later in the day, Chamberlain informed the War Cabinet that the Labour Party had refused to serve under him. Labour had seized their opportunity, forced a change in Government and established themselves as equal partners in the new coalition.

When Chamberlain tendered his resignation, the King 'told him how grossly unfairly I thought he had been treated, and I was terribly sorry that all this controversy had happened.' George VI suggested Halifax as Chamberlain's successor, but Chamberlain told him that Halifax was not enthusiastic. The King confessed that he 'was disappointed over this statement, as I thought Halifax was the obvious man'.

At six o'clock that evening, Winston Churchill kissed hands at Buckingham Palace on his appointment as Prime Minister. He drove back from the Palace, accompanied only by his detective, W.H. Thompson. Neither of them said a word. When they arrived at the Admiralty, Churchill asked Thompson if he had realised why he had gone to the Palace. Thompson congratulated him, and wished him well in his enormous task. As Churchill replied, tears came into his eyes: 'God alone knows how great it is. I hope that it is not too late. I am very much afraid that it is. We can only do our best.' As Churchill turned away, he muttered something to himself, 'Then he set his jaw and with a look of determination, mastering all emotion, he began to climb the stairs of the Admiralty.'

Shortly afterwards, across Horse Guards Parade, in Rab Butler's room at the Foreign Office, Chips Channon opened a bottle of champagne. As Channon noted, together with Butler, Alec Dunglass and Jock Colville, 'we four loyal adherents of Mr Chamberlain drank "To the King [Chamberlain] over the water".'

Chamberlain confided his thoughts a week later:

All my world has tumbled to bits in a moment. The national peril has so swamped all personal feelings that no bitterness remains. Indeed, I used to say to Annie [his wife] before the war came, that if such a thing happened, I thought I should have to hand over to someone else, for I knew what agony of mind it would mean for me to give directions that would bring death and mutilation and misery to so many. But the war was so different from what I expected that I found the strain bearable, and perhaps it was providential that the revolution which overturned me coincided with the entry of the real thing.

Chamberlain was numbed: 'I frankly envy Austen's peace.'

It was a far cry from the hero's welcome which Chamberlain had received a little over eighteen months earlier. Michael Powell and Emeric Pressburger symbolised the about-turn in Chamberlain's political fortunes with the scene in *Contraband*, filmed in 1940, showing a store-room full of surplus busts of Chamberlain.

It is impossible not to feel that, whatever the errors of judgement he made, Chamberlain was unlucky to become Prime Minister at such a desperately difficult time. He was also unlucky in one other respect. For some time, British intelligence had been trying, unsuccessfully, to crack the code used for Germany's secret messages, the so-called 'Enigma'. The vital breakthrough, which would eventually change the course of the war, came just twelve days after Chamberlain left Downing Street.

By the time Chamberlain departed Number 10, the prospect seemed to be getting more daunting by the hour. The army's ill-equipped expeditionary force was suddenly vulnerable to the unexpected speed of the German advance through the Low Countries.

Churchill immediately set about forming his Administration. He recognised that his predecessor continued to enjoy considerable support within the Conservative Party. He was careful to retain Chamberlain in the War Cabinet and appoint him Lord President of the Council. He also thought it important that Chamberlain should continue as leader of the Party. This would demonstrate that his Government was truly a coalition, in which no party leader was pre-eminent. Yet even had Churchill thought differently, there was not much he could do about the Party leadership – only chronic ill-health eventually persuaded Chamberlain to relinquish the position some months later.

Halifax was also allowed to continue at the Foreign Office, and when he requested that Rab Butler should remain there with him Churchill agreed. Some appeasers, at least, fared far better than they had dared hope.

Churchill himself became Minister of Defence, and Eden was appointed Secretary of War. They had discussed these appointments when it became clear that Chamberlain would not continue as Prime Minister. Eden noted his mixed reactions to Churchill's offer:

I told him I would obey orders and serve or not and where he thought I could best help. Position will be very difficult one for state of army is inglorious, and it will not be easy to maintain harmony with W. [Churchill].

The Labour leader, Attlee, became Lord Privy Seal, Greenwood was appointed Minister without Portfolio, and another Labour frontbencher, A.V. Alexander, became First Lord of the Admiralty. The Liberal leader, Sinclair, was appointed Secretary of State for Air.

Attlee persuaded Bevin to become Minister of Labour. As the union leader later recalled, 'I said, "You have sprung it on me." He said "It is sprung on all of us, but we want someone from the industrial movement, from outside Parliament, to come in, not merely to run a Department but to help the State in this critical hour." ' Bevin agreed to take on the job, but only on condition that the Ministry would not remain 'a glorified conciliation board', but would have real powers.

Not until the early hours of 11 May did Churchill finally complete the key dispositions in his Government. As he later wrote,

> I was conscious of a profound sense of relief. At last I had the authority to give directions over the whole scene. I felt as if I were walking with destiny, and that all my past life had been but a preparation for this hour and for this trial.

But there were many doubters. The next day, King George VI wrote, 'I cannot yet think of Winston as P.M. . . . I met Halifax in the garden and I told him I was sorry not to have him as P.M.'

In Whitehall, Cadogan noted, 'I'm not at *all* sure of W.S.C.,' and at Number 10 John Colville was in despair at the prospect of Churchill as Prime Minister.

On the Monday following the change of Government (Whit Monday), Rab Butler and his wife dined at the Berkeley Hotel where they met the secretary of the Tory backbench 1922 Committee, Maurice Hely-Hutchinson. He told Rab, 'You must not underestimate the great reaction which has been caused among Conservative Members [at the news of Hitler's invasion of the Low Countries], among whom you will find over three-quarters are ready to put Chamberlain back.'

When Butler returned to the Foreign Office after the Whitsun break, he found Halifax full of foreboding at Churchill's accession to the highest office:

> I went into Halifax's room early on reaching the Office. He suddenly said 'It's all a great tragedy, isn't it?' I replied 'That is because you did not take the Premiership yourself.' He said 'You know my reasons, it's no use discussing that – but the gangsters will shortly be in complete control.

By the 'gangsters', Halifax had in mind Bracken and Lindemann, rather than Churchill himself.

Chamberlain's first appearance in the Commons after he had lost the premiership prompted the most extraordinary reception. Channon gave a graphic account: 'MPs lost their heads; they shouted; they cheered; they waved their Order Papers, and his reception was a regular ovation.'

By contrast, when Churchill first entered the Chamber as Prime Minister, his own benches greeted him in silence. For some months, the only spontaneous cheers for Churchill came from the Labour and Liberal benches.

Even as Britain's darkest hour approached, she retained her class divided.

# SELECT BIBLIOGRAPHY

Anthony Adamthwaite, 'The British Government and the Media', in *Journal of Contemporary History*, 1983; and 'War Origins Again', in *Journal of Modern History*, 1984.

Paul Addison, *The Road to 1945*, Jonathan Cape, 1975.

Leo Amery, *My Political Life*, Hutchinson, 1955.

Christopher Andrew, *Secret Service*, Heinemann, 1985.

C.R. Attlee, *As It Happened*, Heinemann, 1954; *A Prime Minister Remembers*, ed. Francis Williams, Heinemann, 1964.

Corelli Barnett, *The Audit of War*, Macmillan, 1986, and *The Collapse of British Power*, Alan Sutton, 1984.

Vernon Bartlett, *And Now Tomorrow*, Chatto & Windus, 1960.

Peter Beck, 'England v. Germany 1938: Football as Propaganda', in *History Today*, 1982.

P.M.H. Bell, *The Origins of the Second World War*, Longman, 1986.

Earl of Birkenhead, *Halifax: the Life of Lord Halifax*, Hamish Hamilton, 1965.

Robert Blake, *The Conservative Party from Peel to Thatcher*, Fontana, 1985.

Brian Bond, *British Military Strategy Between the Wars*, Clarendon Press, Oxford, 1980.

Robert Boothby, *Recollections of a Rebel*, Hutchinson, 1978.

C.M. Bowra, *Memories*, Weidenfeld & Nicolson, 1966.

Alan Bullock, *The Life and Times of Ernest Bevin*, Heinemann, 1960.

Trevor Burridge, *Clement Attlee*, Jonathan Cape, 1985.

J.R.M. Butler, *Lord Lothian (Philip Kerr) 1882–1940*, Macmillan, 1960.

R.A. Butler, *The Art of the Possible: the Memoirs of the Lord Butler*, Hamish Hamilton, 1982, and (ed.) *The Conservatives*, George Allen & Unwin, 1977.

Sir Alexander Cadogan, *The Diaries of Sir Alexander Cadogan, 1938–1945*, ed. David Dilks, Cassell, 1971.

Angus Calder, *The People's War*, Jonathan Cape, 1969.

John Campbell, *Nye Bevan and the Mirage of British Socialism*, Weidenfeld & Nicolson, 1987.

David Carlton, *Anthony Eden*, Allen Lane, 1981.

Barbara Cartland, *Ronald Cartland*, Hutchinson, 1945.

Martin Ceadel, 'Interpreting East Fulham', in Cook and Ramsden, 1973; *Pacifism in Britain, 1914–1945: The Defining of a Faith*, Clarendon Press, Oxford, 1980.

Sir Henry Channon, *Chips: The Diaries of Sir Henry Channon*, ed. Robert Rhodes James, Weidenfeld & Nicolson, 1967.

John Charmley, *Duff Cooper*, Weidenfeld & Nicolson, 1986.

Winston S. Churchill, *The Second World War*, Vol. I, *The Gathering Storm*, Penguin, 1985.

Kenneth Clark, *Another Part of the Wood*, John Murray, 1974.

Anthony Clayton, *The British Empire as Superpower, 1919–39*, Macmillan, 1986.

John Colville, *Footprints in Time*, Collins, 1976.

Ian Colvin, *The Chamberlain Cabinet*, Gollancz, 1971.

Chris Cook and John Ramsden (eds), *By-elections in British Politics*, St Martin's Press, 1973.

Diana Cooper, *The Light of the Common Day*, Hart-Davis, 1959.

Duff Cooper, *Old Men Forget*, Hart-Davis, 1953.

Colin Coote, *Editorial*, Eyre & Spottiswoode, 1965.

Maurice Cowling, *The Impact of Hitler: British Politics and British Policy 1933–40*, Cambridge University Press, 1975.

Mary Craig, *Longford*, Hodder & Stoughton, 1978.

Bernard Crick, *George Orwell: A Life*, Secker & Warburg, 1980.

Valentine Cunningham, *The Penguin Book of Spanish Civil War Verse*, Penguin, 1980.

Hugh Dalton, *Memoirs 1931–1945: The Fateful Years*, Muller, 1957.

David Dilks, *Retreat from Power: Studies in Britain's Foreign Policy of the Twentieth Century*, Vol. I: *1906–39*; Vol. II: *After 1939*, Macmillan, 1981.

Bernard Donoughue and G.W. Jones, *Herbert Morrison*, Weidenfeld & Nicolson, 1973.

Roy Douglas, *In The Year of Munich*, Macmillan, 1977; *The History of the Liberal Party, 1895–1970*, Sidgwick & Jackson, 1971.

David Duff, *Queen Mary*, Collins, 1985.

Blanche Dugdale, *Baffy: The Diaries of Blanche Dugdale, 1936–1947*, ed. Norman Rose, Vallentine, Mitchell, 1973.

Roger Eatwell, 'Munich, Public Opinion, and Popular Front', in *Journal of Contemporary History*, 1971.

Anthony Eden, *Facing the Dictators*, Cassell, 1962; *The Reckoning*, Cassell, 1965.

Keith Feiling, *The Life and Times of Neville Chamberlain*, Macmillan, 1946.

Larry William Fuchser, *Neville Chamberlain and Appeasement*, W.W. Norton & Co., 1982.

Franklin Reid Gannon, *The British Press and Germany 1936–1939*, Oxford, 1971.

Martin Gilbert, *Winston S. Churchill*, Vols V and VI, Heinemann, 1976 and 1983; *Winston Churchill: The Wilderness Years*, Macmillan, 1980; 'Horace Wilson: Man of Munich', in *History Today*, 1982.

A.L. Goldman, 'Two Views of Germany: Nevile Henderson vs. Vansittart and the Foreign Office, 1937–39', in *British Journal of International Studies*, 1980.

A.M. Gollin, *Proconsul in Politics: a Study of Lord Milner in Opposition and in Power*, Anthony Blond, 1964.

Sheila Duff Grant, *The Parting of the Ways*, Peter Owen, 1982.

Richard Griffiths, *Fellow Travellers of the Right: British Enthusiasts for Nazi Germany, 1933–39*, Constable, 1980.

John Grigg, *Nancy Astor: Portrait of a Pioneer*, Sidgwick & Jackson, 1980.

Jo Grimond, *Memoirs*, Heinemann, 1979.

Kenneth Harris, *Attlee*, Weidenfeld & Nicolson, 1982.

Brian Harrison, 'Women in a Men's House: the Women MPs, 1919–45', in *Historical Journal*, 1986.

Oliver Harvey, *The Diplomatic Diaries of Oliver Harvey, 1937–40*, ed. John Harvey, Collins, 1970.

Lord Home, *The Way the Wind Blows*, Collins, 1976.

Anthony Howard, *Rab: The Life of R.A. Butler*, Jonathan Cape, 1987.

Samuel Hynes, *The Auden Generation: Literature and Politics in England in the 1930s*, The Bodley Head, 1976.

Robert Rhodes James, *Victor Cazalet: A Portrait*, Hamish Hamilton, 1976; *Anthony Eden*, Weidenfeld & Nicolson, 1986; *The British Revolution: British Politics, 1880–1939*, Hamish Hamilton, 1977; *Churchill: a Study in Failure*, Weidenfeld & Nicolson, 1970.

Storm Jameson, *Journey from the North: Autobiography of Storm Jameson*, Vol. I, Collins and Harvill Press, 1969.

Douglas Jay, *Change and Fortune*, Hutchinson, 1980.

Roy Jenkins, *Baldwin*, Collins, 1987.

Jack Jones, *Union Man*, Collins, 1986.

Thomas Jones, *A Diary with Letters*, Oxford University Press, 1954.

Denis Judd, *King George VI*, Michael Joseph, 1982.

James Jupp, *The Radical Left in Britain, 1931–1941*, Frank Cass, 1982.

David E. Kaiser, *Economic Diplomacy and the Origins of the Second World War*, Princeton University, 1980.

Paul Kennedy, *The Realities Behind Diplomacy*, Fontana, 1981; *Strategy and Diplomacy*, Fontana, 1984.

Ivone Kirkpatrick, *The Inner Circle*, Macmillan, 1959.

Richard Lamb, *The Ghosts of Peace, 1935–1945*, Michael Russell, 1987.

James Lees-Milne, *Ancestral Voices*, Chatto & Windus, 1975; *Harold Nicolson*, Chatto & Windus, 1981.

Roy Lewis, *Enoch Powell: Principle in Politics*, Cassell, 1979.

Elizabeth Longford, *The Pebbled Shore*, Weidenfeld & Nicolson, 1986.

Iain Maclean, 'Oxford and Bridgwater', in Cook and Ramsden, 1973.

Harold Macmillan, *Winds of Change, 1914–39*, Macmillan, 1966; *The Blast of War, 1939–45*, Macmillan, 1967.

John Marlowe, *Milner, Apostle of Empire*, Hamish Hamilton, 1976.

Gordon Martel (ed.), *The Origins of the Second World War Reconsidered*, George Allen & Unwin, 1986.

Christopher Mayhew, *Time to Explain: an Autobiography*, Hutchinson, 1987.

Keith Middlemas, *Diplomacy of Illusion: the British Government and Germany, 1937–38*, Weidenfeld & Nicolson, 1972; with John Barnes, *Baldwin: a Biography*, Weidenfeld & Nicolson, 1969.

Wolfgang J. Mommsen and Lothar Kettenacker (eds), *The Fascist Challenge and the Policy of Appeasement*, George Allen & Unwin, 1983.

Ted Morgan, *FDR*, Grafton Books, 1985.

Sophia Murphy, *The Mitford Family Album*, Sidgwick & Jackson, 1985.

John F. Naylor, *Labour's International Policy: The Labour Party in the 1930s*, Weidenfeld & Nicolson, 1969.

Beverley Nichols, *The Unforgiving Minute*, W.H. Allen, 1978.

Harold Nicolson, *Harold Nicolson: Diaries and Letters, 1930–39*, ed. Nigel Nicolson, Collins, 1966.

R.J. Overy, 'German Air Strength 1933 to 1939: A Note', in *The Historical Journal*, 1984.

Frank Pakenham, *Born to Believe*, Jonathan Cape, 1953.

R.A.C. Parker, 'Great Britain, France and the Ethiopian Crisis, 1935–1937', in *English Historical Review*, 1974, and 'British Re-armament 1936–9: Treasury, Trade Unions and Skilled Labour', in *English Historical Review*, 1981.

G.C. Peden, *British Re-armament and the Treasury: 1932–1939*, Scottish Academic Press, 1979.

Henry Pelling, *A Short History of the Labour Party*, Macmillan, 1968.

Ben Pimlott, *Labour and the Left in the 1930s*, Cambridge University Press, 1977; *Hugh Dalton*, Jonathan Cape, 1985.

Nicholas Pronay and Philip M. Taylor, ' "An Improper Use of Broadcasting . . .", The British Government and Clandestine Radio Propaganda Operations against Germany during the Munich Crisis and After', in *Journal of Contemporary History*, 1984.

John Ramsden, *The Age of Balfour and Baldwin, 1902–1940*, Longman, 1978; *The Making of Conservative Policy: The Conservative Research Department since 1929*, Longman, 1980.

Lord Reith, *The Reith Diaries*, ed. Charles Stuart, Collins, 1975.

Brian Roberts, *Randolph*, Hamish Hamilton, 1984.

Keith Robbins, *Munich, 1938*, Cassell, 1968.

William R. Rock, *Appeasement on Trial*, Archon Books, 1966; and *British Appeasement in the 1930s*, Edward Arnold, 1977.

Norman Rose, *Vansittart: Study of a Diplomat*, Heinemann, 1978.

A.L. Rowse, *All Souls and Appeasement*, Macmillan, 1961.

Conrad Russell, *The Letters of Conrad Russell*, John Murray, 1987.

Gustav Schmidt, *The Politics and Economics of Appeasement: British Foreign Policy in the 1930s*, Berg, 1986.

Robert Paul Shay, Jnr, *British Re-armament in the Thirties*, Princeton University Press, 1977.

Robin Skelton (ed.), *Poetry of the Thirties*, Penguin, 1964.

Philip Snow, *Stranger and Brother: A Portrait of C.P. Snow*, Macmillan, 1982.

Paul Stafford, 'The Chamberlain–Halifax Visit to Rome: A Reappraisal', in *English Historical Review*, 1983; 'Political Autobiography and the Art of the Plausible: R.A. Butler at the Foreign Office, 1938–1939', in *The Historical Journal*, 1985.

A.J.P. Taylor, *Beaverbrook*, Hamish Hamilton, 1972; *A Personal History*, Hamish Hamilton, 1983.

Telford Taylor, *Munich: the Price of Peace*, Hodder & Stoughton, 1979.

Viscount Templewood (Sir Samuel Hoare), *Nine Troubled Years*, Collins, 1954.

Neville Thompson, *The Anti-Appeasers: Conservative Opposition to Appeasement in the 1930s*, Oxford University Press, 1971.

*The History of 'The Times'*, Part II: *1921–1948*, The Times, 1952.

Ronald Tree, *When the Moon Was High*, Macmillan, 1975.

Wesley K. Wark, 'British Intelligence on the German Air Force and Aircraft Industry, 1933–1939', in *The Historical Journal*, 1982.

K.W. Watkins, *Britain Divided: the Effect of the Spanish Civil War on British Political Opinion*, Thomas Nelson, 1963.

D.C. Watt, 'Misinformation, Misconception, Mistrust: Episodes in British Policy and the Approach of War, 1938–1939', in *High and Low Politics in Modern Britain*, eds Michael Bentley and John Stevenson, Oxford University Press, 1983.

Evelyn Waugh, *Vile Bodies*, Eyre, Methuen, 1930; *Waugh in Abyssinia*, Longmans, Green, 1936.

W.J. West, *Truth Betrayed*, Duckworth, 1987.

John W. Wheeler-Bennett, *King George VI*, Macmillan, 1958.

Edward Whitley, *The Graduates*, Hamish Hamilton, 1986.

Francis Williams, *Nothing So Strange: an Autobiography*, Cassell, 1970.

Philip Williams, *Hugh Gaitskell*, Jonathan Cape, 1979.

Ted Willis, *Whatever Happened to Tom Mix?*, Cassell, 1970.

Leonard Woolf, *Downhill All the Way*, The Hogarth Press, 1967.

Virginia Woolf, *The Diary of Virginia Woolf*, Vols 4 and 5, ed. Anne Oliver Bell, Hogarth Press, 1982 and 1984; *The Letters of Virginia Woolf*, Vols 5 and 6, ed. Nigel Nicolson, Hogarth Press, 1979 and 1980.

Lord Woolton, *Memoirs of the Rt. Hon. the Earl of Woolton*, Cassell, 1959.

J.E. Wrench, *Geoffrey Dawson and Our Times*, Hutchinson, 1955.

Lord Zuckerman, *From Apes to Warlords*, Hamish Hamilton, 1978.

# INDEX

Abyssinia, 5, 38, 42, 43,
    44–57, 76, 102, 125, 126–7,
    156, 187
Acland, Richard, 98, 262
Adams, Vyvyan, 31, 75, 86,
    134, 135, 185, 192, 247
Adamthwaite, Anthony, 111,
    193, 250
Admiralty, 157–8, 196–7, 288
AEU, 159, 160
Africa, 114, 117
Aid for Spain, 86, 88, 91
Air Ministry, 10, 112–13, 161
Air Raid Precautions (ARP),
    6–10, 248
Aitken, Max, 80
Albania, 280
Aldington, Richard, 17
Alexander, A.V., 296
All Souls College, Oxford,
    23–6, 252
Allberry, Charles, 228
Allen, Lord, 31, 96–7
Amery, Julian, 263
Amery, Leo, 17, 129, 134, 239,
    275, 286; Abyssinian crisis,
    46, 56, 75; imperialism, 73;
    and the Austrian Anschluss,
    142–3; and the Czech crisis,
    200, 204, 205, 208, 217, 218;
    critical of Chamberlain, 211,
    289–90; and the Munich
    Agreement, 225, 247; calls
    for National Government,
    279; Norway debate, 291–2

Anderson, Sir Alan, 134
Angell, Sir Norman, 97, 220
Anglo-French
    Non-Intervention
    Agreement (1936), 86
Anglo-German Fellowship, 18
Anglo-German Naval
    Agreement (1935), 38, 117,
    280
Anti-Comintern Pact (1936),
    149
Anti-Nazi Council, 74, 97
Anti-Socialist and
    Anti-Communist Union, 16
Asch, 195, 197
Ashton-Gwatkin, Frank,
    165–6, 171
Asquith, Katharine, 228, 231
Astor, John, 25
Astor, Nancy, 23–4, 25, 58,
    59, 130–1, 136, 164, 182,
    207, 241, 281, 291, 292
Astor, Viscount, 25, 58, 118,
    176, 207
Astor, William, 64–5, 207
Asua, Señor de, 94
Atholl, Duke of, 270
Atholl, Katharine, Duchess of,
    86–7, 98, 269–70
Attlee, Clement, 63; and the
    rearmament debate, 39, 41,
    97, 101, 102; and the
    Abyssinian crisis, 45, 54;
    leadership of PLP, 50, 60;
    on the League of Nations,

64, 68; and the Spanish Civil
War, 94–5; on Chamberlain,
108; and Halifax's meeting
with Hitler, 119; and the
Popular Front initiatives,
155; Czech crisis, 191–2,
197, 207, 209; and the
Munich talks, 220; Munich
Agreement debate, 234,
236–7, 239, 246; new
National Government
proposed, 248; Oxford by-
election, 255; Norway
debate, 292; invited to join
Government, 293, 294, 296
Auden, W.H., 17, 89
Austin, John, 263
Austria, 37, 38, 39, 48, 117,
127, 137–43, 146, 152, 278
Auxiliary Air Force, 10

Bad Godesberg talks, 194–5,
196, 198, 201–3, 204, 207,
213, 221, 225, 232, 234, 242,
272
Baldwin, Stanley, 25, 81, 107,
108; on the 'terror of the air',
15, 27; East Fulham
by-election, 30; rearmament
debate, 36, 37, 40, 69, 79,
82–4, 113–14; becomes
Prime Minister, 38; and the
Abyssinian crisis, 45, 51–3,
54, 102; 1935 election, 50,
69; and the occupation of the
Rhineland, 58, 59, 61–2; and
the Spanish Civil War, 87;
and the Abdication crisis,
98, 105; retirement, 106;
foreign policies, 109; Czech
crisis, 154, 207; Munich
Agreement debate, 241

Balfour, A.J., 184
Balfour, Captain Harold, 161
Balkans, 280
Ball, J.R., 111, 112, 126, 130,
135–6
Balliol College, Oxford, 131,
256, 258
Balogh, Tommy, 181
Baltic, 279
Barrington-Ward, Robert, 191
Bartlett, Vernon, 29, 31, 97,
171, 191, 215, 219, 267–9,
274, 284
Baxter, Beverley, 152, 226
BBC, 2, 29, 30, 58, 112, 130,
136–7, 141, 171, 190, 211,
212, 215, 250, 268, 269
Beaverbrook, Lord, 72, 73,
79–80, 152, 175
Beck, Colonel, 279
Belgium, 276
Bell, Julian, 89, 101
Bell, Vanessa, 6, 89
Beloff, Max, 14
Beneš, Eduard, 145, 164, 165,
171, 187–8, 208, 209, 212,
223, 230
Berlin, Sir Isaiah, 24, 223, 252
Bernays, Rob, 244
Berry, Seymour, 219
Bevan, Aneurin, 93, 99, 103–4
Beveridge, Sir William, 262
Bevin, Ernest, 19, 39, 40, 41,
44, 48–50, 92, 93, 95, 96,
100–1, 102–4, 282, 296
Blackshirts *see* British Union of
Fascists
Blake, Lord, 7, 229
Blickling Hall, Norfolk, 25,
58–9, 140
Blum, Léon, 85, 92, 93, 223
Boer War, 117

*Boersen Zeitung*, 267

Bohemia, 144, 168, 182, 242, 278

Bond, Brian, 35

Bonham Carter, Lady Violet, 52, 218, 219, 220, 229, 237, 243, 244, 249, 262, 275

Bonnet, Georges, 164, 177, 179, 187–8

Boothby, Robert, 24, 65, 66–7, 73, 98, 134, 142, 205, 220, 221, 229, 239, 247, 286–7, 290, 292

Bourne, Mrs, 265

Bourne, Captain R.C., 252

Bowra, Maurice, 14, 24, 229

Bracken, Brendan, 73, 135, 197, 220, 239, 243, 247, 286, 297

Brand, Bob, 25

Bridgwater by-election (1938), 267–9, 271, 274

British Army, 113, 157, 187, 243, 295

British Council, 211–12

British Expeditionary Force, 35–6

British Institute of Public Opinion, 130

British Legion, 34–5

British Union of Fascists (Blackshirts), 16, 18, 30–1, 40, 48, 90, 92–3, 254

Brittain, Vera, 17

Brocket, Lord, 31–2, 174, 289

*The Brown Book of the Hitler Terror*, 28

'Brown Shirts', 33

Buccleuch, Duke of, 289

Buchan, John, 25, 140

Burgess, Guy, 190, 230

Burgin, Leslie, 202

Butler, R.A. (Rab), 136, 150, 153, 172, 185, 244, 272, 280, 285, 291, 292–3, 294, 295, 296

Byron, Robert, 81

Cable Street riot (1936), 92–3

Cadogan, Sir Alec, 111, 151–2, 170, 175, 202, 277, 296; assesses German threat, 123; and the Roosevelt initiative, 125; and the Austrian Anschluss, 139–40; Czech crisis, 144, 145–6, 147, 208, 209, 210; and Plan Z, 173; on the Godesberg memorandum, 198; critical of Chamberlain, 199; lectures Halifax, 200, 201; Duff Cooper's resignation, 227; and the fall of Prague, 279; Polish guarantee, 279; on proposed Soviet alliance, 283

Cadogan, Christopher, 229–30

Cadogan, Commander, 229–30

Cambridge Union, 16–17

Cambridge University, 89

Camrose, Lord, 118, 152, 175, 219

Carlton Club, 260

Cartland, Barbara, 72, 134–5, 154, 223, 228

Cartland, Ronald, 72, 98, 134–5, 150, 154, 164, 223, 228, 247, 285

Cazalet, Victor, 46, 51, 52, 53, 56, 59, 63, 80, 87, 127, 129, 139, 159, 225, 274, 277, 280, 287, 292

Ceadel, Martin, 18

Cecil, Lady Beatrice, 162

Cecil, Robert, Viscount, 20,
45, 178, 192, 197, 202–3,
205, 220, 223, 240, 248–9
Cecil family, 290
Chamberlain, Anne, 3, 4, 107,
294
Chamberlain, Sir Austen, 45,
53, 54–5, 56, 57, 63, 65–6,
68, 73–4, 78–9, 98, 106, 126,
291
Chamberlain, Hilda, 106–7
Chamberlain, Lady Ida,
106–7, 126, 148–9
Chamberlain, Joseph, 25, 106,
117
Chamberlain, Neville:
rearmament debate, 21, 76,
81; Ottawa Trade
Agreement, 21; East Fulham
by-election, 30; and Lord
Brocket, 32; doctrine of
'limited liability', 35–6; and
the Abyssinian crisis, 45, 46,
52; and the occupation of the
Rhineland, 62, 63–4; 1935
election, 69; lifts sanctions
against Italy, 74–5;
reluctance to intervene in
economy, 76–8; and the
Spanish Civil War, 94;
background and character,
106–12; becomes Prime
Minister, 106–7; poor
relations with Eden, 109–10,
116, 127–9; management of
the media, 111–12, 118–19,
130, 137; defence spending,
112, 114, 115, 157–8;
diplomatic initiative towards
Germany, 114–21; attitude
towards League of Nations,
121–2, 133–4; and

Roosevelt's peace initiative,
124–7; and Eden's
resignation, 133–4; Austrian
crisis, 138–9, 141; Czech
crisis, 143, 145, 147–52,
163–4, 167–71, 173–88,
189–203; appeases
Mussolini, 156–7; industrial
policy, 159–60; Cabinet
reshuffle, 161–2; Runciman
mission, 164–6; Plan Z
(meetings with Hitler), 169,
170, 173, 174, 179–84,
194–5, 198–202; warnings to
Hitler, 173–5, 176, 207,
208–9, 213; broadcast, 204,
209–12; propaganda
offensive, 211–12; Czech
debate, 214–18; Hitler
invites to Munich, 216–18;
Munich Agreement, 1–5,
219–22, 223–9; Munich
Agreement debate, 230–1,
234–9, 242, 245–8; and the
Oxford by-election, 264,
265–6; Mansion House
speech, 273; cool reception
in Paris, 275; begins
full-scale rearmament, 276;
hopes to appease Mussolini,
276; and the fall of Prague,
277–9; Polish guarantee,
280; introduces
conscription, 282;
opposition to alliance with
Soviet Union, 283; vote of
confidence, 284–5; delays
declaring war, 286;
abhorrence of war, 287–8,
289; declares war, 287–8;
widens Government, 288–9;
criticism of conduct of war,

289–93; resignation, 293, 294–5, 297

Chamberlain, Norman, 14, 107

Channon, 'Chips', 45, 73, 80–1, 115, 150, 213–14, 217, 227, 273, 274, 276, 281, 286, 291, 292, 293–4

Chiefs of Staff, 35, 68, 76, 149, 178, 186–7

Churchill, Clementine, 201, 223

Churchill, Randolph, 16, 97, 152, 181, 261

Churchill, Sir Winston: on the Oxford Union debate, 16; cuts defence spending, 20; calls for rearmament, 27–8, 36, 40; and the Abyssinian crisis, 45, 46–7, 53, 56; Rhineland crisis, 61, 63, 65, 66, 68, 74; focus of Tory rebels, 69–73, 75; wants better relations with Mussolini, 73–4; calls for intervention in economy, 78; attacks Government's defence policy, 82–4; and the Spanish Civil War, 86, 87, 88; and the Popular Front initiatives, 97–8; and the Abdication crisis, 105–6; seconds Chamberlain's nomination, 107; banned from BBC, 112, 215, 250; foreign affairs debate, 120–2; support for Eden, 127; and Eden's resignation, 132, 134, 136; Austrian crisis, 142; and the Czech crisis, 144, 152, 153–4, 167–9, 171, 175, 176–7, 179, 185, 187, 192–3, 197–8, 201,

205–6, 212–13; hopes for coalition, 146; calls for defensive alliance with France, 150–1; visits France, 152; and Chamberlain's meeting with Hitler, 181; House of Commons debate, 215, 217; and the Munich Agreement, 11, 218, 220–1, 223, 230, 231; Beneš asks for advice, 230; Munich Agreement debate, 239–40, 241–4, 245, 247, 272; and the Oxford by-election, 260, 261; and the Kinross by-election, 270; local party tries to drop, 274; and the fall of Prague, 278; calls for National Government, 279; calls for alliance with Soviet Union, 283; asked to join Government, 285, 286, 288; and the invasion of Poland, 286–7; and the declaration of war, 287; Norwegian fiasco, 290, 291; succeeds Chamberlain, 293, 294; forms Government, 295–7

Citrine, Sir Walter, 40, 41, 48, 74, 103, 185, 282

Clark, Kenneth, 32–3, 34, 228, 229, 273

Clarke, David, 270

Clarke, Sir Richard ('Otto'), 218

Cliveden, 23–5, 151–2, 189, 207, 281

Cockburn, Claud, 23, 150

Cocks, Seymour, 98

Cole, G.D.H., 98

Cole, Margaret, 40

Colefax, Lady Sybil, 33, 139
Colville, John, 223–4, 294, 296
Commonwealth, 21
Communism, 79, 106
Communist International, 90
Communist Party (Britain),
    89–91, 96, 99–100, 155, 156,
    253, 254, 255
Conservative Central Office,
    193, 234
Conservative Party: East
    Fulham by-election, 29–30;
    1935 election, 50;
    rearmament debate, 71–3,
    75–9; wants better relations
    with Italy, 73–5; and the
    Spanish Civil War, 87–8;
    Popular Front initiatives,
    96; and Eden's resignation,
    135–6; Czech crisis, 200; and
    the Munich Agreement,
    238–41, 245–6; Oxford by-
    election, 252–3, 260–1, 265;
    Bridgwater by-election, 267,
    269; Polish guarantee, 280
Conservative Research
    Department, 126, 130, 234,
    270
Cooper, Lady Diana, 6–7, 32,
    33, 80, 227, 228, 230, 231,
    237, 285
Cooper, Duff, 80, 112, 169,
    285; and the occupation of
    the Rhineland, 61;
    rearmament debate, 81; on
    Eden, 127; and Eden's
    resignation, 129; Czech
    crisis, 151, 168, 177, 178–9,
    186, 196–7, 200, 202, 203,
    209; defence spending,
    157–8; and Chamberlain's
    meeting with Hitler, 180,
    183, 184; mobilises fleet,
    213; and the Munich
    Agreement, 11, 220–1, 225,
    247; resignation, 227, 228,
    230, 231–3, 234; leaks, 245;
    calls for National
    Government, 279; and the
    invasion of Poland, 286;
    Norway debate, 291, 292,
    293
Coote, Colin, 220, 221
Corbin, M., 2, 172, 176
Cornford, John, 89, 96
Coward, Noël, 16, 274
Cowling, Maurice, 202
Cranborne, Lady, 131
Cranborne, Viscount, 24, 45,
    131, 133, 135, 136, 162, 240,
    247, 275, 281, 290–1
Cripps, Sir Stafford, 19, 47–8,
    49, 98–9, 100, 101–2, 156,
    248, 253
Croft, Sir Henry Page, 86
Croom-Johnson, Reginald,
    267
Crossley, Anthony, 134, 165,
    247
Crossman, R.H.S., 90, 251–2,
    253, 254, 256, 263
Cudlipp, 118
Cummings, A.J., 193
Cunard, 10
Cunard, Lady Emerald, 32
Curtis, Lionel, 25
Czechoslovakia: German threat
    to, 21, 117, 140, 143,
    144–55, 162–6, 167–88,
    189–203; Munich
    agreement, 4, 219–22, 226,
    230, 234–50; defensive
    treaties, 38; and the Austrian
    crisis, 142, 143; Runciman

mission, 164–6, 168; and Chamberlain's meetings with Hitler, 179–84, 194–5, 198–202; rejects Hitler's terms, 203; House of Commons debate, 214–18; International Commission, 272–3; declares martial law, 277; German occupation, 277–9

*Daily Express*, 17, 79, 152, 262–3, 275
*Daily Herald*, 48, 49, 109, 118, 130, 156, 163, 180, 183, 190, 193, 227–8, 249
*Daily Mail*, 30, 34, 45, 118, 175
*Daily Telegraph*, 15, 78, 130, 152, 180, 181, 190, 192, 219, 226, 227
*Daily Worker*, 89
Daladier, Edouard, 2, 164, 212, 216, 235
Dallas, George, 192
Dalton, Hugh, 40, 61, 68, 74, 101, 150, 155, 175, 185, 192–3, 207, 218; and the rearmament debate, 39, 41, 102–4; on Lansbury, 48; and the Rhineland crisis, 58, 64; and the Spanish Civil War, 92, 95; on Chamberlain's talks with Hitler, 181; Munich Agreement debate, 234, 246; and the Munich Agreement, 238, 239; new National Government proposed, 248, 249; Oxford by-election, 255
Danzig, 279, 282, 283

Dartford by-election (1938), 267
Davies, Clement, 290, 291
Davies, Ivor, 252–3, 254, 255, 256, 261, 263
Dawson, Geoffrey, 22–5, 118, 172–3, 194, 207, 226, 233
Day Lewis, Cecil, 17
De la Warr, Buck, 184–5, 189–91, 202, 225, 286
Defence Policy Requirements Committee, 35–6, 76–7
Delbos, 145
Derby, Earl of, 154
Devonshire, Duke of, 277–8
Disarmament Conference, Geneva (1932), 20–1, 27, 28, 29, 37, 43, 62, 268
Disraeli, Benjamin, 4, 231
Dobbie, Williams, 98
Dollfuss, Engelbert, 37, 39, 137, 139
Doncaster by-election (1938), 267
Donner, Patrick, 247
Douglas, Roy, 166
Driberg, Tom, 230
Dugdale, Blanche ('Baffy'), 184–5, 190, 202–3, 211, 217–18, 223, 224, 225, 239, 243, 246, 248
Duggan, Hubert, 292
Dunglass, Lord (Lord Home), 4, 14, 107, 109, 110–11, 216, 221–2, 291, 294
Durbin, Evan, 228, 249

East Africa, 38, 42
East Fulham by-election (1933), 29–30
Ebbutt, Norman, 22, 119

Eckersley, 229
*Economist*, 28, 31, 39
Eden, Anthony, 38, 118,
  160–1; opinion of Hitler, 37;
  and the Abyssinian crisis,
  45; and Hoare's resignation,
  53; as Foreign Secretary,
  55–6, 109; Rhineland crisis,
  61, 62, 63; and sanctions
  against Italy, 74–5;
  rearmament debate, 81; and
  the Spanish Civil War, 87,
  88; poor relations with
  Chamberlain, 109–10, 116,
  127–9; opposition to
  appeasement, 115; and
  Halifax's visit to Germany,
  116; and the League of
  Nations, 117; foreign affairs
  debate, 122; and Roosevelt's
  peace initiative, 125–7, 133;
  resignation, 128–36, 155,
  291; Austrian crisis, 138–9,
  141–2; Czech crisis, 144,
  145, 153, 154, 163, 174,
  175–6, 177, 189, 192–3;
  House of Commons debate,
  217; and the Munich
  Agreement, 220, 238–9, 247;
  new National Government
  proposed, 248; and the
  Oxford by-election, 260–1;
  considers future, 274–5,
  278, 281, 284; and the fall of
  Prague, 278; hopes for
  alliance with Soviet Union,
  283; recalled to
  Government, 288; in
  Churchill's government,
  295–6
Edward VIII, King, 34–5, 98,
  105

Edwards, Bob, 89
Eger, 195, 197
Einstein, Albert, 28
Einzig, Paul, 218
Elizabeth, Queen, 3, 10, 153,
  164, 227
Elliot, Walter, 55, 129, 131,
  184, 185, 189–90, 202,
  217–18, 220, 224, 227,
  246–7, 286
Elton, Lord, 97
Emrys-Evans, Paul, 59–60, 65,
  67, 98, 127, 134, 153, 247
'Enigma', 295
'Establishment', 25
*Evening Standard*, 62, 118,
  152, 165, 193
Eyres-Monsell, Sir Bolton, 19

Federation of British Industry,
  77
Firth, J.B., 15, 16
Fisher, H.A.L., 97
Fisher, Sir Warren, 35, 109
Flandin, Pierre, 62
Fletcher, Reginald, 98
Focus for the Defence of
  Freedom and Peace, 97–8
Foot, Dingle, 98, 262
Foot, Isaac, 97, 262
Football Association, 162
Foreign Affairs Committee,
  71, 136, 153, 286
Foreign Office, 36, 113; and
  the Abyssinian crisis, 53;
  relations with Chamberlain,
  109–10; management of
  media, 111, 118; censors
  BBC, 171; Czech crisis,
  149–50, 172, 177, 188, 206,
  212–13; Munich Agreement,
  223; and the Munich

Agreement debate, 244
Foreign Policy Committee,
  114, 126, 147, 173, 276
Four-Power Agreement
  (Munich, 1938), 1–5, 11–12,
  216–17, 219–22, 234
'Fourth Plan', 171, 173
France: Stresa conference, 38;
  treaty with Czechoslovakia,
  38, 145; and the Abyssinian
  crisis, 50–1; German
  diplomatic proposals, 59;
  Rhineland crisis, 61–2,
  67–8; and the Spanish Civil
  War, 85–6, 92; Czech crisis,
  147–9, 152, 163, 174, 176,
  177, 179, 184, 185–8, 189,
  194–5, 205; Churchill calls
  for defensive alliance, 150–1;
  and the Runciman mission,
  164; rejects Hitler's terms,
  203; mobilisation, 208, 286;
  Munich Agreement, 219,
  221; International
  Commission, 272;
  Chamberlain's unpopularity,
  275; Halifax urges support
  for, 276
Franco, General, 85–8, 92, 100
Fraser, Hugh, 262
Fraser, Robert, 228, 249
Freedom and Peace group, 220
Freikorps, 195, 197
French Air Force, 148, 185
Fulton, John, 259
Fylde by-election (1938), 269

Gaitskell, Hugh, 39, 228, 249
Gallagher, William, 217
Gamelin, Maurice, 205
Gandhi, Mahatma, 15, 258
Gannon, Franklin, 233

Garvin, J.L., 25, 170, 176,
  177, 220, 221, 226
general election (1935), 50, 69
George V, King, 35, 53
George VI, King, 2, 3, 5, 10,
  130, 153, 164, 169, 175, 180,
  185, 227, 248, 290, 293, 294,
  296
German navy, 38
Germany: Hitler's rise to
  power, 13–14, 20, 22–3, 28;
  Geneva Disarmament
  Conference, 20–1, 37;
  withdraws from League of
  Nations, 29; British
  sympathisers, 31–5, 162;
  'Night of the Long Knives',
  33–4; Saarland plebiscite,
  37; Naval Agreement, 38;
  and the Locarno Pact, 41;
  occupation of Rhineland,
  58–68, 71, 73, 74, 79; public
  relations campaign, 79–81;
  and the Spanish Civil War,
  85; Chamberlain's
  diplomatic initiative
  towards, 114–21; Austrian
  Anschluss, 137–43; threat to
  Czechoslovakia, 143,
  144–55, 162–6, 167–88,
  189–203; Italian support for,
  157; Britain's proposed
  warning to, 173–5, 176;
  Chamberlain's meetings
  with Hitler, 179–84, 194–5,
  198–202; Chamberlain
  broadcasts to, 211–12;
  House of Commons debate,
  214–18; Munich Agreement,
  1–5, 11–12, 219–22, 223–50;
  and the Oxford by-election,
  267; 'Krystallnacht', 268,

273; occupies Sudetenland,
272; International
Commission, 272–3;
rumours of surprise attack,
275; occupies Prague,
277–9; seizes Memel, 279;
threat to Poland, 279–80;
pact with Italy, 280; fresh
talks with Britain, 283–4;
pact with Soviet Union, 283,
285; invasion of Poland,
285–6; Britain declares war,
287; invades Norway, 290,
291; invades Low Countries,
293–4
Gestapo, 138
Gilbert, Martin, 223, 247
Gladstone, Lady, 262
'the Glamour Boys', 150, 281,
291
Glasgow *Forward*, 100
Göbbels, Joseph, 9, 117–18,
119, 162
Gollancz, Victor, 17, 28, 91
Gordon-Lennox, Victor, 130
Gordon Walker, Patrick, 90,
251–2, 253, 254–6, 261, 262,
264, 266
Göring, Hermann, 22, 115,
117, 138, 143, 162, 164,
283–4
Graham, Alan, 136
Grandi, Count, 2, 126, 127, 280
Grant Duff, Sheila, 200–1, 212
Graves, Robert, 17
Gray, Frank, 257
Great War, 14, 15, 17, 19, 23,
55, 67, 229
Greece, 280
Greenwood, Arthur, 93, 94,
102, 155, 255, 286, 290, 293,
296

Greenwood, Tony, 14
Greville, Mrs Ronald, 32–3,
280
Griffiths, Richard, 30
Grigg, Sir Edward, 25, 205
Grimond, Jo, 224
Guernica, 1, 5
Guest, Captain Frederick, 97

Hacha, Emil, 277
Hacking, Douglas, 246
Hadley, W.W., 226
Hailsham, Viscount, 19, 129,
202, 252, 264, 291
Haldane, J.B.S., 262
Halifax, Viscount, 18–19, 231,
275; friendship with
Dawson, 24–5; and the
Abyssinian crisis, 52;
relations with Chamberlain,
110; visits Germany,
115–21; tries to influence
media, 118–19, 136–7; and
Eden's resignation, 128;
becomes Foreign Secretary,
136; Czech crisis, 145, 147,
149, 163–4, 167, 169–78,
183–5, 187, 189, 192, 195–6,
200–2, 209–10;
Anglo-Italian accord, 156;
Runciman mission, 164;
censors media, 193; and
Chamberlain's meetings
with Hitler, 2, 199, 202;
statement on Czech crisis,
206, 212–13; calls for
support for France, 276;
increases influence, 279;
Polish guarantee, 279; fresh
talks with Germany, 284;
and Chamberlain's
resignation, 293, 294, 296;

in Churchill's government, 295

Hankey, Maurice, 35

Hardinge, Sir Alexander, 130, 153, 185

Harmsworth, Esmond, 34, 118

Harrisson, Tom, 251, 263, 264

Harrod, Roy, 50, 239–40, 253, 254

Harvey, Oliver, 105, 115, 118, 125, 130, 131–2, 136, 160–1, 170, 175–6, 177–8, 179, 181, 188, 223, 273–4, 281, 282, 285

Healey, Denis, 90, 256, 259

Healey, Edna, 265

Heath, Edward, 87, 131, 256, 259, 261–2

Heathcoat-Amory, Patrick, 267, 269

Hely-Hutchinson, Maurice, 296

Hemingway, Ernest, 17

Henderson, Sir Nevile, 118, 136, 139–40, 145, 162, 165, 167, 174–5, 176, 272

Henderson, Arthur, 20, 98, 220

Henlein, Konrad, 144–5, 152–3, 164, 165, 171, 173, 182, 195

Herbert, Sir Sidney, 240–1, 243, 247

Hess, Rudolf, 162

Hichens, Lionel, 25

Hill, Christopher, 259

Hills, Major J.W., 134

Hindenburg, President, 13

Hitler, Adolf: bombs Guernica, 5; Nuremberg Rallies, 6, 9; rise to power, 13–14, 20, 22–3, 28; withdraws from League of Nations, 29; British sympathisers, 31–5, 162; 'Night of the Long Knives', 33–4; Saarland plebiscite, 37; and the Locarno Pact, 41; occupation of Rhineland, 58–68, 71; public relations campaign, 79–81; and the Spanish Civil War, 85, 86; *Mein Kampf*, 86; Halifax meets, 116, 119–20; Austrian Anschluss, 137–43; threat to Czechoslovakia, 143, 144–55, 162–6, 167–88, 189–203; Italian support for, 157; Britain's proposed warning to, 173–5, 176; Chamberlain's meetings with, 179–84, 194–5, 198–202; speech, 205, 206, 207, 208; Chamberlain's messages to, 207, 208–9, 213; invites Chamberlain to Munich, 216–18; Munich Agreement, 1–5, 219, 221–2, 226–7, 234–6, 242; occupies Sudetenland, 272; rumours of surprise attack, 275; occupies Prague, 277; threat to Poland, 279–80; fresh talks with Britain, 284; invasion of Poland, 285–6; invades Norway, 290; invades Low Countries, 293–4, 295

Hoare, Sir Samuel, 18–19, 33, 109, 169, 245, 289, 293; becomes Foreign Secretary, 38; and the Abyssinian crisis, 45–6, 50–3; resignation, 52–4; and the

Rhineland crisis, 62;
reluctance to intervene in
economy, 78; rearmament
debate, 81, 82; relations with
Chamberlain, 110; Czech
crisis, 175, 176, 179, 183,
184, 196; censors media,
193; and Chamberlain's
meetings with Hitler, 199,
219

Hoare-Laval Pact (1935), 50–5,
61, 70, 105

Hogg, Quintin, 15, 252, 256,
257–8, 261, 262, 263–6, 292

Home, Lord, *see* Dunglass,
Lord

Home Office, 8

Hore-Belisha, Leslie, 109, 157,
186, 187, 202, 262, 276, 292

Horne, Lord, 197, 220

Horner, Lady, 228

'Hossbach memorandum', 145

House of Commons:
rearmament debates, 36,
41–2, 82–3, 103; 1935
election, 50; and the
Abyssinian crisis, 54–5;
Rhineland crisis, 63–7;
foreign affairs debate,
119–22; and Eden's
resignation, 132–5; debates
Austrian crisis, 141, 143;
and the Runciman mission,
164–5; debates Czech crisis,
214–18; debates Munich
Agreement, 230–1, 234–48,
250, 272; Duff Cooper's
resignation speech, 231–3;
adjourned, 249–50; Norway
debate, 291–3

House of Lords, 214, 240

Houston, Lady, 31, 62

Howard, Anthony, 153, 244

Hudson, Robert, 284

Hungary, 21, 188

Hunt, David, 14

Huxley, Aldous, 42

Huxley, Julian, 97

Independent Labour Party
(ILP), 99–100, 246, 253, 254

India, 21, 27, 38, 204

Inskip, Sir Thomas, 58, 59, 62,
76–8, 81, 82, 112, 113–14,
115, 147, 157, 159, 169, 170,
183–4, 186, 196, 209, 275–6

'the Insurgents', 150

International Brigades, 87, 89

International Commission on
the Sudetenland, 272–3

International Committee for
the Application of the
Agreement regarding
Non-Intervention in Spain, 95

*Isis*, 90, 261

Ismay, General, 186–7, 196

Italy, 21; builds-up troops in
East Africa, 38, 42; Stresa
conference, 38; Abyssinian
crisis, 43, 44–57, 76, 125,
126–7, 156; Tory rebels seek
better relations with, 73;
sanctions lifted, 74–5; and
the Spanish Civil War, 85;
Chamberlain and Eden
disagree over, 127–9, 133;
and Austria, 137–8;
Anti-Comintern Pact, 149;
Chamberlain appeases,
156–7, 276; Munich
Agreement, 219;
International Commission,
272; invades Albania, 280;
pact with Germany, 280

James, Robert Rhodes, 116, 154, 261, 275
Jameson, Storm, 7, 18
Japan, 20, 21, 35, 39, 44, 149, 283
Jay, Douglas, 22, 24, 26, 28, 39, 89, 181, 201, 218, 249, 252
Jebb, Gladwyn, 158–9
Jenkins, Roy, 256, 261
Jews, 120, 268, 273
Joad, Cyril, 14–15, 97, 101
John Lewis department store, 141
Johnstone, Harcourt, 80
Jolliffe, William, 229
Jones, Jack, 89, 95–6, 159
Jones, Morgan, 165
Jones, Tom, 25, 27, 30, 58–9, 207
Joyce, William (Lord Haw-Haw), 31

Kaiser, Philip, 131
Kemsley, Lord, 118
Kennedy, John F., 214
Kennedy, Joseph, 193, 276–7
Kent, Duke and Duchess of, 214
Keyes, Sir Roger, 247, 291
Keynes, John Maynard, 26, 151
'King and Country' debate, 14–18
Kinross by-election (1938), 269–70
Kirkpatrick, Helen, 135
Kirkpatrick, Ivone, 194
Kleist, Major von, 169
Koestler, Arthur, 91
Kordt, Theodor, 2, 171–2, 194
'Krystallnacht', 268, 273

Labour Party: East Fulham by-election, 29–30; attitudes to rearmament, 19, 39–42, 100–4; and the Abyssinian crisis, 45, 47–50; 1935 election, 50; Rhineland crisis, 60–1, 64, 68; and the Spanish Civil War, 89, 91–2, 93–6, 99–100; and the Popular Front initiatives, 96, 99, 155–6; and Chamberlain's meeting with Hitler, 181; Czech crisis, 173–4, 185, 191–3, 207; Munich Agreement debate, 236–8, 240, 246; new National Government proposed, 248; policy after Munich, 249; Oxford by-election, 253–6, 262–3, 264, 266; Dartford by-election, 267; Kinross by-election, 270; and the invasion of Poland, 286; invited to join Government, 293, 294
Lacroix, 187, 188
Lambert, Constant, 8
Lang, Cosmo, Archbishop of Canterbury, 140–1, 230, 287–8
Lansbury, George, 19, 39, 41, 45, 47–50, 120, 237, 238, 289, 291
Lascelles, Sir Alan, 185
Laski, Harold, 91, 156
Laval, Pierre, 50–1, 54
Law, Richard, 220, 221, 247
Layton, Sir Walter, 28–9, 31, 58–9, 118, 183, 220
League of Nations, 19, 60, 61, 101, 240, 275; British

attitudes towards, 20; and the collective security debate, 39–40, 42–3; Abyssinian crisis, 44–7, 51, 54, 56–7, 156; Rhineland crisis, 62, 63, 64, 67, 73–4; the Next Five Years Group and, 97; Chamberlain and, 117, 121–2, 133–4; Churchill's support for, 121–2; and the Czech crisis, 152; Labour Party and, 155

League of Nations Union, 42, 218, 225, 248–9

Leeper, Rex, 74, 97, 206, 213

Lees-Milne, James, 32

Left Book Club, 91, 99, 155, 267, 268

Lennox-Boyd, Alan, 146, 217, 247

Liberal Party, 19; East Fulham by-election, 29; and the Abyssinian crisis, 45; Munich Agreement debate, 246; Oxford by-election, 252–3, 256, 262, 263; Kinross by-election, 270

Libya, 156

Liddall, Sir Walter, 217

Liddell Hart, Basil, 187, 220, 280

Lindbergh, Charles, 163, 179, 207, 219

Lindemann, Professor, 62, 220, 221, 260, 297

Lindsay, A.D. ('Sandie'), 254–5, 256–66, 268, 269, 270

Lindsay, Erica, 259

Lindsay, Kenneth, 262

Lindsay, Sir Ronald, 124–5

*Listener*, 215

Lithuania, 279

Litvinov, Maxim, 147, 148, 150

Lloyd, Lord, 82, 197, 205, 220

Lloyd George, David, 19, 25, 26, 45, 64, 81, 86, 106, 127, 207, 220, 291, 292

Lloyd George, Megan, 220, 262

Locarno Pact, 41, 60, 62, 63

Locker-Lampson, Oliver, 98

Londonderry, Marquis of, 19, 32, 79–80, 291

Lothian, Philip Kerr, Marquis of, 25, 26, 31, 58–9, 140, 182, 280

Low, David, 23, 97, 101, 118–19, 152

Low Countries, 76, 113, 293, 295

Luftwaffe, 37, 41, 113, 148, 158, 163, 179, 186, 219

Lytton, Lord, 197, 205, 220

MacCarthy, Desmond, 139

MacDonald, Malcolm, 131, 155, 184, 196, 209

MacDonald, Ramsay, 18, 20, 21, 28, 29, 30, 38, 78, 107

McEwen, John, 98

Macmillan, Lady Dorothy, 178

Macmillan, Harold, 6, 24, 72, 258–9; on the 'Night of the Long Knives', 33–4; and the Abyssinian crisis, 44, 51, 52; and the occupation of the Rhineland, 60; resigns government whip, 75, 97; and the Spanish Civil War, 87, 88; Next Five Years Group, 96–7; and Eden's resignation, 135; calls for coalition, 146; Czech crisis, 178, 205, 208; and the Munich Agreement, 11, 225, 229; Munich Agreement debate, 234, 239, 244–5, 246, 247; proposes new National Government, 248; and the Oxford by-election, 259–60; believes Chamberlain should resign, 278; Norway debate, 292

MacNeice, Louis, 85

Maginot line, 59

Maisky, Ivan, 74, 171, 172

Makins, Roger (Lord Sherfield), 46, 224, 273

Malcolm, Dougal, 25

*Manchester Guardian*, 151, 226, 227, 250

Manchuria, 39, 44

Mandel, 187

Margach, James, 111

Margesson, Captain David, 72, 108, 127, 128–9, 161

Marlowe, John, 26

Martin, Kingsley, 155, 168, 249

Mary, Queen, 214, 248

Masaryk, Jan, 144–5, 197, 172, 187, 203, 247

Masefield, John, 1, 183

Mass Observation, 5, 193

Massey, Vincent, 183

Maude, Angus, 15

Maugham, Lord Chancellor, 202

Maxton, James, 237

Mayhew, Christopher, 90, 261–2

Memel, 279

MI5, 31

Milestone, Lewis, 17

Milne, A.A., 17

Milner, Lord, 25–6

'Milner's Kindergarten', 25–6

Minehead, 267–8

Ministry of Food, 289

Ministry of Labour, 282

Ministry of Supply, 282, 289

Mitford, Jessica, 8, 32, 89

Mitford, Nancy, 32

Mitford, Unity, 32

Monsell, Lord, 80

Montagu, Venetia, 6–7

Morocco, 85

Morrison, Herbert, 61, 92, 93, 97, 102, 103, 155, 185, 246, 248

Morrison, W.S. ('Shakes'), 55, 129, 131

Mosley, Diana, 32

Mosley, Oswald, 16, 30–1, 32, 40, 48, 90, 93, 112, 254

Mountbatten, Louis, 227

Moyne, Lord, 175, 220

Munich Agreement (1938), 1–5, 11–12, 219–22, 223–50, 251–71, 272

Murdoch, Iris, 90–1

Murphy, J.T., 98

Murray, Basil, 90

Murray, Gilbert, 14

Mussolini, Benito, 5, 21, 30, 122, 251; and the BUF, 31; motives for appeasement of, 38; builds up troops in East Africa, 38, 42; Abyssinian crisis, 43, 44–6, 51–2, 56, 67, 126–7; Tory rebels seek better relations with, 73; sanctions against lifted, 75; and the Spanish Civil War, 85; Chamberlain and Eden

disagree over, 128–9; and
  Austria, 137–8; Chamberlain
  appeases, 156–7, 276; and
  the Czech crisis, 213, 214;
  Munich Agreement, 216,
  217, 235; invades Albania,
  280

National Advisory Committee
  on International Relations,
  155
National Council of Labour,
  49–50, 92, 94, 95, 103, 185,
  191, 192
National Defence
  Contribution, 112
National Executive Committee
  (NEC), 41, 47, 48, 60, 93,
  94–5, 99, 101, 156, 173–4
National Labour Party, 184,
  190, 262
National Liberals, 19, 262, 267
National Union of Societies for
  Equal Citizenship, 23
Nazi–Soviet Non-aggression
  Pact (1939), 283, 285
Nazis: rise to power, 13–14,
  20, 22–3, 28; British
  supporters, 31–5;
  Nuremberg Rallies, 87;
  objections to political
  cartoons, 118–19; Austrian
  Anschluss, 137–43; *see also*
  Germany
*New Signatures*, 17
*New Statesman and Nation*, 45,
  49, 55, 60, 104, 105–6, 151,
  155, 168, 249
*New York Times*, 203
Newall, Air Marshal Sir Cyril,
  158

*News Chronicle*, 17, 31, 118,
  130, 163, 164, 165, 180, 183,
  190, 191, 193, 219, 227, 268,
  284
Newspaper Society, 118
Newton, 187, 188
Next Five Years Group, 97
Nichols, Beverley, 16, 18
Nicholson, Godfrey, 218
Nicolson, Harold, 46, 71, 105,
  142, 150, 280–1, 290; and
  the Abyssinian crisis, 54–5;
  Rhineland crisis, 63, 65; on
  Nazi sympathisers, 80; and
  the Spanish Civil War, 86;
  and Eden's resignation, 134,
  136; Austrian crisis, 139;
  Czech crisis, 153, 155,
  163–4, 176, 181–2, 183,
  189–91, 197–8, 205–6;
  defence spending, 158–9; on
  the Cabinet reshuffle, 161;
  BBC censors talks, 171, 215;
  House of Commons debate,
  214, 215–16, 217; and the
  Munich Agreement, 11,
  218–21, 225–7, 231, 233–4;
  Munich Agreement debate,
  241, 243–4, 246, 247, 272;
  renewal of Czech crisis, 277;
  on the invasion of Albania,
  280; and the declaration of
  war, 287
Nicolson, Nigel, 217
'Night of the Long Knives',
  33–4
'1900 Club', 75
Noel-Baker, Philip, 31, 94, 98,
  218, 249
Norway, 290, 291
Nuremberg Rallies, 80, 87,
  166, 170, 173, 177, 178

*Observer*, 25, 59, 170, 176, 201, 226

Olympic Games (1936), 80, 162

O'Neill, Con, 224

O'Neill, Sir Hugh, 224

'Operation Green', 163

Ormsby-Gore, William, 55, 147, 161–2, 291

Orwell, George, 89, 91, 100, 155

Other Club, 220–1

Ottawa Trade Agreement (1932), 21

Oxford, Lady Margot, 219, 248

Oxford City by-election (1938), 251–67, 269, 271

Oxford City Labour Party, 251–2, 256, 262–3

*Oxford Mail*, 254, 255, 256–7, 265, 267

*Oxford Times*, 16

Oxford Union, 14–18, 261–2

Oxford University, 89–91, 131, 251–2, 253, 257–8

Oxford University Carlton Club, 262

Oxford University Conservative Association, 261, 262

Oxford University Labour Club, 89–90

Pakenham, Elizabeth, 108

Pakenham, Frank, 90, 108, 251–2, 253–4, 256, 259

Palencia, Señora de, 94

Palestine, 21

Papen, Franz von, 13

Paramount, 130, 193

Parker, John, 262

Parliamentary Labour Party (PLP), 41, 48, 50, 60–1, 68, 100, 102–3

Pathé, 4–5

Patrick, Mark, 131, 135

Paul, Herbert, 231

Peace Ballot, 42–3, 46

Peace Pledge Union, 42

Peace Society, 69

People's Front Propaganda Committee, 98

Phipps, Sir Eric, 118, 152, 179, 187–8

*Picture Post*, 251, 252, 257–8, 263, 266–7, 269

Plan Z, 169, 170, 173, 174, 177, 179–80

Plunkett-Ernle-Erle-Drax, Admiral Sir Reginald, 283

Poland, 21, 148, 188, 273, 279–80, 283, 284, 285–6

Pollitt, Harry, 96, 112

Ponsonby, Lord, 39, 48

Pope-Hennessy, James, 190

Popular Front, 96–100, 105, 155–6, 253, 254, 255–6, 260, 266–8, 269, 270

Post Office, 212

POUM, 89, 100

Powell, Enoch, 34

Powell, Michael, 295

Pownall, Colonel, 35–6

Prague, 277

Pressburger, Emeric, 295

Pritt, D.N., 156

Pronay, Nicholas, 212

*Queen Elizabeth*, 10

Radio Luxemburg, 211–12

Rathbone, Eleanor, 23, 97, 98

Red Army, 148
Redesdale, Lady, 285–6
Redesdale, Lord, 32, 174,
　285–6
Reed, Douglas, 22
Reith, John, 30, 31, 33, 136–7,
　141
Remarque, Erich Maria, 17
Reynaud, Paul, 187
*Reynold's News*, 228
Rhineland, 58–68, 70, 71, 73,
　74, 79, 140, 187, 278
Ribbentrop, Joachim von,
　31–3, 34, 62, 79, 80, 138,
　141, 162, 175, 191, 284
Richardson, H.S., 255
Ripka, Hubert, 212
Roberts, Sir Frank, 110, 123,
　273
Roberts, Stephen, 114
Robeson, Paul, 86, 89
Röhm, Ernst, 33–4
Romilly, Esmond, 89
Roosevelt, Franklin, 124–7,
　129, 133, 169, 212, 213, 249,
　251, 276
Rothermere, Lord, 30–1, 34,
　78, 80
Rothschild, James de, 98
Rothschild, Victor, 6
*Round Table*, 25
Round Table group, 25–6
Rous, Stanley, 162
Rowse, A.L., 24, 207, 252
Royal Air Force, 27, 36, 37,
　41, 113–14, 115, 158–9
Royal Navy, 38, 157, 169, 197
*Royal Oak*, 289
Rumania, 21, 142, 148, 280
Runciman, Viscount, 164–6,
　168, 171, 173, 183, 215
Rushcliffe, Lord, 282–3

Russell, Conrad, 228, 229,
　231, 237
Russian Revolution, 26
Rutland, Duchess of, 33


SA, 33
Saarland, 37
Sackville-West, Vita, 46, 136,
　161, 181–2, 208
St Stephen's Club, 111
Salisbury, Marquis of, 78–9,
　290–1
Salter, Sir Arthur, 98, 220, 260
Samuel, Viscount, 19, 36, 45,
　63, 224–5
Sanderson, Lord, 262
Sandys, Duncan, 73, 98, 247,
　249, 286
Sargent, Sir Orme, 144, 202,
　223–4
Sassoon, Sir Philip, 27, 34, 80
Sassoon, Siegfried, 17
*Saturday Review*, 31, 62
Savoy Hotel, London, 220
Scapa Flow, 289
Scheme L, 158–9
Schleicher, General von, 33
Schmidt, Paul Otto, 194
Schuschnigg, Kurt von, 137–8,
　139
Secret Service, 31, 113, 122,
　230
Seyss-Inquart, Artur von, 138
'Shadow' factories, 77, 159
Shay, Robert Paul, Jr, 77
Shepherd, George, 255
Sheppard, Canon 'Dick', 42
Sherfield, Lord, *see* Makins,
　Roger
Shinwell, Emmanuel, 102
Sikorski, General, 225

Simon, Sir John, 19, 24, 33, 37, 38, 55, 109, 127, 268, 289, 293; and German disarmament, 20-1; at Disarmament Conference, 29; visit to Germany cancelled, 37; becomes Home Secretary, 38; on Chamberlain, 108; relations with Chamberlain, 110; cuts defence spending, 114; and Eden's resignation, 128, 134; Czech crisis, 147, 173, 176, 196, 202, 205; increases income tax, 157; and Plan Z, 180; and Chamberlain's meetings with Hitler, 199; and Hitler's message to Chamberlain, 216; Munich Agreement debate, 241-2; and the Oxford by-election, 262; and the fall of Prague, 278

Simpson, Mrs, 98
Sinclair, Sir Archibald, 63, 98, 108, 165, 190, 192, 197, 205, 218, 220, 248, 262, 296
Singapore, 35
Skelton, Neil, 55
Slovakia, 277
Smith, F.E., 220
Smyth, Ethel, 34
Snell, 63
Snow, C.P., 228
Snow, Philip, 228
Socialist League, 47, 98-9
South Africa, 117
Southwood, Lord, 118
Soviet Union, 23; contacts with Churchill, 74; and the Spanish Civil War, 86-7, 88, 95; mutual assistance pact with Czechoslovakia, 145, 153; Czech crisis, 147, 148-50, 176, 205-6; and the Munich Agreement, 237; Churchill calls for alliance with, 283; pact with Germany, 283, 285

Spanish Civil War, 5, 79, 85-96, 99-100, 126, 133, 148, 156-7, 187
Sparrow, John, 24
Spears, Brigadier-General Sir Edward, 65, 67, 134, 205, 208, 226
Spears, Louis, 247
*Spectator*, 43, 56, 106, 132
Spender, Stephen, 17, 89
SS, 219
Stalin, Joseph, 23, 91, 148, 283
Stanhope, 202
Stanley, Edward, 154
Stanley, Oliver, 55, 129, 131, 147, 154, 176, 178, 184, 196, 200, 202, 286
Steed, Wickham, 97, 193, 220
Strabolgi, Lord, 262
Strachey, John, 91, 98
Strachey, Lytton, 15
Strang, William, 274, 283
Stresa conference, 38
Stuart, James, 72
Sudeten German Party, 144, 173, 182
Sudetenland, 6, 117, 144-5, 153, 164, 172-3, 177-8, 180, 181-2, 186, 194-5, 199, 209, 215, 234-6, 272, 278
*Sunday Graphic*, 226
*Sunday Times*, 226
Swinton, Viscount, 77, 113-14, 115, 158-9, 161, 291

Tawney, R.H., 249–50
Taylor, A.J.P., 38–9, 40–1
Taylor, Philip, 212
Ten-Year Rule, 20
Tennant, Ernest, 31–2, 34
Territorial Army, 10, 113, 157
Thomas, J.P.L. (Jim), 109,
    126, 128, 131, 135, 154, 239,
    247, 275
Thompson, W.H., 294
Thorneycroft, Lord, 72
Thurtle, Ernest, 238
Tillett, Ben, 224
*The Times*, 3, 5, 6, 7, 8, 9–10,
    13, 16, 22–3, 25, 52, 59, 93,
    130, 134, 140, 146, 172–3,
    175, 177, 178, 183, 190, 191,
    194, 203, 204, 208, 218, 226,
    227, 233, 257, 260, 263, 267,
    278, 282, 292
Tiso, 277
Toynbee, Arnold, 58
Trades Union Congress
    (TUC), 41, 48, 49, 60, 92,
    96, 102, 103–4, 159–60, 289
Transport and General
    Workers Union, 49, 96
Treasury, 21, 35–6, 76, 115,
    158
Tree, Ronald, 59, 130–1,
    135–6, 292, 293
Turkey, 280
Twyford, Sir Harry, 1
Tyrrell, Lord, 160

Unity Campaign, 99, 253, 254
*Unity Manifesto*, 99
University College, London,
    16
University Labour Federation,
    89

United States of America, 124,
    126–7, 129, 133, 207, 221–2,
    237, 276

Vansittart, Sir Robert, 95, 118,
    279; and the rearmament
    debate, 35, 36, 77;
    Abyssinian crisis, 51;
    Rhineland crisis, 61;
    campaign to publicise
    German threat, 74, 97;
    relations with Chamberlain,
    109–10; becomes Chief
    Diplomatic Adviser, 122–3;
    Czech crisis, 144, 169, 170,
    173, 174, 175, 186; and the
    soccer match with Germany,
    162; and Chamberlain's
    meeting with Hitler, 181;
    and the Munich Agreement,
    225, 227
Vega, Rodriguez, 96
Versailles Treaty, 20, 23, 26,
    28, 31, 37, 38, 137, 139, 140,
    237
Vienna, 39
Von Krosigk, 28

Waldron, W.J., 29
Walker, James, 104
Walsall by-election (1938), 267
Wanner, Dr, 31
*War and Peace*, 39
War Cabinet, 288, 294, 295
Ward Price, George, 34
Wardell, Captain Michael,
    118, 119
Wardlaw-Milne, Sir John, 286
'Watching Committee', 290–1
Waterhouse, Charles, 277
Watt, D.C., 279, 284
Waugh, Evelyn, 13, 45

Wedgwood, Josiah, 141
*The Week*, 23, 150
Wehrmacht, 179, 187
Weizsäcker, 272
Welles, Sumner, 124
Wells, H.G., 8, 97, 262
West Lewisham by-election
(1938), 269
*West London and Fulham
Gazette*, 30
Westminster, Duke of, 32, 285
Wigram, Ralph, 61
Wilkinson, Ellen, 86, 91, 156,
262
Williams, Francis, 8, 109
Willingdon, Lady, 228
Willis, Ted, 99
Wilmot, John, 29–30, 249
Wilson, Sir Arnold, 86
Wilson, Sir Horace, 109, 114,
210, 224, 285; influence on
Chamberlain, 110; and the
Roosevelt initiative, 126;
and the Austrian Anschluss,
141; Plan Z, 169; control of
the media, 171; Czech crisis,
173, 175, 185, 186; and the
Bad Godesberg talks, 195,
202; mission to Berlin, 203,
204, 208–9, 213, 232;
notoriety, 282, 283; fresh
talks with Germany, 284
Windle, T.H., 255
Winn, Anthony, 233
Winterton, Earl, 54, 55, 161,
184, 202, 219
Wireless Publicity Ltd, 211
Wohltat, Helmut, 284
Wolmer, Lord, 197, 247
Wood, Alan, 253
Wood, Kingsley, 109, 161,
178, 202, 207
Woolf, Leonard, 95, 249
Woolf, Virginia, 6, 8, 10–11,
34, 89, 95, 163, 226–7
Woolton, Lord, 141

York, Archbishop of, 97
*Yorkshire Post*, 130
Young, Allan, 98
Young, G.M., 30
Yugoslavia, 21, 142

Zetland, Lord, 204
Zuckerman, Solly, 261

# PICTURE ACKNOWLEDGEMENTS

Photographs in the 8-page plate section are from the following collections:
BBC Hulton Picture Library: page 3 above left; page 4; page 5 below;
page 7 below; page 8 below. The Photo Source/Keystone Collection: page
1 above; page 1 below; page 2; page 3 above right, below; page 5 above;
page 6 below left; page 7 above; page 8 above. Cartoons by David Low.
Photographs from the Centre for the Study of Cartoons and Caricature,
Canterbury. © Solo Syndication.